W9-BTF-859

More Than A Pretty Picture

Using Poverty Maps to Design Better Policies and Interventions

Edited by

Tara Bedi
Aline Coudouel
Kenneth Simler

THE WORLD BANK
Washington, DC

The International Bank for Reconstruction and Development / The World Bank
1818 H Street NW
Washington DC 20433
Telephone: 202-473-1000
Internet: www.worldbank.org
E-mail: feedback@worldbank.org

ISBN-10: 0-8213-6931-8
ISBN-13: 978-0-8213-6931-9
eISBN: 0-8213-6932-6
DOI: 10.1596/978-0-8213-6931-9

Library of Congress Cataloging-in-Publication Data

World Bank.
    More than a pretty picture : using poverty maps to design
better policies and interventions.
        p. cm.
    Includes bibliographical references and index.
    ISBN-13: 978-0-8213-6931-9
    ISBN-10: 0-8213-6931-8
    ISBN-10: 0-8213-6932-6 (electronic)
    1. Poverty—Maps—Case studies. 2. Poverty—Government policy—Case studies.
I. Title. II. Title: Using poverty maps to design better policies and interventions.

HC79.P6W65 2007
362.5'561—dc22   2006102151

All dollar amounts (US$) are U.S. dollars unless otherwise noted.

Cover design by Quantum Think.

All maps used with permission.

Printed in Mexico

Contents

PART *One*

Applications and Lessons

1 Maps for Policy Making: Beyond the Obvious
Tara Bedi, Aline Coudouel, and Kenneth Simler

2 Increasing the Impact of Poverty Maps 23
Tara Bedi, Aline Coudouel, and Kenneth Simler

PART *Two*

Country Studies

Boxes

Figures

Tables

Foreword

Location is a powerful determinant of poverty. Spatial patterns of inequality between and within countries have become an important focus of the development community, and research on patterns of poverty and inequality across districts, municipalities, and communities has accelerated over the past decade. While the absence of data once impeded the examination of local information on poverty, a technique developed by the Development Research Group in the World Bank has enabled the estimation of poverty at a local level by combining census and household survey information. The result—the small area poverty map—has deepened our understanding of the determinants of poverty and led to improvements in the design of policies tailored to local conditions.

More Than a Pretty Picture: Using Poverty Maps to Design Better Policies and Interventions draws on the experiences of a dozen countries in Eastern Europe (Albania and Bulgaria), Latin America (Bolivia, Ecuador, and Mexico), East Asia (Cambodia, China, Indonesia, Thailand, and Vietnam), North Africa (Morocco), and South Asia (Sri Lanka). Insights from the diverse experiences of these 12 countries are drawn together in the first two chapters, on key elements in the successful implementation and utilization of poverty maps and on the political economy of poverty maps. The case studies in the volume highlight the wide range of policies and interventions that have been influenced by poverty maps, including, but not limited to, the location of investments and services, the creation of district and municipal development plans, and the allocation of grants and fiscal transfers. They show that successfully implemented and appropriately utilized poverty maps may lead to radical shifts in the perception of poverty and in strategies designed to address poverty.

This publication hopefully offers crucial lessons for policy makers and development experts who may be considering using small area poverty maps as tools of economic development and helps add to our array of tools for dealing with the political economy issues of poverty. It represents a major contribution to a little understood aspect of the well-known adage "location, location, location," demonstrating that the conceptualization of poverty at the local level represents an important step in our fight against poverty.

Danny Leipziger
Vice President and Head of Network
Poverty Reduction and Economic Management
World Bank

Acknowledgments

This volume draws on a work program developed and led by Aline Coudouel and undertaken by a team comprising Samia Amin, Tara Bedi, Ken Simler, and Cécile Wodon under the leadership of Danny Leipziger, Luca Barbone, and Louise Cord. The volume builds on experiences in 12 developing countries. The country case studies have been prepared by Gero Carletto, Andrew Dabalen, and Alia Moubayed (Albania), Omar Arias and Marcos Robles (Bolivia), Boryana Gotcheva (Bulgaria), Tomoki Fujii (Cambodia), Chor-ching Goh and Yusuf Ahmad (China and Indonesia), M. Caridad Araujo (Ecuador), Luis Felipe López-Calva, Lourdes Rodríguez-Chamussy, and Miguel Székely (Mexico), Jennie Litvack (Morocco), Tara Vishwanath and Nobuo Yoshida (Sri Lanka), Somchai Jitsuchon and Kaspar Richter (Thailand), and Rob Swinkels and Carrie Turk (Vietnam).

We would like to extend our profound appreciation to Samia Amin for her valuable involvement in organizing and managing the production of this volume. We wish to thank Markus Goldstein, Peter Lanjouw, Johan Mistiaen, and Berk Özler for their guidance and extensive comments throughout the process, which ensured the quality and relevance of the volume. We are also grateful to M. Caridad Araujo, Shaida Badiee, Julia Bucknall, Gero Carletto, Louise Cord, Andrew Dabalen, Olivier Dupriez, Tomoki Fujii, Björn-Sören Gigler, Michael Goldberg, Boryana Gotcheva, Margaret Grosh, Norbert Henninger, Kai Kaiser, Peter Lanjouw, Danny Leipziger, Mark A. Levy, Jennie Litvack, Johan Mistiaen, Alia Moubayed, Maryvonne Plessis-Fraissard, Sudhir Shetty, Miguel Székely, Carmelle Terborgh, Roy van der Weide, and Tara Vishwanath for their inputs and assistance at the conference held on this topic at the World Bank in May 2006. Acknowledgment of contributions to specific country studies are noted in the relevant chapters. Finally, we are grateful to Susan Graham and Robert Zimmermann for excellent publication and editorial support.

In addition to funding from the World Bank, the work program has benefited from a grant by the Trust Fund for Environmentally and Socially Sustainable Development, supported by Finland and Norway, which is gratefully acknowledged.

For any questions, comments, or suggestions on this volume, please contact Aline Coudouel at the World Bank (acoudouel@worldbank.org). For more information on the small area estimation methodology and on poverty mapping application, please visit http://www.worldbank.org/povertymaps.

About the Contributors

Yusuf Ahmad is a consulting economist with Poverty Reduction and Economic Management, East Asia and Pacific Region, World Bank. Over the past three years, he has been working on poverty assessment in several countries. His research interests include public expenditure reviews, development economics, and income convergence. His ongoing work examines the development effectiveness of aid provided directly to government budgets in recipient countries, as well as income convergence using the nonlinear stationary test. His articles on economic development have been published in international journals. He holds a PhD in economic development from Howard University, Washington, DC, and a BA from the University of Findlay in Findlay, OH.

María Caridad Araujo, an Ecuadorian national, joined the World Bank as a young professional in September 2005. Her first rotation was with the East Asia Human Development Team, working on issues in education and social protection. Previously, she was a visiting assistant professor at the Public Policy Institute, Georgetown University, Washington, DC. She has worked with the Bank as a consultant for Poverty Reduction and Economic Management in the Latin America and the Caribbean Region, the Development Economics Research Group, and *World Development Report 2006*. She holds a PhD in agricultural and resource economics from the University of California at Berkeley. Her previous work has been on issues in poverty, inequality, social networks, impact evaluation, and political economy.

Omar Arias is a senior economist in the Poverty and Gender Group, Latin America and the Caribbean Region, World Bank, where he is conducting research and strategy and policy formulation on labor markets and public policies to reduce poverty and inequality. He also contributes to project design, targeting, and impact evaluation in antipoverty projects and the elaboration of national poverty reduction strategies and country assistance strategies. His research has focused on the application of semiparametric econometrics to explain the impact of growth on the poor, informal markets and sectors, income dynamics, returns to schooling, and the determinants of tax evasion. He has worked at the Centro de Investigación Económica para el Caribe, Santo Domingo, Dominican Republic, and the Inter-American Development Bank. Born in the Dominican Republic, he received a BA in economics from the Instituto Tecnológico de Santo Domingo and was a Fulbright Scholar at the University of Illinois, Urbana-

Champaign, where he obtained his MS and PhD in economics, with a concentration in public finance, labor economics, and applied econometrics.

Tara Bedi worked on monitoring and evaluation as a junior professional associate with the Poverty Reduction Group at the World Bank in 2004–06. She received a master's degree in Public Administration in International Development at the John F. Kennedy School of Government, Harvard University. She has previously worked on the sustainability of nongovernmental organizations, refugee settlement, and health policy. Tara grew up in India and was involved with the nongovernmental organization her parents founded to solicit the participation of the rural poor in addressing issues in social and economic development.

Calogero Carletto is a senior economist in the Development Research Group of the World Bank. His research interests include poverty, migration, and rural development. A member of the Living Standards Measurement Study team, he has extensive experience in the design, implementation, and analysis of household surveys. He holds a PhD in agricultural and resource economics from the University of California at Berkeley.

Aline Coudouel is a senior economist with the Human Development Network, Latin America and the Caribbean Region, World Bank. Over the past two years, she led a team working on poverty analysis, monitoring, and impact evaluation at the Poverty Reduction Group, World Bank. She has focused on Africa and Latin America, particularly on poverty measurement, poverty monitoring, the poverty and social impact of reforms, development impact evaluation, labor markets, social protection, and poverty reduction strategies. Previously, she investigated the welfare situation of children and women in Europe and Central Asia for the United Nations Children's Fund.

Andrew Dabalen is a senior economist in the Europe and Central Asia Region, World Bank. His research interests include poverty, labor markets, and human development. He holds a PhD in agricultural and resource economics from the University of California at Berkeley.

Tomoki Fujii is an assistant professor at Singapore Management University and a Lee Foundation Fellow for 2006–07. He holds one PhD from the University of California at Berkeley and another from the University of Tokyo. He has written journal articles, book chapters, and policy reports and consulted for the World Bank, the World Food Programme, Macro International, and several private companies. His research interests include development, environment, and health.

Chor-ching Goh is a senior economist at the World Bank, where she works on Cambodia, Mongolia, and the Philippines at the Poverty Reduction and Economic Management Unit, East Asia and Pacific Region. She has worked with the Human

Development cluster at the Bank's Operations Evaluation Department. Her recent papers include "Trade Protection and Industry Wage Structure in Poland," with Beata Smarzynska Javorcik, in *Globalization and Poverty* (ed., Ann Harrison, University of Chicago Press 2007) and "Estimating Individual Vulnerability to Poverty with Pseudo-Panel Data," with François Bourguignon and Dae-Il Kim, in *Mobility and Inequality: Frontiers of Research in Sociology and Economics* (eds., Stephen L. Morgan, David B. Grusky, and Gary S. Fields, Stanford University Press 2006). She graduated from Yale University summa cum laude, with simultaneous BA and MA degrees, and received her PhD in economics from Harvard University.

Boryana Gotcheva is a senior operations officer in the Human Development Sector, Europe and Central Asia Region, World Bank, working mostly in Azerbaijan, Bulgaria, and Georgia. She is involved in multisectoral development policy lending and is focused on growth, employment promotion, social service delivery, and education and training. She manages investment projects and grants supporting reforms in general education, child welfare, and the decentralization of social services. She is also involved in research in social protection, child welfare, and poverty monitoring and evaluation. In 2001–2005, she managed an institutional development grant aimed at capacity building for poverty assessment and impact analysis in Bulgaria. The project delivered two sets of regional and municipal level poverty maps that are now used in policy making and targeting in social infrastructure projects. She holds a PhD in international economics.

Somchai Jitsuchon is a research director at the Thailand Development Research Institute. He received his doctorate in economics from the University of British Columbia, Vancouver, in 1999. He specializes in macroeconomic policies, macroeconomic modeling (computable general equilibrium models and econometric models), and theory and empirical applications in poverty and income distribution. His latest poverty research is focused on the construction of a poverty map for Thailand. He has carried out policy research for Thai government agencies, the Bank of Thailand, the World Bank, the Asian Development Bank, and the Inter-American Development Bank. He has been a visiting researcher at the Economic Planning Agency, Tokyo, and a lecturer at the National Institute for Development and Administration and Thammasat University, Bangkok.

Jennie Litvack is a lead economist for human development, Latin America and the Caribbean Region, World Bank. She joined the World Bank in 1992. She was lead country economist for Morocco and was based in Rabat for almost three years. She has also served as country economist for Vietnam and coordinator of the Decentralization Thematic Group. She has published several books and articles on household welfare, decentralization, and health care finance. She holds a PhD from the Fletcher School at Tufts University, Medford, MA.

Luis F. López-Calva holds a PhD in Economics from Cornell University, Ithaca, NY. He is visiting scholar at the Stanford Center for International Development at Stanford University. He has been the director of the office for the *National Human Development Report*, United Nations Development Programme, Mexico City, since 2002.

Alia Moubayed is a country economist in the Europe and Central Asia Region, World Bank. Her research interests include trade and public finance. She holds a BA degree in economics and a master's degree in business administration, finance, and public administration and public policy. Prior to joining the Bank, she worked at the Ministry of Economy and Trade, the Central Bank, and the Council for Development and Reconstruction, Beirut, Lebanon.

Kaspar Richter is a senior economist with seven years of experience in South Asia, East Asia, and Africa at the World Bank, as well as two years of experience in Eastern Europe with the TACIS programme of the European Union, the Economist Intelligence Unit, and the World Bank. He holds a master's degree in econometrics and mathematical economics and a PhD in economics from the London School of Economics and Political Science, as well as a diploma in economics and a diploma in political science from the Freie Universität Berlin.

Marcos Robles is an economist in the Poverty and Inequality Unit, Inter-American Development Bank. He has been coordinator of the Budget and Social Expenditure Project (United Nations Development Programme and the United Nations Children's Fund) and the Program for the Improvement of the Measurement of Living Conditions (Inter-American Development Bank, World Bank, and the United Nations Economic Commission for Latin America and the Caribbean) in Paraguay; adviser, National Institute of Statistics and Informatics and National Institute of Planning of Peru; manager of quantitative methods, Maximixe Consulting, and professor at several universities in Peru and Mexico. He received his bachelor's degree in economics from the National Agrarian University of Peru and a master's degree in Economics from the Center for Research and Teaching Economics of Mexico. Recently, he has supported institutions of the governments of Honduras, Jamaica, Panama, and Paraguay in the production of monetary poverty maps and participated in research on social protection in the Dominican Republic, Mexico, and Paraguay.

María de Lourdes Rodríguez-Chamussy is a PhD student at the University of California at Berkeley. She has worked as coeditor of the *National Human Development Report*, United Nations Development Programme, Mexico City.

Kenneth Simler is a senior economist in the Poverty Reduction Group, Poverty Reduction and Economic Management Network, World Bank. He leads the team working on shared growth and the poverty and social impact of policy reforms. His research interests include the measurement of poverty and inequality, poverty reduction strategies, human capital development, education, and child undernutrition. Prior to joining the Bank he was a research fellow at the International Food Policy Research Institute, Washington, DC, and a research associate at the Cornell Food and Nutrition Policy Program, Cornell University, Ithaca, NY. He holds a PhD in agricultural economics from Cornell University.

Rob Swinkels is a senior poverty economist with the World Bank in Vietnam. He has held this position for the past five years, during which he has worked on promoting and improving poverty measurement and high-quality poverty analysis. He has also supported greater results orientation and poverty focus in national planning and budget processes in Vietnam. Before joining the Bank, he worked as a policy adviser in the Ministry of Agriculture, Bhutan, where he was responsible for strengthening local capacity in the collection and analysis of reliable economic data for policy making. He has also been involved in economic analysis and multidisciplinary research in Kenya aimed at more sustainable and more efficient land use through agroforestry.

Miguel Székely is the undersecretary for secondary education, Ministry of Public Education, Mexico. Between March 2002 and January 2006, he served as deputy minister for planning and evaluation at the Ministry of Social Development. He has also been chief of the Office of Regional Development at the Office of the President of Mexico, vice president of the Territorial Policy Committee at the Organisation for Economic Co-operation and Development, and research economist at the Inter-American Development Bank. He has a master's degree in economics for development and a PhD in economics from the University of Oxford and a BA in economics and a master's degree in public policy from the Instituto Tecnológico Autónomo de México. He has researched widely on the topics of inequality and poverty, with more than 60 academic publications, including seven books, journal articles, and chapters in edited volumes.

Carrie Turk is a senior poverty economist at the World Bank. For the last seven years, she has been based in the Bank office in Vietnam, where her work focuses on bringing high-quality poverty data and analysis to policy-making and planning processes. This work involves substantial engagement with research institutes and government partners to improve local capacity in the production and use of poverty policy analysis. Prior to living in Vietnam, she worked with a British nongovernmental organization on programs in Bangladesh, India, Nepal, and Vietnam. She previously lived in Papua New Guinea, where she worked as an economist in the planning section of the Department of Finance and Planning.

Tara Vishwanath is a lead economist, adviser on Poverty Reduction Strategy Papers, and poverty coordinator for the Poverty Reduction and Economic Management Unit, South Asia Region, World Bank. Before joining the Bank, she was a professor in the

Economics Department, Northwestern University, Evanston, IL. In South Asia, she provides leadership in poverty initiatives, including in survey-based analysis, the development of monitoring tools, the design and evaluation of policy interventions, and strategic policy. She has managed the cash grant program of the tsunami project and supplied technical support for welfare reform in Sri Lanka and the cash grant program of the Earthquake Reconstruction and Rehabilitation Project, Pakistan.

Nobuo Yoshida is an economist in the Poverty Reduction and Economic Management Unit, South Asia Region, World Bank. He has been involved in a number of poverty assessments and development policy reviews and a wide range of analytical work on poverty measurement, including a poverty mapping exercise in Sri Lanka. His research interests are centered on exploring growth and poverty from the spatial angle, such as in poverty mapping, lagging region issues, and the impact of internal migration on poverty and growth. He is currently participating in a poverty mapping exercise in India.

PART One

Applications and Lessons

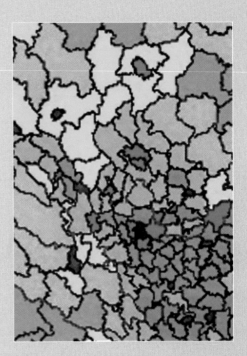

Poverty Maps for Policy Making
Beyond the Obvious Targeting Applications

TARA BEDI, ALINE COUDOUEL, AND KENNETH SIMLER

S mall area estimation poverty maps are a recent innovation that provide detailed estimates of poverty levels in highly disaggregated geographical units (see box 1.1). The presentation of these detailed estimates in the form of maps is a powerful communication tool because the maps summarize poverty estimates for hundreds or even thousands of towns, villages, or urban neighborhoods on a single page and in a visual format that is readily understandable by a wide audience. The presentation as a map not only summarizes a large volume of data concisely, but it also enhances the interpretation of that data by preserving the spatial relationships among different areas, something that simply is not possible in a tabular data format.

A large part of the initial impetus behind the development of these poverty mapping techniques has been supplied by the need to target antipoverty spending more precisely. Because the maps helped identify the areas with the greatest number of poor people and the highest poverty rates (not always the same thing), it was anticipated that policies and programs would be able to make more effective use of scarce resources. Knowing the distribution of the poor helps to ensure that antipoverty programs reach the poor and that the leakage of the benefits to those who are not poor is limited.

Although poverty maps have, indeed, become valuable tools for targeting programs, they have had a much wider impact as well. Besides targeting in specific programs, the maps have also informed the planning process at the subnational level. Patterns of poverty revealed by the maps may assist in regional planning efforts that consider poverty in a particular area and in neighboring areas and examine how the poverty in the two sets of areas may be economically linked.

We are grateful to Norbert Henninger and Peter Lanjouw for their advice and helpful discussions in the preparation of this chapter.

BOX 1.1   Building Poverty Maps: The Small Area Estimation Method

Typical household surveys, which are the basis of most poverty estimates, comprise a sample of several thousand households. Although this provides a rich information base on the living standards of the sample households, the sample size is usually only sufficiently large to estimate poverty to the first subnational administrative unit, such as a province or state.

By combining the detailed information of a household survey with the comprehensive coverage of a national census, one may estimate poverty levels for much smaller areas. Although these small area estimates are indirect and are calculated with a certain degree of statistical error (or uncertainty), they may be suitably precise to be useful for policy purposes (see Elbers, Lanjouw, and Lanjouw 2003).

At least two data sets are required to implement the method. One is a detailed household survey that includes a measure of welfare, which is typically consumption per capita. The other data source is a national census or, alternatively, a large national survey that includes a significant share of the country's population.

In the first stage, the analysts use multiple regression analysis to estimate a model of household consumption. The variables in the model are restricted to those variables that are available in both the survey and the census, and the data sources are examined to ensure that they are indeed comparable.

In the second stage, the estimated model parameters are applied to the census data. Simulation methods are used to introduce a random disturbance term, which is required because the model does not predict consumption perfectly. The simulations provide an estimate of consumption per capita for every household in the census. These estimates are then used, along with the appropriate poverty lines, to estimate poverty measures at various levels of aggregation, such as province, state, district, subdistrict, and municipality. The method also produces an estimate of the standard error of the poverty measure, which is used to construct a confidence interval for the poverty estimate. The estimates are then typically merged with a map in a geographic information system (GIS) to facilitate the presentation and visual analysis of patterns.

Standard statistical software packages may be used, although elaborate programming is required. The initial poverty mapping analyses were conducted using SAS software (originally known as Statistical Analysis System software). The World Bank has since developed special-purpose poverty mapping software, PovMap, that is freely available at http://iresearch.worldbank.org. PovMap has a graphical user interface that greatly simplifies the small area estimation of poverty and inequality.

The increasing decentralization of government authority has also created demand for the information that the maps may provide. Although provincial governors are no doubt interested in how poor their provinces are relative to other provinces, they are probably more interested in knowing which parts of the province are the poorest so that they may focus development efforts where they are needed most. Similarly, a district commissioner would be interested in subdistrict poverty rates so as to help set poverty reduction priorities within the district.

Poverty maps are likewise used to examine the geographical determinants of poverty. By combining the poverty maps with other spatial data sets, one may analyze the extent to which natural geography and climate (for example, elevation, rainfall, and temperatures) and infrastructure (such as roads, railways, and markets) determine poverty levels within an area.

This chapter illustrates the wide range of impacts that small area estimation poverty maps have had on policy making in many countries. Although most small area estimation analyses and the resulting maps appear to have been motivated primarily by the desire for more accurate targeting, the country studies presented in this volume show that the poverty maps have influenced policy in many different ways, some of which have been unexpected. These impacts include (1) a deeper understanding of poverty in a country; (2) a radical shift in the dialogue on poverty, including the motivation for new strategies and approaches; (3) the elaboration of the operational details of specific programs; (4) increased accountability among governments; and, last but not least, (5) the development of capacity and interest in evidence-based policy making.

This chapter briefly discusses these different types and levels of impacts of poverty maps in the countries studied. It also discusses the limitations and potential pitfalls of poverty maps. We hope these discussions will stimulate similar exercises and encourage policy makers and analysts to expand the innovative uses of small area poverty estimates.

Building Awareness, Changing Perceptions, Opening a New Dialogue on Poverty

Opening the dialogue on poverty

By providing new and more detailed insights on the state of poverty, small area estimation poverty maps may be a powerful tool to foster greater awareness on poverty issues in a country. Often, discussion of poverty is dominated by a single number: the proportion of the population that is living below the poverty line (that is, the national poverty headcount ratio). Poverty maps offer rich information about the heterogeneous poverty conditions that underlie the national average, revealing unsuspected pockets of poverty even within relatively well-off areas. Poverty maps may also supply empirical evidence to confirm patterns in poverty that were suspected, but are controversial.

Although the technical aspects of producing a poverty map may be complicated, the maps that are produced may be easily understood by a wide audience, much of which is sometimes at the periphery of policy debates. The maps may thus broaden the dialogue on poverty, the determinants of poverty, and the policy consequences. Because these maps present data that are relevant and important to local communities, local elected officials, and local service providers, they often interest many stakeholders.

The maps create an important opportunity for different actors to join in the public debate on poverty. This space for dialogue is critical because it brings together many actors who probably would not otherwise speak on such issues and creates a forum for them to reflect on poverty. Hence, in many countries, the elaboration of the maps has opened a debate and a dialogue on poverty, much broader than any debate about the maps themselves. Moreover, the maps are an important source of information for actions to reduce poverty.

One of the more dramatic examples of how poverty maps may raise awareness, generate discussion, and lead to action on poverty is the case of Morocco. Although there is less poverty in Morocco than in most countries in Africa, the poverty map in Morocco has highlighted the problem of persistent poverty and sparked a national conversation on poverty. King Mohammed VI has taken an especially keen interest, and the poverty maps have been used to help design and allocate the budget for his signature program, the National Human Development Initiative.

In Vietnam, poverty maps have revealed high levels of inequality both across and within regions. This strong message has resonated with many users and provided empirical evidence of patterns that were only suspected, but never documented. This has shifted the understanding of poverty and welfare in the country and enabled many stakeholders to improve the understanding of poverty in their own organizations and reshape programs accordingly. The maps have also been an important background resource for media articles, other publications, lectures, and organized discussions, such as the Partnership to Assist the Poorest Communes.

Solving issues in the definition of poverty

The development of the poverty maps has often triggered a broader debate among analysts and practitioners on the definition of poverty. The elaboration of the maps has also often been the platform for a larger discussion on poverty measurement and the selection of a particular national definition. For example, in some countries, a variety of tools is used to measure well-being, such as basic needs indexes, consumption per capita, and income. Rarely is there perfect agreement in the ranking of households or regions across the different measures. Moreover, there is frequently disagreement about the appropriate threshold value or values that should be used to distinguish the poor from the nonpoor.

The poverty map alone does not necessarily resolve such disagreements, but the map does foster debate and analysis about what it means to be poor, how one might measure poverty, and what additional perspective each of the various measures may lend to understanding poverty. While the various measures may reflect the multidimensional nature of poverty, the process of constructing a poverty map has sometimes produced closer agreement on official measures of well-being and poverty thresholds.

For example, in Vietnam, the debate generated by the maps and other poverty measures has resulted in the definition of a new poverty line that is closer to the estimates derived from the household survey than were previous official poverty data. The poverty mapping exercise has also demonstrated the need for independent data.

In Sri Lanka, prior to the appearance of the poverty map, many different poverty lines were used by organizations, creating a lack of clarity on the meaning of poverty. Through a consultative approach, stakeholders came together to review the methodological issues involved in estimating poverty and to offer recommendations. Based on these recommendations, another study was carried out to select an acceptable and understandable methodology for calculating the poverty line. One of the key impacts of the map has thus been the establishment of an official poverty line that has attracted a consensus among the various stakeholders.

Revisiting Old Ideas, Exploring New Options

What might we do with a poverty map?

Countries have also used small area estimation poverty maps to analyze existing programs or resource allocation mechanisms and assess their effectiveness. To achieve this objective, countries have integrated the small area estimates with geo-referenced information on various aspects of the programs under scrutiny. This is typically done using a geographic information system (GIS), which systematically organizes data on the location and characteristics of points of service, various sorts of zones, or networks. These features are not specific to poverty maps; indeed, more aggregate poverty estimates from survey data alone may also be projected onto maps. However, more aggregate poverty maps are typically too coarse to provide substantial insights on the spatial correlates of poverty. In other words, until the advent of the poverty maps, poverty data were often a weak link in GIS analysis because the poverty data were at much lower resolution than the other spatial data. The added value of using a GIS is that a GIS makes it relatively easy to bring together and analyze information based on different units of analysis (see box 1.2), and this opens new doors for the analysis of incidence and targeting.

The combination of data from different sources and at various levels of analysis has allowed many countries to deepen their understanding of poverty and its determinants. This may then lead to shifts in the approaches adopted by governments to fight poverty, design new programs, revise strategies, and so on, in addition to changes in existing programs. Sri Lanka provides an interesting example. Overlaying the poverty map and a map depicting access to nearby markets or cities has demonstrated that poverty incidence is highly correlated with geographical isolation as measured by distance to the nearest market or city. This has prompted a shift to an emphasis on reaching areas that are more isolated. A similar exercise has been conducted with GIS data on drought patterns. Although this simple visual correlation does not provide conclusive evidence on causal relationships, it does help identify relationships that merit closer investigation.

The projection of detailed poverty data—together with poverty correlates—onto maps may also improve the understanding of phenomena that exhibit spatial patterns or follow spatial processes. This might apply to processes such as spillover effects (when an intervention has effects beyond its immediate area), diffusion patterns (when knowledge, techniques, or practices are passed from one area to neighboring areas), trade, and other factors related to proximity and spatial interaction.

If the poverty maps are available for more than one point in time, it becomes possible to examine temporal changes in poverty at a level that heretofore has not been possible. In addition to exploring changes in poverty over the given time period, one may also examine how these changes and changes in other variables during the same time period are correlated. For intertemporal comparisons to be useful, it is critical that the welfare measures and poverty thresholds are consistent over time. Ecuador was one of the first countries to construct a series (or panel) of poverty maps. It used data from 1990 and 2001, and the two maps helped identify areas where there had

---

BOX 1.2   What May Be Projected onto the Poverty Maps

Small area poverty data may be integrated with other data, such as information on infrastructure, education, topography, and health, through the use of a graphic information system (GIS). A GIS also allows the analysis of multiple correlations when numerous elements are projected onto maps. For instance, poverty data may be overlaid with geo-referenced data on road networks. A particularly useful feature is the physical representation on the map, which allows the merging of information at different levels of observation, such as subdistrict-level poverty estimates, accompanied by rainfall data that follow a natural pattern rather than administrative boundaries.

A GIS includes data on

- points (for instance, points of service delivery such as schools, health centers, or boreholes),
- networks (networks of infrastructure such as roads, electricity, or telecommunications), and
- areas (areas of administration or livelihood such as enumeration areas, districts, or communities).

For each of these, the GIS includes data on location (geographical coordinates) and may include data on the status of the item (such as the quality of a health center, the number of teachers in a school, the condition of a road, and so on). Natural features such as rainfall, elevation, and agroclimatic characteristics may also be incorporated in a GIS (see figure 1.1 on next page).

For instance, in Kenya, the GIS database contains information on topography, administrative boundaries, population, poverty, election results, public expenditures, schools, health facilities, weather stations, agroecological zones, climatic zones, soil erosion, rivers, lakes, catchment areas, elevation, road quality, and mobile phone masts and coverage areas.

(continued)

BOX 1.2   **What May Be Projected onto the Poverty Maps (*Continued*)**

The Content of a Typical GIS

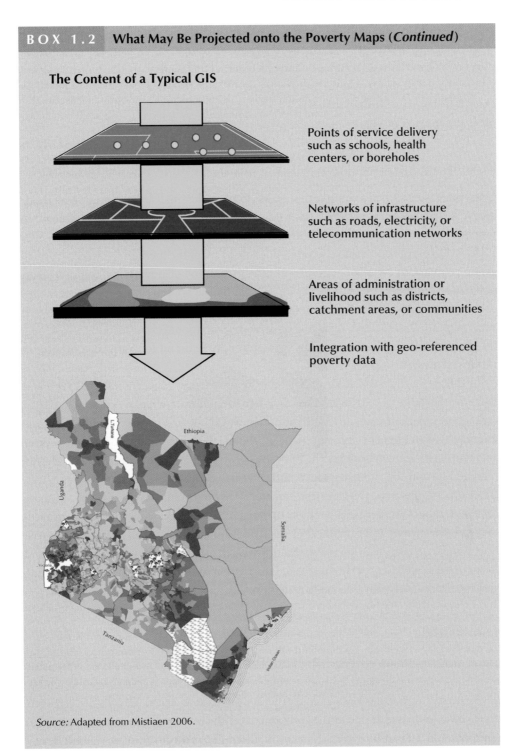

Points of service delivery such as schools, health centers, or boreholes

Networks of infrastructure such as roads, electricity, or telecommunication networks

Areas of administration or livelihood such as districts, catchment areas, or communities

Integration with geo-referenced poverty data

Source: Adapted from Mistiaen 2006.

been a significant increase in poverty over that time (for example, urban areas in the Coast Region, where the 1990 poverty rates were lower), as well as areas where poverty had remained largely unchanged (such as rural areas in the Coast Region, where the 1990 poverty rates were higher). These findings were consistent with expectations, considering that the 1999 financial crisis in Ecuador had hit urban areas the most severely.

Broadening the application of the small area estimation methodology

Once there is a group in a country that is able to apply the small area estimation methodology, it then becomes possible, with guidance from experts in this methodology, to produce small area estimations for other indicators besides poverty, such as nutrition or HIV/AIDS prevalence. It also becomes possible to adapt the method to undertake small group estimations for nongeographical disaggregations of poverty. Many important population subgroups are statistically invisible in typical household surveys because they constitute a relatively small percentage of the population. Common examples of such subgroups are the disabled, orphans, or certain occupational classifications. Analyzing the poverty status of these subgroups separately may be useful for planning purposes in various ministries.

In Indonesia, through the capacity built by producing a poverty map, *Badan Pusat Statistik,* the national statistical office, acquired the skills needed to produce a small area estimation nutrition map. The nutrition map was then used by the World Food Programme to select beneficiary areas. In fact, the nutrition map has also become a valuable tool at the Ministry of Health. Prior to decentralization, the ministry had collected nutrition data at the subdistrict level to use in its yearly plans of action for provinces. After decentralization, the ministry had to rely on the voluntary submission of these data by local governments. A number of provinces no longer collected the data or, if they did, the quality and timeliness of the data were not guaranteed. Because its nutrition map illustrates nutrition estimates down to the subdistrict level, the World Food Programme is able to provide substitute information for the ministry to use in planning and monitoring activities related to nutrition.

Coordination

Small area estimation poverty maps have also assisted policy makers in coordinating the efforts of actors and agencies in setting priorities and devising strategies to achieve goals. An example from Mexico is instructive. In Mexico, the small area poverty estimates have been used as one of the components of the human development index. This approach has helped provide information about the most prominent human development gaps, the areas with the lowest indexes, and the poverty issues in these areas. Using this combined information, the president of Mexico has developed a plan to reduce poverty and promote human development by focusing on the 50 municipalities with the highest poverty rates and the lowest human development indexes. Seven ministries operating 12 different but related programs now focus as a priority on the poor in these 50 municipal areas. These seven ministries have had to coordinate the 12 programs to meet the targets set out in the plan. Previously, each ministry and program had its own priorities and objectives that were implemented in isolation. Now, not only has each of the 50 municipalities seen an increase in its budget, but it is also benefiting from programs that are more effective because of the greater coordination among the ministries.

An example from South Africa is also instructive. Data and maps on poverty, sanitation, clean water, and the incidence of cholera were used to help contain the spread of cholera in KwaZulu-Natal Province in South Africa in January 2001. Poverty and cholera data sets showed that the cholera outbreak had followed a river floodplain and was moving through poor areas toward other poor areas. The use of the data sets assisted in producing a swift, well-coordinated response by national and local government departments (health, water, and so on), which agreed to the following:

- Provide safe water in tankers and portable toilets in affected areas
- Develop epidemiology training and reassign health personnel to affected areas
- Develop health education and awareness of good hygiene practices in affected areas and other potentially high-risk areas
- Provide health material and additional health services in affected areas

This response led to the containment of the outbreak within three months. This meant that fewer people died (the death rate was 0.22 percent among more than 100,000 cases) and helped prevent a massive outbreak across the country.

The collation and use of information from research and administrative sources also encouraged collaboration among institutions, provided an opportunity to offer integrated services, and prompted calls for additional research on the collection of appropriate social and environmental data to facilitate future planning and mitigation activities and to respond to flooding, fires, and drought.

Motivating changes in systems and interventions

Poverty maps have been an aid in motivating and informing efforts to refine programs at several levels, from an overall analysis of public expenditure in Morocco to analyzing the coverage of a particular program, as in the cases of Albania and Vietnam. Poverty mapping analysis has not only revealed patterns that are not otherwise visible, but has also been effective in addressing politically sensitive questions in an objective manner. As a result, locational decisions about programs and project implementation and funding allocation are likely to be less politically charged.

The case of Sri Lanka offers a good example. In Sri Lanka, the small area estimates on poverty at the Divisional Secretariat level were compared to the coverage of the Samurdhi transfer program, the largest welfare program in Sri Lanka. Only a weak correlation was found between the areas targeted by the program and the areas ranked as the poorest in the poverty map. This helped quantify the extent of mistargeting in the Samurdhi program with regard to both undercoverage and leakage.

As a result, the formulas for the allocation of funds in the program were modified. This was very sensitive politically, as many people stood to receive reduced benefits or none at all because of the changes in the allocation criteria. As a compromise, allocations remained fairly constant for existing recipient areas, but the poorest of these areas saw an increase in funding.

As a benchmark for the allocation of resources, the poverty mapping data are a powerful tool. Given the limited budgets of governments for propoor policies and programs, the ability to identify any mistargeting is a valuable asset.

A poverty map may also be used to validate a program's targeting mechanisms. If the correlation between poverty and the distribution of program benefits is high, the map provides evidence that the existing targeting criteria are working as planned. This has been the case of Program 135 in Vietnam, which is coordinated by the Committee for Ethnic Minorities. The poverty map was overlaid with information on communes receiving funds through Program 135. The results of this exercise validated the program's targeting criteria by showing that most communes benefiting from Program 135 were in poor areas and that most poor areas were included in the program, although the analysis did reveal a few gaps in coverage in the Northwest region that needed attention.

In Morocco, an analysis of public expenditure and poverty has provided a measure of the extent to which program allocations have matched the patterns of poverty (the targeting differential approach). Morocco has found a strong correlation between poverty and other local data. This has enabled a deeper understanding of local conditions, the evolution of social conditions, and the effectiveness of government programs in reaching poor areas.

Designing Interventions Tailored to Local Needs

Targeting interventions: location of the intervention

The most common motivation for estimating highly disaggregated poverty indicators and producing associated poverty maps is to improve targeting in interventions. Indeed, a poverty map may be used as the sole criterion or one of several criteria for identifying appropriate intervention locations (see box 1.3).

Poverty maps rank areas from poorest to richest based on poverty estimations, although one needs to bear in mind that the estimates have a corresponding standard

---

BOX 1.3   Geographical Targeting: How Much Does It Help?

Targeting resources to areas where poverty is more acute is an intuitively appealing solution to the budget constraint faced in poverty reduction programs. Elbers et al. (2007) simulate and compare the effects on poverty of uniform transfers (whereby all households receive identical transfers) and transfers that are optimally targeted geographically. They show that the use of more highly disaggregated poverty data in targeting cuts the cost of reducing poverty significantly. For instance, in Cambodia, a transfer program that relies on provincial data in targeting is able to achieve the same level of poverty reduction as a uniform (that is, untargeted) transfer program, but at about one-half the cost. If targeting is carried out at the commune level, the same amount of poverty reduction may be achieved for less than one-third the cost of an untargeted transfer program.

Cost Comparison: Uniform Transfers Versus Optimal Targeting

Transfer type	Rural Ecuador %	Madagascar %	Cambodia %
Uniform transfer	100.0	100.0	100.0
Optimal targeting			
First administrative level	76.0	60.7	54.5
Second administrative level	66.7	46.4	41.4
Third administrative level	58.4	37.6	30.8

Source: Elbers et al. 2007.
Note: The administrative levels (first to third) refer to 21 provinces, 195 cantons, and 915 parishes in Ecuador; 6 faritany (provinces), 111 fivandrona (districts), and 1,248 firaisana (counties) in Madagascar; and 24 provinces, 180 districts, and 1,594 communes in Cambodia.

However, the authors also examine the limitations of geographical targeting. Some nonpoor people are living within poorer areas, so that geographical targeting may still produce errors of inclusion. Similarly, strictly geographical targeting would exclude the poor who are living in wealthier areas. The gains realized with geographical targeting therefore depend on the ability of the data to provide sufficiently disaggregated information on poverty and on the level of inequality within the small areas. In addition, the political economy of geographical targeting might limit the ability of governments to apply such optimal targeting. To reduce the cost of poverty reduction programs further, the authors recommend that geographical targeting should be combined with some other method of targeting within areas, for example, targeting based on individual or household characteristics associated with poverty.

---

error and confidence interval. Nonetheless, this information is objective and transparent. In programs in which the main objective is poverty reduction, this tool is easy to use to prioritize expenditure among areas. In countries in which living standards are relatively homogeneous within small areas, such a tool is helpful in locating pockets of poverty. Even in those countries where there is considerable economic heterogeneity within small areas, the poverty map is a useful tool in implementing a multi-stage targeting strategy.

In Bulgaria, poverty maps account for one of five formal criteria used in allocating social infrastructure projects among municipalities. The other four criteria are the local unemployment rate, the local employment rate, the cost per beneficiary, and the share of cofinancing. The steering committee of the Social Investment Fund has found that the maps are important in the allocation process because they have helped guarantee an objective ranking among municipality applicants. Indeed, the committee has considered the maps so helpful that it has now integrated the small area poverty estimates into the fund's management information system.

In Cambodia, the World Food Programme has integrated several maps, including information on infrastructure and vulnerability to flood and drought, into a GIS, along with small area poverty and nutrition maps. It has used the combined information to identify potential areas for its programs. The maps have also been used for resource targeting by, for example, the Ministry of Agriculture, Forestry, and Fisheries.

Poverty maps may likewise be an important tool for decentralized governments. In Cambodia, the government of Prey Veng Province uses the poverty map, along with its own database, to identify the poorest districts.

Targeting interventions: funding formulas

Another key application of poverty maps is in determining the funding formulas that will cause interventions to vary across areas depending on the level of poverty or some other indicator. If poverty is the main or only criterion used to identify target areas, the funding formula may be designed to vary benefit levels across the entire range of scores instead of relying on a cutoff score to identify locations eligible for a program. In this way, all areas will receive a minimum amount of resources, but the allocations will increase in areas where the poverty level is greater. Such compromises are often a political necessity; sometimes, there is a need to demonstrate that all parts of the country are receiving at least some benefit from a program. Furthermore, because all areas are bound to contain a certain number of poor people, this type of targeting, if it is combined with a method to target individual poor households, will help ensure that all poor people receive benefits.

In Kenya, the allocation formula used in the Constituency Development Fund has been revised so that 25 percent of the allocations are based on the incidence of poverty, and those areas showing higher poverty incidence receive more resources from this portion of the allocations.

In Bulgaria, the poverty map is used to target transfers from the government budget, donor support, and European funds to those municipalities with the highest estimated level of poverty incidence and social exclusion.

In Cambodia, the Department of Local Administration of the Ministry of the Interior allocates commune development funds based on three criteria: a base allocation for all communes (30 percent of the budget), an allocation for heavily populated communes (30 percent), and an allocation for the poorest communes (40 percent). The last relies on an annual communal profile, which is checked against the poverty map.

If a system relies on a score based on several criteria, policy makers will have the opportunity to tailor the intervention to the location. For example, areas with a higher score because of poor infrastructure may become the focus of programs that have a stronger emphasis on building infrastructure, while areas with higher poverty rates might obtain programs that tackle the poverty dimension. Thus, the Albanian Development Fund provides resources for projects that focus on infrastructure and the delivery of social services. Prior to 2003, project designs were standard across all communes. Starting in 2004, the fund has applied a scoring system whereby eight criteria, including the rankings from the poverty maps, are used to rank communes and municipalities. The other criteria revolve around technical, social, and environmental endowments. The fund's resources are then distributed based on the score received by each commune or municipality. Areas with a higher poverty score receive additional resources.

Strengthening Accountability

The information provided by poverty maps has several qualities that contribute to the role of the maps in strengthening accountability mechanisms. First, the information supplied in poverty maps and the visual format are easy to understand. This is especially true when areas are ranked by level of poverty.

Second and perhaps more importantly, the information in poverty maps is relevant to all actors, including local government officials, service providers, civil society organizations, and the public. The maps tell these actors about the level of poverty in the areas where they live, work, and raise their children, and the maps allow for ready comparison with the situation in other communities.

Third, small area poverty maps are objective. They are based on established data sets that are collected and stored in systematic ways. Decisions based on such information help prevent local capture or subjective decision making.

Fourth, poverty maps are also transparent in that they follow a methodology that is well established, systematic, and publicly available. The poverty estimates are derived through standard processes.

For all these reasons, the maps provide citizen groups and local authorities with powerful information they may use to hold officials accountable. Poverty maps have already been used as lobbying tools to promote equitable and objective allocation mechanisms and program processes. For example, in Morocco the maps have been widely disseminated by the government and have supplied citizens and local officials with the information they need to hold central government agencies accountable for program placement and coverage.

Promoting Evidence-Based Decision Making by Building Capacity

Strengthening the capacity of data users

Even in the absence of detailed small area poverty estimates, people typically have some impressions or opinions about the areas that are poorer or richer than others. Poverty maps usually confirm some of these impressions, but also frequently turn some of the conventional wisdom on its head. For example, in Indonesia and Thailand, the small area estimation poverty maps produced counterintuitive results. Subsequent in-depth investigation of some of the apparently anomalous results confirmed that the poverty maps were capturing information about living standards that had been overlooked until then. Such surprises not only foster greater appreciation for empirical evidence (as long as there is confidence in the data and methods), but also stimulate considerable thought and discussion about how casual impressions may misinform.

Poverty maps may thus highlight the usefulness of data collection and the wealth of information contained in surveys and censuses. In part, this is likely because the main data sources—the national census and household surveys—are usually respected as objective sources of information, even if they are not used to their full potential. This is especially true of census data, which are generally underexploited. By accentuating the value of census and survey data, the poverty mapping exercise may raise the profile of the national statistics agency as well.

Because poverty maps supply users with data that are relatively easy to understand and apply, users may, if questioned, easily indicate the data on which they have based their views and readily defend their decisions. This quality is appealing for policy makers.

The poverty maps may also be drawn on to strengthen the understanding of potential users through training, seminars, workshops, and other presentations and thereby help open a dialogue among partners who might not have the skills to engage in a more technical conversation on poverty measurement. In Bulgaria, several poverty mapping training workshops have been conducted among mayors, other municipal authorities, and officials from various line ministries. Likewise, in Vietnam, the poverty maps have played a valuable role in the dialogue between nongovernmental organizations and the government. They have increased understanding among both groups and raised the capacity of nongovernmental organizations to participate in public forums on the relevant issues.

Building analytical and statistical capacity

For the poverty maps to become policy relevant, it is important that further analysis be carried out on the data. This analysis might involve, for instance, performing decomposition calculations and integrating poverty data with other geo-referenced data to examine correlations. Regardless of the exercise, to carry out such studies, experts must possess or acquire certain skills in poverty analysis. By strengthening their skills, statistical analysts become more proficient in accomplishing a wider range of data production and analytical functions. Once developed, such capacity has beneficial spillover effects, as it may then be used in other poverty-related studies. This enhances the value of statistics because they are rendered more reliable and useful.

Experiences in a number of countries have shown that the production of poverty maps alone may have this effect and that the poverty mapping process may be harnessed to strengthen local statistical and analytical capacity.

In Indonesia and Sri Lanka, for example, by producing poverty maps, groups of local experts have been developed that are able to replicate and update poverty maps and undertake the analysis required to make poverty maps more policy relevant.

In Thailand, the government agency at the center of the poverty mapping effort has hired a research institute to train analysts from various agencies on the mix of statistical and software skills needed to produce the poverty maps. The analysts are divided into teams consisting of a leader, a software specialist, and a backup, so that, if one member leaves, there will still be two others who are able to complete the process. In this way, institutional capacity is being emphasized.

In Bulgaria, a Grant for Poverty Monitoring, Evaluation, and Policy Design was secured through the Institutional Development Fund, and a portion was used to build institutional capacity for poverty analysis, policy design, and the ex ante assessment of the poverty impact of government policies and to foster a participatory policy dialogue on poverty issues.

Limitations

While the policy applications of poverty maps are numerous and expanding, it is necessary to keep in mind the limitations of this methodology. If the maps are applied without regard for the limitations, the results may be damaging. Poverty maps should be applied in the appropriate context, respecting the constraints and advantages of the sort of information they may and may not provide. The key areas of concern include the quality of the data inputs; the quality of the poverty mapping analysis; the nearly exclusive focus of poverty maps on consumption poverty; the ability of the maps to demonstrate correlation, but not causation; the constraints on the degree of disaggregation possible; and the typically long intervals between updates of the maps.

The poverty map is only as accurate as the survey and the census

The quality of the output of the poverty mapping methodology is constrained by the quality of the inputs, that is, the census and survey data sets. If there are problems with either data set, these problems will not disappear when the data sets are used to produce the map. It is therefore important to identify the problems that may exist in each data set, determine ways to minimize the impact of these problems on the resulting small area poverty estimates, and be candid about these problems when disseminating the maps. For example, in Ecuador, the 1999 household survey relied on in the production of the poverty map did not include El Oriente Region. No sound alternative was found for these missing data, and, as a result, this region was excluded in the final 2001 poverty map. This limited the policy relevance of the map because it is hard to make policy and program decisions when information from an entire region is lacking.

Poverty maps are built on the assumption that the census and survey data sets represent the same underlying population. This assumption will hold if the data sets are collected in the same timeframe and the survey sampling frame is representative of the larger population. But, if these data sets are based on different time periods or if the survey is not designed to be adequately representative of the population, then the assumption becomes less tenable. This is especially the case when dramatic events occur between the collection of the census and survey data sets, such as a natural disaster or an economic crisis.

Often, censuses are combinations of population and housing censuses, and the accuracy of the data collection systems rely heavily on knowledge of the location of dwellings. This may lead to important omissions in environments where a significant segment of the population lives on the streets or in irregular housing. The effect of such omissions

---

BOX 1.4   Potential Technical Issues and Policy Relevance

In 2006, the World Bank commissioned a panel of top academics to evaluate research conducted within the Bank between 1998 and 2005. The panel expressed doubts about the poverty map research program at the Bank, noting three particular concerns: (1) the poverty estimates may be much less precise than the researchers claim, (2) the U.S. Census Bureau considers the small area estimation method unreliable, and (3) in at least one case (a recent poverty map constructed in South Africa), the Bank has not been sufficiently focused on the client. (For the report, see Banerjee et al. 2006.)

Of these three criticisms, it is the first that concentrates on the basic methodology and is therefore potentially most damning. The review panel correctly observes that, in the estimation of the first-stage consumption model, the intracluster correlation across household disturbances within enumeration areas is likely also to be correlated across these areas. It is possible, even likely, that households in a given area are systematically richer or poorer than a simple consumption model would predict based on the observable characteristics in the model. If this correlation of prediction errors is ignored, the calculated standard errors will overstate the true precision of the estimates, thereby overstating the statistical significance of any differences among small areas. The review panel asserts that the small area estimation poverty mapping method fails to account for this correlation and concludes that the poverty estimates therefore risk being too imprecise to be useful.

In response to these criticisms, Lanjouw and Ravallion (2006) acknowledge that the correlation of prediction errors within and across enumeration areas is an important and valid concern. They note, however, that addressing this concern has been a major focus of the development of the small area estimation poverty mapping methodology and point to an earlier paper (Elbers, Lanjouw, and Lanjouw 2002) that deals with the review panel's concern explicitly. They demonstrate that, far from ignoring these correlations, one may reduce the impact of the correlations

(continued)

on the poverty estimates needs to be considered and communicated in the presentation of the poverty maps.

The quality of the poverty map is only as good as the methodology

The small area estimation method has been developed carefully and subjected to extensive testing and peer review. But it is not foolproof. Even the advent of the user-friendly PovMap software has not eliminated the need for adequate training and proper application of that training. Producing reliable poverty maps requires close attention to detail and good judgment in making the numerous analytical decisions required. Among the most important issues are the comparability of the survey and census variables, the specification of the first-stage regression models, the evaluation of the standard errors in the poverty estimates, and the appropriate presentation of the results in map form. A recent independent review of World Bank research has highlighted potential weaknesses in the small area estimation method (see box 1.4). These weaknesses are all avoidable, and,

---

BOX 1.4   **Potential Technical Issues and Policy Relevance (*Continued*)**

to negligible levels by introducing a variety of enumeration area variables—calculated from the census or from a tertiary data set such as GIS data—into the first-stage model. In addition, they point out, diagnostic statistics may be scrutinized to determine if a given model specification is successful at removing the correlation from the error terms.

The signal lesson here is that, while the small area poverty mapping methodology does provide a mechanism for avoiding the pitfall highlighted by the review panel, it is the responsibility of the analytical team to specify a model that incorporates effects specific to enumeration areas and to perform the tests to ensure that the reported standard errors are not understated. Even convenient specialized software packages such as PovMap do not carry out this step automatically for the analyst: there is no substitute for careful analysis and good judgment. A similar caution applies to users of poverty maps: users should be prepared to challenge poverty map producers to demonstrate sufficient attention to such issues.

Responding to the second criticism, Lanjouw and Ravallion (2006) note that, so far, there has never been an explicit rejection of the Bank's small area estimation approach by the U.S. Census Bureau. Rather, they explain, the U.S. Census Bureau does not need to use the Bank's approach because it collects income and poverty data directly from three million households. Such a sample size is adequate for estimating small area poverty levels without resorting to the estimation of income from econometric models. The resources required to complete such a large survey would be far in excess of the budgets available to statistical agencies in low- and middle-income countries; so, direct estimation is not a feasible alternative there.

On the third criticism, Lanjouw and Ravallion (2006) dispute the basic assertion. They explain that, although Bank researchers were deeply and constructively involved in the development of South Africa's first poverty map using the 1996 census, the Bank was never a participant in the second poverty map, which was assembled by Statistics South Africa on the basis of the 2001 census.

indeed, they do not surface as problems in any of the country studies described in this volume.

Consumption poverty versus other dimensions of poverty

The poverty map only reports consumption or income poverty, it does not represent other attributes of poverty. These other attributes may be equally important in determining who is poor. In Thailand, the nonmaterial dimensions of poverty were central to the Ninth National Economic and Social Development Plan, which thus limited the applicability of the poverty map because the map does not cover these dimensions of poverty. In this context and in similar contexts, the poverty map should be considered an important source of information on poverty, even if it is not the sole source. In general, both the poverty map and other sources of poverty information should be viewed as complementary: together, they facilitate an understanding of poverty and potential poverty reduction policies that is deeper than the understanding produced by any single information source.

Correlation does not imply causality

The poverty map provides estimates of poverty, but it does not provide information on the causes of poverty. Furthermore, when a poverty map is overlaid with other information, the resulting analysis only reveals correlations between poverty and other spatial characteristics, but not the causal pathways. To understand the reasons for poverty, additional analysis and studies are needed. Although poverty maps may serve as an instrument to explore spatial relationships among indicators, these should not necessarily be interpreted as causal links.

Constraints on the degree of disaggregation

The poverty mapping method involves estimating consumption levels for every household recorded in the census, which is usually the entire population. However, to achieve reasonable precision in the estimates, it is necessary to aggregate observations to a unit that is above the household, such as a municipality, subdistrict, district, or other grouping. Thus, even though poverty maps may uncover the heterogeneity that lies behind provincial, state, or national averages recorded by surveys, the disaggregated estimates it provides are averages among smaller units. For example, in Morocco, the analysis revealed that there was large variation in living standards within urban neighborhoods. If there are large inequalities within a neighborhood, then an antipoverty program that relies only on geographical targeting might suffer from many errors of exclusion (excluding the poor in coverage) and many errors of inclusion (including the nonpoor in coverage; see elsewhere above).

More generally, in small areas that are estimated to be more or less poor relative to an average, there is likely to be a range of living standards, and this range is likely to vary considerably from site to site. The poverty estimate for an area may give an impression of homogenous poverty within that area, which is usually not the case. It is therefore important to associate poverty estimates with inequality estimates. It may also help to perform decomposition calculations that disentangle the levels of poverty and inequality within and between local areas (Elbers et al. 2004). In Morocco, it has been found that a large share of rural inequality is attributable to differences between communes. On the other hand, in urban areas, there is a high level of inequality within communes. This implies that, in rural areas, it is a good option to target resources on the commune versus the province level, which some development programs have been doing. At the same time, because there is also inequality within rural communes, it is important in targeting resources to combine the small area estimation tool with other household targeting tools.

The issues in updating poverty maps

If poverty maps are to be policy relevant, one has to be able to update them on a regular basis. The most thorough and straightforward means of updating a poverty map is to use newer census and survey data. But, because censuses are carried out every 10 years or so, updating the maps is a major problem. Policy makers want new data, but, in most countries and, especially, in countries where there have been rapid changes, three- or five-year-old data will not accurately represent the situation.

Initiatives are therefore under way to develop methods for updating poverty maps during intercensal years. The primary alternative now is to combine a new survey with an old census. One way this has been done is to take advantage of the fact that, in certain countries, such as Uganda, household surveys have a panel component. In cases where there is no panel component, a panel structure may be simulated. Any of these methods will involve more assumptions than the standard small area estimation approach and will need to be validated. Furthermore, the accuracy of the maps that result will be weaker than the best-case option, a new census and a new survey.

Conclusions

From their origins as a tool to improve the targeting of antipoverty policies and programs, poverty maps have evolved to serve many other functions in the policy process. By condensing huge volumes of data and sophisticated econometric analysis into an easily understood, visual map format, poverty maps are able to achieve a wider reach and more immediate impact than most analytical outputs. As outlined here and described in more detail in the country case studies, poverty maps may become important catalysts for raising general awareness about poverty and bringing a broader and more diverse set of stakeholders into the public discussion on poverty and poverty reduction policies. In the process, a reconsideration of the meaning of poverty and the way to measure poverty may emerge.

Advances in GIS technology have greatly expanded the uses of poverty maps by making it easier for nonspecialists to overlay or juxtapose poverty maps with other thematic maps. They are thus able to facilitate a better understanding of the spatial correlates and determinants of poverty. Similarly, poverty maps may help promote accountability and transparency because they may be compared with maps showing the allocation of antipoverty program benefits. Extension of the small area estimation methodology to examine poverty among small groups, such as the disabled, has also helped inform policy design and resource allocation.

As with any powerful tool, proper care must be exercised in constructing and using poverty maps. Poverty maps are best viewed not as decision-making tools per se, but as sources of detailed poverty data that may complement information from other sources. Capacity-building efforts should therefore pay attention not only to enhancing the ability of statistical agencies and analysts to produce poverty maps, but also to addressing the need for the effective communication of poverty map results and for training the users of poverty maps to become educated consumers who recognize the strengths and weaknesses of the maps.

References

Banerjee, Abhijit, Angus Deaton, Nora Lustig, and Ken Rogoff. 2006. "An Evaluation of World Bank Research, 1998–2005." With Edward Hsu. Report, World Bank, Washington, DC. http://siteresources.worldbank.org/DEC/Resources/84797-1109362238001/726454-1164121166494/RESEARCH-EVALUATION-2006-Main-Report.pdf.

Elbers, Chris, Tomoki Fujii, Peter F. Lanjouw, Berk Özler, and Wesley Yin. 2007. "Poverty Alleviation through Geographic Targeting: How Much Does Disaggregation Help?" *Journal of Development Economics* 83 (1): 198–213.

Elbers, Chris, Peter F. Lanjouw, Johan A. Mistiaen, Berk Özler, and Ken Simler. 2004. "On the Unequal Inequality of Poor Communities." *World Bank Economic Review* 18 (4): 401–21.

Elbers, Chris, Jean O. Lanjouw, and Peter F. Lanjouw. 2002. "Micro-Level Estimation of Welfare." Policy Research Working Paper 2911, World Bank, Washington, DC.

———. 2003. "Micro-Level Estimation of Poverty and Inequality." *Econometrica* 71 (1): 355–64.

Lanjouw, Peter F., and Martin Ravallion. 2006. "Response to the Evaluation Panel's Critique of Poverty Mapping." Report, Development Research Group, World Bank. http://siteresources.worldbank.org/INTPOVRES/Resources/PovertyMapping_Response_to_the_Evaluation_Panel.pdf?resourceurlname=PovertyMapping_Response_to_the_Evaluation_Panel.pdf.

Mistiaen, Johan A. 2006. "Poverty Mapping, Policy Making, and Operations: Some Applications from Kenya." Presentation at the World Bank conference, "More Than a Pretty Picture: Using Poverty Maps to Design Better Policies and Interventions," Washington, DC, May 11.

2

Increasing the Impact of Poverty Maps

TARA BEDI, ALINE COUDOUEL, AND KENNETH SIMLER

Small area estimation poverty maps provide policy makers and practitioners with poverty estimates at the local level. Because of the amount of detail they offer, the poverty maps are powerful tools. Such maps have initiated dramatic shifts in the dialogue on poverty and the related strategic choices of countries, helped strengthen a culture of accountability, aided in the selection of mechanisms for resource allocation, and promoted informed decision making in many domains.

In Vietnam, for example, there are several competing standards for the measurement of poverty. One necessary early step in the process of developing a poverty map was discussions on an appropriate poverty line. This discussion helped forge a consensus on a suitable poverty threshold. In Mexico, the results of the poverty mapping exercise have been used directly in targeting antipoverty programs on the 50 poorest municipalities. Government accountability came to the fore in Morocco, where local officials used information from the poverty maps as a benchmark in the allocation of resources from the central government.

Yet, while poverty maps are increasingly applied for decision making, their full potential is not being realized. There are many missed opportunities; small area poverty estimates might have informed policies in other countries, but have failed to do so. The Indonesia case study reveals that many government agencies had never even heard about the poverty map, and these agencies had, of course, never benefited from the maps in their policy and program decisions. In Albania, although many stakeholders were aware of the poverty map, there was little application of the map information in public policy making.

We would like to thank Norbert Henninger for his advice and comments on drafts of this chapter.

A reason cited for the lack of a more intensive application of poverty maps is the highly technical nature of certain aspects of the maps. Many policy makers view the small area estimation methodology as a black box, and they do not completely trust the poverty estimates the methodology generates. This shows that ensuring the usefulness of poverty maps requires careful attention to awareness raising and related institutional and political considerations, as well as technical issues. Building support, creating demand, and establishing institutional arrangements need to be undertaken before and during the actual production of the maps. The experiences described in this volume also suggest clearly that a well thought out dissemination strategy is needed to convey the information contained in the poverty maps in a variety of formats and to a wide range of potential users. Consultations must be held with stakeholders to identify interim and long-term goals. Local technical capacity to produce and interpret the poverty maps must be strengthened. All these activities will shape the role of poverty maps in influencing policy and program decisions.

The objective of this chapter is to explore some of these elements that are critical to the broader use of the poverty maps. The chapter draws out the lessons learned in the 12 country case studies in this volume and offers guidance and recommendations that may be considered in mapping poverty. The aim is to be practical.

The chapter is organized around 10 steps, which we refer to as the poverty mapping process. Some of the steps are technical, while others are more institutional. Technical and institutional considerations are both critical to producing a poverty map that is analytically sound and policy relevant. The steps are presented in box 2.1 in a schematic fashion that is loosely chronological, although, in fact, some steps are likely to overlap.

BOX 2.1   **The 10 Steps of the Poverty Mapping Process**

Preproduction

1. *Define the scope of the mapping exercise.* Determine the main objectives of the poverty map and how it is expected to fit in the larger organizational structure. Identify actual and potential stakeholders and the way they may become involved.
2. *Build support.* Identify knowledgeable, well-connected, and senior champions to promote the poverty map. Locate a focal point for the poverty mapping process. Establish contacts early with key agencies and counterparts.
3. *Create demand.* Build a network of potential poverty map users and set up users groups early. Bring agencies together to carry out needs assessments. Explain how poverty maps may be applied and how they may feed into the policy-making cycle. Keep users informed of progress and early findings. Clarify the limitations of the information provided by poverty maps so as to curb unrealistic expectations.

BOX 2.1   The 10 Steps of the Poverty Mapping Process (*Continued*)

4. *Overcome challenges, conflicts, and tensions.* Use an official poverty measure in calculating the small area poverty estimates to avoid undermining the poverty map among government entities and other agencies that rely on government funding or technical support. Emphasize that the variety of tools that a country probably already has for designing antipoverty policies and programs are complementary. Poverty maps may be used to validate whether other tools are efficiently targeting the poor. Without incentives to use new tools, people will continue to apply the tools they have always used.
5. *Establish institutional arrangements.* If no single institute has the requisite skills in statistical and poverty analysis, select several agencies to contribute experts for map production. Create institutional links with users and other stakeholder organizations. Explore how the mapping process may be tied to other antipoverty efforts. Integrate the poverty map within the national monitoring system.

Production

6. *Address data and software issues.* Obtain access to census and survey data to build the poverty map. All the various data sets and platforms must be of good quality, compatible, and comparable, including the sampling frame of the household survey, the coverage of the data, and the number of observations. Seek the participation of experts who have helped collect the census and survey data; they understand the data.
7. *Produce the poverty maps and test their validity.* Establish clear responsibilities and incentives and formally define ownership. The mapping activities should be supported by specific resources and objectives, as well as dedicated personnel in training, production, management, analysis, and follow-up. The poverty mapping process provides an opportunity to strengthen local statistical and analytical capacity. Invest in this capacity by associating and training local staff in the production of the maps from the outset. Validate the poverty map by reviewing the technique, comparing the results to other data sources, and performing field testing. Validate the results among stakeholders, too.

Postproduction

8. *Distribute the poverty mapping products.* The mapping process should include an active dissemination strategy that specifies the distribution objectives, the potential users and key decision makers, and the sources of funding for distribution. Rely on a variety of media and formats so as to reach a wider audience. Be sure to state the assumptions behind the poverty maps and the limitations of the maps.
9. *Support users and provide follow-up.* Help potential users understand the poverty maps and how to apply the information they contain by continuing to build statistical literacy and demonstrating applications. Supply ongoing support services. For reliable comparisons over time, it is important to advocate for data consistency in subsequent surveys and censuses.
10. *Engage development partners.* Bilateral and multilateral donors, foundations, and international organizations may provide technical support, encourage decision makers and other key actors behind the scenes, supply funding, and contribute in distribution and use within the development community.

Step 1: Defining the Scope of the Mapping Exercise

Define the objectives

At the outset, the team proposing to develop the poverty map should decide on the scope of the effort. Is the mapping process intended as a narrow research exercise or as a regular and important contributor to poverty analysis? Is there a significant capacity-building component? Is the process being undertaken in response to the request of an organization or government agency? What is the political economy of information in the country?

The main objective of the poverty map should be identified clearly, including how it fits into the larger organizational structure. An efficient way to do this is to create a detailed overall work program in which the motivation behind the poverty map plays an appropriate role. Then, it will be easier for participants to work together because they will understand the expected outcome of the mapping process.

In Sri Lanka, a central objective of the poverty mapping process was to incorporate it into the regular poverty monitoring framework of the Department of Census and Statistics so that the department might update the poverty map on its own. Given this objective, a central component of the work program was comprehensive internal capacity building.

In Cambodia, the World Food Programme contributed to the production of the small area poverty and nutrition maps with a clear objective: to produce a tool to guide resource allocations. The World Food Programme has been one of the main users of these tools and has used them to rationalize decision making. This has increased the returns to the resources it has invested in the development of the maps.

The Bulgaria and Ecuador case studies provide a contrast. In both countries, the first poverty maps were produced as a research exercise. However, in Bulgaria, the interest generated by the results sparked demand for information that resulted in a second poverty map. The second map was produced entirely by local experts and was used for allocating resources. In Ecuador, meanwhile, the poverty map remained a research exercise with little country ownership or continuity.

Carry out a stakeholder analysis

Conducting a stakeholder analysis helps identify the actual and potential stakeholders who may become involved in the various phases of the poverty mapping process. A thorough analysis enables the collection of information on stakeholder needs, interests, capabilities, and views. This will facilitate the participation of stakeholders in the poverty mapping process—as producers, disseminators, or users—in line with the objectives of the stakeholders. It will also assist in determining openings in the policy process where poverty maps may be introduced as tools. This type of analysis should be ongoing to capture the changing dynamics in stakeholder contributions.

Step 2: Building Support

Identify champions

In several countries, support for the poverty maps has been built up early by creating awareness about the practical information the maps would provide for the design of policies and programs. Identifying and engaging champions who are willing to put their names behind the poverty maps and actively make a case for such applications may greatly influence how the maps are perceived and used. The ideal champion has the following characteristics:

■ *Knowledgeable.* The champion should understand the methodology behind the mapping tool and the significance of the tool for policy. A champion should have an ability to position the poverty map conceptually so as to respond to needs.
■ *Well connected.* Champions should be well established in their organizations and possess strong ties to a wide range of actors so as to help ensure that key players inside and outside government are aware of the poverty map early in the process.
■ *Senior.* Senior policy makers have the influence to help ensure the acceptance of the poverty map. High-level involvement in the mapping process signals the importance of the map tool. This may help overcome resistance and generate demand.

In Morocco, as part of the production of the poverty map, key actors were brought on board so that, when the map was completed, applications would be supported, and the map would not remain solely a research activity. Indeed, the initial request for the production of a poverty map was generated from within the government by an individual who had read about the methodology and understood its potential.

In Bulgaria, the impact of the poverty maps has been enhanced because champions have been identified at several levels of government. The main champion is the minister of labor and social policy. The minister has encouraged the extension of the poverty mapping program by including overlays of the small area poverty estimates and other data and cluster analysis so that the maps are more policy relevant. The minister has also played an important role in expanding the awareness and use of the poverty maps among other ministries. Meanwhile, the deputy minister of labor and social policy has been instrumental in the adoption of the poverty maps as targeting instruments for government programs.

In contrast, in Albania, few champions have been cultivated, and some have been lost to staff turnovers. As a result, the poverty maps have been promoted mainly by the analytical mapping team without the advantage of well-placed champions within the government.

Locate a focal point for the mapping process

Critical to the poverty mapping process is the identification of an appropriate focal point. It is important to discover an agency that has an adequate budget, but the reputation of the agency that is the home of the poverty map will also affect how well the map is accepted and used. The focal point must therefore be well positioned and well connected so that it is able to communicate easily with other ministries. Internal or external frictions may greatly inhibit the support for the tool.

Establish contacts early with key agencies and counterparts

Poverty maps are relevant to a wide range of governmental and nongovernmental actors. Identify these actors and recruit them early into the poverty mapping process as counterparts. The involvement of such counterparts will stimulate interest in the mapping outcomes. It will also provide a channel through which the mapping team may learn more about the needs of users. Keep these counterparts in the loop on the progress of the mapping process. Likely counterparts include national statistics institutes, international and national research institutes, national development organizations, multilateral and bilateral donors, parliament, local governments, and ministries of health, labor, education, finance, and infrastructure (see annex 2.1).

In Morocco, supportive counterparts have been identified in several government ministries. Early and regular interactions between the mapping team leader and these counterparts have been a powerful means of promoting the use of the poverty maps in these ministries.

Step 3: Creating Demand

The mapping process also involves creating and maintaining demand for the poverty maps well beyond the initial distribution effort. How this demand is generated and sustained will affect whether the maps are used widely and whether additional resources will be invested in updating the maps. The country case studies in this volume suggest a variety of methods, including awareness raising initiatives to explain possible applications and demonstrate the power of the results at an early stage through clarifications about the data limitations of the maps, as well as collaboration with potential users early in the process. It is critical that these efforts be part of the initial steps in producing the maps.

Set up users groups early

The production of the poverty map represents an opportunity to bring users from various agencies together into groups. Such groups play two main roles. First, they facilitate a dialogue so that the needs of users may be assessed. Users may then influence the technical exercise, for example, the level of map resolution, the software, and the presentation format. Second, the users will be well positioned to provide feedback as the results emerge and to communicate these results to a wider audience, including other organizations and policy makers.

For the groups to be effective, they should consist of users who have some decision-making power and are situated close to policy makers. The groups should also be invited into the heart of the poverty mapping process so that they may experience this process first hand and develop strong ties with the mapping team. Local government personnel should not be overlooked. As countries decentralize, funds are increasingly being allocated at the local level. There is thus a rising demand for data for decision making at the local level.

In Bulgaria, the poverty mapping process began with a series of discussions among the production team, policy makers, and experts. The needs expressed by the users in these discussions helped determine that the poverty map should be disaggregated to the district and municipal levels. These levels were selected because of their relevance in the administration of European funds, including European structural funds following accession.

A similar collaborative process took place in Vietnam, where interaction between the producers and users of poverty maps helped build interest and support by ensuring that poverty maps would address the information needs of users.

Explain possible applications

To generate demand, the strengths and uses of poverty maps must be explained clearly and put into a practical context, including for policy makers. Users should understand how poverty data may feed into the policy-making cycle. They need exposure to the broad range of potential applications. By outlining a variety of concrete applications in other countries, one may create a better sense of what the map tool may achieve.

For instance, in Morocco, even though the initial interest was focused on using poverty maps as targeting aids, demonstrations of applications in other countries helped bring together stakeholders for more general discussions on targeting, the spatial aspects of poverty, and the need for transparency and objectivity in antipoverty programs.

Keep users informed of progress and early findings

Users and key policy makers should be apprised of emerging issues and of any early results in a timely manner during the mapping process. The explanations should be appropriate to the audience. Such explanations will help sustain interest and will provide users and policy makers with the means to consider the implications of the results and possible ways they might use the information.

In Morocco, for example, the team leader of the poverty map effort has kept the principal government counterparts informed on progress in the mapping process and highlighted politically interesting findings for these counterparts. This has helped generate much interest.

Explain the limitations of poverty maps

It is imperative that future users be aware of the limitations of poverty maps as descriptive and analytical tools. Avoid building expectations that may not be met. Users should understand that the mapping data are estimates that have a degree of measurable, but unavoidable statistical error. Moreover, they are estimates for certain levels of aggregation and may not be disaggregated further. In addition, one of the key potential limiting factors of the poverty mapping process is the quality of the census and household survey data upon which the mapping is based. These data are time sensitive. A number of countries that have produced poverty maps are experiencing rapid changes in migration, prices, income distribution, infrastructure, and so on. These changes may render the small area poverty estimates obsolete after a few years. It is therefore important to explore how the maps might be updated regularly. Finally, the maps depict poverty as measured by consumption (a proxy for income) and may not reflect other dimensions of poverty such as housing conditions or access to health care, education, and other social services.

In Vietnam, poverty has been decreasing by 3.5 percentage points per year. This diminishes the relevance of poverty estimates that were disseminated in 2003, but that were based on 1999 census and household survey data.

Similarly, in Cambodia, a number of people interviewed for the case study felt that, while the poverty map did reflect the poverty situation in 1998, it did not reflect the situation in 2006. Between these years, there had been significant infrastructure development and migration. Furthermore, some communes had benefited from market integration, rendering them less poor, while communes dependent on natural resources had become poorer.

Step 4: Overcoming Challenges, Conflicts, and Tensions

The poverty mapping process may lead to conflicts and tensions of many kinds. It is critical that such situations be identified early and tackled head on so as to dispel skepticism and build understanding. For example, stakeholders may rely on several definitions of poverty. The variance in definitions may have arisen from differences in the concept of poverty, such as consumption-based welfare measures versus broader notions of poverty based on the capabilities framework. If these poverty measures are compiled by separate agencies, these agencies have a natural interest in promoting their own measures. Or, the differences in definitions may have a technical origin, as often occurs with poverty lines. Even if the definitions are clear, tensions may have arisen because of the institutional division of labor, whereby one entity is responsible for data collection, another for poverty analysis, and a third for cartographic work. Often, it is helpful to use the diversity of definitions to help validate the poverty map and thereby build cooperation and consensus around the map as an important, complementary source of information.

Issues in the selection of an official measure of poverty

Separate data may be needed for different objectives, and poverty may therefore be measured in many ways. The results do not always agree. When there are discrepancies among various poverty measures and there is no systematic method to explain these discrepancies, conflicts may arise among the parties that produce the poverty measures.

For example, in Sri Lanka, several poverty lines were used by various organizations. There was not only disagreement on the overall levels of poverty, but also on the geographical profile of poverty and on the trends in poverty. Given the differences in poverty measurement, there was a high probability that the poverty map would be treated as merely one more set of poverty measures.

Another sort of difficulty is encountered when different poverty measures are used to estimate poverty at separate administrative levels in a country. For example, in Thailand, the national poverty estimate is determined by a monetary poverty line based on the Thailand Household Socio-Economic Survey of the National Statistical Office. Meanwhile, village poverty indicators are determined based on a more elaborate basic minimum needs data set compiled by the Ministry of Interior.

In such cases, the various poverty estimates must be examined to determine their comparability. This must be done delicately because there is a fine line between a valuable versus a discriminatory comparison. One way of approaching this issue is to lay out the objectives and uses of each measurement and the underlying data so as to advocate for a consensus on the concept of poverty, even if there are differences in the ways to measure it.

In Sri Lanka, this was achieved by bringing the various stakeholders together in a workshop to examine the relevant poverty estimation methodologies. A number of recommendations were put forward, and then a detailed analysis was produced. A new official poverty line was established on the basis of this analysis.

Poverty maps are typically constructed using the most recent national census and a nationally representative household survey carried out within a few years of the census. Although national household surveys are often designated as the official source of poverty data, this is not always the case; sometimes, official poverty estimates are based on another data source. The official status of the poverty map may be undermined in the latter situation, thereby severely limiting the application of the map in official contexts.

In Vietnam, for instance, official poverty data are produced by the Ministry of Labor, War Invalids, and Social Affairs. As the poverty map is based on the poverty line generated through national household surveys conducted by the General Statistics Office, it is not considered official. Stakeholders are therefore reluctant to use the poverty map formally in decision making and government work.

It is obviously important to recognize this problem and find a way to build credibility into the poverty map, possibly through a consensus-building exercise such as in Sri Lanka.

Tools may be complementary

Most countries already possess a variety of tools for the design and implementation of antipoverty policies and programs. While each tool may have a special purpose, a new tool, such as a poverty map, may be considered a threat to the agencies that produce and invest resources in the existing tools. This may result in an unwillingness by some to apply the poverty map. It is therefore important to present the poverty map as a complementary tool whenever possible.

For example, in Mexico, separate indicators are used to measure human development, marginality, welfare, and deprivation. The role of the poverty map as a complementary source of information was established by using the mapping estimates as inputs for the existing human development index. A potential conflict was thus sidestepped, and a constituency was formed. The poverty map came to be published officially and used in policy design.

There is frequently a debate about which targeting tool most accurately identifies the poor and minimizes the leakage of benefits and funds toward the nonpoor. The main argument for household targeting rather than targeting through the small area estimation methodology is that, while the poverty map provides an estimate of poverty within a small area, it does not tell us precisely which households in that area are poor. Indeed, experience shows that the best targeting strategy usually combines a few complementary tools, taking advantage of the relative strength of each one. One appealing option is to develop a two-stage targeting process. The poverty map is used in the first stage to identify the poorest locations, and, in the second stage, targeting is based on household- and individual-level indicators to ensure that resources go to the poorest groups within these poor areas.

Poverty maps may be used as validation tools

The Integrated System of Social Indicators of Ecuador has not included the results of the poverty mapping exercise on a compact disc it distributes widely on socioeconomic indicators at various levels of disaggregation. Part of the reason is that the discs incorporate maps on unmet basic needs that have been developed and produced by this government unit, and there are discrepancies between the two map instruments in the assessment of levels of poverty and in poverty rankings.

Clearly, a potential area of conflict exists if the poverty map yields results that are different from the results of other poverty measurement or targeting tools. Yet, if this situation is viewed from another perspective, it may become an important selling point for the poverty map. First, by comparing the poverty map and other antipoverty tools, one may be able to identify discrepancies among the data. If there are many discrepancies, it will signal a need to reexamine the data before using them to make decisions. It may be that there are errors in the tools or simply that the poverty map and the other tools are measuring distinct aspects of poverty that are imperfectly correlated. Ignoring discrepancies may actually do more harm. Second, the poverty map may also be used to measure the effectiveness of targeting tools in helping programs and expenditures reach poor areas.

Address inertia and the need for incentives to change practices

The agencies that produce poverty measurements or policy design tools possess a corresponding incentive structure consisting of objectives, budgets, and staffs. If they do not use their own data and tools, it becomes difficult for them to justify allocating resources to collect the data. Political factors are often key motivators in this structure and have an important influence on which tools are used and how resources are allocated, although this may not be explicitly acknowledged. Thus, even if it is demonstrated to government agencies that a new, more efficient tool has been developed or that their programs are not entirely effective in reaching the poor, there may be little follow-up. Furthermore, in many instances, if program allocations are to be politically acceptable, all areas must receive some amount of the funding, regardless of the poverty targeting criteria. A first step in introducing new techniques and tools is therefore to understand the existing incentive system. With such an understanding, one may be better positioned to adjust the incentive system and motivate change.

There are also incentives connected to the poverty mapping exercise, which may involve significant investment in resources, training among local counterparts, new equipment, and so on. This may also generate struggles among data producers and other stakeholders to obtain a share of these resources.

In Kenya, the poverty mapping process began as a capacity-building exercise that involved substantial resource investments in the producer of the poverty map, the Central Bureau of Statistics. A poverty analysis unit and a geographic information system (GIS) research laboratory were set up at the bureau. As a result, the profile of the bureau has been enhanced.

Step 5: Establishing Institutional Arrangements

It is important to identify the institutional structure in which the poverty mapping process is to be embedded. The success of the effort depends partly on linking the process to relevant components of the larger institutional structure. Establishing and strengthening these links will help ensure the proper production, distribution, and application of the poverty maps.

Choose a location for poverty map production

In many countries, the agency that will be the home of the poverty mapping process is an obvious choice. Often, this is the national statistical institute. Such agencies usually have the appropriate skills in statistical and poverty analysis to produce the poverty map or, at least, the institutional mandate to acquire these skills. Yet, it is important not only to determine the institution that will produce the poverty map, it is also important to give clear responsibility within the institution to the most able and relevant unit.

In Indonesia, *Badan Pusat Statistik*, the national statistical office, was the natural choice to lead in the production of the poverty map. While it had clear ownership, the assignment created a conflict within the agency. Responsibility for production was given to the Mapping Division, which lacked the poverty analysis and statistical skills of the

Poverty Division. The choice therefore not only alienated the Poverty Division, but it also meant that the map could not be readily produced by the Mapping Division. This problem was later resolved, but it represented a setback that affected the outreach of the final product.

Multiple agency ownership and the interagency approach

The production of a poverty map involves a series of related, but distinct stages, including data processing and analysis, the technical write-up, the policy write-up, and distribution. As in the case of Indonesia, there is sometimes no single institute capable of performing all these tasks. Thus, joint arrangements among several agencies or units that are specialized in each task may be suitable.

It is important in this case to identify the tasks will be involved in producing the poverty map and the agencies that may be best able to undertake them. A task force consisting of representatives of these agencies might also be organized to oversee the entire mapping process. This might also have the advantages of enabling a larger number of stakeholders to become involved and of drawing on a wider range of skills and resources, and the task force might also help ensure a smooth transition among the various stages of the process. However, if the task force is to be sustained, it is important that each agency's responsibilities be clearly defined, along with the resources that are to be allocated to each task and each agency.

China, Mexico, and Vietnam have implemented the multiple agency approach. In China, three departments in the National Bureau of Statistics were responsible for producing the poverty map, the Rural Survey Department, the Urban Survey Department, and the Population Department. This was the first time these departments had worked together on a shared output. It was also the first time that the databases for which each of the departments was responsible were processed and analyzed together. The poverty mapping experience thus helped strengthen these units by developing capacities and relationships that would enhance their work in other areas.

The multiple agency approach in Vietnam relied on a steering committee that was headed by a representative from one institute, but included all key antipoverty agencies. This approach set a precedent for cross-agency collaboration that thereby became more commonplace in government operations.

Create institutional links

It is also important to establish links between the institution that produces the map and other government agencies and civil society organizations. These links should enable the flow of information to relevant stakeholders and potential users and help stimulate interest and eventually ensure access to the poverty maps and related findings. The existence of such links should not be assumed, even among governmental agencies that appear to communicate well.

Embed the poverty map in a broader policy-making process

Linking the poverty mapping program with other antipoverty projects, studies, and products helps promote dialogue, ensure ongoing interest and involvement among key stakeholders and eventual users, strengthen the capacity of the map production unit, and facilitate the dissemination of the end product.

In Morocco, work on the poverty map was linked to a wider study of poverty, which took place over the course of 18 months. The poverty study was accompanied and followed by analytical work that enabled capacity building and a sustained dialogue on poverty with the government, the palace, and civil society. This helped facilitate discussions on targeting during the preparation of the poverty map and generated significant interest in the map even before it was published.

In Cambodia, one of the completed poverty maps was featured in the National Poverty Reduction Strategy document. Because this document is central in guiding government policy, the inclusion of the map made it easier for people involved in programs and projects in poor areas to use the map to support and justify their work.

Integrate the poverty map within the national monitoring system

Most countries possess national monitoring systems on poverty and other outcomes of interest. These systems are usually embedded within the structure of government administration, with regular staffs and budgets. If poverty maps are produced and updated regularly, the maps may be used to monitor changes in poverty over time. This effort may be readily merged into the national monitoring system, which would help make the poverty mapping process sustainable.

Step 6: Addressing Data and Software Issues

Obtain access to census and survey data to build the poverty map

Access to census and survey data is needed to construct the poverty map. In most countries, the access to census data is the more difficult to obtain. Because of the comprehensive coverage of the census, the data are often regarded as highly sensitive, even though the questionnaires are generally far less invasive than the typical household survey. A principal reason for restricting access to census data is to protect the privacy of respondents. However, the identity of individual respondents is not important in the construction of poverty maps. Only the codes that link census modules and identify geographic units down to the level of the enumeration area are required. It should therefore be easy to address privacy concerns simply by removing the specific names and addresses linked to households. Nonetheless, gaining access to census data may take considerable time and negotiation and needs to be planned for. Clear guidelines should be established on the selection of the analysts who will have direct access to the data and on the identification of those individuals who may see the data.

In Mexico, the producers of the poverty map needed 18 months to secure full access to census data from the National Institute for Statistics, Geography, and Informatics.

In Vietnam, full census data have not been made available, although the General Statistics Office does provide samples for a fee. Like many statistical organizations, the statistics office requires that a formal request be filed indicating the purpose for which the data will be used and the census variables needed. At the time the poverty map was produced, the statistics office was willing to release only a 33 percent sample, that is, data on every third household randomly selected from the entire census database.

Check the compatibility of the data sets

The various data sets must be compatible. In most cases, the primary compatibility issue revolves around the geographical location identification codes that are attached to the census and survey data. These codes must match if the poverty map is to refer to a consistent set of locations. This is often a problem because, in many countries, there is a time lag between the census and the household survey. During this time, new administrative units may be created, boundaries may be redrawn, and the classification of areas, such as rural or urban, may change.

To make them comparable, the data need to be matched to unique boundary specifications. This usually requires a major commitment, as the data may have to be matched manually, a tedious task that expands with the degree of disaggregation, sometimes exponentially.

Problems with geographical identification codes also render the mapping outcome less accurate. Greater use of consistent geographical codes for census and surveys and more thorough documentation of changes would greatly improve this aspect of the poverty mapping process. If all changes in the structure of census tracts and administrative units and the dates they occur are fed into a central database, matching locations would become easier.

For example, because of decentralization, the national statistical office had not kept up with changes at the lowest administrative unit in Indonesia, the village. Therefore, the village codes did not match in the three sources used for the poverty mapping process.

The poverty mapping team in Ecuador had to track down each of the changes in administrative units on paper maps. This took a considerable amount of time, and it also limited the level of disaggregation of the poverty map. The team was able to document the changes down to the level of provinces and cantons, but not parishes. Therefore, cantons were the lowest level of disaggregation in the poverty map that resulted.

Ensure data quality

The quality of the poverty map depends directly on the quality of the census and survey data. These two inputs must therefore meet acceptable standards. The country studies in this volume have highlighted several relevant issues:

■ *Representativeness of the survey data.* The adequacy of the sampling frame of a household survey may affect the poverty mapping results. In some countries, the sampling frame may not be updated frequently, and the data collected in the survey will therefore not be representative.

   In China, the sampling frame for the rural household survey was designed in 1984. Since then, there have been substantial changes in the distribution and other characteristics of the population. This affects any inferences based on survey data. The reliability of poverty maps has therefore been called into question.

■ *Coverage.* Because of a lack of funds, security issues, or other factors, some areas may not be covered by a census or survey. In other cases, certain population groups may be excluded in the design of a survey. It is important to identify these missing areas or groups, understand how the omissions may influence the results of the mapping, and determine if there are ways to compensate. Even if a substitute model may be estimated, the results for these areas or groups will be tentative. This may affect the usefulness of a map as a policy tool. These issues should be explained to users, but also to those responsible for data collection so that the problem may be minimized in the future.

   In Ecuador, to save on costs, El Oriente Region was not included in one of the household surveys. It was thus not possible to measure the special structural relationships between welfare and the characteristics of households in El Oriente. Alternative estimation approaches proved unsuccessful. So, the region was not included in the poverty map based on this survey.

   In Indonesia, an effort is made to ensure that all populations are represented in the census, including migrants and the homeless. For migrants, a reference period of six months is used so that whoever has lived in a location for six months is included. Likewise, a special population category has been created to record the homeless.

   In Vietnam, the household survey does not include highly mobile populations. These populations may be small, but they may still affect the level of poverty in an area, particularly if they are concentrated in, for example, urban areas. If they affect the level of poverty, their omission would color the small area poverty estimates.

■ *Census data.* In some countries only a portion of the census data is made available. This means that the small area poverty estimates may only be based on a sample from the census. Enough data need to be available so that there are sufficient observations on sparsely populated areas to produce poverty estimates with reasonable standard errors.

   In the 1994 census in Morocco, only 25 percent of the household responses to questionnaires were computerized. In provinces with small populations, 100 percent of the census data had been entered by the census takers. In medium-size (by population) provinces, 50 percent of the census questionnaires had been entered. The shares decreased to 25 percent and 10 percent in larger and the largest provinces, respectively. This helped ensure an adequate sample size even in lightly populated areas, thus minimizing the impact of the lack of computerized census data.

Identify cost-effective software

Initially, a major barrier to poverty mapping was the significant cost and complexity of the mapping software. The software must be able to merge the two data sets, process a huge amount of data, identify common variables in the data sets, and run the consumption models. Until recently, it was necessary to acquire licenses to use the Stata or SAS software, which are expensive and which are difficult to use in poverty mapping applications because of the expertise required. A research group at the World Bank has now developed PovMap, a Windows-based poverty mapping software that is available at no cost and works with a variety of data file formats.

Include experts who have helped collect the census and survey data

If the poverty mapping team is not familiar with the attributes of the data with which it is working, it will have trouble merging the data, matching the variables in the data sets, and minimizing the effects of data problems. One way to deal with this is to include on the team experts who have been involved in producing the data.

In Bulgaria, experts from the National Statistical Institute who had been involved in carrying out both the household survey and the census were made part of the poverty mapping team. They helped determine whether matched variables from the two data sets represented the same sort of information.

Step 7: Producing the Poverty Maps and Testing Their Validity

Establish clear responsibilities and incentives and formally define ownership

If an entity is formally recognized as the owner of the poverty mapping process, then it will be more willing to commit staff, invest resources, and undergo training. It will receive credit for the outcome, but it will also have a corresponding responsibility to ensure the quality of the product. Recognizing ownership is a way to establish incentives and mainstream poverty mapping into the agenda of an organization.

Dedicated technical and financial resources

Facilities and equipment are needed to produce the poverty map. Computers on which data may be entered, processed, and stored are essential. Sufficient financial resources also need to be allocated. If government departments are to incorporate these new activities in their work programs, the activities must be supported by specific budgets and be tied to fixed objectives.

In the short term, seeking grants and linking up to existing poverty studies may be a way to secure funding. Over the longer term, building institutional capacity will probably require government funding. One approach might be to align the poverty mapping program with a regular product of the map producer. This will ensure that the mapping is funded through the government rather than donors and that staff time is specifically allocated to the mapping activity. This is also a more stable approach because grants may dry up. Oftentimes, if resources are limited, governments may only be inclined to fund regular activities. If poverty mapping is viewed as an ad hoc activity, it may be more difficult to secure government funding. This is another reason to create demand. If there is demand, there will be a greater inclination to fund the process.

In Bulgaria, capacity building, technical assistance, goods, and services for the poverty mapping process were financed through various grants.

In Morocco, the second poverty map was completely funded by the government and became a high priority. This was partly because of the demand generated by the first map.

An opportunity to strengthen statistical and analytical capacity

A common theme that emerges in the country studies in this volume is that, while there may be technical capacity to produce poverty maps, most staff are already overcommitted. Dedicated staff must therefore be freed up, assigned to poverty mapping, and trained in production, management, analysis, and follow-up.

The poverty mapping process provides an opportunity to build statistical and analytical capacity in a country. The skills will include facility with the management of data sets, the estimation of consumption models, and the calculation of correct standard errors. Staff will need to be trained in the relevant software, programming, and the use of a GIS.

By becoming technically self-reliant, staff will gain confidence and a strong sense of ownership of the mapping products. Not only will they be able to understand the poverty maps, they will also be able to explain the mapping process, and this will also affect how stakeholders view the maps that are likely to be developed in the future.

Capacity building should be ongoing. In such an endeavor, because of staff attrition, it is important to maintain a focus on institutional capacity rather than on individuals. If institutional capacity is established and maintained, a country will be able to update poverty maps, produce new ones, create sector-specific maps, and apply new small area estimation techniques that are likely to be developed in the future.

Periodic capacity reviews should be conducted to identify gaps. Common bottlenecks highlighted in the case studies are shortages in facilities and equipment, technical skills, staff time, data quality, GIS resources, funding, and local capacity. Appropriate training programs should be instituted.

In Bulgaria, local experts were involved only minimally in the creation of the first poverty map, and there was no large-scale effort to build local capacity. This first poverty map has not been much used. In contrast, the second mapping exercise was accompanied by a substantial capacity-building component and was produced entirely by a national team, which consisted of an econometrician, two statisticians, a GIS expert, and two social policy experts. This map, including overlays, has been widely used in poverty analysis, policy making, and the identification of priority areas for funding.

In Cambodia, three staff members at the National Institute of Statistics and the Ministry of Planning underwent three training sessions while the poverty map was being produced. At the end of the sessions, they had not gained the skills needed to perform the poverty map calculations nor were they able to transfer their skills. It appears that capacity building was not a priority, and insufficient attention was paid to building sustainable capacity.

In Thailand, the National Statistics Office has set a goal to foster institutional development for greater ownership and sustainability in poverty mapping. It has hired a research institute to train analysts at various agencies on mapping skills. The analysts are organized into teams of three, consisting of a leader, a software programmer, and a substitute in case another member leaves. Because of this systematic approach, institutional capacity in the small area estimation methodology has been strengthened in the National Statistics Office and in other ministries.

Technical and participatory validation exercises

The reliability of the sources, methods, and procedures involved in the poverty mapping process is central to the widespread acceptance of the map. The soundness of the mapping data and other outputs must be tested. Trust must be established with policy makers. One doubtful estimate may jeopardize the credibility of other results because potential users may assume that the estimates are generally questionable.

There should be both technical and participatory validation exercises. The technical exercise would involve a review of the procedures, a comparison of the results to other data sources, and field testing. The technical procedures should be checked to ensure that they have been followed properly. Any apparent errors or contradictions should be examined. Comparisons between the small area poverty estimates and other poverty data help highlight issues. Field trips would allow the results on a sample of areas to be tested based on direct contact.

The participatory exercise should focus on surveying users and other stakeholders to determine if their perceptions of the poverty situation in the various areas correspond with the mapping results. Such an approach may help build interest, demand, and support. The stakeholder feedback would represent additional information on the accuracy of the mapping estimates that may be taken into account prior to completion of the map.

In Cambodia, the poverty mapping data were compared with a welfare index derived from commune- and village-level indexes included in the commune database prepared by the Seila Task Force Secretariat. Two areas were found, one in the northwestern part of the country and another in the northeast, where the poverty map seemed to be off the mark. This acted as a signal that these areas needed to be reexamined. It was discovered that the northwest was not included in the sampling frame of the household survey; therefore, the consumption model may not have been applicable there. Meanwhile, the northeast faced a different rural pricing structure relative to other parts of the country. These results allowed the team to understand these two areas and the reasons for the discrepancies and thereby improve the poverty map.

In Thailand, during field visits, official documents were reviewed and local economic conditions were directly observed, including housing quality and the amount of commercial activity. The analysts also collected information from local officials, residents, and entrepreneurs on their perceptions of the accuracy of the poverty maps.

In China, during two field trips, the small area poverty estimates were evaluated against the perceptions of local officials. The poverty mapping team followed up on the reasons for any differences. They discovered that there was a data shortage in one area in which a different poverty threshold applied.

Step 8: Distributing Poverty Mapping Products

Dissemination is one of the weakest elements in the country experiences studied here. In many of the countries, numerous potential users were not aware of the poverty maps or had not understood their value. The poverty mapping process needs to include an active information distribution strategy. Dissemination is often an afterthought in terms of planning and the mobilization of resources, but it influences the reach of the product and is therefore an essential element in determining the impact of poverty maps.

In Ecuador, one commentator pointed out that the poverty mapping process involved a great deal of investment in the methodology and the preparation of the product, but little investment in dissemination and awareness raising.

In Cambodia, representatives of a number of organizations had not received a copy of the poverty map report, but thought it would be useful to have one. Officials in many districts also had not received the report and did not know where to obtain a copy.

Need for funding and a plan of distribution

The development of a carefully planned dissemination strategy that specifies how potential users will access and use the poverty maps is crucial. A successful strategy will be initiated before the poverty map is completed by identifying the potential users, the formats of the products, the internal and external distribution outlets, and the limitations of the poverty map. Articulating the objectives of the strategy will help focus the strategy on the activities and resources needed. If there are not enough resources to support the strategy, the poverty map may not be used.

Availability and access are key factors in the effect poverty maps will have in a country. Therefore, at an early stage in the development of the dissemination strategy, agreement should be reached on who may have access to the maps and to the small area poverty estimates and the census and survey data used to construct the maps. In some countries, it may be necessary to make this issue the subject of a legal decree or directive. Most map users may not be interested in the background data, but an unambiguous policy on access rights should nonetheless be established in advance to deal with requests that might occur.

In Bulgaria, the distribution strategy aimed at explaining the methodology, building institutional capacity to apply the poverty map in policy making, and surveying other possible applications. The poverty mapping team regularly briefed central and local officials on the progress of the poverty mapping process. The team thus built awareness and acceptance of the poverty map before it had been completed.

In Morocco, the government was initially skeptical of publishing the poverty maps. However, once external funding had been secured, the maps and the data were readily made available.

Identify the audience

The many sorts of possible audiences for the maps may have already been identified during the stakeholder analysis; if not, the potential audiences and their needs should be identified now. Key audiences might include antipoverty program decision makers and specialists, members of the legislature and other government policy makers, staff at national and international nongovernmental organizations and at national and international antipoverty research organizations, users of other antipoverty data sources, civil society experts, representatives of trade associations, donors, the diplomatic community, the media, and so on (see annex 2.1). It is important to consider ways that the information might be distributed internally within these organizations. A focal audience should be local governments, especially in countries with decentralized governance.

In Bulgaria, the dissemination strategy has been reasonably successful within the Ministry of Labor and Social Policy, but other relevant ministries lack an understanding of the poverty maps. One reason is that there has been little effort to engage these other ministries.

In Vietnam, the Ministry of Finance has been part of the poverty map task force, but there has been little effort to distribute key poverty map messages within the ministry. As a result, others in the ministry are unaware of the poverty maps. Moreover, few in provincial or local government offices know about the maps.

Use various media and formats

The dissemination strategy should seek to spread public awareness through various media and formats to reach all stakeholders. The mapping products should be made available in all languages in which the government works, including regional or provincial governments. The countries examined in this volume have experimented with several approaches, including reports, press releases, compact discs, posters, the Internet, and linking the maps to other initiatives such as Poverty Reduction Strategy Papers.

- Reports are the most common sort of publication through which the poverty maps have been disseminated. A public report on the maps provides civil society, nongovernmental organizations, and the media with a concrete reference on which they may draw. In Indonesia, 1,000 hard copies of the poverty map report were distributed during the launch of the map.

- Compact discs are an effective medium to provide users with poverty mapping data and maps in a user-friendly format. If possible, the discs should be interactive. In Vietnam, a compact disc was produced that included the small area poverty estimates and other relevant data. Through the discs, users were able to generate maps of areas of interest.

- The Internet is central to dissemination. A user-friendly map and related data that are Web compatible and available online allow users to gain easy access to the mapping products in one place. In Cambodia, no Web site material on the poverty map is in Khmer. This has been an important roadblock to the application of the poverty map.

- Press releases and news articles explaining the poverty mapping methodology, the results, and potential applications represent an easy way to inform the general public about the maps. The media is also thereby provided with information that may be readily passed along. In Bulgaria, special press releases describing the mapping methodology and the related data were provided to journalists, who helped attract wider media coverage.

- Posters may be used to display a poverty map as part of a public awareness campaign. Easy to understand and colorful, posters draw the attention of potential users. In Vietnam, a range of poverty map posters have been printed and widely distributed.

- Linking the poverty map to other products ensures the distribution of the map and confers a formal status on the map, thereby making it easier for stakeholders to use, especially users in government agencies. Poverty maps have been linked to poverty assessments and Poverty Reduction Strategy Papers. In Cambodia, the poverty map was associated with the National Poverty Reduction Strategy, and this connection helped increase the number of people who saw the map. In Ecuador, the poverty map was included in the 2004 poverty assessment. This meant that the map was made publicly available through the World Bank Web site.

Public events and data outlets

The poverty maps may also be distributed during specially organized public events such as project launches, workshops, and informal presentations. The events usually have different purposes and different sorts of audiences. They may be narrowly targeted to convey particular aspects or findings of the poverty maps.

Formal data outlets are another valuable channel for distribution. In most countries, national statistics offices are associated with bookstores or other locations where data users may purchase various products. The advantage of relying on these is that data users already know about the outlets.

In Morocco, the poverty maps were introduced during a significant launching event that included speeches by ministers and the World Bank country director. The event was covered by the media.

In Albania, two workshops were organized. Covering the mapping methodology and the related data, the first workshop targeted experts who would be involved in the future development of the poverty maps. The second workshop targeted journalists, and the event was followed in at least four newspapers.

In Indonesia, the national statistical office has a bookstore where its regular publications are available. Because the poverty map is not a regular publication, it is not stocked there. This represents a missed opportunity given that the bookstore is used frequently by staff in other government departments.

In Cambodia, the network of staff members at the Vulnerability Analysis and Mapping Unit of the World Food Programme in Phnom Penh has provided a convenient, rapid method to distribute the poverty map.

Explain the assumptions and limitations

In conveying information to users, including users with little literacy in statistics, one should explain the assumptions and limitations of the maps and the underlying data. This helps ensure that there are no false expectations and that inappropriate applications are avoided.

For example, in Sri Lanka, according to the poverty headcount ratio, the poverty rate is 6 percent in Colombo. However, the number of poor is high in Colombo because of population density. So, arguments in favor of various policies may be made based on one or the other of these poverty figures, though none of the arguments may convey complete information. For sound policy, both figures should be understood and taken into consideration.

In Thailand, local data collection by the Ministry of Interior is not based on uniform criteria and is somewhat subjective, and the data are not interpreted consistently. This must be clearly understood by map users.

Step 9: Supporting Users and Providing Follow-Up

Demonstrate applications

Demonstrating applications may be an effective method to help users understand how poverty maps may be adapted to their needs and become beneficial in their programs. One way to demonstrate applications is through training events targeting policy and operational staff, such as staff in line ministries. In training events for middle-level policy makers, for example, one might focus on the logic behind poverty maps and the various subtleties of policy applications. Among higher-level policy makers, short presentations showing the range of map applications, but with little technical emphasis might be more constructive.

In Bulgaria, several training sessions were held among staff at line ministries. The training provided an overview of the mapping methodology, explained the mapping results, and examined applications in policy design.

Build statistical literacy and mapping capacity

The creation of poverty maps relies on data processing and econometric estimation techniques that may sometimes appear obscure to people who participate in planning and decision making, especially at the local level. Moreover, there may be anomalies and inconsistencies among the data sets. The production of the map should therefore be accompanied by an effort to ensure that potential users fully understand the small area poverty estimates, the variations in data quality, and the standard errors so that they may interpret the data appropriately and translate the map information into program and policy decisions. The capacity of local users to conduct additional analysis with the data, such as merging the poverty map data with other geo-referenced data, should also be developed. This will help in updating poverty maps and in constructing new poverty maps.

In Cambodia, there were no technical guidelines and supporting mechanisms for applying the poverty maps. Moreover, users tended to rely only on hard copies. The standard errors associated with the small area poverty estimates were often ignored. This sort of approach may result in misapplications of the estimates, which may jeopardize confidence in the mapping process.

Without full understanding of the maps, local statistical staff in the Indonesia office must rely on the central office to explain and promote use of the maps, but the central office has many responsibilities. The capacity of local staff must therefore be strengthened. Meanwhile, local development planning boards are the primary implementation agencies for a wide range of programs, and, thus, educating them about the maps might enhance the propoor impact of their projects and investments.

Provide ongoing support

Building user capacity to understand the poverty maps may not be sufficient. Experience shows that providing support services to users is valuable. Users, especially those who simply apply the data without additional processing, may need to contact experts who are familiar with the technical features of the maps. More advanced users may need assistance in overlaying the mapping data with other information of interest, merging the information with other data sets, and so on.

In Thailand, staff at the National Statistical Office are helping staff at provincial statistical offices understand the mapping technique and how to verify the results. They have established guidelines for provincial statistical offices so as to promote the use of the poverty maps in the context of local poverty reduction efforts, and they have placed background material on the mapping process on the Web site of the National Statistical Office.

Maintain data consistency so that maps may be updated

Consistency in the periodicity, sample size, questionnaires, and geographical location identification codes is not necessarily maintained in successive rounds of household surveys. In the collection of survey data, countries face a trade-off between the frequency with which they update their survey instruments and the comparability of the estimates they will be able to produce from the data. The trade-off will affect the accuracy of updates of the poverty map.

In Ecuador, one of the first problems encountered in the mapping exercise was the fact that each of the household surveys had incorporated changes in the consumption modules in the questionnaires. As the small area poverty estimates are based on consumption aggregates, this meant that the two sets of consumption aggregates and poverty lines had to be made comparable. The lesson learned from the experience was that, while it is preferable to maintain consistency in the survey instruments, this may not be possible, and, so, it is also important to document all the changes and adjustments that are undertaken over time. Moreover, during the analysis stage, specific corrections are crucial in making sure that the survey instruments are actually comparable. While these steps may be time consuming, they should never be neglected.

Setting up a GIS lab

One way of extending the usefulness of the poverty map is by overlaying and integrating the small area poverty estimates with other geo-referenced data. This will enable cross-sectoral analysis and provide critical information for policy makers at the various levels of government. A common problem is that, in most countries, these data are collected and analysed at many different government agencies and external organizations.

The establishment of a GIS laboratory would facilitate the compilation in one location of geo-referenced data from various ministries and sectors. This might then become a regular activity whereby all geo-referenced data are periodically fed into a central location. The minimum requirements for a small GIS laboratory might include desktop GIS tools, a laptop or larger computer with significant data storage capacity, staff training in the software application, access to administrative data on areas with the same geographical boundaries and the consistent location identification coding required for the small area poverty estimates, and additional geo-referenced data such as data on health care facilities and transport networks. The sources of the data should all be clearly identified, and the data should be examined carefully for comparability.

In Kenya, a GIS research laboratory was set up as part of the poverty mapping process. The laboratory is being used to construct a GIS database that integrates the geo-referenced small area poverty estimates with data on topographic features, administrative boundaries, geo-political boundaries, service facility locations, agroclimatic zones, digital elevation models, and infrastructure networks. Among other things, the laboratory is using the integrated geo-referenced database to design and monitor a primary school infrastructure expansion and renewal program.

Step 10: Engaging External Development Partners

The role of development partners influences the extent to which poverty maps may become institutionalized. The prominence of this role, the location of the staff of these partners, the amount of funding, and the involvement of the partners in dissemination are factors in the influence these partners exert.

Providing technical support

External partners that are intimate with the technical aspects of the small area estimation methodology are needed to provide support in the poverty mapping process. Such partners may also have an important role in ensuring the quality of the data and the maps and in continuing to build capacity.

For example, in Bulgaria, the second poverty map was compiled by a national team of experts. The World Bank provided a consultant who independently carried out the same steps the team was using and was therefore able to answer questions that arose. The consultant also discussed with team members the strengths and weaknesses of research decisions made by the team during the process.

Behind the scenes

External partners should avoid upstaging local counterparts or seeming to exert ownership over the process. This will help the local counterparts understand their own contribution and gain confidence in their abilities, both of which are important in building long-term institutional capacity.

In Sri Lanka, the Department of Census and Statistics was always the focal point of the poverty mapping process. All questions and requests about the mapping process were referred to this department.

In Morocco, the World Bank published its report on the mapping process two months after the government's report had been published. The World Bank report cross-referenced the government report.

Location of staff

If the staff of the external partners involved in the mapping process are close by, especially team leaders and senior experts, this may influence the role the poverty map plays in the country. A team leader who is nearby will become more aware of the motivating factors behind the mapping project and the uses to which the poverty map may be put. The team leader may also then more readily act as a bridge between the technical counterparts, other government agencies, and the external partners. The team leader will thereby become better positioned to respond to needs and help resolve problems.

In Morocco, the team leader from the World Bank was in close, regular contact with the principal government counterparts to ensure that information reached the counterparts in a timely manner.

Multiyear approach and funding

Embedding the poverty mapping process within a multiyear program and providing regular financial assistance appear to be effective ways for external partners to help sustain the mapping effort.

In Morocco, the poverty mapping process was associated with a poverty study carried out by the World Bank and conducted over a span of 18 months. This was followed by programmatic economic and sector work by the Bank. The combination of these two initiatives provided a sufficient time frame for capacity building and a sustained dialogue with the government on poverty and the mapping process.

Contributing to dissemination and use within the development community

As they support countries in the elaboration of small area estimation poverty maps, donor agencies must also take steps that mirror those described in this chapter. Indeed, promoting the wider use and application of these maps within development agencies also requires building support, creating demand for the maps, overcoming potential tensions with users who traditionally rely on alternative sources of data, distributing the poverty map products widely, educating colleagues on the maps' potential and limitations, and supporting users in the application of the maps.

Annex 2.1 Key Counterparts in the Poverty Mapping Process

National statistical institutes

Oftentimes, national statistical institutes are the organizations that produce the poverty maps or, at least, provide most of the data for the maps. It is therefore necessary and appropriate to involve them in the process.

In Vietnam, the General Statistics Office was included in the mapping process, but it did not have a central role. A complication faced during the production of the map revolved around access to census data. If the General Statistics Office had played a more important role, it might have become more committed to the success of the process and done more to facilitate access to the data.

National research institutes

Research institutes usually possess some of the skills needed to produce poverty maps. Such organizations have led in the production of poverty maps in Indonesia and Vietnam and in training staff in mapping techniques at the National Statistical Office in Thailand.

National development organizations

Governmental development organizations may play a central role in the dissemination of poverty maps and in linking the maps into the policy cycle. Such organizations are usually more closely aligned with the policy makers than are the statistical institutes and often possess research and policy skills. Examples of such organizations are the Ministry for National Development Planning in Indonesia and the National Economic and Social Development Board in Thailand.

International donors and bilateral organizations

These entities are key users of poverty maps. They have also provided funding and technical assistance for poverty mapping in many countries.

Providers of poverty data

Most governments produce more than one type of poverty data, some of which are updated yearly. These data do not necessarily always confirm the small area poverty estimates used in poverty mapping and may even contradict these estimates. However, because these other poverty data are regularly updated, the providers, as well as users, have a key interest in supporting the collection of the data. It is therefore important to identify the providers and explore how they may become involved in the poverty mapping process.

Other ministry stakeholders

Most ministries collect and use their own data. Some key ministries, including health, education, finance, and labor, might find the small area poverty estimates valuable in program design and targeting. In Indonesia and elsewhere, small area estimation nutrition maps have attracted the interest of the Ministry of Health. In most countries, the ministry of finance requires good tools for the allocation of resources; this ministry is thus a potential stakeholder in poverty mapping.

Legislatures

Central, provincial, and local legislative bodies are key stakeholders in policy making. Often, they rely on official data, which tends to be produced by national statistical institutes. This is one reason one should seek official recognition for poverty mapping.

Local governments

Numerous countries are involved in government decentralization. Local policy makers are therefore important potential stakeholders in the poverty mapping process given that the small area estimation methodology disaggregates data to the local level.

PART Two

Country Studies

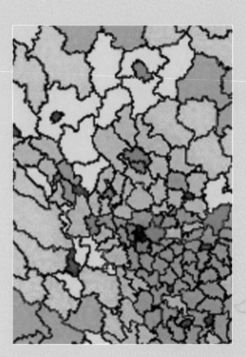

3

Constructing and Using Poverty Maps for Policy Making

The Experience in Albania

CALOGERO CARLETTO, ANDREW DABALEN, AND ALIA MOUBAYED

ACRONYMS AND ABBREVIATIONS

ADF	Albanian Development Fund
INSTAT	Institute of Statistics
lek	the Albanian currency
LSMS	Living Standards Measurement Survey
MDG	Millennium Development Goal
MOLSA	Ministry of Labor and Social Affairs
NSSED	National Strategy for Socio-Economic Development

The small area estimation methodology used to construct poverty maps may become an essential policy tool in Albania for several reasons. First, despite substantial growth and a sizable reduction in poverty, Albania remains one of the poorest countries in Southeastern Europe. The share of the population with per capita consumption under the poverty line of lek 5,272 per month (US$54) was estimated at about 18.5 percent in 2005. Moreover, although these poor are concentrated in rural and mountainous parts of the country, there are pockets of poverty even in regions that are more well off. Poverty reduction is therefore still high on the agenda, particularly in view of these large spatial disparities.

We are grateful to the Institute of Statistics for providing access to the data and to Tara Bedi for excellent comments and suggestions throughout the preparation of this chapter. We thank Arjan Rukaj for collecting useful background information.

Second, the country is pushing to decentralize the delivery of services to local governments, which may be expected to develop independent local strategies and interventions. However, the lack of information at the local level has hampered this effort.

Third, like most countries, Albania has a number of antipoverty programs that are designed to help the most vulnerable groups in society. While the programs appear to be functioning reasonably well, their coverage and effectiveness may be improved. There is thus room to rethink the criteria for the allocation of resources through antipoverty programs so as to foster transparency and equitability, especially in a highly contested political environment. A methodologically sound poverty map may provide the basis for carefully designed geographical targeting in specific antipoverty programs.

Several methodologies are available to produce finely disaggregated poverty maps. The small area estimation methodology described in this chapter is based on a methodology developed at the World Bank and now also adopted in Albania. This estimation technique provides several benefits relative to alternative poverty maps based on composite thematic indicators using administrative data, such as maps based on a basic needs index. First, maps based on composite indicators are rather arbitrary in both the choice of variables and the weights assigned to the variables, yielding ad hoc, easily disputable outputs. Also, drawing a connection between these composite indicators and income poverty is not straightforward and often prone to criticism. Small area estimation, in contrast, by using a clear and transparent methodology, may produce easily interpretable results the statistical precision of which may be properly gauged. Despite this and many other advantages, however, small area estimation has some drawbacks, too. The first concern is related to the significant data requirements; in fact, as we will show, small area estimation poverty maps rely on large and sequenced survey data collection and censuses. Thus, given the low frequency of census undertakings, small area estimation maps may only be updated every decade or so. In addition, the analytical skills and human resources needed for the production of small area estimation maps are substantial and often beyond the available skill level in many developing countries; this also makes the full transfer of ownership and acceptance by local policy makers more difficult to accomplish in a short time. Finally, there is a limit to the level of disaggregation that may be achieved with small area estimation given the increasing level of imprecision at smaller geographical levels. Overall, small area estimation is widely regarded as a more reliable and sound methodology, now applied in a large number of countries.

In the next section, we look at the process involved in the preparation of finely disaggregated poverty maps in Albania using the small area estimation methodology. We also look at subsequent steps to distribute and facilitate the use of the poverty maps. In the section thereafter, we identify the impact (or lack thereof) of poverty maps in the country. The penultimate section summarizes the lessons learned. The last section concludes with considerations on the sustainability of poverty maps in Albania.

Preparation and Dissemination of the Poverty Maps

By late 2000, Albania had no reliable, nationally representative survey to assess the living conditions of the population adequately.[1] The available sources were fragmented and poorly documented, and they provided only partial information of dubious quality. Previous attempts at undertaking household surveys included a survey in Tirana in 1995, followed by a somewhat complementary exercise in 1996 that covered rural and urban households beyond Tirana. More recent efforts have included the 1998 Household Living Conditions Survey and the 2000 Household Budget Survey. While the latter was only carried out in urban areas, the former was nationwide, though it relied on an outdated sampling frame. However, neither supplied complete information for a proper computation of a consumption aggregate measure. Thus, in view of the rapid transformation of the economy and the dramatic population movements in the country, neither survey offered a valid snapshot. In any case, it became clear that, whatever the strengths or weaknesses of the available data, none of these surveys could be used to produce spatially disaggregated poverty maps of Albania.[2] This was simply because there was no reliable population census available.

That changed in 2001 when the Institute of Statistics (INSTAT), with donor support, carried out the country's first census since the end of the communist era. The following year, using the census as a sampling frame, INSTAT implemented a nationally representative multitopic household survey, the 2002 Living Standards Measurement Survey (LSMS). The survey was carried out as part of a program of support to the government of Albania by the U.K. Department for International Development and the World Bank to establish a reliable and sustainable system of household surveys to monitor poverty and policy outcomes. During the same year, the World Bank began to prepare for a full poverty assessment. Finally, in 2002, the government completed the preparation of its first Poverty Reduction Strategy Paper (the National Strategy for Socio-Economic Development, or NSSED). It was understood that the LSMS program, together with the 2001 population census and available administrative data, would form the core information for policy makers in the design, implementation, and evaluation of the NSSED. The convergence of these multiple events within a short time span and the related data that were generated provided the ideal opportunity to construct small area estimates of poverty and inequality, as well as the poverty maps, to understand the spatial distribution of welfare at a finely disaggregated level of much potential use to policy makers.

The creation of the poverty maps followed four steps:

Step 1

The first step involved *awareness raising* through presentations and workshops on the value and methodological innovation represented by small area estimation techniques. The presentations were made by technical assistance teams from the World Bank to technical and policy staff at various line ministries that were responsible for resource allocation and service delivery and that were therefore considered potential users of the poverty maps. The initial demand for the poverty map exercise emerged directly from within the government. However, although much discussion had been held in the country about poverty maps, there was still confusion about the pros and cons of different mapping methods. The confusion arose in part from the failure to distinguish the new small area poverty maps from existing thematic poverty maps based on composite indicators derived from administrative data. Clarifying the differences required patience. Moreover, there was limited knowledge of the scale and scope of small area poverty map applications, the proper interpretation of the results, the technical hurdles to be overcome, and the human capacity required to produce and use the maps. A champion of the small area estimation methodology in one of the ministries was instrumental in creating and maintaining interest in the exercise.

Step 2

The second step aimed at the *formation of the mapping team, institution building,* and *strengthening interministerial collaboration* and joint efforts. This was fostered by the preparation of the Social Services Delivery Project, the objective of which included support for the poverty monitoring system in Albania. By linking the LSMS program to an investment operation spanning several years, both the government and the World Bank showed their long-term commitment to the establishment of a sustainable survey system. This proved key to the successful implementation of the LSMS program.

Step 3

The third step involved hands-on *capacity-building activities,* including technical assistance through international consultants, and the *preparation of the first map*. The team working on the poverty maps consisted of staff members at INSTAT and the Ministry of Labor and Social Affairs (MOLSA), consultants from the University of Siena, and staff at the World Bank. International experts were brought in to train Albanian team members on sampling, questionnaire design, survey techniques, poverty analysis, and the small area estimation methodology. INSTAT staff also attended training abroad on the use of statistical software and on poverty analysis. The preparation of the poverty map took place as part of a poverty assessment that was carried out in collaboration with INSTAT. However, then, as now, the technical capacity of INSTAT was too limited to undertake such a task independently. So, it is fair to say that, although the role of INSTAT expanded over time, much of the work was performed, at least initially, by consultants, primarily from the University of Siena, supervised by World Bank staff.

Step 4

The *dissemination of the results* of the mapping exercise was organized by INSTAT. This followed two parallel tracks. The first track involved the distribution of the maps to the Office of the Prime Minister, the Office of the President, INSTAT regional offices, regional and local government offices, the Tirana municipal government office, economics faculties at several local universities (Elbasan, Gjirokastra, Kamez, Korca, Shkoder, Tirana, Vlora), media outlets, the National Library of Albania, the Library of the People's Assembly, and international institutions and foreign embassies in Albania. The poverty and inequality rankings down to the municipality level were published as maps and also as tables. The reports that contained the maps were made available to the public in various formats, including as monographs, which were published and widely distributed by INSTAT in Albanian and English.

The second track involved the organization of events at which the small area estimation methodology and the data on poverty and inequality were presented to various audiences. There was a number of formal and informal presentations at the Ministry of Finance and MOLSA. Two workshops were also held. The first targeted technical staff at line ministries who were expected to be involved in future policy applications of the maps. The second was organized among journalists at media outlets. As an outcome of this event, the results of the mapping exercise were published in four newspapers. The poverty map work was also presented at the international conference "How to Use Statistics as a Development Tool" held in Tirana on May 18–19, 2003, to disseminate the results of the 2001 census.

In the remainder of this section, we highlight some of the technical issues that the team had to resolve (in Step 3) in order to produce the maps.

Data sources

The preparation of the maps relied on the use of three data sets: the 2001 Population and Housing Census, the 2002 LSMS, and the 1998 General Census of Agricultural Holdings.

2001 Population and housing census

The population census was conducted during April 2001. The questionnaire had four parts: a building questionnaire (filled out by inhabitants of the first or main dwelling in each building), a dwelling questionnaire, a household questionnaire, and an individual questionnaire (to be completed for all members of each household, including those members absent for less than a year). The country was divided into 9,834 enumeration areas for purposes of the census, and data were collected on 726,895 households, comprising about 3.1 million people.

2002 LSMS

The 2002 LSMS was fielded between April and June 2002 by the Living Standards Unit of INSTAT, with support from the U.K. Department for International Development and the World Bank. The 9,834 enumeration areas in the 2001 census provided the sampling frame for the LSMS. A total of 450 primary sampling units were selected, and eight households, plus up to four substitute households, were chosen in each primary sampling unit, for a total of 3,600 households. The sample was stratified into four areas drawn along agroecological and socioeconomic lines: the coast, the center, and the mountains, as well as the city of Tirana. The first three areas were further stratified into major cities, other urban areas, and rural areas, and each primary sampling unit was drawn with probability proportional to its size. In Tirana, the primary sampling units were selected systematically, according to an implicit stratification. The LSMS is representative of urban and rural areas, as well as each of the four strata. The household questionnaire consisted of a total of 15 modules, including food, nonfood consumption, housing and dwelling characteristics, utilities and durables, education, health, fertility, child anthropometric outcomes, migration, income sources, and participation in social assistance programs. A community questionnaire and a price questionnaire were also administered.

1998 General census of agricultural holdings

The agricultural census was fielded in June 1998. It involved interviews among managers (or owners) of agricultural holdings. About 466,809 private and public holdings were covered. The data collected through questionnaires included number of holdings, total area of holdings, total cultivated land by type of tillage (manual, machine, and so on), and livestock assets.

Estimation

Administratively, Albania is divided into 12 regions, 36 districts, 374 municipalities and communes, and 11 submunicipalities within the municipality of Tirana. The purpose of the poverty mapping exercise was to estimate poverty and inequality for each of the regions, districts, and municipalities or communes, as well as for each submunicipality of Tirana.

One of the issues in imputing consumption for census households based on information from the LSMS involved identifying the variables to be used in the prediction model of consumption. After careful cross-checks of both the census and the LSMS, 38 variables common to both data sets were selected. This unusually large match is not completely surprising: because the census was conducted a year prior to the household survey, it was easier for the organizers of the LSMS to ensure that relevant census questions, especially those on housing and durables, were closely matched to those that would be asked in the household survey. Of the 38 overlapping variables, 23 were from the sections on housing characteristics and the ownership of durable goods, 8 were related to the characteristics of heads-of-household, and the last 7 were on household demographic characteristics. Missing values on selected variables in the LSMS data were imputed using statistical imputation techniques. This initial stage, that is, the selection of variables common to the census and the survey, yielded satisfactory results.

A separate per capita consumption model was estimated for each LSMS stratum and substratum, namely, the coast (rural and urban), the center (rural and urban), the mountains, and Tirana.[3] The cluster-specific component of the residuals appeared correlated with the covariates, and a generalized least squares method was adopted. The consumption for each household in the census was simulated using the parameter estimates from the LSMS consumption model (see Elbers, Lanjouw, and Lanjouw 2003 for more on the methodology). Using the LSMS-based parameter estimates, consumption was estimated for households in the census given the observed household characteristics. The parameter estimates and the predicted residual were drawn a second time, and the consumption was recalculated. The process was repeated 100 times, providing the expected value of consumption for each household in the population. For each of the regions, districts, and municipalities and communes, the usual Foster-Greer-Thorbecke poverty measures, the Sen measure of poverty, and the Gini and generalized entropy (0,1) measures of inequality were estimated based on these simulated consumption values. Standard errors of the estimates at the different levels of aggregation were computed to assess the precision of the estimations. The small area estimates showed acceptable margins of error down to the municipality and commune level.

The charts in figure 3.1 show the final estimates of the poverty headcount at the three levels of geographical aggregation, namely, regions (12), districts (36), and municipalities and communes (374).

Awareness and Policy Outcomes

Now that we have described the process for the preparation and dissemination of the maps, we turn to the use and impact of the maps in the policy discourse in Albania. Who were the users? How have they used the maps? To answer these questions, individuals involved in the preparation of the maps and potential users of the maps were interviewed. The methodology was simple. First, we identified a list of potential users of the maps. These included front-line social service delivery ministries or departments, such as education, health, and labor and social assistance, plus the Ministry of Finance, local government offices, nongovernmental organizations, and bilateral development agencies. Next, we drew up a set of questions. For instance, are the staff of the department or agency aware of the maps? If so, have they used them? And, if yes, how have the maps been used? If the staff are not aware of the maps, we ask why not and, now that they are aware, how they might use the maps in future.

During the interviews, we found that there were three ways in which poverty maps have been used in Albania.

A benchmark against existing resource allocation criteria

One example of benchmarking against existing resource allocation criteria is a recent exercise by MOLSA with regard to Ndhima Ekonomika, the main social assistance program. The origins and the performance of this program have been the subject of a number of studies (see early evaluations by Alderman 2002 and Case 1997). Ndhima Ekonomika began in 1992/93 as a safety net program for the urban and rural poor during the chaotic transition of the country from central planning to a market economy. Soon, it became the largest income support program for the poor, covering as much as 20 percent of the population. In 1994, the implementation of the program was decentralized to local governments, which were assigned block grants from the central government and acquired discretionary authority over eligibility criteria and the level of benefits per recipient.

While the decentralization of the program may have improved targeting at the local level, concerns remain that benefits continue to flow to politically favored communes. This concern is reinforced by the fact that the allocation of grants is based on a 1999 decision by

Figure 3.1 Poverty Headcount Ratio in Albania by Region, District, and Commune/Municipality

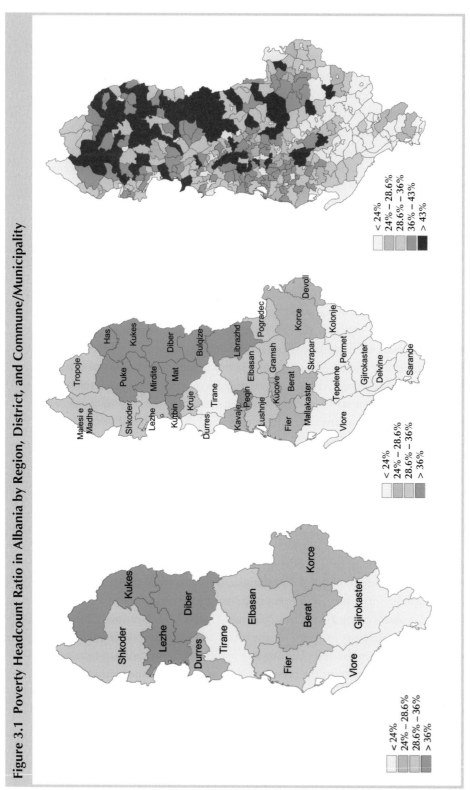

Source: INSTAT 2004.

the Council of Ministers that specifies conditions that may not all be closely linked to poverty.[4] Moreover, there was no explicit formula that linked the proposed indicators with grant levels. Finally, grant levels were determined at a time when the country's information base was weak. There was thus no monitoring and evaluation in place. So, itis quite possible that the decision of the Council of Ministers was not applied uniformly everywhere.

As part of a strategy to build evidence-based policy making in government, the NSSED and the policy unit of MOLSA undertook a study to assess whether block grant allocations correlate with the poverty rates of communes. The objective of the study was to "raise awareness on the use of available statistical information to evaluate whether policies achieve the desired results and how effectivenessof public expenditure and the design of public policies can be improved" (NSDI 2005, page 1). In effect, the study looked at how well the first-stage allocation, that is, block grants from the central government to local governments, was targeted. It does not assess second-stage allocation or distribution to households. The study concludes that there is low correlation between the distribution of block grants for social assistance and the distribution of poverty in the country and that there is scope for revising the methodology used for allocating the block grants.

Figure 3.2 illustrates the results of this study. It plots the implied poverty rates of the block grant system for each commune, measured as the share of the commune population that receives Ndhima Ekonomika benefits (vertical axis) in the State Social Services data and the commune-level poverty rates as measured through the poverty mapping exercise (horizontal axis). Each municipality is represented by a point.

Explicit geographical targeting

To our knowledge, the only explicit use of poverty map data for targeting public spending occurred through the Albanian Development Fund (ADF). The ADF is a community-driven development fund that supports infrastructure and social service delivery projects. It began in 1993 as a rural development fund to transfer resources to rural areas, initiate community works programs, and generate employment, but, by 2000, it had expanded activities to every commune in Albania.

Prior to 2003, the ADF allocated funds on the basis of one commune–one project, but, after 2004, the criteria for allocating investment funds changed to include, in an explicit way, the poverty ranking of communes and municipalities, which had become

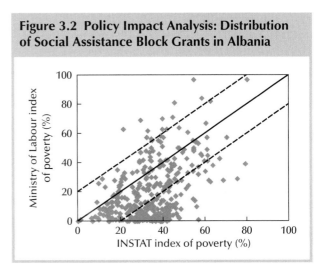

Figure 3.2 Policy Impact Analysis: Distribution of Social Assistance Block Grants in Albania

Source: MOLSA 2005.

available in 2003. Now, municipalities and communes obtain a score from 1 to 8 on the basis of their technical, social, and environmental endowments and their poverty ranking as calculated in the poverty mapping exercise. The ADF funds are subsequently allocated according to the scores so that municipalities and communes with higher than average poverty scores receive additional resources. It is important to note that, though poverty ranking is one criterion among the many criteria used in allocating resources, this is currently the only instance where poverty ranking enters directly into a score used to determine the allocation of resources. A careful evaluation has not yet been made, but there is a general belief by staff at the ADF that the introduction of the poverty ranking has improved program targeting. The explicit inclusion of the poverty map data among the criteria for the allocation of ADF projects has been rendered straightforward because of the desire and efforts of the ADF staff to improve the targeting.

Monitoring MDGs at the central and local levels

Another way poverty maps have been used is to provide data for monitoring progress toward achieving the Millennium Development Goals (MDGs) in Albania. This contribution has occurred through two channels. In the first, with the assistance of the United Nations Development Programme, regional development strategies aimed at achieving the MDGs were identified. These strategies use the poverty map data as the baseline for monitoring progress toward the first MDG (halving extreme poverty and hunger). At least four regional development strategies (Durrës, Fier, Tirana, and Vlora) and one regional progress report (Fier) have been prepared. The United Nations Development Programme has worked with INSTAT to create an integrated development database, DevInfo, to monitor progress toward the MDGs at the national and regional levels. The poverty map data for the municipalities and communes have been entered into the database. Parallel efforts are under way to gather data on health and vital statistics, education, and infrastructure. Once completed, the integrated database will provide policy makers at the central and local levels with tools to monitor and benchmark their progress in achieving the MDGs.

In the second channel, the NSSED has used the poverty map data to prepare the MDG progress report. Once again, the poverty map data set the baseline against which to measure the country's overall progress in poverty reduction.

Finally, we note that several nongovernmental organizations have relied on the poverty maps in supplying advisory services to local governments and donor agencies in Berat, Dibër, Durrës, Elbasan, Lezha, Shkodra, and Vlora regions and in designing joint intervention strategies with them.[5]

While there is a general awareness of the mapping results, especially among nongovernmental organizations, development partners, and even among technical people in some line ministries, public policy making overall has not been much affected by the maps. This is a missed opportunity in an environment in which ongoing reforms in areas such as decentralization, public finance, and service delivery might benefit significantly from the maps. Why has the policy impact of the maps been small? We provide four possible explanations in the next section.

Lessons Learned

The dissemination strategy is key

The key to widespread use of poverty maps is a good dissemination strategy. In the case of Albania, two workshops (one for technical experts and the other for journalists) and an international conference, plus many formal and informal presentations, did not appear to expand the policy impact of the poverty maps. Although these events led to the publication of articles on the mapping exercise in daily newspapers, there was no sustained effort to use the mapping evidence in policy making.

In retrospect, there were two concrete ways in which the dissemination strategy might have contributed more to the policy impact. First, the value and the many possible applications of the poverty maps needed to be emphasized among advisers to key policy makers. In particular, it would have been useful to highlight the advantages of poverty maps by demonstrating how, for example, Ndhima Ekonomika, or the road investment programs, or a new program might benefit from the maps.

Second, the dissemination strategy needed to focus on reaching a wider audience, including policy makers in regional councils and local governments, professional associations, and civil society groups. The visual representation of the mapping information might have been made more widely available through user-friendly media. Specifically, a poster might have been produced and exhibited in government buildings, universities, and the offices of international organizations. For an example of such a poster, see FIVIMS (2005).

Weak capacity, high staff turnover, and inertia

Another reason for the limited policy impact is the fact that poverty maps and, indeed, the idea of the measurement and assessment of poverty are new and unfamiliar in Albania. To understand the importance of this issue, recall that a routine poverty assessment and a poverty headcount based on internationally accepted standards were first carried out in Albania in 2003. For many technical staff in the line ministries, these are new ideas, and it is understandable that there has been resistance to adopting the innovations quickly. Moreover, even in cases in which able staff have received training in the new methodology, high staff turnover and attrition have been a barrier to the acquisition of skills and the foundation of institutional memory. INSTAT has, however, started a data users group that brings together staff at several governmental institutions. This is a positive step.

By contrast, technical staffs and policy makers are familiar with the current rules and criteria for targeting and the allocation of resources. For instance, the Ministry of

Finance allocates unconditional grants to regions and municipalities and communes on the basis of a formula that considers population share, size of the commune (surface area), own revenue effort, and poverty (defined as the share of the population receiving social assistance). There are merits and flaws in this method, particularly with regard to the definition of poverty that has been adopted. A new methodology based on poverty maps would have represented a radical departure from existing practices. The reluctance to use the poverty maps is amplified because the maps are not readily updated given that census data are typically collected only once every decade.

Sequencing

To produce the poverty maps, both census and household surveys must be available, ideally for the same year. The fact that a household survey had been conducted soon after the census has been an important ingredient in the successful production of the poverty maps in Albania. Because there was no census, this would not have been possible prior to 2001 even though household surveys were available. However, such sequencing between the census and a survey requires patience and persuasion not least because, of the two, a census is less easily and less quickly carried out in terms of both costs and logistics. However, proper sequencing should be attempted by planning the household survey around the time of the census.

Political economy

Many observers of the political landscape in Albania have noted the incredible transformation from a very insular communist regime to a highly open and robust multiparty democracy. However, although there are numerous parties, the political system is dominated by two parties, the Democratic Party and the Socialist Party, each with smaller coalition partners. As is common throughout the world, parties in such democracies may favor flexible rules that allow them to allocate resources on the basis of criteria other than economic needs, as would be the case with poverty maps, so as to reward areas that provide support or increase their chances of winning elections. Indeed, Case (1997) shows that the size of social assistance block grants received by a commune in Albania depends on the commune's political leanings.

Conclusion: Increasing and Sustaining the Policy Impact of Poverty Maps

Since 2001, Albania has made tremendous strides in laying the foundation for a poverty monitoring and evaluation system. In particular, it has accumulated a wealth of administrative and household survey data that offer all the potential benefits of an integrated information system. Moreover, there is a general consensus on the need for and direction of policy reform. Demand is also growing for policy making grounded on information derived from the integrated system. There is thus a huge potential for the use of poverty maps and similar tools to support transparent and evidence-based policy making.

The current government was elected in 2005 on a wave of reform promises. These include (1) revising and updating the NSSED (now renamed the National Strategy for Development and Integration) to sustain growth, improve service delivery, and reduce disparities among regions; (2) increasing the efficiency of public resource use through the modernization of government administration and integrated budgeting and planning; and (3) improving the effectiveness of intergovernmental transfers by decentralizing government functions. To augment and sustain the impact of the poverty maps on policy, support is crucial in maintaining the momentum of government reform. This may be accomplished in part by raising the interest of policy makers in poverty maps, creating local demand for the maps through public displays on the Web sites of INSTAT and MOLSA, and supporting local researchers in acquiring the skills to create and make use of the maps.

Now, there are opportunities to update the small area estimation poverty maps in Albania and make them relevant for policy. However, aside from the formidable technical hurdles to be overcome, it is not realistic to expect policy makers to shift policies and resource allocations by relying entirely on maps based on census data that are five or six years old. This is especially true in Albania, where population movements have been massive, and structural changes dramatic. However, it would be important to undertake the exercise to update the poverty maps so that capacity is built, especially in the small area estimation methodology, in advance of the next census, which is less than four years away. It is also important to keep up the effort at dissemination and generate ownership and widespread use of the maps. It is hoped that the prospects for reaching these goals will be enhanced by multiyear analytical programs such as public expenditure and institutional reviews, poverty assessments, and development policy loans.

Notes

1. This section draws heavily on INSTAT (2004) and Betti, Neri, and Ballini (2003).
2. It should be noted that, despite their shortcomings, these surveys have been underutilized. For instance, the 1996 survey provided the information necessary to assess the targeting effectiveness of the Ndhima Ekonomika (Social Assistance) Program for the first time. See Alderman (2002).
3. Because the mountain sample was mostly rural, no separate models for urban and rural were estimated for the mountains.
4. According to the decision of the Council of Ministers, seven indicators are supposed to be monitored for each municipality and commune and used to determine block grant levels. These indicators include (1) the population of the municipality or commune, (2) the number of public sector employees, (3) the number of private sector employees, (4) the number of people receiving unemployment benefits, (5) the number of people with real estate, (6) the number of pensioners, and (7) the numbers of households possessing land, little land, or no land. See NSDI (2005).
5. The nongovernmental organizations include Oxfam, the National Albanian Center for Social Studies, the Human Development Promotion Centre, and Sustainable Economic Development Agencies.

References

Alderman, Harold. 2002. "Do Local Officials Know Something We Don't?: Decentralization of Targeted Transfers in Albania." *Journal of Public Economics* 83 (3): 375–404.

Betti, Gianni, Laura Neri, and Francesca Ballini. 2003. "Poverty and Inequality Mapping in Albania: Final Report." Unpublished working paper, World Bank and Institute of Statistics, Tirana, Albania.

Case, Anne C. 1997. "The Decentralization of Social Assistance: Evidence from Albania." Unpublished working paper, Research Program in Development Studies, Woodrow Wilson School of Public and International Affairs, Princeton University, Princeton, NJ.

———. 2001. "Election Goals and Income Redistribution: Recent Evidence from Albania." *European Economic Review* 45 (3): 405–23.

Elbers, Chris, Jean O. Lanjouw, and Peter F. Lanjouw. 2003. "Micro-Level Estimation of Poverty and Inequality." *Econometrica* 71 (1): 355–64.

FIVIMS (Food Insecurity and Vulnerability Information and Mapping Systems). 2005. "Country Activities: Publications, Madagascar." Newsletter of the FIVIMS Initiative 7 (1): 1–2, Secretariat, Inter-Agency Working Group on Food Insecurity and Vulnerability Information and Mapping Systems, Food and Agriculture Organization of the United Nations, Rome. http://www.fivims.net/upload/recentletters/406/FIVIMS_Newsletter__Nov_2005.pdf.

INSTAT (Institute of Statistics). 2004. "Poverty and Inequality Mapping in Albania." Report, Institute of Statistics, Tirana, Albania.

MOLSA (Ministry of Labor and Social Affairs). 2005. "Policy Impact Analysis: Distribution of Economic Assistance Block Grants." Report, June, Ministry of Labor and Social Affairs, Tirana, Albania.

NSDI (National Strategy for Development and Integration). 2005. "Utilizing Data to Evaluate Policies: Economic Assistance Block Grants." Briefing Note, October, National Strategy for Development and Integration Unit, Council of Ministers, Tirana, Albania.

4

The Geography of Monetary Poverty in Bolivia
The Lessons of Poverty Maps

OMAR ARIAS AND MARCOS ROBLES

During the 1990s, Bolivia followed the practice of many Latin American countries by developing poverty maps based on unsatisfied basic needs (UBN) almost immediately after the execution of the population census. These maps have been influential in the portrayal of geographical disparities in living conditions and in access to basic services. However, while census data often allow considerable geographical disaggregation (for example, at the municipal level), they do not capture household income and expenditure. Meanwhile, household surveys rarely allow for reliable estimation of income and consumption poverty in small geographical areas (such as municipalities).[1]

The small area estimation method developed by Elbers, Lanjouw, and Lanjouw (2003) allows one to circumvent these restrictions. It permits consumption poverty maps to

The authors would like to thank Milenka Figueroa, Wilson Jimenez, and Fernando Landa for invaluable support and input during the development of this chapter and Björn-Sören Gigler for useful comments.

be derived by combining census and household survey data so as to supply missing expenditure data in the census at adequate statistical confidence levels using hedonic regression models. This methodology has been successfully applied in several countries in Latin America and other regions.

In Bolivia between November 2002 and June 2003, the method was used to create consumption poverty maps at the level of municipalities. The maps were developed by a joint team at the *Unidad de Análisis de Políticas Sociales y Económicas* (Social and Economic Policy Analysis Unit, UDAPE) and the *Instituto Nacional de Estadística* (National Institute of Statistics, INE) that was supported through World Bank technical assistance. The purpose was to generate local indicators of monetary poverty and consumption inequality for the measurement of municipal disparities and to provide an additional tool for planning and targeting within Bolivia's poverty reduction strategy and the ongoing process of decentralization and local participation.

This chapter documents the Bolivian experience in developing and using these monetary poverty maps. It focuses on the impact of the consumption poverty maps developed by the World Bank and the Bolivian government in 2003 on the design and targeting of public policies in the country. It draws on lessons from the experience of the authors and numerous interviews with diverse stakeholders in and outside government in Bolivia (see Figueroa 2006).

The chapter is structured as follows. The next section provides a brief description of the context and the process of the development of the consumption poverty maps. The subsequent section describes succinctly the main methodological aspects of this process. The section thereafter illustrates some of the main results that highlight the policy relevance of the poverty maps to Bolivia. The penultimate section reports on the field interviews. The chapter concludes with an examination of the main lessons that arise from the Bolivian experience and that may help tap more effectively into the policy potential of monetary poverty maps.

The Demand for Poverty Maps in Bolivia

Bolivia underwent important economic, political, and social changes in the 1990s. Macroeconomic stabilization in the late 1980s was followed by market reforms to deregulate the economy, liberalize trade, simplify taxes, reform the pension system, privatize nonperforming public companies, and decentralize public resources to municipalities. The decentralization process gained impetus with the development of the Bolivian poverty reduction strategy through the broad participation of various sectors and donors as part of the Heavily Indebted Poor Countries Initiative in 2000–01 (see World Bank and IDB 2004; World Bank 2005).

Bolivia's reform efforts swiftly paid off through high rates of investment and growth. The economy expanded at an average annual rate of 4.7 percent (2.2 percent per capita) during 1993–98. Exports diversified; social spending increased substantially; and living conditions improved, particularly as measured by education, health, and other Millennium Development Goal indicators.

Expenditure decentralization started with the *Ley de participación popular* (law on public participation) in early 1994 and the *Ley de descentralización* (law on decentralization) in 1995, which transferred primary responsibility for the planning and implementation of public investment to the municipalities and prefectures. These advances were augmented by the 2001 law on national dialogue. These reforms, aimed at smoothing the large regional disparities in living conditions, established mechanisms to allocate public resources, expand the abilities of local governments to deliver basic services, and increase community participation in the formulation and execution of social programs. In particular, the Bolivian government developed a poverty map using 1992 census data and the UBN method to guide social investment allocations (see Ministry of Human Development 1995). This map was later updated according to the 2001 census and became the basis for the formula that was established in the 2001 law on national dialogue and that guided the allocation of intermunicipal transfers under the Heavily Indebted Poor Countries Initiative. These maps revealed the country's large regional disparities in living conditions, particularly between urban and rural areas and between the central highlands, where many of the indigenous people live, and the lowlands of Santa Cruz.

The decentralization process, supported with growing tax revenues, had a positive impact on social expenditure and service delivery in the poorest municipalities. Social spending rose from 2.5 percent of gross domestic product in 1986 to 18.5 percent in 2001. This was the second highest share in Latin America and the Caribbean and led in turn to greater human capital and social investments in localities with poor indicators in literacy, nutrition, and connection to water and sewerage services (see World Bank and IDB 2004; Faguet 2004; Bossert 2000).

However, progress was limited in many areas and not sustained. After several external and internal shocks in 1999, economic growth decelerated to an average rate of only 1.7 percent during 1999–2002. Fiscal imbalances and financial sector difficulties weakened macroeconomic stability, reducing job creation and poverty reduction. In 2002, 65 percent of the population was living in poverty, of which nearly 40 percent were in extreme poverty. Bolivia remained one of the poorest and most unequal countries in Latin America, and the opportunities for income generation among the poor, particularly the poor indigenous population, continue to be a critical issue today.

Two factors made this situation ripe for the production of disaggregated data on monetary poverty. First, the Bolivian poverty reduction strategy and the law on national dialogue required an evaluation every three years of the impact of the strategy on poverty conditions, and the resources from debt reductions were to be distributed using poverty indicators on municipalities. Second, the UBN poverty maps only illustrated the nonmonetary aspects of the geographical distribution of poverty, and they were therefore inadequate tools to help improve the impact of public expenditures on monetary poverty at the municipal or even departmental level. In fact, some government officials were concerned that the system of intermunicipal transfers based on targeting according to the UBN poverty maps (the formula of the law on national dialogue) was less responsive to the conditions in the many municipalities with entrenched pockets of monetary poverty.

UDAPE thus made a request to the World Bank for technical support in the development of monetary poverty maps using the small area estimation method of Elbers, Lanjouw, and Lanjouw (2003). This was followed by an official request from the Bolivian government to the World Bank for technical and financial support for the joint development of the new poverty maps. A team of highly qualified technical staff from the INE, UDAPE, and the World Bank started preparing a consumption poverty map on Bolivia in early 2003.[2] UDAPE undertook the related technical production and overall project coordination, and the INE provided the data platform for the exercise, while the Bank supplied technical support and some financial assistance. The basic data requirements and methodological details were defined during a technical mission by Bank staff with the local team. During a second visit, initial results were examined, and data consistency was assessed. A map was completed in June 2003, and, by the end of August, the local team had prepared and published a report on the results.[3]

The consumption poverty map document was launched successfully, and the results were well received in Bolivia, although the impact of the instrument on policy making has been limited by several factors (see elsewhere below). We now discuss some of the methodological aspects of the development of the consumption poverty maps and some of the findings that highlight the policy relevance of such a map for Bolivia.

Data and Methodology

The main data sources for the exercise were the National Population and Housing Census of 2001 and household surveys that were conducted through the *Programa para el Mejoramiento de las Encuestas de Hogares y la Medición de Condiciones de Vida* (Program for the Improvement of Household Surveys and the Measurement of Living Conditions) and carried out in 1999, 2000, and 2001 by the INE. Data from these sources were combined to obtain a larger sample that could be disaggregated according to the main administrative regions (departments) and areas in Bolivia. The approach followed closely the small area estimation method used in other applications elsewhere. The approach was tailored to the data and country context of Bolivia. The methodology linked household consumption expenditure with variables measured in the household surveys and the census so as to impute the missing expenditure data (see INE and UDAPE 2003; Elbers, Lanjouw, and Lanjouw 2003). The approach involved the following steps:

- An econometric model of per capita household expenditures was estimated (through generalized least squares) as a function of variables in the surveys and also collected in the census. The variables included household structure, household durable goods (including appliances and other equipment), basic services, and the sociodemographic characteristics of household members.[4] Separate models were developed for the urban and rural sectors in each of the country's departments. There were thus a total of 16 models. (There are nine departments, but Beni and Pando were combined for purposes of the exercise.)

- The estimated parameters of the models were applied to the census data to obtain conditional estimates of average per capita consumption. From these, several indexes of poverty and inequality were derived for each locality (the headcount index, the poverty gap and the severity of poverty, the Gini coefficient, the Atkinson index, and three generalized entropy inequality indexes).

- The errors of estimation in the model have two parts: one attributed to geographical or location effects, and the other related to individual or idiosyncratic errors. The first indicates the presence of nonobservable characteristics that affect household consumption in a certain area or community; to address this, explanatory variables were generated for each community or area (the average characteristics of the urban and rural areas) that predicted the location error with fixed effects. The idiosyncratic error was then estimated through random draws of the unexplained regression residuals from a normal or t distribution, while account was taken of the dependence of the dispersion of the residuals on the observed variables.

- The data samples of the 1999, 2000, and 2001 household surveys were pooled to obtain more reliable estimates of indicators on localities.[5] The small area estimation method presumes that survey samples have been split into homogeneous area clusters so as to render more accurate and robust estimates and statistical inferences. However, the surveys closer in time to the 2001 census had smaller sample sizes that were representative only at the regional level and in the urban and rural sectors. (There are three regions: the western and central highlands, the valleys at the eastern slopes, and the eastern lowlands.) The three independent surveys were therefore pooled to obtain a higher frequency of observations in the primary sampling units common to the three surveys. Since the sample frames were different (the 1999 and 2000 surveys used the 1992 census, while the 2001 survey was based on the 2001 census), the sampling expansion factors were adjusted to maintain the consistency with a single sample frame (that of the 2001 census). Based on the list of common primary sampling units and the corresponding number of dwellings, the expansion factors were recalculated on the assumption that the primary sampling units had been randomly selected in each of the 16 geographical territories modeled (see elsewhere above).

- The computation of poverty lines (extreme, low, and high) for each of the 16 geographical units was based on data from the 1990 household expenditure survey (urban areas) and the impact evaluation survey for the Social Investment Fund (rural areas). The required minimum per capita daily caloric intake was set at 2,120 kilocalories. The poverty lines were adjusted according to the consumer price index corresponding to the reference period of the survey. The household reference group was composed of households that showed food expenditure levels capable of covering the minimum nutritional requirements within an interval of 1 percent, 5 percent, and 10 percent above and below the minimum caloric intake. The poverty lines were obtained by averaging the values of the household expenditures for each interval. Besides the extreme poverty line, two other lines were used: a high poverty line that reflected an upper limit on the value of nonfood products and a lower poverty line corresponding to an inferior, survival limit.[6]

The data and statistical strategy summarized in the final two points above may be instructive in other country contexts. Too often, the sample size in a household survey permits the reliable estimation of consumption expenditure regression models only at a regional level, which is too broad. In our case, the pooling of time-adjacent surveys offered a way to circumvent the problem. Moreover, in practice, few households meet the totality of basic caloric and protein intake requirements. Combined with expenditure measurement errors, this supports the use of interval rather than ordinal estimation in assessments of the robustness of locality poverty rankings (Wodon 1997).

Policy Lessons from the Monetary Poverty Mapping Exercise

The mapping exercise has corroborated many suppositions about the concentration of the income poor in Bolivia, while shedding light on the geographical patterns in monetary poverty and the links to inequality in the country. Poverty and inequality in Bolivia transcend rural-urban and regional boundaries. The exercise has pinpointed more unequal areas and localities with the highest concentrations of poverty and the implied relative indicator rankings. It also shows that the variability in the levels of extreme consumption poverty is greater than indicated in the UBN poverty maps.[7]

The heterogeneity of poverty and inequality in Bolivia

The poverty mapping exercise demonstrates in detail the heterogeneity of monetary poverty and inequality in Bolivia and helps identify the places where greater public policy efforts are needed. While poverty is widespread, there are important differences across locations. Figure 4.1 shows the incidence of consumption poverty and the intensity of consumption poverty (the poverty gap) across municipalities.

Although an overwhelming portion of the rural populace is living in consumption poverty, there are also large pockets of urban poverty. Nonetheless, many intermediate cities and small municipalities also have low poverty rates. The main results may be summarized as follows:[8]

■ Monetary poverty is concentrated in the valleys and the western and central highlands, especially in the departments of Chuquisaca and Potosí, then Beni, La Paz, and Oruro (with minor differences in the rankings according to low or high poverty lines). The urban conglomerations of Cochabamba and Santa Cruz show the lowest poverty rates, while Beni and La Paz present the highest levels of poverty (over 50 percent for the low poverty line). About 40 percent of the population in the department of Santa Cruz is poor, but the poverty rate is only 20 percent in the capital; the situation observed in Cochabamba is similar. Urban development in Cochabamba and Santa

Figure 4.1 Incidence and Intensity of Consumption Poverty in Bolivia, 2001

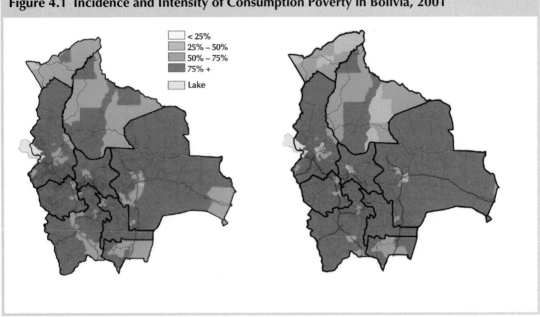

- < 25%
- 25% – 50%
- 50% – 75%
- 75% +
- Lake

Source: INE and UDAPE 2003 using data from the 2001 census and household surveys in 1999–2001.
Note: The intensity of poverty (poverty gap) is the total consumption shortfall (expressed in proportion to a poverty line) of those households showing consumption below the poverty threshold, divided by the total number of households.

Cruz has created broadbased income opportunities. However, owing to their higher population density, the two cities contain the largest number of poor people in absolute terms.

- Rural areas throughout the country are overwhelmingly poor regardless of the poverty line used. In fact, in rural areas, the incidence of extreme consumption poverty is almost as high as the incidence of total poverty. The rural areas of Cochabamba and Santa Cruz exhibit a poverty incidence as high as the incidence of poverty in rural Chuquisaca and Potosí.

- Monetary poverty is widespread in a large number of municipalities in terms of magnitude and intensity and regardless of the poverty line. Many municipalities exhibit poverty above national levels, and a significant fraction exhibit poverty above 80 percent. In at least 20 municipalities with dispersed populations (such as Buena Vista, Morochata, Ravelo, San Pedro in Pando, and San Pedro in Potosí), most residents are unable to cover their basic food needs.

- Bolivia also exhibits high levels of inequality in consumption at the local level. In the more egalitarian departments (Beni, Pando, and Tarija), inequality may be attributed mainly to rural-urban disparities. However, in the most unequal (Chuquisaca, Cochabamba, and Potosí), inequality is pervasive within both urban and rural localities. Chuquisaca, Cochabamba, and Potosí show the highest inequality with regard to consumption expenditures. The more equitable distribution of consumption expenditures in Beni, Pando, and Tarija partially reflects greater economic opportunities by virtue of the location along the borders with Argentina and Brazil and the lower proportion of indigenous populations, among other factors.

Poverty, average consumption, and inequality

The results of the poverty mapping exercise reveal core connections at the local level among increases in average consumption (such as would occur with economic growth), consumption poverty, and inequality. Poverty incidence is lower in municipalities with higher average consumption, but the association is mediated by inequality. Many localities may be caught in poverty traps (Azariadis 2004). Such patterns should be taken as tentative since they may reflect cross-sectional correlations, but they illustrate the rich interrelationships revealed by the monetary poverty mapping exercise.

Figure 4.2 shows the relationship between per capita consumption and the incidence and intensity of consumption poverty in municipalities. It is clear that increases in consumption are weakly correlated with poverty reduction in the poorest municipalities, but that this association becomes stronger among the less poor municipalities. Municipalities with an average consumption far below (above) the national average register poverty rates above (below) the national level. These municipalities are typically located in more economically dynamic urban areas. Around the average per capita expenditure level, several municipalities perform below and above national poverty levels. This reflects, in part, the differences in poverty intensity among localities. As shown in the chart on the right in figure 4.2, higher per capita consumption correlates with lower poverty intensity almost linearly, but the association becomes more dispersed among

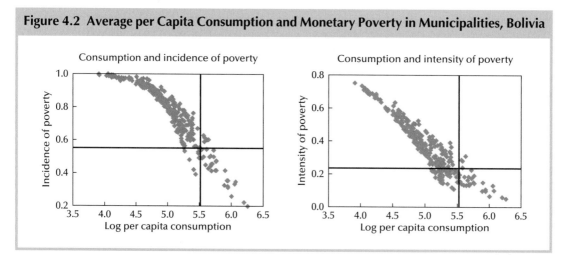

Figure 4.2 Average per Capita Consumption and Monetary Poverty in Municipalities, Bolivia

Source: INE and UDAPE 2003 using data from the 2001 census and household surveys in 1999–2001.
Note: The results correspond to the low poverty line. The poverty gap is the total consumption shortfall (expressed in proportion to a poverty line) of those families (households) showing consumption below the poverty threshold, divided by the total number of families (households).

municipalities at average per capita consumption. This pinpoints the role of programs targeted at the poorest municipalities in complementing or reinforcing the impact of economic growth.

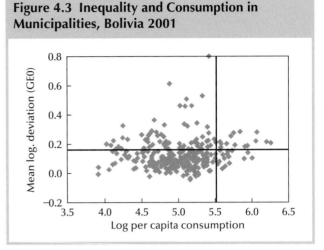

Figure 4.3 Inequality and Consumption in Municipalities, Bolivia 2001

Source: INE and UDAPE 2003 using data from the 2001 census and household surveys in 1999–2001.
Note: The y axis depicts the mean log deviation of family consumption from the average per capita consumption within each municipality.

Meanwhile, figure 4.3 shows no clear-cut correlation between municipal average consumption and inequality. While most municipalities at low consumption also exhibit low inequality, we find both low and high inequality among municipalities at higher average consumption. Thus, for most municipalities (the mass of points at the bottom of the figure), there is little evidence that higher average consumption necessarily entails higher inequality. Municipalities at average per capita consumption show greater variation in inequality.

The municipal data also illustrate that inequality is a key factor in the country's significant poverty rates. Figure 4.4 shows the relationship between inequality and the incidence and intensity of extreme consumption poverty. The horizontal and vertical

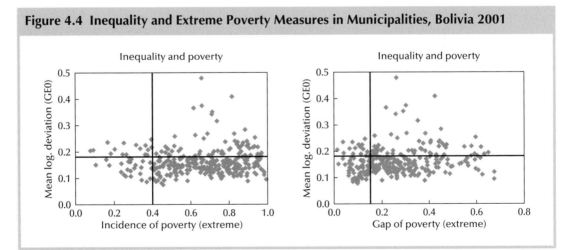

Figure 4.4 Inequality and Extreme Poverty Measures in Municipalities, Bolivia 2001

Source: INE and UDAPE 2003 using data from the 2001 census and household surveys in 1999–2001.
Note: The y axis depicts the mean log deviation of family consumption from the average per capita consumption within each municipality. Poverty rates are based on the extreme poverty line. The poverty gap is the total consumption shortfall (expressed in proportion to a poverty line) of those families (households) showing consumption below the poverty threshold, divided by the total number of families (households).

lines depict the national levels for each variable and divide each of the charts into four quadrants. High inequality and high extreme poverty are pervasive in many localities, but there is significant variation. Three groups of municipalities are worth distinguishing:

- The largest group is comprised of municipalities with high extreme poverty and low inequality (the quadrants at the bottom and on the right in each chart), which are mostly low-population, remote, indigenous communities living at a subsistence level.
- The second largest group includes those municipalities with *high extreme poverty and high inequality* (the quadrants at the top and on the right in each chart), which are generally larger urban localities with better resource endowments and small cities involved in mineral exploitation or the border trade with Argentina or Brazil. Small, wealthier groups typically coexist with large pockets of poverty.
- The third group consists of municipalities with *low extreme poverty and low inequality* (the quadrants at the bottom and on the left in each chart), which are mainly more economically dynamic urban areas.

This typology suggests that a wide range of interventions may be needed depending on the poverty and inequality levels, location, and resource endowments of the various municipalities. For instance, in many municipalities in the first or second groups, poor basic infrastructure, costly access to markets, limited natural resource endowments, low returns to human capital, and ineffective protection from natural and idiosyncratic risks may all prevent poor households from engaging in higher-yield economic activities and long-term investments in human capital. Low incomes also restrict the demand for local goods and services, especially given the importance of the consumption of home production in rural areas.

In this situation, raising consumption through growth alone may be insufficient, and targeted interventions may be required to increase the incomes of the poor in these areas. Such interventions might include growth-enhancing investments; targeted programs to develop human capital, community assets, and income generation; and investments that promote gradual integration among communities by migration. Moreover, in high-poverty, high-inequality municipalities, there may be a greater risk of the elite capture of local public investments, highlighting the need for mechanisms to ensure accountability and community participation in budget development and investment.

An additional tool for targeting

These results confirm that monetary poverty and UBN measurement tools may capture closely related, but distinct aspects of welfare. Figure 4.5 shows that UBN and consumption or monetary poverty are not always coincident (the dark areas do not coincide). The map on the incidence of extreme poverty captures welfare from the perspective of current income-generation and consumption capacity. The map on UBN reveals the

Figure 4.5 UBN and Consumption Poverty Maps on Municipalities, Bolivia 2001

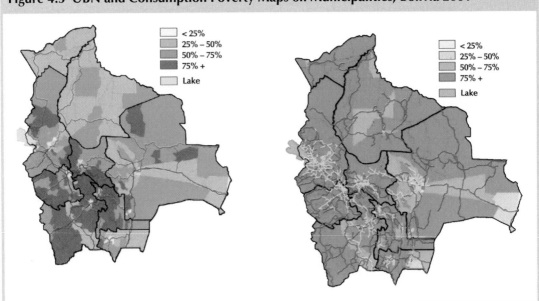

Source: INE and UDAPE 2003 using data from the 2001 census and household surveys in 1999–2001.

welfare landscape of the structural aspects of poverty related to differences in household physical assets (such as housing quality and access to basic infrastructure).[9]

Figure 4.6 shows the direct relationship between UBN poverty and poverty incidence and intensity (high poverty lines) with the corresponding national levels (the horizontal and vertical lines). Severe poverty—high proportions of a population with UBN and

Figure 4.6 Poverty and UBN in Municipalities, Bolivia 2001

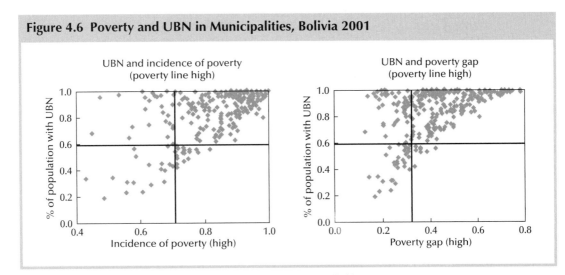

Source: INE and UDAPE 2003 using data from the 2001 census and household surveys in 1999–2001.

low consumption levels—characterizes a large number of municipalities in Bolivia (note the sizable concentration in the quadrants on the top and to the right in the charts). However, the relationship between consumption and UBN measurements is weak among municipalities at moderate levels of poverty, which are precisely the municipalities where the need to go beyond geographical targeting is greater.

In this sense, the UBN and monetary poverty maps should not be viewed as substitutes. Rather, they represent complementary targeting tools. Each map or a combination of the maps might be used as a means of targeting in various, specific types of interventions or to track the evolution of different aspects of poverty. The UBN map is well suited for targeting investments in basic infrastructure or policies that promote the accumulation of assets or for monitoring the progress in closing gaps in living conditions between municipalities. The monetary poverty map is better suited for targeting income transfers or programs aimed at raising the skills of the poor, employment, or minimum income protection against risks or for tracking the impact of economic growth on different localities. Meanwhile, the consumption poverty map is better suited for studying geographical differences in the distribution of welfare within localities through indicators on the intensity and severity of poverty and Gini consumption inequality.

Multisectoral projects and monitoring of the national poverty reduction strategy might benefit by exploiting information from each of these maps. This view is in line with the concerns expressed by several observers in Bolivia that the current system of intermunicipal transfers based on targeting according to the UBN poverty maps (the formula of the 2001 law on national dialogue) tends to be less responsive to the needs of municipalities with entrenched pockets of monetary poverty. This observation is meant simply to highlight that monetary poverty maps offer important insights into the interaction of poverty and inequality at the local level and that they might help inform social investment allocations and policy design.

More Than a Technical Exercise: Uses and Impact of the Monetary Poverty Map

In this section, we discuss the extent to which, in practice, the potential of the monetary poverty mapping tool has been realized in Bolivia. To investigate the actual uses and impact of the monetary poverty map in the country, a local consultant conducted on-site interviews with potential users in February and March 2006 (Figueroa 2006). The initial list targeted interviewees at 24 institutions. Of these institutions, 14 were government agencies, including central planning and line ministries involved directly in poverty and social policy (9 of 15 government ministries), while 10 were international cooperation agencies (such as multilateral and bilateral donors) operating in the country. The interviewees were to be managers, program officers, or technical staff who were likely to be exposed to or make use of the poverty maps. In five cases, it was not possible to conduct the interviews because of staff rotations (that is, changes associated with the transition to the new government) or nonresponses.[10]

Interviewees were asked about their knowledge about and use of poverty maps in their work (the results of the mapping exercise, the map tool, or the mapping publication). Five levels of knowledge or application were identified: (1) planning, (2) prioritization or targeting, (3) reference within studies, (4) general knowledge, and (5) no knowledge or awareness. The results may be summarized as follows (see figure 4.7; also see annex 4.1 for a list of the institutions and their responses):

- More than half the public institutions that responded were unaware of the monetary poverty maps, while this was true of only one of the international institutions.
- Among public institutions, only UDAPE, one of the main partners in the project, has used the maps for planning purposes. UDAPE has included the map statistics on its municipal data sheets, and all the map information may be found on its Web site. Meanwhile, three

Figure 4.7 Uses for and Awareness of Monetary Poverty Maps among Institutions, Bolivia

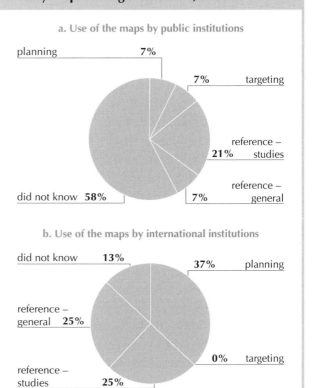

a. Use of the maps by public institutions

planning 7%
7% targeting
reference – studies 21%
reference – general 7%
did not know 58%

b. Use of the maps by international institutions

did not know 13%
37% planning
reference – general 25%
0% targeting
reference – studies 25%

Source: Based on field interviews described in Figueroa 2006.

of the seven international institutions that took part in the interviews used the maps in planning strategies, activities, and programs in Bolivia. For instance, as part of the assistance it has provided through the Programa de Apoyo a la Democracia Municipal (Program to Support Municipal Democracy), the Swiss Agency for Development and Cooperation has included consumption and poverty indicators from the mapping exercise in the program database used by all municipalities in the country. Similarly, the United Nations Development Programme has used the municipal estimates of per capita consumption in calculating its municipal human development indexes.

- Only one public agency, the *Directorio Único de Fondos* (the Unified Directorate of Funds, which, until 2005, was part of the Ministry of Popular Participation), has used the maps to target resources. This is the entity charged with administering funds for public productive and social investments and for regional development. It has an important role in the coordination and financing of poverty reduction interventions at the local level. It has used the maps in the selection of the beneficiary municipalities for the *Programa Contra la Pobreza y Apoyo a la Inversión Solidaria* (Program against

Poverty and in Support of Solidarity Investments), a community investment program funded at US$36.6 million and sponsored by the Inter-American Development Bank. It has also used the maps in setting budget limits for selected municipalities. The maps were also used in a study by a private consultant for the directorate that sought to select beneficiary municipalities for the support provided by the German Agency for Technical Cooperation to strengthen institutions in Bolivia. The initiative was never completed because of the change in the administration in government. Among international agencies, no organization has used the maps for targeting purposes.

■ One-third of the public institutions and one-half of the international organizations that participated in the interviews were aware of the results of the poverty mapping exercise, but had not used the maps in strategy or program design. This included the Japan International Cooperation Agency, which financed the second printing of the publication on the poverty maps, but which did not make extensive use of the maps in targeting interventions. Most of the institutions used the publication in the development of other studies or tools. For example, the Division of Health Reform Planning of the Ministry of Health compared the municipal rankings on extreme poverty with the rankings from a composite health index that had been developed to identify localities needing special interventions to ensure the achievement of the Millennium Development Goals in health. This highlights the potential use of poverty maps in monitoring the Millennium Development Goals at the local level (Gigler and Terborgh 2006). The World Food Programme likewise used the municipal poverty data and the human development indexes of the United Nations Development Programme (which in turn uses per capita municipal consumption as a main component) as a check on its food vulnerability index. Similarly, the Planning Division of the Ministry of Education used the information on municipal poverty incidence as a reference in the development of its multiannual operations program, 2004–08.

Overall, these results suggest that monetary poverty maps have had a modest impact on policy making in Bolivia. More than half the interviewees were not aware of the existence of the maps, although, having learned about them, many expressed interest and thought the maps might be valuable to their work. Even among the interviewees who knew about the tool, the use of monetary poverty maps in planning and targeting has been limited. Indeed, although a major motivation for the development of the tool was to help meet the requirements of the formula established for intermunicipal transfers by the law on national dialogue, this use has not materialized. While the decentralization of expenditures and targeting based on UBN have had positive effects in reducing disparities in access to basic services, investment allocation policies have not yet exploited the potential of monetary poverty maps for the more accurate targeting of interventions aimed at expanding the opportunities for income generation among the poor.

The prevailing economic and social environment in Bolivia and the interviews with stakeholders suggest three main factors behind these limited impacts: (1) the country's generally fragile political and institutional context in recent years; (2) the weak effort in dissemination and outreach; and (3) the lack of sustained, broad capacity building, including plans to update or develop applications of the mapping tool. We discuss these three factors in the next sections.

A Challenging Political and Institutional Context

It is not possible to isolate the reasons for the limited adoption, use, and impact of monetary poverty maps from the political and social turmoil in Bolivia in recent years. The country's political situation changed dramatically in late 2003. Discontent and social unrest over the economic and social situation and the export policy on natural gas forced President Gonzalo Sánchez de Lozada to step down. He was succeeded by Vice President Carlos Mesa, who later resigned as a result of social and political pressure to hold national elections. Social and political conflict dominated the political landscape. It became difficult to adopt policy innovations or reforms. Policies were devised in an incremental fashion so as to avoid resistance and social unrest. Public institutions lacked the stability or focus to formulate and implement plans with longer-term objectives.

Reforming the criteria for public resource allocation was particularly difficult. There was a legitimate and shared concern over the narrow policies on basic infrastructure investment, which did not address the need to create employment opportunities and income generation among the poor. This led to a renewed focus on production and income-generation policies in sectors supported by the general economic policy, known as *Bolivia Productiva*, established through the law on national dialogue. However, while some voiced alarm at the inequities in the UBN-based formula for intermunicipal transfers (particularly in municipalities with moderate poverty levels), those localities that stood to lose from the new allocation criteria opposed changing the existing criteria the most fiercely. Moreover, there was clear evidence that the UBN-based allocation formula of the law on national dialogue had enabled improvements in the access to basic services among the neediest municipalities. Hence, policy makers saw no urgency to change the criteria.

UDAPE and the INE, the two institutions that championed the development of the monetary poverty maps, lacked the support to promote the use of the maps. In early 2003, UDAPE, which had been part of the Ministry of Sustainable Development and Planning, was attached to the Ministry of the Presidency. At the end of 2003, it was placed under the Ministry of Economic Development, and it recently became part of the Ministry of Planning and Development. During these shifts, UDAPE was transformed from a technical unit with responsibilities in planning and analysis, to an entity responsible for interministerial coordination. Meanwhile, the INE was underfunded and experienced significant turnover in personnel. These factors severely limited the ability of these organizations to assume ownership and engage in the proactive diffusion of the mapping tool.

In January 2006, Evo Morales became Bolivia's first indigenous president, and the country regained some political stability. The government has faced numerous, more urgent, and overarching concerns involving the constitutional assembly and the reassessment of the economic policy framework and use of natural gas resources. Government policy is constrained by the need to avoid social and political polarization and reconcile diverging priorities among the multicultural populations of the country. However, the creation of opportunities for income generation among the poor, particularly the indigenous population, remains one of the main goals of the new government. The use of monetary poverty maps is being considered in several of the proposed initiatives. In particular, the 2006 *Plan Nacional de Desarrollo* (National Development Plan) includes the programs *Comunidades en Acción* (Communities in Action) and *Comunidades Recíprocas* (Reciprocal Communities) that are said to rely on the consumption poverty map to identify municipalities for priority intervention.

Weak Effort in Dissemination and Outreach

One of the most obvious reasons for the modest impact of the monetary poverty maps, corroborated in the interviews, has been an inadequate, underfunded dissemination strategy. Dissemination and the promotion of the application of the monetary poverty maps were not provided for in the initial project of collaboration between UDAPE, the INE, and the World Bank or in the individual plans of the three institutions. There was no involvement of other institutions or potential users at the beginning or during the development of the maps. Outside the team members, few knew about the initiative. No resources were contemplated for the timely publication and dissemination of the results.

The mapping publication has been substantially underfunded. The distribution of the publication was launched during a seminar at the INE in July 2003. The participants included the directors of the INE and UDAPE and representatives of many public and private institutions that were considered potential users. However, there was no serious planning behind the distribution effort. The first printing of the mapping document— 300 copies financed by the U.K. Department for International Development—was quickly distributed among high-level officials concerned with social policy and representatives of international cooperation agencies. The second printing, a run of 250 copies in January-March 2006 financed by the Japan International Cooperation Agency, was also exhausted within a few weeks. Further dissemination efforts were curtailed by the country's social and political instability. As a result, the publication has been distributed among only a few local entities, mainly in the municipalities of Chuquisaca, El Alto, and La Paz.

Moreover, the format and limited distribution of the results of the poverty mapping exercise are not amenable to access by a wide audience. Many of the institutions that reported using or knowing about the maps find the publication too dry and academic. They complain that it contains too many complicated tables, which makes it difficult for nonspecialists, particularly policy makers. The methodology remains obscure for many; the main concepts and the various indicators of poverty and inequality are not explained in lay terms. This undermines the usefulness of the results. In addition, there is no interface to render the data results accessible for easy consultation by users.[11] The mapping publication is currently available on the Web sites of both UDAPE and the INE (see http://www.ine.gov.bo and http://www.udape.gov.bo). Meanwhile, the data are only available, upon request, as spreadsheets as a component of the geographic information system on UDAPE's Web site; there is little documentation or guidance on their use.

Thus, intermediate technical staff in and outside government who may want to use the tool are not likely to be able to do so. Both UDAPE and the INE have lacked sufficient support to make these tools more friendly to users.

The limited dissemination that has taken place has been traditional and has not effectively emphasized the innovative aspects of the work. For example, characteristics that make the poverty mapping tool especially relevant for Bolivia—such as the measurement of the extent of monetary poverty in some areas where UBN poverty has not been so severe, as well as the availability of municipal indicators of inequality and the intensity and severity of poverty—have not been widely publicized. Little is known about the contribution of the monetary poverty maps to decision making or more effective resource allocation among local governments.

However, there is a latent unsatisfied demand for the maps. The majority of the institutions that participated in the interviews, but had not known of the maps, found the results of great interest for their work and were therefore surprised and disappointed at the limited distribution. Many, including staff at the Ministry of Public Works, the Ministry of Agriculture and Rural Development, and the Ministry of Health, indicated that, if they had been aware of the maps, they would have used them in targeting through ongoing programs and activities. Nonetheless, there are currently no other plans for additional distribution of the maps.

Lack of Broad, Sustained Capacity Building

While local capacities have been created for updating or developing new maps, this has not been sufficiently broad to be sustained and generate demand for the mapping tool among potential users. This is related to the lack of an effective distribution plan from the start of the project and to the high turnover among technical staff because of the weak civil service, which is a common feature in most of Latin America.

The direct responsibility of UDAPE for the actual production of the maps means that the methodologies have been acquired by the local team and might still be applied today with little technical guidance from specialists from the World Bank or elsewhere. This is certainly a positive accomplishment. However, this has involved only a small number of local people, several of whom are no longer with UDAPE or the INE. Indeed, some of the institutions that participated in the interviews and that had been unaware of the existence of the mapping tool had requested municipal data on poverty from the INE, but were only given data from the UBN poverty maps, even though the monetary poverty mapping results have been available on the INE Web site since late 2003. Most prominently, this reportedly happened to the Division of Local Economic Development in the Undersecretariat of Decentralization.

There has been no systematic attempt by the poverty mapping team to train other local staff, researchers, or potential users on the main methodological underpinnings and possible uses of the maps. Most of the interviewees remarked that there was no training being offered in the application of the tool and that the publication offered no examples of how the tool might be applied to help solve problems in development policy. Many of the interviewees showed a lack of understanding of fundamental concepts, such as the differences between UBN and monetary poverty measures, the reason for the differences in estimates based on different poverty lines, the suitability of different poverty lines for different purposes, and the reason for statistical errors in estimates derived from population census data. None of the interviewees knew the poverty maps also covered indicators of inequality that greatly expanded the potential application of the maps to the design of local development policies and programs.

There were also two significant criticisms of the monetary poverty maps themselves that related to applications. First, a number of institutions participating in the interviews indicated that the aggregation level of the mapping data was insufficient to be useful in certain, specific activities. For example, the World Food Programme, the German Agency for Technical Cooperation, and the Ministry of Indigenous Affairs all reported on initiatives at a community rather than municipal level and called for the development of a targeting tool disaggregated at the community level. Second, several interviewees criticized the UBN and monetary poverty maps because they are not periodically updated. If regularly updated maps were available, they would be able to track changes in indicators of poverty and social inequality in the localities in which they operate.

Conclusions and Lessons Learned

Poverty maps effectively reveal the heterogeneity of poverty in its multiple dimensions and the contrasting inequality levels in a country. In the case of Bolivia, the UBN poverty maps have effectively influenced the investment allocation process, facilitated the redirection of resources to the neediest municipalities, and helped these municipalities close gaps in access to basic services. Developed in 2003 using the small area estimation method to enable more effective targeting of interventions aimed at improving income opportunities among the poor, the monetary poverty maps have not lived up to their promise. Interviews with experts at a significant number of entities in and outside the government show that over half the potential users were still unaware of this tool, while those who were aware were not exploiting it fully in the formulation and targeting of their strategies and programs.

Three main factors have hindered monetary poverty maps from having a bigger impact. First, the social and political turmoil in Bolivia in recent years and the weak institutions in the country have caused public policy horizons to be limited to the short term, have stalled reform, and have contributed to high turnover among technical staff in public institutions. Second, there has not been an adequate program of dissemination and outreach to spread awareness of the maps. Third, the initiative did not contemplate broad capacity building and the training of potential users to ensure the sustained application of the tool to real development policy problems. While some of these factors are common elsewhere in Latin America and the developing world, other countries have been more effective in overcoming them to take advantage of poverty maps to improve public policy.[12]

The interviews with stakeholders suggest that there is significant latent demand in Bolivia for the monetary poverty mapping tool. While the country's political situation imposes numerous challenges and short-term imperatives, the creation of opportunities for income generation among the poor remains a critical issue for the government and international cooperation agencies. The experience so far points to a few lessons that might help Bolivia and other countries tap more effectively into the potential offered by poverty maps to improve the design and impact of poverty reduction policies:

- *The development of poverty maps should be viewed as part of a broader reform agenda, not as a narrow technical exercise.* Maps may be effective tools to enhance the planning, targeting, and evaluation of public policies. Hurdles common to other reforms or policy innovation must be overcome in the application of these tools. These hurdles include short-term planning horizons, weak institutional capacities, and capture by special interests. Thus, it is critical to adapt the development of these tools according to the country context and political economy considerations and to approach them as building blocks of broader incremental reforms.

- *Seek to build effective dissemination, outreach, and capacity-building objectives and strategies at the onset.* Without effective means to convey findings, encourage applications, and establish a broad base of trained staff and competent users, poverty maps are likely to represent a significant untapped potential to improve public policy. They will remain merely pretty pictures of a sad reality. Beginning with the effort to develop the maps, one should therefore contemplate the creation of the institutional means necessary to achieve sustained country ownership, identify the intended audience, and devise effective ways to attract interest and enable potential users to apply the tools.

  For instance, offering training to academics and graduate students, independent researchers, and technical staff in selected government institutions may help form a broader base of skilled practitioners and users of the tool. It is essential to ensure accuracy and credibility by fostering transparency and exercising methodological rigor in the publication of results, but it is also essential to supply clear, careful explanations of methods, findings, and applications suited to potential users. This requires reliance on numerous avenues for distribution, including nontechnical pamphlets, computer-based presentations, and data sheets, as well as an electronic interface that allows agile data search and cross-tabulation with other disaggregated data on the multiple determinants of poverty (for example, agroclimatic conditions, road infrastructure, and the supply of education and health services). It is particularly important to reach out to local government bodies in these efforts.

- *Continue to work on the development of methodologies to enable periodic updating of the maps.* The updating of UBN poverty maps is certainly restricted by the need to be tied to population censuses. However, ways to track changes in monetary poverty regularly at the local level through extensions of small area estimation map applications is a current area of research at the World Bank. Since regular updating would enhance the value of the maps for users, including in the local monitoring of the Millennium Development Goals, the development of the related methodologies should be supported.

Annex 4.1 Use of the Monetary Poverty Maps by Governmental and International Institutions, Bolivia

Institution	Indicator	Purpose
Governmental Institutions		
Ministry of Economic Development, Vice-Ministry of Urban Development and Housing	Was unaware of the poverty maps	UBN maps and maps based on human development indexes are used to allocate resources to urban and rural settlements
Ministry of Sustainable Development and Planning, Vice-Ministry of Planning and Territorial Development	As above	Develops its own maps and uses them in the selecting of municipalities for various purposes
Ministry of Public Works, Vice-Ministry of Basic Services	As above	The food vulnerability index map was used to select high-poverty areas
Ministry of Popular Participation, Directorate for Social Development	As above	The monetary poverty maps might have been used for interventions to provide health care, education, school feeding, and so on
Ministry of Health, National Program for Health Coverage Extension	As above	The UBN maps were used to target interventions
Ministry of Agriculture and Rural Development, General Directorate for Agriculture	As above	The food vulnerability index map has been used to select areas of intervention
Ministry of Agriculture and Rural Development, Vice-Ministry of Microenterprises and Rural Development	As above	The monetary poverty maps will be used to transfer resources within the National Strategy for Agriculture and Rural Development
Ministry of Popular Participation, Vice-Ministry of Decentralization	As above	The UBN maps have been used as a reference
Ministry of Indigenous Affairs	As above	The UBN maps have been used in the identification of local needs
Ministry of Labor	As above	Has shown no interest in the mapping results
UDAPE	Consumption and extreme poverty	Infant, child, and adolescent development index in municipalities, local booklets, dissemination results on the Web site

Institution	Indicator / document	Use of monetary poverty maps
Ministry of Popular Participation, Unified Directorate of Funds	High poverty rates	The monetary poverty maps have been used to select beneficiary municipalities for the Program against Poverty and for Social Investment and to establish budget limits on selected municipalities
Ministry of Health, Division of Health Reform Planning	Extreme poverty rates	The monetary poverty maps have been used to check a map of municipalities identified as priorities for health interventions that were part of the effort to achieve the Millennium Development Goals on health
Ministry of Education, Planning Division	Full document	The monetary poverty maps have been used as a reference during the development of the multiannual operations program, 2004–08
International institutions		
German Agency for Technical Cooperation, Decentralized Governance to Support the National Poverty Reduction Strategy Programme	The map document was known only as a reference	The monetary poverty maps were not used
Japan International Cooperation Agency	The map document was known only as a reference	The monetary poverty maps have not been used; however, the organization financed the second printing of the mapping publication
United Nations Development Programme	Consumption	Development of municipal human development indexes
United Nations Children's Fund	Extreme poverty	Development of the municipal infant, child, and adolescent development index
World Food Programme	Consumption	The monetary poverty maps have been used to validate the food vulnerability index
Swiss Agency for Development and Cooperation, Program to Support Municipal Democracy	Consumption and extreme poverty	The monetary poverty maps have been used to add information to the municipal database for use by local governments
Food and Agriculture Organization of the United Nations	Was unaware of the mapping document and the maps	The food vulnerability index and human development index maps have been used to select intervention areas

Source: Based on field interviews by Figueroa 2006.

Notes

1. In this chapter, monetary poverty and consumption poverty are used interchangeably. The terms refer to the inadequacy of resources (both cash expenditures and home produced goods consumed by the household) relative to a poverty line that is specified in monetary terms. This is in contrast to the UBN approach to poverty measurement, which uses an index based on the possession of specific assets and the access to specific services.
2. The team included Wilson Jiménez and Susana Lizarraga from UDAPE, Gustavo Canavire and Javier Monterrey from the INE, and Werner Hernani, Peter Lanjouw, and Quentin Wodon from the World Bank.
3. See INE and UDAPE (2003). By 2004, three poverty maps had been developed, all using data from the 2001 census and the latest household surveys. The first followed on the methodology of the 1994 UBN poverty map. The second relied on the small area estimation method, and the third used the human development index of the United Nations Development Programme. Only the small area estimation method explicitly emphasizes the monetary dimension of poverty.
4. Consumption is proxied by expenditures on goods and services acquired by the household for consumption purposes (per family member, excluding domestic employees). These cover household production for personal consumption, durables, and the implicit rental of housing. The independent variables include the characteristics of the household (number of members, type of household, number of children under 6 years old, and so on), the dwelling (number of rooms, quality of walls and floors, electricity, water, sanitation, cooking fuel), durable assets (televisions, stereos, cars), the household head (schooling, mother tongue, migration status, employment, occupation, age, gender), and the surrounding community (basic infrastructure and services).
5. The single survey sample sizes were 3,247, 4,994, and 5,845 dwellings, respectively. In the end, the pooled sample contained 1,501 primary sampling units and 13,328 dwellings.
6. The low and high poverty lines are, on average, 32 and 68 percent higher, respectively, than the extreme poverty line.
7. The variation in poverty levels is actually larger than depicted in figures 4.1 and 4.5, where municipalities have been grouped according to only four poverty categories.
8. The complete results are described in World Bank (2005), annex 1.2.
9. The divergence and variation in UBN and consumption poverty levels are larger if one compares the concentration of the poor (that is, the absolute number of the poor rather than poverty rates) and, also, if one contrasts individual municipal indicators rather than grouped data.
10. This occurred particularly with the Ministry of Justice, the Vice-Ministry of Women's Affairs, the Pan American Health Organization–World Health Organization, the United Nations Population Fund, and the European Union. See Figueroa (2006) for details on the institutions and interviewees.
11. UDAPE staff have told us that there are many technical (equipment) barriers to the development of an online interface that allows users to obtain poverty map statistics tailored to their specific needs.
12. See, for example, the experience of Brazil and Ecuador elucidated in Henninger and Snel (2002) and the experience of other countries discussed in this volume.

References

Azariadis, Costas. 2004. "The Theory of Poverty Traps: What Have We Learned." Draft chapter for Samuel Bowles, Steven N. Durlauf, and Karla Hoff, eds. 2006. *Poverty Traps.* New York: Russell Sage Foundation; Princeton, NJ: Princeton University Press.

Bossert, Thomas J. 2000. "Decentralization of Health Systems in Latin America: A Comparative Study of Chile, Colombia, and Bolivia." Latin America and Caribbean Health Sector Reform Initiative 29, Data for Decision Making Project, Harvard School of Public Health, Boston.

Elbers, Chris, Jean O. Lanjouw, and Peter F. Lanjouw. 2003. "Micro-Level Estimation of Poverty and Inequality." *Econometrica* 71 (1): 355–64.

Faguet, Jean-Paul. 2004. "Does Decentralization Increase Government Responsiveness to Local Needs?: Evidence from Bolivia." *Journal of Public Economics* 88 (3–4): 867–93.

Figueroa, M. 2006. "Evaluación y experiencias del uso del mapa de pobreza y desigualdad en municipios de Bolivia." Unpublished working paper, Social and Economic Policy Analysis Unit, La Paz, Bolivia.

Gigler, Björn-Sören, and Carmelle Terborgh. 2006. "Poverty Maps as a Tool to Target Development Interventions and to Monitor the MDGs." Paper presented at the Global Spatial Data Infrastructure Association GSDI-9 Conference, "Spatial Information: Tool for Reducing Poverty," Santiago, Chile, November 6–10.

Henninger, Norbert, and Mathilde Snel. 2002. *Where Are the Poor?: Experiences with the Development and Use of Poverty Maps.* Washington, DC: World Resources Institute; Arendal, Norway: United Nations Environment Programme–Global Resource Information Database.

Hernani, Werner. 1999. "La pobreza en el área urbana de Bolivia, período 1989–1997: evolución, perfiles, determinantes y políticas de alivio." Bachelor's thesis, Universidad Católica Boliviana, La Paz, Bolivia.

———. 2002. "Mercado laboral, pobreza y desigualdad en Bolivia." *Revista Estadísticas y Análisis* 1 (October), National Institute of Statistics, La Paz, Bolivia.

INE (National Institute of Statistics) and UDAPE (Social and Economic Policy Analysis Unit). 2002. "Mapa de Pobreza 2001: Necesidades Básicas Insatisfechas." National Institute of Statistics and Social and Economic Policy Analysis Unit, La Paz, Bolivia.

———. 2003. "Pobreza y desigualdad en municipios de Bolivia: estimación del gasto de consumo combinando el censo 2001 y las encuestas de hogares." Report, National Institute of Statistics and Social and Economic Policy Analysis Unit, La Paz, Bolivia.

Jiménez, Wilson, and Ernesto Yáñez. 1997. "La pobreza en las ciudades de Bolivia." Social Policy Analysis Unit, La Paz, Bolivia.

Landa, Fernando. 2002. "Pobreza en Bolivia 1999 y 2001." July, Social and Economic Policy Analysis Unit, La Paz, Bolivia.

Ministry of Human Development. 1995. *Mapa de pobreza: una guía para la acción social.* 2nd edition. La Paz, Bolivia: Ministry of Human Development.

Pereira, Rodney, and Tito A. Velasco. 1994. "Estimación de la pobreza urbana en Bolivia." *Revista de Análisis Económico* 8, Social Policy Analysis Unit, La Paz, Bolivia.

UNDP (United Nations Development Programme). 1990. "La pobreza en Bolivia." United Nations Development Programme, La Paz, Bolivia.

UNDP (United Nations Development Programme), INE (National Institute of Statistics), and UDAPE (Social and Economic Policy Analysis Unit). 2004. "Índice de Desarrollo Humano en los Municipios de Bolivia." United Nations Development Programme, National Institute of Statistics, and Social and Economic Policy Analysis Unit, La Paz, Bolivia.

Urquiola, Miguel. 1994. "Participando en el crecimiento, expansión económica, distribución de ingreso y pobreza en el área urbana de Bolivia." *Cuadernos de Investigación* 2, Social Policy Analysis Unit, La Paz, Bolivia.

Wodon, Quentin. 1997. "Food Energy Intake and Cost of Basic Needs: Measuring Poverty in Bangladesh." *Journal of Development Studies* 34 (2): 66–101.

World Bank. 2001. "Bolivia: Poverty Diagnostic 2000." Report No. 20530-80, Poverty Reduction and Economic Management Sector Unit, Latin America and the Caribbean Region, World Bank, Washington, DC.

———. 2005. "Bolivia Poverty Assessment: Establishing the Basis for Pro-Poor Growth." Report 28068-BO, Poverty Reduction and Economic Management Sector Unit, Latin America and the Caribbean Region, World Bank, Washington, DC.

World Bank and IDB (Inter-American Development Bank). 2004. *Bolivia: Public Expenditure Management for Fiscal Sustainability and Equitable and Efficient Public Services.* Report 28519-BO. Washington, DC: World Bank.

5

The Poverty Mapping Exercise in Bulgaria

BORYANA GOTCHEVA

ACRONYMS AND ABBREVIATIONS

BIHS	Bulgaria Integrated Household Survey
EU	European Union
Eurostat	Statistical Office of the European Communities
IDF	Institutional Development Fund
Lev	lev (plural leva), the Bulgarian currency
MLSP	Ministry of Labor and Social Policy
MTHS	multitopic household survey
NSI	National Statistical Institute
OECD	Organisation for Economic Co-operation and Development
SIF	Social Investment Fund

Bulgaria is a well-performing middle-income country that joined the European Union (EU) on January 1, 2007. After a difficult transition from central planning that culminated in a severe crisis in 1996–97, the country has made impressive progress toward long-term stability and sustained growth. Macroeconomic stability has been reestablished and maintained through prudent fiscal policies and strict discipline in income policy anchored on the currency board arrangement adopted in 1997. A broad structural reform agenda has contributed to solid economic performance. Continued growth since the 1996–97 crisis has led to poverty reduction and improvements in living standards generally, although deep pockets of poverty persist. Per capita income increased from US$1,200 in 1997 to US$2,740 in 2004 (gross national income, Atlas method). Nonetheless, per capita gross domestic product, at the purchasing power standard in 2003, was only 30 percent of the EU average, so that continued growth and the convergence of living conditions toward EU standards remain a core policy goal. Poverty fell sharply from 1997 to 2001 and more slowly thereafter.[1] The most recent assessment of poverty in the country indicates that, measured at two-thirds of median consumption, relative poverty fell by 2.1 percentage points between 2001 and 2003 (Teşliuc 2005). Indicators of the depth and severity of poverty also improved. Extreme poverty remained low, at 4.8 percent of households in 2003, while food poverty (a proxy for malnutrition) was virtually nonexistent. Even as poverty has fallen, the profile of poverty has been changing. Poverty is increasingly concentrated among certain vulnerable groups, especially single-parent families with children, households where the head is long-term unemployed or disabled, and the Roma ethnic minority.

In the beginning of the decade of the 2000s, the government of Bulgaria and the World Bank reinstated their dialogue on poverty issues, starting with a high-level workshop opened by the prime minister. The participants—cabinet ministers, the Bank country and social sector teams, the ambassador of the EU delegation to Bulgaria, and the United Nations resident coordinator and the United Nations teams—discussed the findings of the Bank poverty assessment and analytical and advisory work on poverty and living standards in the 1990s. The joint agenda they set for actions focused on the following:

- Strengthening the social development impact of macroeconomic and sectoral polices
- Responding to the needs of the vulnerable
- Establishing institutional arrangements for antipoverty policy development and implementation; ex ante and ex post poverty impact analysis and poverty monitoring and evaluation for antipoverty policy design emerged as one of the main cross-cutting agenda items and one of the main areas of Bank support for the government in the following years

In Bulgaria, the poverty mapping methodology and related concepts were first introduced by the World Bank in the beginning of the decade of the 2000s in the context of the Bank's poverty-related analytical work. The Bank's aim was to advance the policy dialogue with the government based on solid knowledge of poverty at the level of districts (oblasts) and municipalities. The Bank team tasked with the poverty work in Bulgaria conducted a multitopic household survey (MTHS) in April and May 2001, and the National Statistical Institute (NSI) conducted a methodologically similar survey in October and November 2003. The two surveys were used in the preparation of two poverty assessments that were carried out in 2001–02 and 2003–05 (World Bank 2002 and NSI 2006, respectively). Both poverty assessments pointed to the clear regional dimension of poverty in Bulgaria and showed that poverty is a spatially heterogeneous phenomenon with concentration in rural areas. However, aggregated national-level poverty data, as well as an urban-rural breakdown of poverty, obscured considerably the subnational variations at the level of the 28 districts (oblasts) and, most importantly, the 262 municipalities. At the same time, policies and programs to reduce poverty required solid and detailed information about where the poor live and what resources they need to improve their welfare.

Because the 2001 MTHS data were representative at the national and district levels, the Bank's analytical team first suggested, in 2002, testing the small area estimation methodology in the measurement of poverty at the district and municipal levels. In parallel, the team started engaging the government, the Ministry of Labor and Social Policy (MLSP) in particular, with ideas and proposals about using the results achieved with the small area estimation methodology to design geographically targeted antipoverty policies and to allocate resources for poverty reduction interventions tailored to conditions in the municipalities.[2]

The MLSP approved the concept of using poverty maps in targeting policies and resource allocations and requested consultancy support in the application of the small area estimation methodology to produce poverty maps because the in-house capacity did not exist at that time. As a result, an international consultant developed the first poverty and inequality maps on Bulgaria in 2003. These maps measured and illustrated mean per capita consumption by municipality, the poverty headcount index and the poverty depth index using upper (two-thirds of the median consumption) and lower (one-half of the median consumption) relative poverty lines, and the Theil mean log deviation index and the Theil entropy index by municipality (see Ivaschenko 2004). After the collection of more recent household consumption data at the end of 2003, the poverty mapping exercise was replicated in 2004–05.

The objective of this chapter is twofold. First, it aims to introduce and to discuss the Bulgarian experience in the development of poverty maps and to reflect on the use of the maps in policy making and on the range of policy decisions influenced by the maps. Second, it aims at drawing lessons with regard to process (what is involved in preparing the maps and understanding how to apply them) and with regard to the areas of application and the effective use of the maps in taking policy decisions.

The chapter is organized as follows. The next section provides background on how the idea to produce poverty maps evolved in Bulgaria. The subsequent section reviews the technical aspects of the elaboration of poverty maps, but without considering methodological and technical issues in detail. The following section summarizes the main findings of the analysis of the spatial distribution of poverty. The section thereafter describes the users of poverty map, the ways in which the poverty mapping results have been applied in the country, and the impact of the maps on policy. The penultimate section examines the determinants of the long-term sustainability of poverty mapping in Bulgaria. The chapter concludes with a brief outline of the lessons learned.

Background

The first poverty maps in Bulgaria were developed on the initiative of the World Bank in 2003 using the data collected in April and May 2001 through the Bulgaria Integrated Household Survey (BIHS), the first MTHS. The desire to improve the quality of the analysis of the regional dimensions of poverty drove that effort. The World Bank hired an international consultant to apply the methodology developed by Elbers, Lanjouw, and Lanjouw (2002) to obtain accurate estimates of consumption-based poverty and inequality at the disaggregated district level by combining census and household (consumption) survey information. The NSI provided access to the anonymized household-unit data from the 2001 Population and Housing Census, as well as support with data processing during the preparation of the maps. The consultant linked the 2001 census data to the household-unit data from the 2001 BIHS. For the data processing, the consultant applied the special-purpose World Bank software developed in SAS (originally known as Statistical Analysis System software) by Gabriel Demombynes. A report summarized the estimated poverty and inequality indicators at the district (28) and municipal (262) levels for 2001, together with the set of corresponding maps. It also provided sufficient technical details on the process of poverty mapping to allow the mapping steps to be replicated (see Ivaschenko 2004). Policy makers recognized the analytical value of the first municipal-level poverty maps, and these maps were included among the criteria for ranking municipalities by poverty status in assessing the eligibility of municipalities for social infrastructure project financing through the Social Investment Fund (SIF).

The development of the second set of poverty maps became a joint effort of the World Bank and the government. The effort was driven by the desire to update the analysis of the regional dimensions of poverty using more recent household consumption data and to test whether a team of national experts would be able to apply the small area estimation methodology. For this purpose, a joint team composed of staff at the MLSP, the NSI, and the World Bank, along with representatives of academic institutions (the Institute of Economics of the Bulgarian Academy of Sciences, the University of National and World Economy, and the University of Sofia), was set up under the leadership of Mariana Kotzeva, a statistician and econometrician. The poverty mapping took place in 2004 and 2005. It was based on data from the 2001 census and the new MTHS conducted in October and November 2003. The main findings are summarized in Kotzeva and Tzvetkov (2006) and other analytical reports (see also Kotzeva 2006).

Conceived as a part of the World Bank poverty assessment, the main goal of the poverty mapping exercise was to display the spatial dimension of poverty and identify pockets of poverty across the country. The poverty maps were also aimed at serving as a basis for the targeting of disadvantaged areas and for a general evaluation of geographically oriented actions and programs involved in the national poverty reduction strategy. The purposes and intended uses of the maps determined the scope and the level of precision and resolution (disaggregation) of the poverty maps.

Extensive discussions with policy makers and experts confirmed that there was a need to measure the incidence of poverty at the district and municipal levels. Districts (oblasts) and municipalities are the basic administrative-territorial units in the country. Because they are self-governing communities, municipalities have the required administrative capacity to initiate local antipoverty measures and policies, and they are developing the structures and administrative capacity needed to absorb European structural funds. Given financial decentralization and the enhanced role of local governments, a poverty analysis at the subnational level would facilitate the identification of directly relevant and appropriately specific antipoverty policies.

The World Bank supported the preparation of the 2003 and 2005 poverty maps through technical assistance, training, capacity building, and the provision of computer equipment and software. The main instrument for the delivery of the Bank's support was an Institutional Development Fund (IDF) grant.[3] The focus of the grant was the creation of a policy analysis directorate in the MLSP and capacity building in antipoverty policy design and related data collection and analysis.[4] For this reason, the grant was extended to the MLSP on condition that the NSI would participate jointly in the realization of the related initiatives. Several bilateral agreements confirmed and reinforced the implementation arrangements, including the division of responsibilities, the distribution of grant resources, and the obligation of counterpart financing by the two implementing institutions. Two other agreements between the NSI and the World Bank defined protocols covering the ownership of the data collected and processed by the NSI and the subsequent access to these data.

In the NSI, the grant supported institutional capacity building in the systematic production of good quality data and improved data processing.

In the MLSP, the grant supported the promotion of a participatory policy dialogue on poverty issues and institutional capacity building in poverty analysis, policy design, and the ex ante assessment of the poverty impact of government policies. The grant helped establish the Social Analysis, Prognosis, and Policy Directorate at the MLSP and strengthen its institutional capacity.

The grant also facilitated the establishment of a multiagency, multisectoral stake-holder forum (the data users group) to discuss all aspects of the poverty monitoring and analysis work, including the preparation and application of the poverty maps.

A part of the grant resources was allocated for the provision of technical assistance, equipment, and training for the analysis of the spatial distribution of poverty using small area estimations and for the promotion of the use of poverty maps in the policy-making process.

The IDF grant was supplemented by a Bank-executed two-year multiteam learning grant aimed at supporting learning among the government-Bank-academia team and facilitating team coherence and a team focus on common objectives.

Technical Aspects of Poverty Mapping

Data sources

In Bulgaria, the 2003 and 2005 poverty maps were produced by applying the small area estimation methodology to combine information from the 2001 census and two successive MTHSs conducted in 2001 and 2003.

The 2001 census is the most recent census. It provides comprehensive information on housing and on household sociodemographic conditions, along with the characteristics of individual household members such as age, educational attainment, and employment status, thus allowing for the finest geographical disaggregation. However, on the downside, in Bulgaria as elsewhere, the census is carried out once every decade and collects information on only a limited set of indicators. Most importantly for our purposes, it does not provide the information necessary to construct a consumption aggregate.

Meanwhile, the MTHSs permit the construction of reliable consumption-based welfare measures.[5] The Bank commissioned a private company, BBSS Gallup International, to carry out the data collection for the first MTHS, the 2001 BIHS. The fieldwork was conducted in April and May 2001 and based on precensus listings so as to draw up a nationally representative sample of 2,500 households. The 2001 BIHS was used as a data source on households for the 2001 Bulgaria Poverty Assessment (World Bank 2002). The NSI conducted the second survey, the 2003 MTHS, in October and November 2003 on a sample of 3,023 households. The completion of the survey was one of the activities included in the IDF grant. Due to the relatively small sample sizes in both surveys, reliable welfare estimates were not possible at a more disaggregated level than Sofia city (the capital), other urban areas, and rural areas.

The Bank played the leading role in the initiative to combine the two types of data sets, thus obtaining information on poverty that was sufficiently disaggregated to capture heterogeneity. The government and the academics undertook the expansion of the analysis. The census and MTHS survey information, in the case of the 2005 poverty maps, was overlaid with an additional data set of more than 30 district and municipal indicators. The results were used to calculate regional poverty and, eventually, to analyze pockets of poverty.

Methodological notes

The poverty maps produced in Bulgaria are grounded in the concept that poverty is a multidimensional phenomenon that affects economic, social, and other aspects of human well-being. The maps are based on consumption as the most appropriate indicator for measuring the living standards of the population under current conditions. The large informal sector in the economy and the reluctance of respondents to report their incomes are among the main reasons for preferring consumption over income in the measurement of welfare.[6]

In 2001 and 2003, the consumption aggregates were calculated in similar ways; however, the composition of the aggregates was different following modifications to the 2003 questionnaire.[7] The approach to the definition of the poverty line was also different in 2003 and 2005. In the case of the 2003 poverty maps, two poverty lines were used to estimate poverty: a lower poverty line equal to Lev 46.1 per capita per month and a higher poverty line equal to Lev 61.5.[8] These poverty lines corresponded to, respectively, one-half and two-thirds of the mean per capita consumption in the previous BIHS

(1997) expressed in 2001 prices. The use of two poverty lines allowed the sensitivity of the poverty rates to be investigated relative to different poverty lines. The main purpose of the poverty mapping exercise was not to obtain absolute numbers (since any poverty line is, in a way, arbitrary), but to understand which districts and municipalities are the poorest and which are the richest (at a given poverty line).

In the case of the 2005 poverty maps, the team of Bulgarian experts decided to work with one poverty line that reflected a definition combining elements of the approaches and definitions of the Organisation for Economic Co-operation and Development (OECD), the World Bank, and the Statistical Office of the European Communities (Eurostat). The relative poverty line was set at 60 percent (as defined by Eurostat) of the monthly median consumption (World Bank) per equivalent adult (Eurostat, OECD equivalence scale).[9] It amounted to Lev 102, and all households and persons living in these households having consumption per equivalent adult of less than Lev 102 were identified as poor. The three most popular measures of poverty—the poverty rate (headcount ratio), poverty depth (poverty gap), and severity of poverty—were calculated for each district (28) and municipality (262) in the country. In addition, the team estimated Gini coefficients to measure inequality at the district and municipal levels.

The poverty mapping exercise followed the standard estimation procedure (see Elbers, Lanjouw, and Lanjouw 2002).[10] At the first stage, the content and statistical compatibility of survey and census data were established. The following two points proved to be key for the success of the map at this stage. First, when defining and selecting comparable variables common to the sample survey and census, it is important to include key experts from the NSI who have been involved in carrying out the census and household sample survey. Such collaboration may help in comparative assessments that determine whether a survey variable may be reasonably assumed to contain the same information as the corresponding census variable. Often, even if the survey and census variables are identically worded, a different ordering of questions, different ways of asking the questions by interviewers, and variations in defining and understanding concepts across a country may cause the information content to vary between census and survey. Sometimes, it is necessary to construct new variables or to redefine response categories. In all these cases, the participation of the data producers—statisticians from the NSI— is crucial to obtaining reliable regional poverty estimates.

Second, a high degree of comparability between census and household data is important. The poverty mapping in Bulgaria benefited from the high degree of comparability between the 2001 BIHS and the 2003 MTHS on the one hand and the 2001 census on the other. During the preliminary phase of the preparation of the 2005 poverty maps, 30 common questions that appear in both questionnaires were identified and grouped. The verification showed that the sample is representative for the main demographic and social characteristics of heads-of-household, including gender, educational attainment, ethnicity, and mother tongue, as well as for the main structural household characteristics such as number of children, presence of people with disabilities in the household, the highest level of educational attainment in the household, and employment status.

These variables constitute the most important factors in the welfare of households. Their presence in the survey and, above all, their proven representativeness ensured that an adequate consumption model would be developed. Consequently, to the extent this model applies to the census data, exact and reliable consumption estimates for each household may be derived.

At the second stage of the mapping exercise, a set of econometric consumption models was developed. One model was identified as the most appropriate and then extrapolated onto the census data. There were two options for assessing the model: based on the whole sample or based on individual subsamples, which, however, had to be representative of the total population.

At the third stage, the parameters of the assessed consumption model were applied to census data to obtain the predicted consumption for each household in the census and calculate general poverty indicators. The reliability and precision of the estimates thus obtained were verified statistically, and the results showed that, in the case of Bulgaria, the poverty mapping exercise produced reliable estimates of poverty at the district and municipal levels, but not at the town or village level.

Findings of the Poverty Mapping Exercise

Key findings

The poverty maps permitted the analysis of the spatial distribution of poverty in Bulgaria. The main purpose of the analysis was to study the incidence, depth, and severity of poverty among the 28 districts and 262 municipalities in the country and to identify pockets of poverty, that is, the territorial units where large numbers of poor people are concentrated, as well as to rank the districts and municipalities according to poverty rates in an attempt to develop a differentiated approach to geographical targeting in poverty reduction programs. The key findings from the 2003 and 2005 poverty maps indicate that the differences in poverty across the districts and municipalities are substantial. The poverty map shown in figure 5.1 illustrates the spatial distribution of poverty across municipalities divided into five groups based on poverty headcount ratios.

The disparities in the level, depth, and severity of poverty among municipalities are more substantial than the corresponding disparities among districts. For the districts, the 2003 map revealed that, at a poverty line of Lev 61.5, the poverty headcount varied from a mere 3 percent in Sofia city to 19 percent in Kardzhali and Razgrad. For the municipalities, it was estimated that the share of the poor varied from 3 percent in Sofia city and Belene (Pleven Oblast) to above 40 percent in Kaynardzha (Silistra Oblast) and Nikola Kozlevo (Shumen Oblast). The 2005 poverty maps revealed that, among the districts (oblasts), Sofia excluded, the difference in the level of poverty between the district with the lowest and the district with the highest percentage of poor (Varna and Silistra, respectively) was only 1:2 (see figure 5.2), while the corresponding difference at the municipal level was almost 1:5.[11] To carry out a rigorous analysis of disparities in

Figure 5.1 Poverty Headcount Ratio by Municipality, Bulgaria

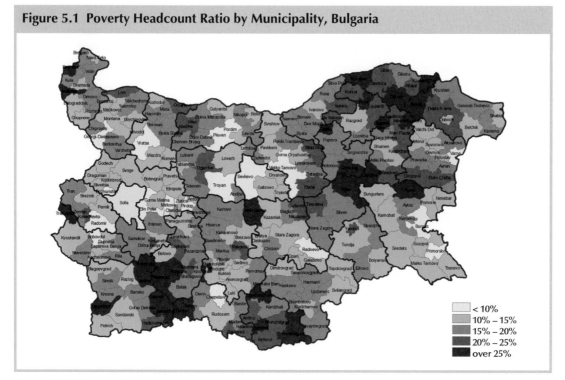

Legend:
< 10%
10% – 15%
15% – 20%
20% – 25%
over 25%

Source: NSI 2006, page 93.

poverty at the district level, the collection of data on the municipalities is clearly extremely important.

At the district level, the share of the population below the poverty line ranges from 10 percent (in Varna Oblast) to 21.7 percent (in Silistra Oblast). The incidence of poverty is also quite high in the oblasts of Kurdjali, Pazardjik, and Turgovishte, where one-fifth of the population is living below the poverty line. These districts, along with seven other districts with a poverty rate of 17 percent or higher, namely, Plovdiv, Razgrad, Shoumen, Sliven, Smolyan, Vidin, and Yambol, are characterized by a relatively higher share of ethnic Roma and Turk households that were considerably poorer than the Bulgarian ethnic households in both the 2001 BIHS and the 2003 MTHS.

The capital city, Sofia, shows the lowest incidence of poverty, and it differs substantially from the rest of the country. The unemployment rate in Sofia is close to zero; the opportunities for informal employment are greater; and the share of more highly educated working-age people in the population is the highest in the country. In other district centers, the percentage of the poor is three times higher than in Sofia, and, in the small towns and villages, it is approximately four times higher.

The country's poorest people are living in districts with the largest share of the poor. There is a strong positive correlation among poverty indicators (level, depth, and severity) in districts. The correlation coefficients between the level and depth of poverty and between the level and severity of poverty are 0.98 and 0.94, respectively.

Figure 5.2 Poverty Headcount Ratio by Oblast, Bulgaria

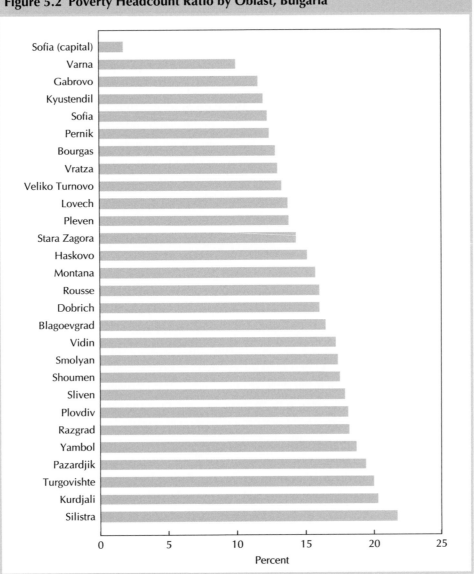

Sources: 2003 MTHS and NSI 2006.

Although poverty is mostly concentrated in rural areas, where, on average, the poverty rate is almost twice as high as the poverty rate in urban areas (excluding Sofia city), there are remarkable differences in welfare within both rural and urban areas. For instance, according to the 2003 poverty map, the poverty headcount ratios in rural areas in the districts ranged from about 8 percent in Kyustendil and Pernik to 28 percent in Dobrich, Shumen, and Targoviste, and the headcount ratios in urban areas fluctuated from around 3 percent in Sofia city to about 13 percent in Pazardzhik and Sliven. The standard of living was found to vary greatly even among municipalities in single districts.

For example, within Silistra Oblast, the poverty headcount ratio ranged from 10 percent in Silistra municipality to 44 percent in Kaynardzha, and, within Shumen Oblast, it varied from 8.8 percent in Shumen municipality to 42 percent in Nikola Kozlevo. Consumption inequality was higher in rural areas in all districts. Measured according to the Theil mean log deviation index, inequality reached 16.3 percent and 12.6 percent in rural and urban areas, respectively.

Compared to the 2003 poverty maps, the maps produced in 2005 reveal a reduction in the difference between urban and rural areas in the depth and severity of poverty. The 2001 BIHS indicates that the poverty headcount in urban areas (Sofia excluded) was close to two times lower relative to the poverty headcount in rural areas, while the poverty headcount in the 2003 MTHS indicates that this difference was much lower at the time of the survey (see table 5.1). In 2003, the poverty rate was significantly lower in towns that are district centers than it was in other towns that are not district centers (by close to 5 percentage points) and in villages (by 5.7 percentage points), while the differences in the poverty rates between small towns and villages are less pronounced and not statistically significant.

There are various possible explanations for the lower welfare disparities. The job opportunities in small towns are almost as restricted as they are in villages. Households in both small towns and villages have similar lifestyles and common strategies for coping with poverty, which involve heavy reliance on household agriculture. Meanwhile, the villages benefiting from good road infrastructure and proximity to the capital or to district centers show much lower poverty rates, and their poverty profile is closer to that of urban residents. The poverty in district centers may be more clearly expressed monetarily, while the poverty in small towns and villages is also related to greater limitations in employment, education, health, and other social services.

The distribution of poverty by municipality indicates that, in 173 of the 262 municipalities in Bulgaria, where 58 percent of the population lives, the poverty headcount rates range from 10 to 20 percent (see table 5.2). A relatively small group of 19 municipalities (the municipalities of Bobov Dol, Bourgas, Bozhurishte, Chelopech, Chepelare,

Table 5.1 Poverty Headcount Ratio by Strata in Bulgaria, 2003 and 2005 Poverty Maps

Strata, place of residence	Poverty headcount, 2001 BIHS (%)	Poverty headcount, 2003 MTHS (%)
Capital, Sofia city	2.34	4.3
Urban, district center	—	12.2
Other urban	9.25	17.0
Village	17.72	17.9
Total (all country)	10.85	—

Sources: 2001 BIHS and 2003 MTHS.
Note: Data for 2001 and 2003 are not fully comparable because of differences in methodologies and consumption aggregates and should be taken for reference only. The poverty line for the 2001 BIHS poverty headcount is Lev 61.5 per month at 2001 prices. The poverty line for the 2003 MTHS is Lev 102 per month at 2003 prices.
— = no data are available.

Table 5.2 Distribution of Municipalities by Poverty Headcount Ratio, Bulgaria

Poverty headcount ratio (%)	Number of municipalities	Population (in 1,000s)	Share of total population (%)
Up to 10	19	2,250.8	28.8
10–15	82	2,148.1	27.6
15–20	91	2,371.6	30.4
20–25	40	633.1	8.1
Over 25	30	397.6	5.1
Total	262	7,801.3	100

Source: 2003 MTHS.

Elin Pelin, Mirkovo, Pirdop, Plevel, Primorsko, Radnevo, Radomir, Sevlievo, Troyan, Varna, Veliko Turnovo, and Vratsa) shows poverty rates of less than 10 percent of the population. In 30 municipalities, more than one-fourth of the population is living under the poverty line. Within this group of poor municipalities, there is a subgroup comprised of the poorest 13 municipalities, in which over 30 percent of the population is living in poverty.[12] The poor municipalities are concentrated in five districts that are also experiencing high poverty. These are the municipalities in the oblasts of Kurdjali, Silistra, and Turgovishte in the northeastern part of Bulgaria and the municipalities on the borders of the oblasts of Blagoevgrad and Smolyan, which are located in southwestern Bulgaria.

Disparity indicators measuring the deviation of the poverty rate in each municipality from the district poverty rate suggest that, as regards the share of the poor population, municipalities in one and the same district differ significantly in poverty rates. Therefore, poverty indicators at the district level may not be considered indicative of the level of poverty in the municipalities within the district (Kotzeva and Tzvetkov 2006). However, when the level of poverty in a district is higher, the municipalities in the district tend to be more homogenous in terms of poverty.

Follow-up research findings

The key findings of the 2005 poverty maps were supplemented by additional research that allowed the development of a typology among the municipalities based on poverty measures, the definition of the profile of the municipalities with the highest poverty rates, and the determination of the factors that trigger the spatial heterogeneity of poverty.

By using district poverty estimates (produced through poverty mapping) and cluster analysis, relatively homogeneous groups of municipalities were identified. The cluster analysis identified six clusters of municipalities. They were clearly defined on both ends, that is, the two clusters of poor municipalities and the two clusters of richer municipalities, while the two middle clusters consisted of 243 municipalities and were less stable and not so easily defined. The two bottom clusters included the municipalities in which over 30 percent of the population were poor. In 10 of these (Belitsa,

Boynitsa, Kainardja, Kotel, Makresh, Omurtag, Rakitovo, Satovcha, Vurbitsa, and Yakoruda), along with the high poverty rate, the depth of poverty was also high. Quite close to these municipalities in poverty terms were the municipalities of Dospat, Nikola Kozlevo, and Opaka.

These 13 municipalities with the highest poverty rates share a number of common characteristics and have a distinct profile. Most of them are situated close to each other, thus forming spatial pockets of poverty. By overlaying the results of the municipal poverty mapping with other municipal level data, including data on municipal road infrastructure and another 30 district and municipal social and economic indicators, one may see that the poorest municipalities appear to have undeveloped road and social infrastructure, less industry and fewer services, higher unemployment rates, and poor educational attainment among the population.[13] The majority of people have only completed primary or lower secondary education, while only 2–4 percent have higher education. Unemployment is in the range of 35–80 percent, and there is a particularly large share of long-term unemployed, exceeding 70 percent of all unemployed.[14] Most poor municipalities are located in underdeveloped rural or mountainous areas, where income and employment opportunities are limited and industry is virtually nonexistent. The population lives mainly on agriculture and livestock breeding in the areas with favorable conditions for such activities, on woodcutting, or on gathering herbs, berries, and mushrooms in mountainous areas.

The economic, social, and demographic profiles of the 13 poorest municipalities are sufficiently specific that these municipalities require a differentiated policy approach to the solution of their problems.

- Boynitsa and Makresh are typical small rural municipalities. They have 2,270 and 2,550 inhabitants at retirement age, respectively.[15] These two municipalities have one of the most unfavorable demographic structures in the oblast of Vidin and nationwide. Boynitsa has the highest age dependency ratio in the country, 134 percent, and only 10 percent of the population is under 15. This implies that policies must be aimed at supporting elderly people (most of whom live alone) through health and social services, the improvement of living conditions, and access to services and markets by way of local infrastructure development.

- In the rural municipalities of Kainardja, Nikola Kozlevo, Omurtag, and Opaka, the unemployment rates exceed 50 percent, the shares of the long-term unemployed surpass 70 percent, and the youth unemployment rate is much higher than the country average. Over 50 percent of the people living in these municipalities are of Turkish or Roma ethnic origin and have completed only primary or lower secondary education or have no education at all. They live mainly through farming (mostly temporary jobs in spring and autumn) or on social assistance. There are no industrial enterprises except in the municipality of Omurtag. The promotion of agriculture to create new jobs is a policy option there. It would provide an opportunity for a sustainable increase in incomes and poverty reduction.

■ The municipalities of Belitsa, Dospat, Kotel, Rakitovo, Satovcha, Vurbitsa, and Yakoruda are located in semimountainous and mountainous areas. Most of the population belongs to the Turkish ethnic minority. Agriculture, particularly potato and tobacco growing, is the main source of income. Tourism is underdeveloped, although all the municipalities have good potential for hunting and agritourism. The unemployment rate in some of the villages is high, up to 90 percent. Children under the age of 15 comprise over one-third of the total population. Child mortality rates are relatively high. The municipalities in this group generally have well-developed water and sewerage systems. Several small wood-processing, furniture, and clothing factories provide jobs, mainly in the municipal centers. In the past few years, there has been an increasing interest in the cultivation of herbs, for which the conditions are also favorable. This group of municipalities might benefit from policies aimed at the substitution of tobacco growing, where the market demand is declining, by the cultivation of mushrooms, herbs, and other, similar crops. There is potential for the creation of new jobs in tourism and organic farming, as well as scope for the development of small and medium enterprises.

In response to the demand to improve targeting in government expenditures and poverty reduction programs, the follow-up research on the 2005 poverty maps also included analysis of the factors behind the spatial heterogeneity of poverty. The analysis assumed that the incidence of poverty at the local level is caused by two main groups of factors: factors related to the quality of human capital, such as education and the demographic structure of the population, and location-related factors, such as social and economic development, the available natural and geographical resources, and the state of infrastructure (see Bigman and Fofack 2000).

For this reason, the poverty mapping data were overlaid with geographically referenced data collected and processed by the NSI on natural resource endowments; access to health, education, and social care; human resources; local labor market conditions; and the degree of infrastructure development. A multivariate regression analysis identified the correlation of the incidence of poverty at the municipal level with a set of variables. (Detailed results of the regression models may be found in Kotzeva and Tzvetkov 2006 and NSI 2006.) Among the variables were human capital (the age, gender, and ethnicity structure of the population; the level of education and literacy), the labor market (the share of the registered unemployed; the share of the long-term unemployed; the share of the unemployed under the age of 29; average salary; employment and labor force participation rates; the share of the employed in services, industry, and agriculture), economic development (per capita municipal gross domestic product, net municipal income from services, the share of own revenues, the net per capita revenue from sales, the share of arable land, the share of urban population), and infrastructure (percentage of houses without sewerage or without indoor toilet facilities, the density of the road network, the number of telephone lines per 100 inhabitants).

The multivariate regression revealed several determinants of the differences in poverty by municipality:

- First and foremost, poverty rates were higher in the municipalities with concentrations of low human capital endowments, especially educational attainment and literacy. The lower the literacy rate and the smaller the share of persons with higher than secondary education, the higher the poverty rate in a municipality.

- Poverty was closely related to employment opportunities and the availability of jobs. The multivariate analysis indicated that the municipalities with a higher average wage had lower poverty rates, although the impact of economic development, employment, and wages was less than the impact of educational attainment. The importance of economic development as a factor in poverty reduction was substantiated empirically by the negative regression coefficients of the variables "net revenue from sales per capita (in 1,000s of leva)" and "share of own revenues in the municipality." In other words, the more efficient the local economy, the higher the incomes and the lower the level of poverty in a municipality.

- The quality of the road network and of communications was crucial for the development of commerce and services, as well as for attracting investments. Phone service availability and the share of people who had access to sewerage and indoor toilet facilities were used as proxies for the quality of social infrastructure. The coefficients of these variables emerged as statistically significant and negative, which confirmed the assumption that infrastructure improvement is an important factor in poverty reduction at the local level.

The Use of Poverty Maps and the Impact of the Maps on Policy

Users

The main users of the poverty maps have been the political leadership of the MLSP, directorates and departments in the MLSP, and the SIF, an independent legal entity subordinate to the MLSP.

The political leadership of the MLSP (the Political Cabinet of the minister of labor and social policy) is a primary user of the poverty maps for policy-making purposes. The work of the Bank team with the political leadership began with awareness raising among the MLSP leadership on the value of the poverty maps. The Bank envisaged meetings with the minister and deputy ministers, discussions with members of the Political Cabinet and public communications officers, and the participation of the MLSP leadership in all workshops and dissemination events related to the poverty maps. The Bank strategy emphasized that the maps represent an advanced methodology that renders more sophisticated and objective assessments relative to composite indexes. It also emphasized the reliability of the mapping data and the extensive informative and analytical potential. Finally, the engagement strategy focused on the need for continuity and the need to transfer the ownership of the maps from the cabinet that endorsed the launch of the poverty mapping exercise to subsequent cabinets. These strategic messages were reinforced by the positive outcome of the practical application of the 2003 poverty maps.

The 2001–05 cabinet and, especially, the then minister of labor and social policy and the deputy minister responsible for social security policy took the principal decisions that set the stage for using poverty maps in the policy-making process in three main ways:

- The poverty monitoring mechanisms developed through the IDF grant, including the poverty maps, were incorporated in strategic government documents addressing the issue of poverty reduction. The national poverty reduction strategies and action plans, the national strategy for the attainment of the Millennium Development Goals, and the Joint Memorandum on Social Inclusion signed with the European Commission on February 3, 2005, require robust mechanisms for the identification of regional disparities. They also require sound evaluation systems for targeting EU grants to the poorest municipalities and for evaluating the antipoverty impact of policies and projects. The Joint Memorandum on Social Inclusion monitoring mechanism involves updating information on income status and living conditions at the national, district, and municipal levels, while a new poverty map might be a way to update information on the spatial distribution of poverty.
- Targeted antipoverty interventions were developed for the poorest municipalities as an immediate response to the updated information provided by the poverty maps in 2005.
- Antipoverty policies directed at the municipalities identified as the poorest were mainstreamed into national strategic documents aimed at the reduction of poverty, the promotion of employment, and the elimination of social exclusion.

Because the poorest municipalities had been singled out and because of the understanding gained about the poverty profile of these municipalities, a number of geographically targeted initiatives and programs were launched. This focused approach had not been common in MLSP policies before the existence of the poverty maps. Immediately after the 2005 maps had been completed, the MLSP organized consultations with the mayors and other representatives of the 13 poorest municipalities. This resulted in the development of an ad hoc Program for Poverty Reduction in the Poorest Municipalities. This program was built entirely on the 2005 municipal poverty rankings. It concentrated only on the 13 poorest municipalities and was launched shortly after the consultations with the representatives of these municipalities. It identified priority areas for intervention and the allocation of resources, including the generation of employment, especially among the long-term unemployed and disadvantaged groups in the labor market, and the enhancement of the quality of the workforce. The program was considered a pilot undertaking, and the outcomes were to serve as a basis for designing future antipoverty policies, measures, and programs.

In 2005, to sustain the impact of the pilot program, the program was included in the National Plan for Poverty Reduction 2005–06. This plan focused on increasing employability and labor force participation; promoting entrepreneurship and job creation through access to financial resources, training, mentoring, and other, related services; and reintegrating marginalized social groups in the labor market. It also sought to overcome the social isolation emerging through regional disparities; foster equal access to health care, education, and training; optimize the access to productive assets and infrastructure; and increase employment-related incomes.

One of its components, the Program for Training and Employment for Poverty Reduction in the Municipalities of Opaka, Omurtag, Nikola Kozlevo, Vrabnitza, Makresh, Belitsa, Boynitsa, Yakoruda, Satovcha, Dospat, Kotel, Kainardja, and Rakitovo, was specifically tailored to the needs of the unemployed in these municipalities. The program was initiated by the MLSP and the Employment Agency and is being implemented by municipal authorities, labor offices, social assistance offices, and private employers. The program was started in 2005 and had a budget of Lev 2 million (US$1.25 million), which was allocated to support projects among local employers aimed at training and at creating new jobs in several sectors. It had been determined through research after the poverty mapping exercise that these sectors were important to the economic development of these municipalities. The sectors included tourism, agriculture, food processing, and organic farming. Activities designed to enhance local infrastructure and public services were also viewed as eligible for project expenditures. In 2006, an additional Lev 1.3 million was allocated for the program.

The program created sustainable employment for 685 unemployed individuals in 2005 and 518 unemployed individuals in 2006. It also led to the creation of 195 private sector jobs in 2006. The job creation activities under the program were combined with literacy courses, training, and skill enhancement so as to increase employability. Inclusion in the program was guaranteed as a priority to unemployed people who were receiving monthly social assistance benefits, the long-term unemployed, unemployed individuals who had not completed secondary education or who had no special skills, and unemployed who lacked basic literacy. In 2005, through the program, 150 poor unemployed took literacy courses, 380 received training, and 60 were supported in becoming self-employed.

In 2006, the MLSP initiated the Overcoming Poverty Program, which also targeted the 13 poorest municipalities. Through the program, individuals from these municipalities improved their employability by taking literacy and vocational training courses or were involved in initiatives to boost employment and self-employment through the creation of business plans for independent activities. The allocations for this program amounted to close to Lev 1.7 million (US$1.1 million). The number of beneficiaries reached 1,818, of which 107 took literacy courses, 182 underwent vocational training, and 1,529 participated in employment programs.

The main goal of the new Strategy for the Reduction of Poverty and Social Exclusion, 2006–08, has been to reduce poverty in the 13 most disadvantaged municipalities by promoting employment. The strategy is targeted at the unemployed who are registered with local labor offices and especially at disadvantaged groups on the local labor market, including youth and young people up to 30 years of age, people over 55, social assistance beneficiaries, and people with low educational attainment. It addresses the issue of the regional disparities that are a focus of the Regional Development Plans for the six planning regions for 2007–13 by including socioeconomic analyses of the situation in the respective regions, along with other measures to eliminate the disparities.

District Development Strategies for 2005–15 and Municipal Development Plans were also elaborated to foster the development of infrastructure, the competitiveness of the economies, and human resources. A number of smaller-scale programs and projects are being implemented that contribute to reducing poverty in the disadvantaged municipalities by creating alternative income sources such as agroindustries, biofuels, rural tourism, local crafts, woodworking, carpentry, apiculture, horse breeding, aquacultures, mushroom growing, and the processing of essential oils, herbs, and mushrooms. These initiatives include the Sustainable Development of Rural Areas Project, the Program for Agriculture Development in Northwest Bulgaria, the Program for Alternative Agriculture Development in the Rhodopi Mountains, and the Bulgarian Forest Restoration Program.

Other users of the poverty maps in the MLSP are the policy directorates. The Social Analysis, Prognosis, and Policy Directorate, the Policy and Strategy of Social Protection Directorate, and the Policy of Labor Market Directorate were aware of the poverty mapping exercise from the beginning and now use the maps in analysis and in drafting policy initiatives and other measures. Representatives of these directorates have been actively involved in the design of the maps, in the seminars on the methodology, and, subsequently, in the seminars on the outcomes and in the discussions on policy options. Experts from these directorates understand the innovative character of the poverty mapping methodology; they believe in its usefulness for in-depth district and municipal social and economic analysis and for designing relevant social policies to reduce poverty. They recognize the poverty map as a useful, multifunctional, and intrinsically objective and impartial governance tool. Their experience is still limited; however, they have a positive outlook and are open to a more extensive application of the tool in future analysis and in the development of and reporting on the Joint Memorandum on Social Inclusion and plans to combat poverty that are already in place. Experts at the newly established Directorate of Demographic Policy, Social Investment, and Equal Opportunities are also familiar with the methodology and the outcomes of the mapping exercise because they have worked on the project and are interested in using the maps in their activities.

The SIF is another main user of the 2003 and 2005 poverty maps. The SIF was legally established in 2002 under the MLSP and tasked with channeling grant funds from the government budget and other sources, including the World Bank's Social Investment and Employment Promotion Project, which is funded at US$50 million, and smaller-scale grant schemes. SIF grants go to municipalities and communities to improve social infrastructure.

SIF projects have clear-cut poverty reduction objectives that require reliance on credible criteria to rank municipalities according to poverty status. After the preparation of the first poverty maps, the SIF steering committee immediately incorporated the maps among the set of formal criteria applied to rank the municipalities by poverty status to target SIF projects on the poorest municipalities.

The poverty maps became one of the five formal tools for social infrastructure project assessment. They were first applied to rank (prioritize) applicant municipalities according to poverty status. The rank of a municipality according to the poverty maps is the criterion with the largest comparative weight in assessment. Therefore, it is extremely important that the data serving as the basis for the poverty maps be reliable and up to date. The SIF staff views this as a major prerequisite in determining the appropriate allocation of resources to reduce poverty.

SIF project identification and selection began before the production of the first municipal poverty maps, but it was anticipated in the SIF operations manual that the maps would be used. Because the poverty maps were not ready at the time of the SIF launch, several interim arrangements were considered during the initial period. These included the following:

- The level of municipal development index of the Ministry of Regional Development and Public Works, applied since 1998, was legitimate in the sense that it had been developed and was used by a government agency. However, it served different purposes. Moreover, it had not been regularly updated and was not suitable for poverty ranking among municipalities. Also, the coefficients, methodology, and data used for the calculation of the index were not publicly available, and an independent update proved infeasible.
- Human development indexes had been calculated by the United Nations Development Programme for the districts (28) and municipalities (262) (see UNDP 2001). The district and municipal composite indexes had been calculated for 2000 and 2001 and were publicly available at the launch of the Social Investment and Employment Promotion Project. The use of the index ratings was discussed with mayors, policy makers, and academics, but rejected because of data gaps and methodological challenges during the production of the indexes that had led to some inexplicable results.
- A municipal development index had been prepared by Club Economika 2000, a local interdisciplinary research organization, specifically to meet the needs of the Social Investment and Employment Promotion Project as an interim solution until the completion of the poverty maps.

Taking into consideration the deficiency of the two more general indexes, the SIF steering committee and the World Bank decided to apply the third index, the municipal development index prepared by Club Economika 2000, until the poverty maps were ready. This index was based on credible municipal social and economic data produced by the municipalities and the Ministry of Finance. The index was used to rank the municipalities and target the first 79 SIF projects in 2003. Subsequently, when the municipal poverty map based on the BIHS was ready, it was applied to target 132 projects in 2004 and 102 projects in 2005. The replacement of the 2003 maps by the 2005 maps took place at the beginning of 2006. By the end of April of that year, the municipalities that were going to be the beneficiaries of 40 new SIF social infrastructure projects had been identified through the 2005 municipal poverty map.

Since 2004, the steering committee and project management of the SIF have applied the poverty maps to identify municipalities and local communities that are eligible for social infrastructure project funding. Among municipalities, the level of poverty is one of the five criteria used to rate and evaluate microproject proposals.[16] The other four criteria include the local unemployment rate, the local employment rate, the cost per beneficiary, and the share of cofinancing. Eligible communities are those that: (1) are poor according to national standards, (2) are marginalized with respect to job opportunities, (3) lack clear prospects to improve living standards, and (4) show limited access to credit markets and productive assets and therefore lack opportunities for self-employment and to share in the benefits of economic growth.

In 2006, before taking the decision to replace the 2003 maps with the 2005 maps, the SIF steering committee evaluated the results of the application of the poverty maps in 2003–05. The committee decided to continue using the tool, but, beginning in 2006, only for ranking and evaluating municipal social infrastructure projects. The experience of the SIF staff and the steering committee had revealed that the application of the poverty maps to target community projects is hindered because the poverty status of a given municipality revealed through the poverty maps is not always representative of the poverty status of the communities within the municipality. (Projects submitted by communities in the same municipality are assigned equal weight as regards the poverty rate, which means that the specific poverty profile of an individual community or disadvantaged group is given insufficient consideration.)

Independent evaluation of the application of the poverty maps has confirmed the following (see Chengelova 2006):

■ SIF staff and the steering committee rated the poverty maps highly as a targeting tool. They considered the maps to be reliable, objective, and easy to use. The SIF representatives had contributed to the development of the poverty maps as participants in the data users group and in the training and dissemination events. As a result, SIF staff members had acquired a sound preliminary understanding of the poverty maps and their implementation potential in evaluating social infrastructure projects.

■ The trade unions were the only party that voiced doubts about the poverty maps as evaluation tools for infrastructure and community projects. These doubts were related, however, to the poverty line that was applied. The trade unions considered this poverty line too low. They did not criticize the concept of using poverty maps for geographical targeting in the allocation of municipal social infrastructure investments. During these debates, the possibility of regularly and quickly upgrading the poverty line and alternative approaches to the definition of the poverty line were also discussed.

■ The poverty maps are generally considered an indispensable part of the initial evaluation of microprojects and the best tool for evaluating and targeting infrastructure projects. The maps ensure objective ranking and comparison among applicants for financing. The readiness and willingness to use the maps were reaffirmed recently when the maps were incorporated in the management information system of the SIF.

Enhancing policy making

By providing high-resolution data on key poverty indicators and by widely distributing the results of the mapping exercise, the developers of the poverty maps managed to focus the attention of the government, academics, independent research organizations, international donors, and private users on the advantages of the maps. The close interaction between map producers and map users promoted several immediate applications of the maps in the policy-making process. These applications included the targeting of services and transfers, the targeting of projects, selection across policy options, the identification of appropriate poverty reduction interventions and approaches, and the design of interventions in rural areas and municipalities with ethnically mixed populations.

Targeting of services and transfers

The poverty maps are recognized by policy makers as an instrument for targeting transfers from the government budget, the EU preaccession funds, and other donor support, including World Bank loans, to municipalities with the highest incidence of poverty and social exclusion. Along with other targeting instruments, the maps are expected to influence coming decisions regarding the absorption of European structural funds and, notably, grants that will be provided through the European Social Fund.

Targeting in projects proposed for funding through the SIF

Since 2004, the municipal poverty maps have been applied in determining the eligibility of municipalities and their ranking in targeting SIF social infrastructure development grants (see elsewhere above).

Selection across policy options

Poverty maps have been used as a starting point for additional analyses aimed at informing policy makers about the best among a number of policy options to reduce poverty and about the details of policy design. After the preparation of the 2005 poverty maps had been completed, the MLSP assigned a research team to identify the characteristics held in common among the poorest municipalities. Using the poverty mapping estimates and multivariate statistical techniques (that is, cluster analysis), the team grouped the municipalities into six clusters within three relatively homogeneous groups: poor, rich, and other. This classification highlighted the need to undertake geographically targeted policies, for example, conditional cash transfers; investments in municipal road infrastructure, sewerage, and water supply; the expansion of subsidized public works programs; active labor market policies targeted at youth and elderly long-term unemployed; alternative income-generation programs; and microcredit or subsidized credit schemes. The government designed the antipoverty policies at two levels—nationwide and targeted at the 13 poorest municipalities—and chose among different policy options depending on whether the targeted municipalities were located in mountainous or rural parts of the country, had higher or lower population densities, were experiencing steeper demographic decline and population aging, or benefited from investment inflows.

Identification of appropriate poverty reduction policy interventions and approaches

Among the 13 poor municipalities, cluster analysis indicated that, in 10 of the municipalities, over 30 percent of the population was poor and the depth of poverty was high. These were the municipalities of Belitsa, Boynitsa, Kainardja, Kotel, Omurtag, Makresh, Rakitovo, Satovcha, Vurbitsa, and Yakoruda, while, in the other three municipalities, Dospat, Nikola Kozlevo, and Opaka, the poverty rate was close to 30 percent. A more detailed study of poverty prevalence helped determine appropriate measures and policies to reduce poverty and smooth out the drastic differences in living standards relative to other municipalities (see elsewhere above). After excluding the two extreme groups (the 13 poorest municipalities and the richest municipalities, which were in the capital), the research team found, through the cluster analysis, that, among the other municipalities in Bulgaria, poverty showed a rather uniform profile, and that, wherever disparities in poverty existed, these were not sufficiently significant to justify separate clusters. The recommendation of the team to policy makers for all these municipalities was therefore to implement a mainstream antipoverty strategy.

Design of specific interventions in rural municipalities and municipalities with ethnically mixed populations

The municipal poverty indicators and poverty maps have been especially helpful in emphasizing the need for and giving guidance on the nature of poverty reduction interventions in rural municipalities and municipalities with large ethnic minorities, mainly Turks and Roma. In 2005, while designing targeted poverty reduction policies for the cluster of the 13 poorest municipalities, the MLSP also undertook the design of interventions to address the specific characteristics of poverty in municipalities with ethnically mixed populations, including, for example, the persistence of long-term unemployment, combined with a high level of dependence on social assistance among the working-age population. The policies and programs have therefore aimed at increasing employability by building up skills and by literacy training. As a result, a greater share of the populations in these mixed areas is now benefiting from antipoverty actions.

The use of the poverty maps, though substantive, has been limited mainly to the SIF and the MLSP. Currently, poverty mapping is not well understood in other relevant ministries, especially the Ministry of Regional Development and Public Works and the Ministry of Agriculture. The reasons for this are manifold. Since no representatives of these entities have been involved in the development of the maps, the maps have failed to garner proper consideration. Upon submitting the maps to the public, no concerted effort was made to engage other government agencies. In view of the positive results of the application of the maps in the activities of the MLSP, key ministries involved in fostering economic and social welfare through employment, training, and the development of human resources ought to be exposed to the results of the poverty mapping exercise as a next step.

Another untapped audience is the district and local structures of the MLSP. Pursuant to the Employment Promotion Act, each district has established a district employment commission to facilitate, coordinate, and guide the allocation of resources to foster employment creation at the district and local levels, conduct monitoring to ensure effective implementation of social policies and programs, generate subsidized and unsubsidized employment, and encourage self-employment. These commissions are potential recipients of training in poverty map applications. In addition, district administrations, municipal councils, and mayors of municipalities should also be made aware of the findings of the poverty mapping exercise. This would enhance their capacity to identify the needs of local communities, as well as improving the quality of their project proposals.

User views on the value of poverty maps

A qualitative survey among the users of poverty maps has revealed a positive attitude toward the instrument, appreciation of its value in policy and program targeting, and a high level of confidence in the mapping results. The users of the poverty maps have confirmed that the maps have been appropriately applied in the formulation of social policies to reduce poverty. They have understood the value of the methodology and the maps mainly because of the ability of the maps to help identify the geographical locations, especially municipalities, that are the deepest and most persistent pockets of poverty and that are in need of targeted policy support. The maps have also helped highlight relevant antipoverty measures. The users of the maps who participated in the qualitative survey identified several areas where the efficiency of the instrument and the scope of its practical implementation might be increased (see Chengelova 2006). Their recommendations are primarily geared toward scaling up the poverty mapping exercise by producing or updating the maps more regularly, by increasing the number of indicators monitored, and by expanding the analysis. Their recommendations may be summarized as follows:

- The poverty map is used as a governance tool in designing social policies to reduce poverty and in evaluating projects to promote employment creation at the district and municipal levels. To be effective in this role, the maps must be regularly updated. According to the users, it is an imperative that new maps be prepared annually or at least every two years to accommodate the dynamics of the economies in individual municipalities, the changes in the characteristics of the workforce in districts, and the development of human capital. Although the country has developed the capacity to carry out high-quality household surveys and produce new poverty maps, it still faces a data constraint in that census data are typically collected at 10-year intervals. Thus, the more frequent updating of poverty maps is contingent on the identification of a suitable methodology for intercensal years (see chapter 1).

■ To increase the potential for practical applications of the poverty maps, the users suggested that data might be gathered on a larger number of indicators. In this way, one of the shortcomings of sample-based poverty surveys that feature an adequate number of units, but a limited number of indicators and variables, would be minimized.

■ A number of users suggested that the information value of the poverty maps might be increased if the maps were not limited to modeling consumption. Since information on a wide range of indicators is collected, they proposed preparing maps focused on specific issues, such as maps on employment and unemployment status and characteristics, school attendance, and school drop outs. MLSP experts in social and economic analysis and labor market policies voiced their agreement with this idea not only through the survey, but also at the workshops on the value and applications of the maps.

■ The potential for raising the number of users of poverty mapping products and outcomes is enormous. In the first place, this would include the European Funds Programs and Projects Directorate of the MLSP. This directorate is the managing authority for the absorption of grants from the European Social Fund. It is responsible for defining the operational objectives of the Human Resource Development Program of the National Development Program and for targeting resource allocations at the most disadvantaged final beneficiaries. Other ministries such as the Ministry of Regional Development and Public Works, the Ministry of Economy and Energy, the Ministry of Finance, the Ministry of Agriculture, and the Ministry of Education and Science would also benefit from the maps in acquiring a better understanding of the socioeconomic situation in municipalities and in improving program targeting. Other potential user entities include district employment commissions, district administrations, municipal councils, and mayors of municipalities.

■ According to some of the users, the maps might help deepen the analysis of poverty through more extensive studies of poverty in the districts and municipalities. The maps might become the starting point for follow-up surveys in selected districts or municipalities. For example, three pilot sample-based surveys might be conducted: one in one of the poorest districts, another in a district showing medium values in the poverty headcount and in the depth and severity of poverty, and another in one of the most prosperous districts. Extensive data would be gathered on these districts, and disparities and specifics among the three types of districts would be highlighted. At a later stage, these pilot models might be used in exploring poverty factors locally elsewhere. Another approach would be to deepen the analysis of the determinants of poverty or the impact of a combination of poverty factors in the municipalities that emerge as outliers, as in the case of the municipality of Boynitsa.

The interviews with map users showed that nearly all of them advocated broader dissemination of the mapping results, combined with discussions on the causes of poverty and on poverty reduction initiatives that might be targeted through the maps. Two of the specific suggestions in this area were the following:

- Prepare and release a pamphlet describing the mapping methodology in general and the findings of the poverty mapping exercise. The pamphlet might be distributed to a broad audience of potential users. It might be aimed, for example, at municipal authorities given that, because they are objective and the selection criteria robust, the maps would boost the transparency of municipal targeting in project financing.
- Continue training initiatives in mapping among central government officials outside the MLSP and among district and municipal administrators. This will facilitate the improvement of individual and institutional capacity for more efficient and broader use of the map findings and for the proper allocation of resources to reduce poverty.

The Long-Term Sustainability of the Poverty Maps

The capacity and sustainability goals of map production

The building of national capacity and the optimal use of capacity are major preconditions for the long-term sustainability of the poverty maps. A new cadre of national experts was created during the production of the poverty maps. The mapping teams accumulated valuable experience in applying the small area estimation methodology and in working with policy makers in using the map results. This experience and capacity were demonstrated in the success of the 2003 MTHS and the 2005 poverty maps. A substantial share of the acquired capacity resides with the NSI. NSI experts possess the necessary theoretical knowledge in the mapping methodology. They also acquired practical experience during the 2005 mapping exercise and will be able to apply this knowledge and experience in the course of upcoming poverty studies and evaluations.

Capacity is also concentrated in the MLSP. One of the objectives of the IDF grant was to institutionalize poverty impact evaluation in the MLSP. The Social Analysis, Prognosis, and Policy Directorate in the MLSP was established for this purpose, and core MLSP staff were trained in poverty and labor market analysis. However, for some time, the ministry was unsuccessful in finding an appropriate director at the directorate, and this affected operations.[17] The present director was appointed in the autumn of 2005. Since then, poverty analysis capacity has been consolidated at the MLSP, and the directorate is now leading in the design and implementation of analytical work on poverty and living standards and in the dialogue with international financial institutions active in this area.

An important source of sustainability is the data users group, which includes policy makers, other experts from public institutions, and representatives of academia and private interdisciplinary research organizations. It brings the cross-agency perspective to the agenda, as well as strong analytical skills and expertise in econometrics, statistics, macroeconomics, regional policy, and the social and economic aspects of poverty.

The World Bank has played a major role in developing the technical elements of sustainability. The Bank was able to provide technical expertise of the highest level for the production of the first set of poverty maps. However, the quality of the outcome depended not only on the expertise and commitment of the consultant who was directly involved in the mapping exercise. A significant factor in the success of the effort was also the high quality of the data collected, the thoroughness in data cleaning and processing, the soundness of the MTHS questionnaire, and the competence in the production of the consumption aggregate. The work in 2001–03 was accomplished in a truly professional manner that set high standards for the national mapping research team in 2003–05. The quality of the 2003 MTHS and subsequent 2005 poverty mapping exercise was strongly influenced by the implementation of the IDF grant. While the field survey was carried out entirely by the NSI and the MLSP, the Bank provided ongoing support over four years starting with the survey planning, the design of the questionnaire, the sampling, and the training for the field data collection, the data cleaning, and the processing to produce the consumption aggregate. The Bank clearly had a significant technical influence on the quality of the data set used for the 2005 maps. More specifically, the Bank undertook the following:

- The Bank provided methodological guidance by hiring a consultant who worked with national experts on the MTHS questionnaire, the training of enumerators, and the training of trainers. Two Bank specialists in the Living Standards Measurement Survey supplied guidance in the overall planning and implementation of the MTHS, including the training of enumerators, sampling, data collection, data entry, and data cleaning.
- The Bank provided overall management and supervision of the process and helped in integrating the poverty mapping exercise into policy dialogue. An operations officer supervised the implementation of the IDF grant. Another operations officer monitored the use of the poverty maps in targeting for SIF projects. Within the framework of the IDF grant, the poverty mapping exercise was monitored through the joint Bank-government portfolio reviews and examined during high-level meetings between the Bank and the government.
- The Bank introduced quality control over the fieldwork and the data processing. The quality control over the fieldwork was carried out by BBSS Gallup International. It included revisiting 15 percent of the households in the sample.[18] The conclusions of the related report were positive with respect to the execution of the methodology and the commitment to best practice in conducting a nationally representative survey. A separate quality control arrangement was applied for the 2003 MTHS consumption aggregate prepared by Bulgarian institutions. A Bank expert in Living Standards Measurement Surveys independently retraced all the steps involved in the preparation process and discussed with the Bulgarian team the strengths and weaknesses of certain research decisions the team had made. The Bank expert concluded that the process had been generally appropriate.

The Bank did not participate except minimally in the production of the 2005 poverty maps. This decision had an important impact on sustainability. After verifying that there was a national capacity in place, the Bank team was comfortable with supplying only marginal feedback through the international consultant who answered specific technical questions that arose during the mapping exercise. The detailed description of the small area estimation methodology and the well-documented steps in the mapping process that the consultant had previously provided contributed greatly to the final success of the endeavor.

The national research team approached the preparation of the poverty maps not as a discrete, one-time task, but as an integral part of its overall poverty analysis capability. Before undertaking the preparation of the maps, the team explored the experiences in poverty mapping in more than 15 developing countries and reviewed the literature on the subject. One of the team members developed a new user-friendly poverty mapping software program based on the SPSS package for applications suited to the equipment and human capacity resources available in Bulgarian institutions. The team members participated in individual and group training and also provided training that had a positive impact on long-term sustainability.[19] Major outreach activities are highlighted in box 5.1.

Dissemination of the results and sustainability

A coherent dissemination strategy for the results of the mapping exercise contributed to long-term sustainability. The strategy raised awareness and helped ensure acceptance of the poverty maps as a powerful tool in decision making by governments at both the central and municipal levels. The key dissemination event was a high-level workshop organized in April 2005 at which the poverty mapping results were presented and discussed with potential users involved in the design and implementation of social policy in Bulgaria. Another important element of dissemination was the regular briefing of senior officials at the MLSP by the poverty mapping team on the progress and interim results of the work.

For both sets of poverty maps, the dissemination of results focused on achieving the following main goals:

- Explain the methodology used to derive poverty estimates on small geographical areas
- Analyze the spatial dimensions of poverty that have been identified through the poverty maps, as well as the causes of this poverty
- Build institutional capacity for the application of poverty maps to policy making
- Build a consensus on the need to apply poverty maps in the policy-making process and in policy and program targeting on disadvantaged groups and pockets of poverty

The official launch of the 2003 MTHS report, including the 2005 poverty maps, took place in July 2005. This was a major event at which the results of the regional analysis of poverty were presented to a wide audience consisting of ministers, district governors, municipal mayors, the leaders of key trade unions, employers associations, diplomats, representatives of the international donor community, experts from ministries, researchers, and the media. At that time, the potential contribution of mapping in the formulation of antipoverty policies was discussed in detail. A special press packet provided journalists with a description of the poverty mapping methodology and the results. This attracted a great deal of interest among civil society organizations and academics and received wide media coverage.

BOX 5.1   Major Dissemination, Training, and Capacity-Building Events, Bulgaria

1. *Training for the Purpose of Establishing and Strengthening the Institutional Capacity for Poverty Mapping, Bankya, March 28–30, 2004.* This training event was conducted by the international consultant and Bank staff who had been involved in the 2003 poverty mapping exercise. It targeted two sorts of audience members: (1) decision makers from the MLSP, the NSI, and other public agencies, district labor and social assistance offices, and municipal authorities and (2) the media. This was the first exposure of the Bulgarian national print and electronic media to the poverty mapping methodology and the mapping results. It was extensively covered by the media, but the overall impact in fostering a general understanding of poverty mapping was limited mainly because of the narrow scope of the event.

2. *Poverty Reduction Policies Based on Data from the 2003 MTHS, Petrich, October 7–9, 2004.* This seminar was attended by 19 participants and was more specialized. It examined strategies and methods for measuring poverty, the identification of criteria in the definition of poverty lines, factors determining poverty risk, and poverty reduction policies. The poverty monitoring process was also introduced.

3. *Mapping Poverty, Bankya, April 8, 2005.* A total of 29 persons were trained at this event, predominantly experts and staff at the SIF and the MLSP, mainly the Social Analysis, Prognosis, and Policy Directorate, the Policy of Labor Market Directorate, and the Policy and Strategy of Social Protection Directorate. Participants were acquainted with the poverty mapping methodology and with the main outcomes of the poverty mapping exercise using the 2003 MTHS and the 2001 census. A separate module focused on the use of mapping in the regional focus of social policies.

4. *Workshop with the mayors of the 13 poorest municipalities.* In January 2005, the MLSP organized a one-day workshop with the mayors of the 13 poorest municipalities. At the workshop, the poverty mapping team presented its analysis of the causes of the existence of pockets of poverty. The possibility of geographically targeting antipoverty policies was discussed. Part of the workshop was dedicated to capacity building and information sharing aimed at increasing the quality of municipal proposals for social project funding.

5. *Consultations with the research community.* In February 2005, immediately following the completion of the 2005 poverty maps, a launching event for academics and researchers was held in Sofia. The event focused on the mapping methodology, the data, and the potential analytical applications of the poverty maps. The reasons behind the ranking of certain municipalities and groups of municipalities were also discussed in relation to poverty headcounts. The event produced some interesting proposals for further analyses based on the poverty maps and household consumption data more broadly.

The results of the 2003 poverty mapping exercise are summarized in a report that was presented to an expert group consisting of the minister of labor and social policy, the three deputy ministers, and senior MLSP experts in September 2004. The report was widely covered by the media. The 2005 poverty maps, along with the main results and findings from the spatial analysis of poverty, are summarized in NSI (2006), which has been published in Bulgarian and English.

Despite the success of the mapping exercise, several issues represent a challenge for the long-term sustainability of the process. The first challenge is related to the data needed to update the maps. The two sets of poverty maps produced in Bulgaria made use of the MTHS, which is not conducted regularly. The latest versions were conducted in 1995, 1997, 2001, and 2003 with the financial and technical support of the World Bank. In addition, methodological differences in survey design, the measurement of welfare, and the definitions of poverty lines have impeded direct comparisons of the results of these surveys and have therefore limited the robustness of the conclusions that may be reached about changes in the incidence and depth of poverty over time.

The second challenge is related to the technical aspects of the poverty mapping methodology. As a new member of the EU, Bulgaria is now committed to reporting on poverty based on the EU Statistics on Income and Living Conditions surveys that measure welfare through income data, monitor income poverty, and apply OECD equivalence scales, while the Bank uses a per capita consumption index to measure poverty. Some of the new EU member states are discussing possible ways to combine the strengths of the two approaches within the limits allowed by Eurostat (see Eur-Lex 2003, article 8). In Bulgaria, the Bank and the government are also exploring steps to allow the best use of all the data collected by whatever methodology to update the information on the poverty characteristics of municipalities. They are implementing a joint multiyear program on poverty monitoring and analysis aimed at evaluating the overall impact of the Bank's involvement in social sector reform in Bulgaria through development policy lending in support of reforms in health care, education, and social protection; investment projects on social inclusion and social infrastructure; and analytical and advisory work. Reforms in the social sector are expected to have a significant influence on the spatial distribution of poverty. There is an understanding that, in poverty analysis, including analysis of the dynamics of the geographical dimensions of poverty, optimal use should be made of all data on households collected through various surveys or stakeholders.

The national poverty mapping team is also exploring the possibility of overlaying data on employment, health, and school attendance on municipal poverty data and undertaking a pilot project to update the poverty maps using more recent data on incomes (see Kotzeva 2006). The eventual development of income-based poverty maps will constitute a new strand of small area estimation applications. It appears that the production of poverty maps through small area estimates has always relied on consumption as the welfare measure. As awareness grows about the appropriate uses of poverty maps in targeting antipoverty actions, it is quite likely that there will be an increase in the demand for updated maps. The methodology through which this will be accomplished has yet to be determined.

The third challenge is related to the fact that the municipal poverty maps do not show the specifics of poverty in individual communities. This challenge was clearly articulated by the SIF steering committee in early 2006 after it began shifting to the newly available 2005 poverty maps. The committee decided to stop applying the poverty maps in targeting poor communities, while retaining them as the principal criterion in targeting poor municipalities.

The forth challenge is related to the need for political will to continue producing and applying poverty maps. Political will is essential in sustaining the institutional structures developed to support poverty mapping, supplying financing for this time-consuming and costly process, and providing an appropriate regulatory environment for the application of the maps in policy making, project targeting, and the identification of beneficiary groups.

The poverty mapping process and its contribution to long-term sustainability

Poverty mapping was carried out in two stages in Bulgaria: first, the provision of technical assistance for capacity building in the small area estimation methodology and the application of poverty maps and, second, the field-testing of the methodology by Bulgarian experts.

The main function of the first poverty mapping exercise was to expose experts and policy makers to the analysis of the spatial distribution of poverty. This was done by demonstrating that sample household survey data may be combined with broader census data to yield estimates on the value of poverty indicators for the population covered by the census.

At this first stage, the poverty map was developed on the initiative of the World Bank by an international consultant because the small area estimation methodology was unknown in the country. The consultant, who was hosted by the NSI, did the data processing there and provided hands-on training to key NSI staff. In December 2002, the consultant conducted a training session for MLSP and NSI experts on the main methodological aspects of the development and use of poverty maps, as well as the strengths and disadvantages of the methodology. However, the involvement of national experts in the process was still limited, and no systematic, larger-scale effort was made to build up local capacity outside the NSI. Moreover, the 2003 poverty and inequality maps were never the focus of additional analysis. The consultant recommended verifying the municipal rankings that were an outcome of the exercise against other available empirical evidence, field visits, qualitative surveys, and the perceptions of outside specialists. Nonetheless, a systematic attempt to link the poverty maps with other spatial data was far beyond the scope of the funding grant. Despite its narrow use in policy design and implementation, the first poverty maps represented a positive step in the analysis of the spatial distribution of poverty.

In 2004–05, Bulgarian experts applied the small area estimation methodology to develop a new set of poverty maps. This effort was driven by the demand of the MLSP and the SIF for maps updated through more recent MTHS data and the emerging capacity among these institutions and the mapping team for which the IDF grant had provided technical assistance and learning opportunities. The success of the second poverty mapping exercise was due in large part to the composition of the team (an econometrician, two statisticians, a geographic information system specialist, and two social policy experts) and the team management. Mariana Kotzeva, a statistician and econometrician, provided leadership on the technical aspects, while Valeri Apostolov, a deputy minister at the MLSP, was responsible for policy guidance. Relative to the first stage, the second poverty mapping exercise was more participatory in that the methodological steps were discussed within the data users group, and key research choices were made based on consensus.

Key factors of success

The key factors in the success of the process are described below:

- The collaborative interagency approach through a multiagency team of experts with an appropriate mix of expertise was effective.
- The high level of involvement of direct and potential users at all stages of map design, preparation, analysis, and application to decision making was positive. The diversity in the backgrounds of the data producers, researchers, and users on the team ensured a clear division of tasks and the efficient allocation of human resources in response to the various needs to be filled by the maps.
- The involvement of the NSI in the poverty mapping exercise helped ensure full, timely access to the data of the 2001 census. Experience with poverty mapping has shown that many governments are reluctant to release household data and other census data to outside experts because of legitimate confidentiality concerns (see Henninger and Snel 2002). However, since the work was done cooperatively, the sharing of household-level census data for research purposes was facilitated.
- The support of senior officials has been crucial to the success of the poverty mapping exercise. Key was the role of the deputy minister of labor and social policy who oversaw the implementation of the IDF grant and was charged with responsibility for the quality and relevance of the outcomes. The deputy minister's decision-making power was instrumental in including the poverty maps in the array of SIF project-targeting instruments, as well as in the timely provision of counterpart funds for all activities not eligible for funding through the grant. The minister of labor and social policy played a major role in soliciting high-level political support for the use of the poverty maps in policy making. The minister was the one who initiated face-to-face meetings with mayors and targeted poverty reduction policies on the poorest municipalities even before the official launch of the maps. The minister extended the terms of reference of the second poverty mapping team so that the team would be able to try to

overlay other available municipal socioeconomic data on the poverty mapping data and perform cluster analysis. The support of the minister and deputy minister, along with the support of the president of the NSI in data collection, data processing, and data sharing, resulted in the provision of substantial cofinancing for the data collection and mapping work; the allocation of staff time; and the conclusion of protocols on data ownership, sharing, and distribution.

- The flexibility to adapt to local circumstances without compromising the methodology was important. For example, due to the limited popularity of the SAS software in Bulgaria and the high license and maintenance fees associated with SAS, the custom World Bank poverty mapping software in SAS was replaced by a new mapping software in SPSS developed by one of the team members, a senior expert at the NSI, and adapted to local conditions and areas of application. The software runs on the most commonly available computers in Bulgaria, requires little hard drive memory, and has easy-to-use import and export functions.
- The high quality of the input data in the MTHS and the census and the quality and availability of additional data used in modeling heteroskedasticity in the consumption model appear to have been important factors facilitating the poverty mapping exercise.

More might have been done to engage a larger number of stakeholders in the poverty mapping exercise, such as ministries, government agencies, district and municipal authorities, academics, and the media. More might have been done to explain the methodology, which seems sophisticated to the mayors and municipal officers who must manage the application for SIF social infrastructure grants. More people might have been trained to sustain mapping capacity given the generally high turnover rates among qualified staff in public service.

Summary of the Lessons Learned

Poverty mapping has only a brief history in Bulgaria, but the experience accumulated so far has generated important lessons that might be useful for other countries undertaking similar mapping exercises. The lessons may be summarized as follows:

Lessons concerning the production of poverty maps

- Close cooperation among map producers, users, and the principal stakeholders from the outset enhances the results of the poverty mapping.
- A collaborative interagency approach supported by senior officials greatly facilitates map production and use.
- Early assessments of poverty mapping needs helps identify properly the resources required (technical, human, financial) and aids in effective planning for map production, distribution, and application.

- Ensuring access to data from household surveys and censuses through the close involvement of national statistics departments in the poverty mapping exercise is critical for the final success and accuracy of the poverty estimates.

Lessons concerning the impact and uses of poverty maps

- The Bulgarian experience has confirmed that poverty maps are powerful tools for the presentation of information to nonspecialists and for the easy location of pockets of poverty that need appropriate policy action. In addition, poverty maps are being used in targeting resources and interventions aimed at reducing poverty.
- The active distribution strategy and widespread access to district and municipal poverty estimates and poverty maps have facilitated the broader use of the maps and ensured greater demand for poverty information and more accountable policy making.
- Because of decentralization in social sector initiatives to the local level, the distribution of maps and the provision of welfare information to local authorities and communities may be useful in local empowerment and policy making.
- Poverty mapping has contributed to strengthening institutions in the country. In addition to the improvement of the technical skills of experts participating in the mapping exercise, the poverty maps have led to the recognition by institutions, mainly the MLSP and the NSI, of the need for better coordination, especially in conducting household surveys and in census design.

Lessons concerning the sustainability of poverty maps

- It is essential to view poverty mapping as critical to long-term capacity development and institutional strengthening.
- The creation of a group of Bulgarian experts capable of implementing the latest poverty mapping methodology and working with policy makers is a prerequisite for the long-term sustainability of poverty mapping.
- Poverty mapping represents not only a technical effort, but also a political effort. To ensure that poverty mapping will be sustained, it is necessary to obtain significant political, institutional, and technical support from the government.

Notes

1. Measured at two-thirds of the median per capita consumption in 1997, poverty fell from 36 percent in 1997 to 12.8 percent in 2001 (World Bank 2002).
2. Henninger and Snel (2002) summarize experiences with the development and use of poverty maps in 14 developing countries.
3. Recipient-executed IDF Grant TF 050333 "Poverty Monitoring, Evaluation, and Policy Design" in the amount of US$338,000, extended to the MLSP on December 13, 2001, and executed jointly with the NSI.
4. IDF grants are used to finance the building of capacity in the implementation of Living Standards Measurement Surveys and MTHSs. In this particular case in Bulgaria, the experience of carrying out a nationally representative household survey and constructing the poverty maps was part of the learning and capacity-building process. There was no certainty beforehand that the

quality of the poverty data collected would be sufficient for poverty analysis. However, after a follow-up (control) survey was conducted by BBSS Gallup International in 15 percent of the household sample that was randomly selected, the quality of the field data collection was found to be satisfactory. In a similar way, when Bank experts examined the steps taken by the local experts during the production of the consumption aggregates, they found the work up to standard. Only after applying these safeguards did the IDF team decide to proceed with data analysis, including the application of the small area estimation methodology.

5. The 2003 MTHS provided comprehensive information on a broad range of dimensions of living standards and their determinants or correlates. The survey questionnaire comprised 10 separate modules: data on the household and its members; housing characteristics, furnishings, and durables; employment status, unemployment, and work-related income; agricultural activity; household income; loans, credits, taxes, and transfers; household consumption; education; health status and health care; and subjective indicators.

6. The European Commission estimates that the level of undeclared employment and income in Bulgaria represents 22–30 percent of gross domestic product. This is considerably higher than the corresponding share in the EU 15, which ranges between 1.5 and 6.5 percent (except for Greece and Italy, where the informal sector is larger). This is also higher relative to the new EU members, where the share of undeclared employment is in the range of 8–10 percent in the Czech Republic and Estonia and up to 18–19 percent in Hungary, Latvia, and Lithuania.

7. Comparability issues related to the 2001 and the 2003 consumption aggregates are addressed in Teşliuc (2005) and NSI (2006).

8. The reported results were based on the estimates that use the higher poverty line of Lev 61.5.

9. The original OECD equivalence scale was used instead of the per capita measurement. The 2005 poverty mapping team argued that the OECD scale is more accurate in countries, such as Bulgaria, where food expenditure occupies a large part of total household expenditures. The scale assigns a value of 1 to the first adult, 0.7 to each additional adult, and 0.5 to each child under 15.

10. The stages in the mapping exercise are discussed in detail in the report prepared by the international consultant after the completion of the first exercise. See Ivaschenko (2004).

11. The municipal-level analysis excluded the municipalities of Boynitsa and Sofia because the values registered there are too extreme: 1.8 percent in Sofia and 53.8 percent in Boynitsa.

12. The poorest municipalities are Belitsa, Boynitsa, Dospat, Kaynardja, Kotel, Nikola Kozlevo, Makresh, Omurtag, Opaka, Rakitovo, Satovcha, Vurbitsa, and Yakoruda. The 13 poorest municipalities were the subject of a more detailed analysis aimed at determining the specificity of the poverty profiles and the design of municipal-level targeted antipoverty interventions. More details on the poverty profiles are contained in the following sections, where the follow-up research and the use of poverty maps for the purposes of policy development are discussed.

13. For example, in the municipalities of Makresh and Boynitsa, the share of households without a supply of water is as high as 80 percent, and 84 percent and 99 percent of the households, respectively, do not have indoor toilet facilities. Both municipalities collect only a negligible amount of their own revenues.

14. The municipality of Satovcha is an exception. For the past two years, it has had an unemployment rate close to the average for the country.

15. All demographic data are taken from the 2001 census.

16. Participation in these projects has helped municipalities reduce income differences by giving poor and socially disadvantaged people opportunities to receive incomes. In addition, the situation in poor communities and municipalities with limited growth potential is improving.

17. On four occasions following the onset of the IDF grant, the MLSP undertook a competitive process for the selection of candidates for the position of director of the Social Analysis, Prognosis, and Policy Directorate, including through professional search agencies. However, the MLSP leadership was not satisfied with the performance of the various appointees and released each of them after the six-month trial period. This had a negative impact on the overall reputation of the directorate and, hence, on staff turnover and the quality of the retained staff.

18. BBSS Gallup International performed the data collection for the 2001 BIHS and was well positioned to oversee and comment on the data collection by the NSI in 2003.

19. Within the framework of the IDF grant, several training workshops were conducted in March and October 2004 at which experts from various line ministries were introduced to the poverty mapping methodology. Individual team members attended flagship courses on poverty analysis in Hungary and on labor market analysis in the United States.

References

Baker, Judy L., and Margaret E. Grosh. 1994. "Measuring the Effects of Geographic Targeting on Poverty Reduction." Living Standards Measurement Study Working Paper 99, World Bank, Washington, DC.

Bigman, David, and Hippolyte Fofack. 2000. "Geographical Targeting for Poverty Alleviation: An Introduction to the Special Issue." *World Bank Economic Review* 14 (1): 129–45.

Chengelova, Emilia. 2006. "Using Poverty Maps for Social Policy Development and Targeting of Resource Allocation in Bulgaria." Background paper, World Bank, Washington, DC.

Datt, Gaurav, and Martin Ravallion. 1993. "Regional Disparities, Targeting, and Poverty in India." In *Including the Poor: Proceedings of a Symposium Organized by the World Bank and the International Food Policy Research Institute,* ed. Michael Lipton and Jacques van der Gaag, 91–114. World Bank Regional and Sectoral Studies. Washington, DC: World Bank.

Davis, Benjamin. 2003. "Choosing a Method for Poverty Mapping." Monograph, Food and Agriculture Organization of the United Nations, Rome.

Demombynes, Gabriel M., Chris Elbers, Jean O. Lanjouw, Peter F. Lanjouw, Johan A. Mistiaen, and Berk Özler. 2002. "Producing a Better Geographic Profile of Poverty: Methodology and Evidence from Three Developing Countries." WIDER Discussion Paper 2002–39, United Nations University–World Institute for Development Economics Research, Helsinki.

Elbers, Chris, Jean O. Lanjouw, and Peter F. Lanjouw. 2002. "Micro-Level Estimation of Welfare." Policy Research Working Paper 2911, World Bank, Washington, DC.

Eur-Lex. 2003. "Regulation CE No 1177/2003 of the European Parliament and of the Council of 16 June 2003 Concerning Community Statistics on Income and Living Conditions (EU-SILC)." Official Journal of the European Union L 165/1 (3.7.2003), Eur-Lex, Office for Official Publications of the European Communities, Luxembourg. http://eur-lex.europa.eu/.

Henninger, Norbert. 1998. "Mapping and Geographic Analysis of Human Welfare and Poverty-Review Assessment." Monograph, World Resources Institute, Washington, DC.

Henninger, Norbert, and Mathilde Snel. 2002. *Where Are the Poor?: Experiences with the Development and Use of Poverty Maps.* Washington DC: World Resources Institute; Arendal, Norway: United Nations Environment Programme–Global Resource Information Database.

Ivaschenko, Oleksyi. 2004. "Poverty and Inequality Mapping in Bulgaria: Final Report." Unpublished report, World Bank, Washington, DC.

Kotzeva, Mariana. 2006. "Development and Use of Poverty Maps in Bulgaria." Background paper, World Bank, Washington, DC.

Kotzeva, Mariana, and Alexander Tzvetkov. 2006. "Regional Dimensions of Poverty." In *Bulgaria: The Challenges of Poverty,* 86–104. Sofia: National Statistical Institute.

NSI. 2006. *Bulgaria: The Challenges of Poverty.* Sofia: National Statistical Institute.

Teşliuc, Cornelia M. 2005. "Poverty Trends in Bulgaria, 2001–03." Background paper, World Bank, Washington, DC.

UNDP. 2001. *National Human Development Report 2001, Bulgaria: Citizen Participation in Governance, from Individuals to Citizens.* Sofia: United Nations Development Programme.

World Bank. 2000. *World Development Report 2000/2001: Attacking Poverty.* Washington, DC: World Bank; New York: Oxford University Press.

———. 2002. *Bulgaria: Poverty Assessment.* Report 24516. Washington, DC: Human Development Sector Unit, Europe and Central Asia Region, World Bank.

———. 2006. *Country Partnership Strategy for the Republic of Bulgaria for the Period FY07–FY09.* Report 36146-BG. Washington, DC: World Bank and International Finance Corporation.

6

To Use or Not to Use?
Poverty Mapping in Cambodia

TOMOKI FUJII

ACRONYMS AND ABBREVIATIONS

CSES	Cambodia Socio-Economic Survey
NPRS	National Poverty Reduction Strategy (Poverty Reduction Strategy Paper)
WFP	World Food Programme

Poverty maps have become popular among researchers and policy makers in many regions over the last few years, including Southeast Asia, where Cambodia has been a leader in this trend. Cambodia was the first country in Asia to produce poverty maps based on the small area estimation methodology developed by Elbers, Lanjouw, and Lanjouw (2002, 2003), which is now the standard method for poverty mapping.[1]

This chapter describes poverty mapping in Cambodia and the lessons that have been learned there and are potentially applicable to other countries. In particular, the chapter provides a detailed account of the contributions poverty maps have made to policy making and the challenges involved. The discussion is based on the author's own experience, as well as on extensive interviews with key stakeholders.

The chapter is organized as follows. The next two sections examine poverty mapping and other initiatives involved in efforts to reduce poverty in Cambodia. The two subsequent sections describe the ground-truthing and nutrition mapping projects that were undertaken to add value to the poverty mapping exercise. The section thereafter

The author would like to thank the two local consultants, Din Virak and Prom Tola, who conducted the interviews in Cambodia. Without their efforts, this chapter would not have been possible. He also thanks all the interviewees who took time to answer the questions. Tara Bedi gave useful suggestions for this chapter, and Sophal Chan also helped form the ideas.

summarizes the interviews conducted with stakeholders. The following sections analyze the information gathered through the interviews with regard to the general awareness about and the use of the maps, map accuracy, the distribution of the maps, capacity
building in mapping, and other challenges. The final section outlines the lessons learned
during the mapping exercise.

Poverty Mapping in Cambodia

Poverty maps were produced in Cambodia in 2002 as a result of a collaborative effort
of the Ministry of Planning of Cambodia, the World Food Programme (WFP), and
the World Bank. Comments and inputs were solicited from the Ministry of Education,
the Ministry of Health, the National Institute of Statistics, the U.S. Agency for International Development, the European Commission, the Asian Development Bank, the
International Fund for Agricultural Development, the United Nations Children's
Fund, the United Nations Development Programme, the United Nations Educational,
Scientific, and Cultural Organization, the United Nations Population Fund, and the
World Health Organization. The initial stage of the work was completed in August
2002, and the finished maps were distributed in Phnom Penh that same month. The
Ministry of Planning and the WFP then published a report describing the details of the
poverty mapping exercise (Ministry of Planning and WFP 2002), and the WFP conducted several regional workshops to disseminate the results of the exercise. Related
research on the applications of poverty mapping to education in Cambodia has also been
published (Fujii 2006).

The standard method used to construct poverty maps combines a census data set
and a survey data set to produce poverty estimates for small geographical areas
(Elbers, Lanjouw, and Lanjouw 2002, 2003). In Cambodia, the Cambodia Socio-
Economic Survey (CSES) for 1997 and the National Population Census for 1998
were used, and poverty estimates were produced for 1,594 communes (after villages,
the smallest government administrative units). The average commune contained approximately 1,300 households.

The primary objective of the poverty mapping exercise in Cambodia was, from the
outset, to develop a tool for policy making and, especially, for the allocation of resources.
That the poverty mapping exercise was more policy oriented probably stems from the
way the exercise began. The exercise started as a refinement of a similar exercise conducted by the Ministry of Planning and the WFP prior to 2002 (see Ministry of Planning and WFP 2002). Before 2000, the WFP produced poverty maps on Cambodia
based on unsatisfied basic needs. For those maps, key indicator variables were weighted
in an ad hoc manner to form one index. Then, in 2001, the Ministry of Planning and
the WFP produced a preliminary version of the next stage of poverty maps by combining a census data set and a survey data set (see Ministry of Planning, WFP, and UNDP
2001). However, unlike the standard method, the method used at that time did not generate the standard errors associated with each poverty estimate. Moreover, the results

were not consistent with the survey observations because the small area estimates of poverty were quite different from the estimates at the level at which the survey was representative, the stratum level.

While the results reported in Ministry of Planning and WFP (2002) have a much more solid theoretical underpinning than the maps produced earlier, they are by no means perfect. Poverty maps may not reflect the current poverty situation correctly for a number of reasons. They only give a snapshot of the poverty situation; that is, poverty maps show the poverty situation during the census year only. Hence, poverty maps do not account for changes that may have taken place after the census year. Given the fact that, when the poverty mapping exercise was completed, four years had already passed since the census year, it is reasonable to expect that there are at least some discrepancies between the poverty maps and the current poverty situation.[2]

Moreover, as reported in Ministry of Planning and WFP (2002), there were a few other well-known data problems. First, the sampling frame used in the survey did not cover the entire country; parts of the country had not been accessible because of security concerns at the time of the survey. Second, for a similar reason, parts of the country had not been covered in the census. Third, the poverty line had to be redrawn to maintain consistency with the widely accepted poverty estimates of 36.1 percent reported in Ministry of Planning (1998), even though these estimates had been based on an analysis of the survey data undertaken before data cleaning was carried out. Finally, some households covered in the census had to be removed from consideration so as to be consistent with the survey definition of household. Because these data sets were not designed specifically for the small area estimation method, data issues like these have been inevitable to some extent.

Poverty Reduction

To understand poverty mapping in Cambodia, it is important to understand the policy environment on poverty reduction in the country. In particular, the role that the National Poverty Reduction Strategy (NPRS) has played in increasing the general awareness about poverty mapping has been noteworthy.

Poverty reduction has been one of the major challenges faced by the government. The government has been adopting detailed strategies and plans to battle poverty since 1993. These include the National Programme to Rehabilitate and Develop Cambodia (1994), the first and second Five-Year Socio-Economic Development Plan (1996–2001 and 2001–05), and the Royal Government Platform for the Second Term (1998–2003). In December 2002, the Council for Social Development published the NPRS, a key document on poverty reduction covering virtually every aspect of poverty in Cambodia (see Council for Social Development 2002). The NPRS includes one of the poverty maps presented in Ministry of Planning and WFP (2002) in an annex. This map, based on commune-level poverty estimates, is the poverty map that will be referred to throughout the rest of this chapter.

The government and donors have only limited resources available for poverty reduction. It is therefore imperative that they allocate the resources they do have to confront poverty effectively and efficiently. Including the map in the NPRS was part of the plan behind the poverty mapping exercise from the beginning, and the development of the map has also been part of the government's efforts to help the line ministries and donors coordinate their antipoverty activities and identify areas on which to target programs and projects aimed at the poor. While the NPRS did not provide guidance on how the poverty map should be employed, the map has obviously been valuable in certain respects. For example, as noted in the NPRS, the Ministry of Health was going to target service delivery toward the poor, including by reallocating resources in favor of poorer geographical areas. So, the availability of the map may assist the ministry in this antipoverty initiative.

The NPRS recognizes the limitations of the map as well. Thus, the NPRS points out that the estimates of the incidence of poverty in Pailin, a municipality (*krong*) in the northwest near the border with Thailand, may be unrealistically high. Also, the map reflects the poverty situation in 1998 and thus does not indicate changes that have taken place since then in Cambodia. These changes include rapid economic development in some areas and droughts and flooding that have occurred in other areas. The NPRS refers to the ground-truthing exercise, which, at the time, was about to be conducted, as a way to capture these changes. (An account of the ground-truthing exercise is contained in the next section.)

The inclusion of the map in the NPRS seems to have had at least two effects. First, because the NPRS is a key document on poverty reduction, many people involved in the struggle against poverty have had a chance to see the map.[3] While the role that the NPRS has played in Cambodia is not entirely clear, the interviews with stakeholders suggest that numerous people were aware of the map's existence and application potential (see below). The situation would have been very different if the poverty mapping exercise had been oriented more toward research and the map had been excluded from the NPRS.

Second, because the NPRS is an official document of the government, people fighting poverty or, indeed, addressing other socioeconomic development issues in poor areas that are highlighted in the map have found it easier to justify their programs and projects. This result would be unequivocally desirable, at least for the purpose of poverty reduction, if the map were irreproachably accurate. In reality, however, the map is subject to various types of errors, including model errors, idiosyncratic errors, and computational errors, as well as errors stemming from the data issues mentioned above. The interview results suggest that, fortunately, the limitations of poverty maps are reasonably well understood in Cambodia. This may be partly because the NPRS is explicit in pointing out the possible limitations.

Ground Truthing

Two related exercises were carried out in Cambodia after the completion of the poverty map: a ground-truthing exercise and a nutrition mapping exercise (discussed in the next section). The ground-truthing project was undertaken by the Ministry of Planning and the WFP, with financial support from Italian Development Cooperation and the International Fund for Agricultural Development (Ministry of Planning and WFP 2003). The purpose of the exercise was to verify the accuracy of the poverty estimates shown through the map and to determine the areas where people were truly in need.[4] The poverty estimates reflected in the map were compared with a welfare index derived from commune-level and village-level indexes included in the commune database prepared by the Seila Task Force Secretariat (Ministry of Planning and WFP 2003).[5]

The exercise revealed that the poverty estimates of the map may be off the mark in two regions. One region is in the northwestern part of the country and includes the municipality of Pailin. This inconsistency may have arisen because the 1997 CSES did not include this region in its sampling frame. Thus, the consumption model used for the poverty mapping may not have been applicable to the region. (This issue is also raised in Ministry of Planning and WFP 2002.) While the statistical evidence was inconclusive, a test was performed to determine whether the consumption model drawn from the 1997 CSES is generally applicable to the areas excluded from the sampling frame of that CSES. The test involved the application of the same model to these excluded areas, but on the basis of the 1999 CSES data set.[6]

The second region showing inconsistency is in the northeast and includes the provinces of Kratie, Mondulkiri, Rattanakiri, and Stung Treng, where the poverty estimates of the map seem too low. A possible explanation mentioned in Ministry of Planning and WFP (2003) is prices: to calculate the poverty estimates for the map, it was assumed that there is only one price system in rural areas, but prices are actually quite different across rural Cambodia. In the case of these northeastern provinces, analysis of 1997 CSES data suggests that the cost of basic goods is especially high, which inflates the nominal consumption aggregate, even though real consumption and the standard of living are not high. In fact, poverty estimates for these provinces calculated using only the 1997 CSES are low, although the numbers are not representative. The low poverty estimates for these provinces may therefore have arisen from the 1997 CSES data, not from the small area estimation methodology used for the poverty mapping.

The experience of the ground-truthing exercise has confirmed the commonsense lesson that one should not expect to eliminate problems in the original data sets simply because one is using a rather sophisticated technique such as the small area estimation methodology. It is always necessary to examine a data set carefully for inconsistencies. The problem in the sampling frame may have been unique to Cambodia, but the problem with prices will likely be observed in many countries. This is an important lesson. As the use of the small area estimation methodology becomes more widespread in policy making and as more user-friendly software is developed for poverty mapping, individuals with less technical expertise will be able to produce poverty maps, and they may not be sufficiently aware of the need to be wary of data consistency issues.

Nutrition Mapping

The nutrition mapping exercise involved estimating indicators of the nutritional status of children at the commune level. It was carried out as a collaborative effort by the Ministry of Health, the WFP, and the Measure Demographic and Health Surveys Project of Macro International, with financial support from Italian Development Cooperation, the U.S. Agency for International Development, and the International Fund for Agricultural Development. The methodology used in the exercise is similar to the standard poverty mapping methodology. However, instead of a consumption aggregate, anthropometric indicators from a demographic and health survey data set were used for the dependent variable in the regression model that was predicted for each child record in the census. A description of this exercise may be found in Ministry of Health, WFP, and Macro International (2003). The results were later revised by Fujii (2005) to take into account issues specific to anthropometric indicators.

Many people seem to believe that poor nutrition should be synonymous with poverty, but the nutrition mapping exercise did not support this belief. Poverty and poor nutrition among children were not strongly correlated at the commune level. This apparent lack of correlation may be partly due to statistical error. However, it is also important to recognize that there may be fundamental differences between the causes of poverty and the causes of poor nutrition. Poor nutrition status may arise among children because of a lack of adequate caloric intake, which may possibly be linked to poverty, but poor nutrition status may arise also because of a lack of proper childcare or because of exposure to diseases, such as diarrhea or malaria, the incidence of which may not be strongly related to poverty. Nutrition mapping provides a way to identify and elucidate the differences between poverty and child nutritional status in small geographical areas.

The nutrition mapping experience imparted at least three lessons. First, the precise interpretation of anthropometric indicators is complicated and requires careful analysis, but it is important to make every effort to include potentially meaningful indicators. Information on a variety of geographical variables is available in Cambodia. These have helped increase the explanatory power of anthropometric models substantially. Second, an appropriate method must be found to estimate anthropometric indicators accurately (see Fujii 2005). Third, nutrition maps may help people become more aware of the differences between poverty and poor nutrition among children. For example, in our case, one may decide that the lack of correlation between poverty and the poor nutrition found among children in various places has arisen from incorrect estimates. However, the estimates of both poverty and nutrition are consistent with the survey observations. Indeed, poverty appears to be quite heterogeneous across the country, whereas the nutrition indicators are quite homogeneous.

It would be premature to conclude that these lessons are applicable in other countries. Nonetheless, the experience in Cambodia still offers a useful reference point for nutrition mapping elsewhere.

The Interviews with Stakeholders

We have described the context in which poverty mapping and the two related exercises have been conducted. Now, let us examine the extent to which the poverty map has become known among stakeholders, how it is viewed by them, and how they have used it. For this purpose, we have carried out interviews with various stakeholders to plumb their experiences with the map and the related poverty estimates.

The interviews were conducted by two local consultants from late January to mid-March 2006. A list of appropriate organizations was tentatively identified for the interviews. The list was prepared to reflect a variety of perspectives as much as possible; it covered local and national government authorities, bilateral and multilateral aid agencies, research institutions, nongovernmental organizations (NGOs), and others. Of the 75 organizations included on the list, 72 responded.

Most of the interviews were conducted in person, but, in the three instances when this was not possible, the interviews were done by phone or e-mail. The interviews typically lasted 30 to 90 minutes.

The interviews generally took place in Phnom Penh, where the majority of the organizations are based. However, because the provinces may represent a different set of opportunities and challenges, field trips were undertaken to the provinces of Kampong Cham, Kampong Thom, Kandal, Prey Veng, Siem Reap, and Takeo. The views of individuals working in the provinces are particularly important since organizations may use the map for decentralization, devolution, or deconcentration.

Potential questions were identified in advance. These were formulated so as to elicit information about the stakeholders' familiarity with the map, their views on the map's usefulness, including its advantages and disadvantages, and their suggestions for poverty mapping in the future. The questions were meant only as guidelines; the interviews were not supposed to be tightly structured. In some cases, there were follow-up questions to acquire additional information.

The interviewees are not necessarily representative of the development community in Cambodia. Moreover, while poverty reduction is an important issue for most organizations on the interview list, it is not the primary area of interest for some organizations. Likewise, the knowledge and expertise of the interviewees with regard to poverty issues varied substantially, even though they all probably tended to be somewhat familiar with such issues given the nature of the organizations with which they work.

One of the interviewers pointed out that some of the users of the map are certainly international consultants who visit Cambodia only briefly during short-term assignments or missions. These consultants may rely heavily on the map in the design of donor projects or programs, but few international consultants were interviewed because of the obvious constraints on time and opportunity. Meanwhile, local officers and managers for these same donor programs and projects who were interviewed may not realize the significance of the map to their work.

While some summary statistics are reported in the sections that follow, the goal is not to provide summary statistics that represent the development community in Cambodia. Rather, the goal is to capture prevalent views about the impact and usefulness of the map and the related poverty estimates so as to derive practical lessons from the experiences in Cambodia. It would be safe to say that the interviews have been carried out on a sufficiently large scale to accomplish this purpose.

Hearing about and Using the Poverty Map

More than 80 percent of the interviewees said they had seen or heard about the poverty map. Staff at all the major bilateral and multilateral aid agencies were aware of the map. A majority had heard about the map from the WFP, and the rest had heard through the Ministry of Planning or other government sources. Despite the high level of awareness about the map, only about 40 percent of the interviewees had used the map. Of these, most had used the map in decision making and analysis and to advance the credibility of their organizations. Some had used the map in fund-raising and in communication and coordination with other organizations as well. Only a fraction of the interviewees thought that the map was being used widely.

Most of the interviewees who were aware of the map also knew about the ground-truthing exercise. However, only about half of those who were aware of the map knew about the nutrition mapping exercise. This included staff at some international NGOs active in addressing health and nutrition issues. There are at least three possible reasons for the lower awareness about nutrition mapping. First, unlike the poverty map, the nutrition maps were not highlighted in the NPRS. Second, the scale of dissemination of the nutrition maps has been much more limited than that of the poverty map. Third, the nutrition maps were oriented more toward research because the methodology had not been well established.

The poverty map users tended to rely on hard copies. This means that they only saw the colored version of the map, where each color corresponds to a range of poverty rates among the communes. This is rather unfortunate because Ministry of Planning and WFP (2002) included a compact disc containing commune-level poverty estimates in a spreadsheet format.

Having played a central role in the production of the poverty map and the nutrition maps, the WFP has been one of the most prominent users of these maps. The Vulnerability Analysis and Mapping Unit of the WFP developed a number of other maps, including maps of infrastructure, vulnerability to flood and draught, and education, and integrated them into the poverty map and the nutrition maps using a geographic information system.[7] The poverty map, the nutrition maps, and the combined maps, along with field observations, are a fundamental tool of the WFP in the identification of areas for program intervention.

In some cases, the poverty map is used because of the influence of the WFP. A good example is the Ministry of Rural Development. The ministry has been actively cooperating with the WFP in various areas, including rural road building, canal irrigation, and construction. The WFP supports these projects through a food-for-work program. Because the WFP uses the poverty map to screen all project proposals submitted to it by the ministry, the map is an indispensable tool for the ministry. However, this approach is also a source of rigidity in the selection of communes for WFP projects. According to an interviewee from the ministry, many communes identified as poor in 2002, but now relatively better off, remain targets of the food-for-work programs.

The technical departments of the Ministry of Agriculture, Forestry, and Fisheries have used the poverty map and the nutrition maps independently of the WFP in planning and policy making and in advising development agencies on resource targeting among poor districts and communes. For example, the Department of Agricultural Extension of the ministry has used the poverty map as a guide in selecting target areas for agro-ecosystems analysis through the Cambodia-Australia Agricultural Extension Project. The Department of Planning and Statistics of the ministry has used the poverty map and the nutrition maps to target the poorest communes for agricultural productivity improvement and crop diversification. The department implemented the Food Insecurity and Vulnerability Information and Mapping System to synthesize estimates from the poverty map, the nutrition maps, and the ministry's database on annual agricultural statistics. The department has also used the map to develop project proposals for donors.

The map may have been used indirectly in the allocation of resources to poor communes. With assistance from the Department of Local Administration of the Ministry of the Interior and the Seila Task Force, each commune receives commune development funds on the basis of three criteria. First, 30 percent of the budget represents the base allocation to every commune. Second, another 30 percent is allocated only to heavily populated communes. Finally, the remaining 40 percent is earmarked for the poorest communes based on a poverty ranking. While the interviewee from the department did not know how the poverty ranking is determined, the interviews with staff at the Seila Task Force Secretariat suggests that the ranking is based on the annually updated commune profile, which is checked against the map (though the map has been deemed unreliable on some communes; see elsewhere above).

Some bilateral aid agencies use the map. For example, the local program officer of the Swedish International Development Cooperation Agency said during the interviews that the map is used in dialogue with the government. He said that the map gives policy makers a bird's-eye view of the poverty situation.

Some local government authorities use the poverty map. The Provincial Department of Planning and the Provincial Department of Rural Development in Prey Veng Province, for instance, are carrying out a district pilot program for the provincial investment fund. They have used the poverty map, in combination with their own database, to find the poorest districts within the province. This is a good example of the use of the map for decentralization and devolution.

The map has been used outside the government as well. The Fisheries Action Coalition Team is a partnership among 35 local and international NGOs that focuses on environmental issues, particularly the fisheries sector around Tonle Sap Lake. The team has introduced the poverty map to its NGO network to help provide information on poverty issues in the provinces surrounding the lake. The map is used as a main reference for network studies. It is also used to ensure the credibility of team proposals to donors and to complement its own experience.

At the Department of Environmental Science of the Royal University of Phnom Penh, the map has been used as reference text for students. The department has worked on a United Nations Development Programme project on the human development index with a focus on AIDS and migration. The map has been used in discussions with provincial stakeholders on poverty issues related to AIDS and migration. The map is also widely used for educational and research purposes by students and lecturers at the departmental library.

Save Cambodia's Wildlife is running a project called Atlas of Cambodia: National Poverty and Environment Maps with funding from the Danish International Development Agency. The poverty map is covered in one of the main chapters in the atlas (see Save Cambodia's Wildlife 2006).

The Cambodia Daily has used the poverty map as part of the background material for articles on domestic violence and poverty in rural Cambodia.

The Accuracy of the Map

There are three major challenges facing the effort to produce poverty maps in Cambodia. First, whether poverty maps accurately reflect the situation in the country is arguably the most important issue. Second, the distribution of the maps is also important because, if they are not distributed, the maps cannot be used and are wasted. Third, capacity building in mapping is key in a country such as Cambodia, where skilled professionals are at a premium. This section discusses the issue of accuracy; the next two sections examine distribution and capacity building.

A number of organizations have not used the map because they believe it does not reflect the current poverty situation very well. Thus, only 4 of the 11 interviewees who clearly responded on this issue indicated that the map reflects the current poverty situation. Meanwhile, 11 of the 14 interviewees who clearly responded to a similar question indicated that the map accurately reflects the poverty situation as of 1998, the year of the census that formed part of the database for the mapping exercise. Thus, according to these opinions, while the map may have provided reasonable estimates of poverty as of 1998, the estimates may well have already been outdated in 2006, when the interview was conducted.

Several interviewees said that the government has put considerable effort into infrastructure development. As a result, some communes have moved out of poverty thanks to better integration with markets. Other communes that have traditionally relied on natural resource exploitation have been negatively affected by declines in the natural resource base. A national planning advisor at the Seila Task Force Secretariat said that

Kratie Province used to be more populated because of the province's abundant forest resources, but that people have been leaving to seek better jobs along the border with Thailand and in Phnom Penh and Sihanoukville.

Many of the interviewees thought the map is inaccurate on Siem Reap Province and the northeast. In Siem Reap, the area around the town of Siem Reap has developed substantially since 1998 as a result of a rapid expansion in tourism. While the map indicates that Siem Reap is one of the poorest provinces, it seems not generally to be so considered any longer. Indeed, while the Ministry of Rural Development and the WFP have allocated more resources for Siem Reap Province, it has become more difficult to identify poor communes suitable for a food-for-work program there. This is because the local people tend to prefer to migrate to the town of Siem Reap, where they may earn more.

Nonetheless, government officials in Siem Reap do not seem to consider the province to be well off. For example, the deputy director of the Provincial Department of Planning in the province, who uses the map to plan community development initiatives, says that Siem Reap is poor in every way. Another government official in Siem Reap made similar remarks.

When the author visited the province in 2003, he observed rapid development in the town of Siem Reap. However, he also observed a number of poor areas in rural Siem Reap, many of them hard to reach. While there is no doubt that the map has not captured the rapid expansion in tourism that has significantly contributed to growth in the province, poor areas still seem to exist there. Indeed, according to a preliminary analysis of the CSES 2003–04, the poverty rate in Siem Reap was 51.8 percent then, while the national average was 35.1 percent.

In provinces in the northeast such as Kratie, Mondulkiri, Rattanakiri, and Stung Treng, the poverty estimates illustrated in the map are often considered too low. For example, an interviewee from the Wildlife Conservation Society said that the estimates on Mondulkiri and Ratatnakiri do not reflect the experience of the society and other NGOs, which suggest that the poverty rates in those provinces must be significantly higher. During field visits in 2003, the author observed relatively poor living conditions in these two provinces. Some people find that the map is also inconsistent with the NPRS, which treats Mondulkiri and Rattanakiri as poor areas.

Preliminary analysis of the CSES 2003–04 shows that poverty in these provinces is high. While the survey is not representative at the level of provinces, the region that includes the provinces of Kratie, Mondulkiri, Oddar Meanchey, Pailin, Preah Vihear, Rattanakiri, and Stung Treng has a poverty rate of 46.1 percent according to the analysis. While the exact reason the map shows low poverty rates in the northeast is unclear, plausible reasons are provided in Ministry of Planning and WFP (2003). One possibility is the problem with the assumption that there is only one price system in rural Cambodia (see elsewhere above). In any case, it is obviously important to make efforts to increase accuracy so as to improve the ability of poverty mapping to reassure policy makers and respond to their need for accurate pictures of poverty.

Map Distribution

The poverty map has been distributed through formal and informal channels. Informally, the map has been distributed through the personal networks of the staff at the WFP's Vulnerability Analysis and Mapping Unit. Formally, distribution has been conducted by the WFP, in collaboration with the National Institute of Statistics, through ad hoc regional and national workshops. The national workshop took place in Phnom Penh in April 2003; key stakeholders, including the line ministries, NGOs, and bilateral and multilateral development agencies, were invited. To make sure that the poverty map and nutrition maps reach a wider audience, regional workshops have been conducted by the WFP in several provinces, including Kampot, Kampong Cham, Prey Veng, and Siem Reap. Representatives of NGOs, commune councils, district officials, and provincial departments from the host provinces were invited to attend the regional workshops, but only representatives from provincial departments were invited from the neighboring provinces.

Despite these efforts, many of the people who were interviewed had never seen or heard about the poverty map, especially in the provinces, and some organizations in the provinces were aware of the existence of the map, but had not received copies. Only a small fraction of the interviewees thought the map had been distributed appropriately. This is somewhat surprising given that the overwhelming majority of the interviewees knew about the map. Still, because of the relatively limited use of poverty maps, distribution should be improved.

Organizations that do not know about or have not received the map tend to use alternative data sources to select project areas. These sources include their own field surveys, the rural transport infrastructure plan prepared by the International Labour Organization, and the Seila commune database of the Seila Task Force Secretariat. Interviewees from all these organizations thought the map might be useful in its own right and as a complement to these other data sources and would consider using it if it is made available.

Distribution would be facilitated if people in the provinces were able simply to go online and download the map and other relevant documentation. However, there appears to be no Web site for the map in Khmer.[8] Creating a Khmer Web site would be an obvious way to enhance the distribution of the map. Yet, this would probably not be sufficient because many organizations in the provinces do not have the technical capacity to use the map digitally even if they are able to download it from the Internet. Hence, making soft and hard copies of the map readily available to potential users in the provinces is reasonable.

It may not be practical for the Ministry of Planning and the WFP to distribute the map in every province and certainly not in every district or commune. It may be possible, however, to distribute the map by passing it along down the governmental or organizational hierarchy. For example, the Ministry of Planning and the WFP might be responsible for transferring the map and the related data from the national level to the regional level. The regions might then distribute the material among the provinces in a decentralized manner. The process would continue to the districts and communes. Thus, a technical expert at each Provincial Department of Planning might be made responsible for passing the poverty mapping material on from the regional center to district chiefs. A Khmer Web site would be useful as a supporting tool in this pass-it-on process by allowing people downstream to deepen their understanding and find responses to any questions they may have. The producers of poverty maps might also benefit from such a loop because feedback from the provinces and other administrative levels would help them evaluate and fine-tune the maps.

The comments of the governor of the district of Bantheay in Kampong Cham Province are indicative. He had heard about the poverty map for the first time on television. When the map was shown to him during the interview, he said it represented the poverty situation in his district accurately. There was already a five-year development plan for the district, but he thought the map might form a basis for discussion and analysis to draft such plans in the future.

As an interviewee from the Cambodia Development Resource Institute suggests, a formal distribution system might be worthwhile. Regular announcements about new products might be made through such a system, which would include links to relevant development agencies.

A senior advisor at the Agri-Business Institute of Cambodia said that the map and similar publications are generally sent to the head of relevant units and that they are often not circulated or used, whereas technical experts, such as poverty specialists, who would be able to use them never obtain access. He also pointed out that the lack of a library system in Cambodia is a constraint on access by potential users of maps and other documents.

Capacity Building

Without capacity building, a poverty map will, at best, be like a picture on a wall: nice to look at, but not otherwise useful. For this reason, three staff members at the National Institute of Statistics and the Ministry of Planning underwent three training sessions in Phnom Penh while the poverty map was being produced. Otherwise, however, capacity building was not a major focus of the mapping exercise, and the interviews suggest that this was a shortcoming.

The deputy director general of the General Directorate of Planning of the Ministry of Planning felt that the lack of wider participation in map production was a failing. She said that three persons participating in three training sessions does not foster a transfer of technology. She thinks that the next round of poverty maps should be created with the involvement of Ministry of Planning staff so as to transfer technology and build the capacity of the ministry.

For the effective application of poverty maps, two types of capacity building are required. The first type is capacity building among individual users. The interviews highlighted that individuals who are not skilled in working with geographic information systems or statistics are often reluctant to use poverty maps. They have difficulty accessing the map estimates. Likewise, people with only limited research skills often use only hard copies of poverty maps. As a result, standard errors associated with point estimates, for example, tend to be ignored. Clearly, an effort must be made to build capacities so that map users may become familiar with the map production process, the applications of the maps, and the potential pitfalls. If knowledge about geographic information systems and statistics is imparted, this would also help significantly.

The interviewee from the Cambodia Development Resource Institute said that the value of the poverty map depends on the capacity of users. The institute, for example, has been able to use the map, in conjunction with the Seila commune database, to identify poor areas during the participatory poverty assessment around Tonle Sap Lake. However, the interviewee pointed out that those who are not familiar with a geographic information system have had difficulty gaining access to the poverty estimates.

The second type of capacity building required for the effective application of poverty maps is organizational. The deputy director of the Provincial Department of Planning of Kampong Thom Province said that his organization had never used the map even though the map had been transmitted to the department by the Ministry of Planning and even though he thought the map would be useful for strategy development and planning. The department had not used the map because it has limited resources and capacity. Instead, the department had been using a diagram sent by the Ministry of Planning.

Staff at the Seila Task Force Secretariat pointed out that no instructions accompany the map. The lack of technical guidelines and a supporting mechanism for implementation such as regulations and standards may represent an obstacle. The staff members also pointed out that training is conducted only on an ad hoc basis by donor organizations and that this is inadequate.

The director of Srer Khmer, an independent nonprofit organization dedicated to the development of farmer-led environmentally sound agriculture, said that, while training is not really necessary for users with a background in statistics, mathematics, or economics, a regular two-day workshop should be held to show other users how to use the maps through application exercises. At the national level, the workshop might be held among trainers by the map production team. The trainers might, in turn, conduct local courses. This echoes the distribution scheme discussed elsewhere above.

The director of the office of the Canadian International Development Agency in Cambodia and a poverty consultant for the Asian Development Bank said that the map may seem quite technical to some. A short descriptive text written in simple language might be helpful for many potential users. Such a summary should be published both in Khmer and in English and be made available on the Web. Research and additional accumulation of experience would be essential in determining the contents of such a publication.

Other Challenges

Several other challenges noted by the interviewees include the updating of the maps, the fact that the map does not enlighten on the root causes of poverty, the integration of databases, and the outlook of donors. All these points are relevant for future poverty mapping.

The methodology for updating poverty maps is an ongoing research topic, and it may be some time before an updating process is fully integrated into the poverty mapping exercise. Many of the interviewees thought that the poverty map should be updated at least once every three years and possibly every year if budgets permit.

Some interviewees were dissatisfied because the map did not directly elucidate the root causes of poverty, that is, the map only supplies a numeric measure of poverty for each commune, but it does not point the way to reasons for the poverty in the commune. Obviously, poverty maps are not designed to describe the causes of poverty. However, to fill this need for more enlightenment, users might be provided with a map showing several different indicators, including potential causes or covariates of poverty, overlaid on the poverty map. The interviewees suggested the inclusion of information on natural resources, landlessness, ethnicity, gender, flood, and drought. The WFP has produced a number of such overlays using geographically referenced data sets, including data on educational attainment, flooding, drought, agricultural productivity, and nutrition. However, these overlays have been circulated even less widely than the map.

Some interviewees from research-oriented organizations said that the integration of various different sorts of data in one database would greatly benefit analysts. Besides the Seila commune database (see elsewhere above), the CamInfo database system also provides helpful indicators for decision making. CamInfo has been created by the National Institute of Statistics, with support from the German Agency for Technical Cooperation and the United Nations Children's Fund. It allows users to access indicators organized by sector, goal, theme, and other monitoring frameworks.

Several interviewees mentioned the outlook of donors. For example, the director of the Provincial Department of Rural Development in Kampong Thom Province says that donors do not like to work in the district of Sandan, which is remote and has bad roads. Poverty maps do not directly relate to or change the attitude of donors. If the maps are widely known and used, it would be difficult for donors arbitrarily to choose to work in relatively more well off areas. On the other hand, if they are used in a rigid manner, then areas that have moved out of poverty since the census year will continue to receive assistance, while areas that have become poor will not receive the needed assistance. This point is particularly important in a country such as Cambodia, where poverty is transient in many ways, that is, people who are not poor one year may easily fall into poverty if they are affected by a natural disaster such as drought or flooding. Hence, serious efforts should be made among donors to share the most recent information on poverty to help tackle poverty issues in a more efficient and timely manner.

Lessons Learned

The poverty map is generally well known among organizations dealing with poverty in Cambodia, especially organizations in Phnom Penh, and the map's potential usefulness is also recognized. At least partly, this is because the mapping exercise has been oriented toward policy making from the beginning, and the map has been included in the NPRS, a key document on poverty reduction. It is also encouraging that the potential pitfalls of the map are understood. Projects related to poverty mapping, especially the ground-truthing exercise, but also the nutrition mapping exercise, have also attracted the interest of researchers and policy makers.

While application of the map has been limited relative to the level of awareness about the map, organizations have used the map in a number of different ways. Most users have relied on the map in decision making and analysis and to enhance their expertise and credibility. Other uses have included fund-raising, dialogue among organizations addressing poverty, education, and the publication of newspaper articles and atlases. These applications are also relevant in other countries.

Stakeholder interviews suggest that there are three major challenges that inhibit the use of poverty maps in Cambodia. First, the accuracy of the map has been questioned, particularly with regard to Siem Reap Province and the northeastern region. Many interviewees thought that the poverty estimates are out of date. Hence, updating the poverty map or creating a new map is necessary to ensure the relevance of poverty maps in policy making. A more well-coordinated data collection and monitoring scheme would also be beneficial for donors and beneficiaries.

Second, despite the dissemination efforts of the Ministry of Planning and the WFP, too many staff in organizations remain unaware of the existence of the map. This is especially noticeable in the provinces. In some cases, people know about the map, but have not received copies. A pass-it-on scheme to distribute the map down governmental or organizational hierarchies might be more efficient. Embedding the distribution process within a wider development context such as regional development plans would also help. The more active involvement of stakeholders in dissemination in Phnom Penh and in the provinces would be desirable.

Third, capacity building among users both at the individual level and at the organizational level is also essential. It is important for the producer of the poverty maps to accommodate the lack of capacity among users. The previous poverty mapping exercise was not sustainable because the training provided for staff at the Ministry of Planning and the National Institute of Statistics was not sufficient. As a result, these organizations do not have the capacity to carry out the poverty mapping exercise on their own. Moreover, no technical guidelines or supporting mechanism have been supplied for the map. These points should be addressed in the next round of the poverty mapping exercise.

Cambodia has a great opportunity to strengthen the link between poverty mapping and development planning. A new round of household survey and census is planned for 2008. By embedding the poverty mapping exercise in the overall planning process, Cambodia would be able to produce an updated poverty map as early as 2009. The timely production of an updated poverty map would help policy makers formulate plans and policies, including the new National Strategic Development Plan for 2011–15. The new poverty map would provide a solid foundation for geographical targeting over the following five years.

Notes

1. Minot (2000) produced a poverty map in Vietnam using a similar, but distinct methodology.
2. Poverty mapping was not a part of the plan when the census and the survey were conducted. There was a four-year gap between the census and the completion of the poverty mapping exercise because the poverty mapping technology was not yet readily accessible.
3. While the assessment of the overall impact of the NPRS is beyond the scope of this chapter, one should note that the NPRS seems to have had limited impact on the implementation of development plans. For this reason, the fact that many people are aware of the poverty maps through the NPRS may not automatically translate into a tangible impact on development planning. For an assessment of the NPRS, see IDA and IMF (2003).
4. Ground-truthing is carried out in the field by experts who measure and observe features, objects, or phenomena on or in the ground within a determined area. The information thus gathered is used to confirm, calibrate, interpret, or analyze an image, map, or other remotely acquired or manipulated collection of data. Thus, for example, ground-truth information might be gathered by social scientists seeking to understand the socioeconomic forces behind modifications in land cover or water quality that have been detected through remote sensing. In our case, ground-truthing involves checking the accuracy of the poverty map against other observations considered reliable.
5. The activities carried out through the Seila program, which came to a close in December 2006, are now under the mandate of the National Committee for the Management of Decentralization and Deconcentration Reform.
6. The 1999 CSES was not used for the poverty mapping exercise because the 1997 CSES was believed to be of better quality (see Ministry of Planning and WFP 2002).
7. See http://vam.wfp.org/country/docs?country=116; http://www.methodfinder.com/wfpatlas/.
8. The poverty map and other, related maps on Cambodia may be downloaded from the Global Distribution of Poverty Web site of the Center for International Earth Science Information Network, Columbia University, at http://www.ciesin.columbia.edu/povmap/.

References

Council for Social Development. 2002. *National Poverty Reduction Strategy, 2003–2005.* Phnom Penh: Council for Social Development, Royal Government of Cambodia.

Elbers, Chris, Jean O. Lanjouw, and Peter F. Lanjouw. 2002. "Micro-Level Estimation of Welfare." Policy Research Working Paper 2911, World Bank, Washington, DC.

———. 2003. "Micro-Level Estimation of Poverty and Inequality." *Econometrica* 71 (1): 355–64.

Fujii, Tomoki. 2005. "Micro-Level Estimation of Child Malnutrition Indicators and Its Application in Cambodia." Policy Research Working Paper 3662, World Bank, Washington, DC.

———. 2006. "Commune-Level Estimation of Poverty Measures and Its Application in Cambodia." In *Spatial Disparities in Human Development: Perspectives from Asia,* ed. Ravi Kanbur, Anthony J. Venables, and Guanghua Wan, 289–314. Tokyo: United Nations University Press.

IDA (International Development Association) and IMF (International Monetary Fund). 2003. "Cambodia Poverty Reduction Strategy Paper: Joint Staff Assessment." Report, January 23, International Development Association and International Monetary Fund, Washington, DC.

Ministry of Health, WFP (World Food Programme), and Macro International. 2003. "Micro-Level Estimation of the Prevalence of Stunting and Underweight among Children in Cambodia." Report, Ministry of Health, World Food Programme Cambodia, and Macro International, Phnom Penh.

Ministry of Planning. 1998. "A Poverty Profile of Cambodia, 1997." Report, Ministry of Planning, Phnom Penh.

Ministry of Planning and WFP (World Food Programme). 2002. "Estimation of Poverty Rates at the Commune Level in Cambodia: Using the Small Area Estimation Technique to Obtain Reliable Estimates." Report, Ministry of Planning and World Food Programme Cambodia, Phnom Penh.

———. 2003. "Commune-Level Poverty Estimates and Ground-Truthing." Report, Ministry of Planning and World Food Programme Cambodia, Phnom Penh.

Ministry of Planning, WFP (World Food Programme), and UNDP (United Nations Development Programme). 2001. "Identifying Poor Areas in Cambodia: Combining Census and Socio-Economic Survey Data to Trace the Spatial Dimensions of Poverty." VAM baseline report, Vulnerability Analysis and Mapping Unit, World Food Programme, Phnom Penh.

Minot, Nicholas W. 2000. "Generating Disaggregated Poverty Maps: An Application to Vietnam." *World Development* 28 (2): 319–31.

Save Cambodia's Wildlife. 2006. *The Atlas of Cambodia: National Poverty and Environment Maps.* Phnom Penh: Save Cambodia's Wildlife.

7

Poverty Maps of Yunnan Province, China

Uses and Lessons for Scaling Up

YUSUF AHMAD AND CHOR-CHING GOH

ABBREVIATION

NBS	National Bureau of Statistics

Country Context

The history of the Chinese government's more recent poverty reduction programs may be divided into three stages. During the first stage, from 1978 to 1985, the government, through higher product prices, encouraged rural households to raise agricultural output. As a result, greater agricultural output translated into increases in the incomes of farm households. Official poverty incidence declined from 30.7 to 14.8 percent during this period. In the second stage, from 1986 to 1993, the State Council Leading Group Office of Poverty Alleviation and Development was established to provide coordination on targeted antipoverty interventions. This entity has since become the key agency responsible

The authors would like to thank the following people for taking their time to provide them with suggestions and feedback: Yaxiu Dong of the National Bureau of Statistics; He Xiaojun of the State Council Leading Group Office of Poverty Alleviation and Development; Guo Hongquan of the Ministry of Civil Affairs, Grace Poi Chiew Tan and Zhou Peng of the Badi Foundation; Peter Zetterstorm of the United Nations Development Programme; Sangui Wang of the Chinese Academy of Agricultural Sciences; Wang Xingzui, Wu Peng, and Bai Zheng of the China Foundation for Poverty Alleviation; and Wu Guobao of the Chinese Academy of Social Sciences. Special thanks to Wang Ping Ping of the National Bureau of Statistics for her invaluable insights and assistance.

for interventions related to poverty. It has more than US$2 billion in annual funding. During this period, the government introduced several large-scale programs focused on reducing rural poverty, and the number of the rural poor fell from 125 million to 80 million. In 1994, in the third stage, China launched the ambitious 8–7 Poverty Reduction Plan to eradicate absolute poverty. The plan called for amassing the manpower, materials, and financial resources necessary to help the remaining 80 million poor in China exit poverty within seven years (8–7). The number of poor fell from 80 million in 1994 to about 58 million in 1997.

Despite the successful government effort in poverty reduction, more than 30 million people are still poor in China today. Rapid economic growth has been a major factor in China's success in reducing poverty. However, the progress has been most notable when growth has been concentrated in the agricultural sector and in poorer regions. In earlier years, substantial poverty reduction might be achieved through general economic growth and broadly targeted programs. Today, the poor are more difficult to track: they may be found in resource-deficient areas and in remote uplands in the interior provinces of northern, northwestern, and southwestern China, as well as in periurban regions with high population densities. However, the central government's poverty reduction funding is available only to counties designated as poor, and the poor residing in counties not designated as poor are excluded from this support. Thus, a tool such as a poverty map might significantly improve the targeting of the poor.

Urban poverty in China is a relatively new phenomenon and the government has little systematic information about the location, profile, and nature of urban poverty. The main motivations for constructing poverty maps include the serious need for subprovincial information to improve the effectiveness and efficiency of current poverty reduction programs and the potential help offered by poverty maps to the government in designing poverty reduction programs in urban areas.

The latest effort undertaken by the government to identify the poor is a new poverty database, the poor household register, launched by the Poverty Alleviation and Development Office of the State Council. However, there are a number of shortcomings in the register. First, the register is very costly to maintain, and the data collection process relies on the judgment of village leaders to identify who are the poor. There is a tendency toward overreporting. Other weaknesses include the lack of clear guidelines about the poverty threshold across counties and villages, which leads to inconsistencies and arbitrariness, and the difficulty in differentiating between near poor households and poor households. Some of the advantages of the poverty mapping approach include the statistical robustness of the estimates (that is, confidence), transparency, consistency, and objectivity based on observed information.

The Mapping Process

The World Bank and the National Bureau of Statistics (NBS) collaborated in 2002–03 to apply the poverty mapping methodology in Yunnan Province. Yunnan Province was selected because of its ethnic diversity and relatively high poverty incidence. The objective was to test whether the methodology might produce reliable poverty incidence estimates down to the township level in rural areas and down to the district level in urban areas.

There were two stages to the study. During the first stage, a poverty map on rural Yunnan was produced based on the First National Agricultural Census, which was conducted in January 1997, and the 1997 Rural Household Survey.[1] The second stage consisted of expanding the exercise to all of Yunnan Province based on the Fifth Population Census (2000), combined with the 2000 Urban Household Survey and the 2000 Rural Household Survey, to produce poverty estimates both for urban and for rural areas. In addition to the censuses and surveys, supplementary county-level administrative data from the county statistics database (1996 and 1999) were used.

Three NBS departments—the Rural Survey Department, the Urban Survey Department, and the Population Department—were involved in the construction of the maps, and each department carried out its responsibilities according to its data expertise. The poverty map project brought together the three NBS departments to produce a common output for the very first time. It was also the first time that all three data sources (that is, the urban and rural household surveys and the census) were merged and used together.

Data Issues

Several data issues arose during the process of the construction of poverty maps of Yunnan. First, there was a sampling issue that might affect the comparability of the household survey and the agricultural census. For the 1984 survey, 40 sampled counties were selected from among the 126 counties in the province. The county sampling has not changed since then. In 1984, the sample was designed to be self-weighting according to the probability-proportional-to-size method of sampling. However, by 1997, the sample was no longer self-weighting because of variations in population growth across clusters at all three levels of administrative division in the province (prefecture, county, and township). The 40 counties in the sample showed quite diverse population growth rates from 1985 to 1997, ranging from 12.5 percent to 60 percent. Counties with a higher income growth rate attracted more residents. It was therefore necessary to construct a household sampling weight to reflect the changes in the cluster population.

On the issue of representativeness, the variation in income growth across clusters raised the question of whether the 1984 sample of counties would still be representative of the 1997 population. For instance, in 1984, all counties were ranked according to average net per capita income over the previous three years, and the counties were selected systematically for the sample so that each selected county would also represent its neighboring counties on the ranking list. But, after 1984, some counties grew more rapidly than others, and the original ranking was no longer accurate by 1997. Similarly, the Urban Household Survey samples were selected in the early 1980s and have never been updated. The representativeness of that survey is even more doubtful because of the rapid urbanization over the past decade that has been motivated by market liberalization and policy changes.

Another issue encountered during the merging of the rural survey, the urban survey, and the population census involved the sampling frames. Both the rural survey and the urban survey used different sampling frames from the population census.

When the simple rule was applied of splitting the population census to match the sampling frames of the rural survey and the urban survey, 10 percent of the population in Yunnan Province remained unaccounted for; the corresponding share was as high as 25 percent in large cities. Neither the urban survey nor the rural survey had been designed to reflect the migration issue. A small fraction of the population temporarily residing in urban areas has been ignored in both surveys. Information on the income and population of primary sampling units would be used to address this issue in both cases.

Field Validation

As measured by the reasonably small standard errors, the poverty estimates used to produce the poverty maps are rather precise all the way to the township level. However, the results at the village level (below the township level) are no longer so precisely measured; the standard errors are relatively high. Two examples of the poverty maps are presented in figures 7.1 and 7.2.

To verify the accuracy of the results, World Bank and NBS staff undertook two field validation trips to Yunnan. The first trip found that the preliminary results on poverty headcount rates by county derived from the First National Agricultural Census and the Rural Household Survey were consistent with the perceptions of local officials. During this trip, the team was able to discuss many issues regarding the methodology for the collection of census and survey data with local NBS officials. These discussions helped in the merging of census and survey data. The second field trip was conducted to distribute and discuss the findings using the population census, the rural survey and the urban survey. Meetings were held at the provincial, prefecture and county levels. All local government officials and researchers agreed that the results of the pilot study at the prefecture level were reasonable. The results on the poverty headcount rate in only one of the 16 prefectures might be viewed as an underestimate; this was the prefecture of Diqing.

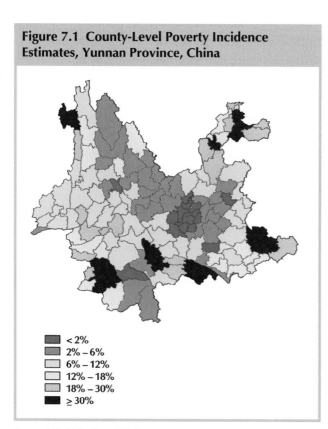

Figure 7.1 County-Level Poverty Incidence Estimates, Yunnan Province, China

- < 2%
- 2% – 6%
- 6% – 12%
- 12% – 18%
- 18% – 30%
- ≥ 30%

Source: World Bank and NBS 2003.

NBS staff then visited Diqing to meet with officials from various government departments. The prefecture officials echoed that the estimated poverty headcount rate seemed lower than anticipated, but the ranking of counties by poverty headcount was reasonable. Contributing to the underestimation was a shortage of data and the difference between the poverty threshold in Diqing and the poverty threshold in the other 15 prefectures.

Dissemination

The results of the poverty mapping exercise were distributed to various government agencies, donors, non-governmental organizations (NGOs), and researchers through two seminars organized by the NBS and the World Bank. Since the poverty map of Yunnan was only a pilot exercise to test the methodology, the results

Figure 7.2 Township-Level Poverty Incidence Estimates, Yunnan Province, China

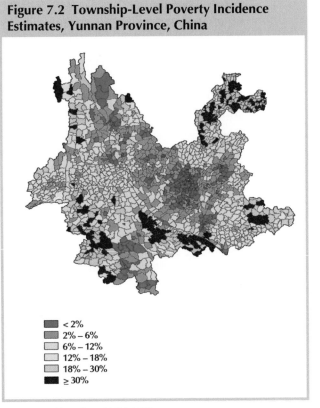

- ■ < 2%
- ■ 2% – 6%
- □ 6% – 12%
- □ 12% – 18%
- □ 18% – 30%
- ■ ≥ 30%

Source: World Bank and NBS 2003.

were not published by the NBS. The participants were not allowed to quote the results, and only hard copies were distributed to participants at the seminars. NBS also did not actively promote the use of the maps at that stage. Many participants regarded the poverty map as a way to fulfill the demand for poverty information at the prefecture and township levels. However, many others were skeptical whether the poverty map may be used in practice to allocate resources to the poor. The government agencies felt that more validation exercises had to be carried out to confirm the reliability of the poverty map findings. While most of the government agencies were well aware of the poverty maps and appreciated their usefulness, they were skeptical of the reliability and robustness of the results. The methodology is still new to them, and they need time to understand and become familiar with it. Also, the tool has only been applied in one province, and further tests on the results or additional applications in other provinces will be necessary. Many of the officials who were interviewed expressed the need to conduct a new round of poverty maps once the Second National Agricultural Census is completed in 2007. While local officials were eager to use the poverty maps, they were worried that any mistargeting will have severe political consequences because of heavy scrutiny through central government audits of antipoverty funding.

Other reasons cited to explain the possible lack of usefulness of the poverty maps echo concerns expressed in other countries: (1) the need for poverty information at the lowest administrative unit (that is, the village); (2) the need for additional indicators, especially indicators on the nonmonetary dimension of poverty, besides poverty and inequality estimates; and (3) the need for regular updates of the maps given that a single map produced to coincide with the census every 10 years is not sufficiently accurate to be useful. These are all issues that may be successfully addressed. To have robust estimates on the lowest administrative unit, additional village-level information will have to be made available, and such a process might be incorporated into the regular data collection of the NBS. Additional indicators might also be constructed, as in other countries. And, lastly, the updating of the maps during between-census periods is being developed and applied in several countries in the region, for example, the Philippines and Thailand.

Impacts of the Maps

Actual uses

The only government agency that has used the poverty maps is the National Development and Reform Commission. The commission has made use of the poverty map to review the county-level allocation of project funding, as well as the incidence of poverty in all Yunnan counties. The commission has found the poverty map less useful for its food-for-work program because poverty headcounts on villages are not available in the map.

The World Bank and the U.K. Department for International Development have used the poverty map of Yunnan to help select beneficiary areas for their Poor Rural Communities Development Project.[2] The project was approved by the Board of the World Bank in June 2005. It covers three provinces: Guangxi, Sichuan, and Yunnan. The project will help the Chinese government to improve resource targeting on the poorest and reduce leakage to the nonpoor.

The poverty mapping exercise has motivated important changes at the NBS. The data issues uncovered during the exercise have been particularly valuable in improving the next rounds of data collection by the NBS. The NBS has also used the poverty mapping results as a guideline in designing the questionnaire for the Second National Agricultural Census, which is being fielded in 2006–07. Additional indicators that may be calculated in future poverty maps are being incorporated in the second agricultural census. The census will now also include data on all households in rural areas rather than merely households with specific types of production. To ensure comparability with the population census, the NBS will be matching the household survey domain with the census domain.

Potential uses

While there has been only limited use of the maps of Yunnan so far, our interviews with various government agencies, donors, and NGOs suggest that there is a tremendous demand for poverty maps in China. The government of China is very conscientious in its efforts to reduce poverty, and a significant amount of funds is designated for poverty reduction. Most donors rely on the government poverty indicators in targeting their programs. Thus, reliable and robust poverty information is crucial.

The government is the main potential user of poverty maps because it oversees a large amount of program funds. The central government plays a major role in distributing antipoverty funds to counties through various government departments and state-owned banks. There are four main government organizations responsible for delivering and managing government antipoverty funds: the Leading Group Office of Poverty Alleviation and Development, the Agricultural Bank of China, the Ministry of Finance, and the National Development and Reform Commission. Each organization uses its own scoring system to channel poverty funds to provincial and county governments. Only counties that have been designated as poor are eligible for the funds. The poverty map tool might provide poverty estimates of the counties in a more systematic, cost-effective, and transparent way.

The following are some of the many programs that might also benefit from the information in national poverty maps.

The subsidized loan program

The objective of this program is to provide credit support in poor areas to boost economic development and improve the incomes of the poor. The bulk of the subsidized loans are supplied to households or enterprises in poor counties. The program is managed by the county office of the Leading Group for Poverty Reduction and the county branch of the Agricultural Bank of China. The county offices select the projects and households in poor areas. Wang (2004) finds that the project has failed to target the poor.

The food- and cash-for-work program

The objective of this program is to make use of the surplus labor resources in poor areas to build infrastructure such as roads, water management structures (for example, reservoirs), and drinking water treatment facilities. The program aims at providing poor farmers with job opportunities and sources of income. The program is managed by the National Planning and Development Commission. Program wage payments are given out as coupons to exchange for grain, clothing, and other daily necessities. Some of these coupons may also be exchanged for cash through state-run commercial banks. It is unclear how the commission determines the villages that will receive the coupons to implement the program.

The budgetary development fund

The objective of this fund is to support productive construction projects and investments. The budgets of local governments in poor areas tend to be in deficit, and the poor areas are unable to make any infrastructure investments. The Budgetary Development Fund was launched by the Ministry of Finance. Many villages are chosen for the program from among counties that are not officially designated as poor, and many people believe that the leakage to the nonpoor is substantial.

The compulsory education project

The objective of the project is to improve the conditions for basic education in poor counties. The program has been running for nearly 10 years and is managed by the Ministry of Education. The project has constructed new primary and secondary schools, renovated and expanded old school buildings, purchased equipment and furniture for schools, and trained teaching staff. The project covers 522 poor counties, mainly in mountainous, pastoral, border, and minority areas.

Nongovernmental programs

The NGO representatives interviewed for this study were generally not aware of the existence of the poverty maps, but expressed interest in learning more about them. Some of the interviewees were disappointed that they had never been informed about the maps, and some would also like to become involved in the mapping process and map construction. They found the information in the maps valuable in their activities. For example, the largest of the NGOs that dealt only with poverty directly, the China Foundation for Poverty Alleviation, is eager to acquire poverty information disaggregated at the county level. While the foundation's programs mostly target individual households, organized, structured information on poverty in counties and townships would be immensely valuable.

The Badi Foundation is a successful local NGO that deals with capacity building. The foundation provides training for the poor, particularly poor rural women. The foundation uses data supplied by the government, usually the NBS, to identify poor villages. While Badi staff had never heard of the poverty maps, they indicated that poverty information on lower-level administrative units would be very useful not only for them, but for other organizations dealing with poverty issues.

Reducing the diversion of poverty funds to other usages

Local governments have, at times, utilized poverty reduction funds for other purposes. One reason is that the revenues of the counties are generally not sufficient to cover county expenditures, and poverty funds are therefore diverted to uses other than poverty reduction. Many observers believe that the poverty maps may help reduce the diversion of poverty funds to other uses because the central government would be able to apply the maps in assessing resource allocations and monitoring the impacts of related projects and polices.

Lessons for Scaling Up

Involve potential users in all stages of map construction

The main concern of government agencies with regard to the poverty maps has been the issue of reliability. Because the methodology is relatively new, there is still much doubt and skepticism. Collaboration between the producer of the maps (that is, the NBS) and potential users at the early stages of map development and continuing all the way through to the completion of the mapping project is vital. Each government agency requires different types of data for its programs, ranging from consumption data and nutrition data to data on educational attainment, illiteracy, access to safe drinking water, and infrastructure. It is important that potential map users be able to provide inputs and suggestions at an early stage so that the end product may better serve their needs. Also, it is important to undertake a process of data validation at the local level; this process should also directly involve potential map users.

Informal discussions on updating and expanding the scope of the poverty maps are currently under way with various government agencies that deal with poverty. The NBS is proposing that a working committee be established, consisting of at least the line agencies, with the main task of discussing the development and construction of poverty maps.

Disseminate actively, widely, and effectively

Besides actively engaging potential users during the development stage and on through construction to the validation of the maps, the NBS must also actively, widely, and effectively disseminate the results. Holding seminars to discuss the results, as in the case of Yunnan, is not sufficient or effective in promoting wider use of the maps. The poverty maps should be published formally, and both soft and hard copies ought to be distributed to potential users. A Web site should be created for the purpose of dissemination and also to educate users on the application of the maps. Dissemination across the country at the local level is equally important. The donor and NGO communities are likewise important users that should be involved from the start.

Improve data quality through better coordination among NBS divisions

During the poverty mapping exercise, a number of data shortcomings were uncovered. These issues should be addressed in future rounds of data collection to improve data quality and the poverty estimates shown on the map. To address these shortcomings, the NBS must improve internal coordination in data collection, processing, analysis, data standard-setting, and data sharing. For example, the household survey data and the population census depend on different sampling frames. It is poor internal coordination within the NBS that has led to the development of incompatible data sets.

The NBS has expressed an interest in updating the poverty maps on Yunnan and constructing maps for several more provinces as soon as the second agricultural census becomes available. The new census has incorporated many improvements and includes additional indicators that should be used in future poverty maps.

Increase the capacity of the NBS

The construction of a poverty map on the entire country is a huge task, and the NBS will need substantial technical assistance. Additional manpower will also be necessary to support field validation, the collection of additional local information, and so on.

Conclusions

The pilot study of Yunnan province was intended to test the applicability of the poverty mapping approach and the relevant data in China. Despite the data shortcomings that were uncovered, it has been a productive endeavor. As reflected in the relatively small standard errors, the poverty estimates were measured with good precision at the county and even township levels. The results suggest that there is substantial geographical heterogeneity in poverty in Yunnan. Even considering the large number of counties, there is considerable variation in the incidence of poverty across townships. A change in the targeting rules for the national poverty reduction program from county-based targeting to township-based targeting might therefore enhance the program's effectiveness in reaching the poor.

If future poverty maps of China are to have an impact, the NBS should ensure that potential users, especially various government agencies, have an adequate understanding of the uses and applications of the maps. Moreover, it is important that users become engaged and involved from the start of the project on through map construction to validation and dissemination. It appears that the NBS is already taking steps to engage various agencies in discussing additional work on the poverty maps, which would include updating the Yunnan poverty map and extending the exercise to other provinces as soon as the second agricultural census becomes available.

Notes

1. See http://www.theinternetfoundation.org/China/Ag/FirstAgriculturalCensusChinaTOC.htm for the agricultural census.
2. See http://www.dfid.gov.uk/pubs/files/PRCDP-en.pdf.

References

Elbers, Chris, Jean O. Lanjouw, and Peter F. Lanjouw. 2003. "Micro-Level Estimation of Poverty and Inequality." *Econometrica* 71 (1): 355–64.

Henninger, Norbert, and Mathilde Snel. 2002. *Where Are the Poor?: Experiences with the Development and Use of Poverty Maps.* Washington, DC: World Resources Institute; Arendal, Norway: United Nations Environment Programme–Global Resource Information Database.

Wang Sangui. 2004. "Poverty Targeting in the People's Republic of China." ADB Institute Discussion Paper 4, Asian Development Bank Institute, Manila.

World Bank and NBS (China, National Bureau of Statistics). 2003. "Developing a Poverty Map for China: A Pilot Work in One Province." Unpublished monograph, December, World Bank, Washington, DC.

8

The 1990 and 2001 Ecuador
Poverty Maps

MARÍA CARIDAD ARAUJO

Motivation

Ecuador was one of the first countries for which two household surveys and two population censuses were available that allowed a panel of poverty maps to be created. The first Ecuador poverty map was developed in the mid-1990s. It was one of the earliest experiences in the small area estimation of poverty. It is frequently cited in the methodological literature on poverty mapping (Elbers, Lanjouw, and Lanjouw 2003). The second poverty map was constructed almost 10 years later.

The experience described in this chapter will focus mostly on the second poverty map, which was developed in 2003. The objectives of the chapter are (1) to document

---

Valuable comments have been offered by Tara Bedi, Aline Coudouel, Carolina Sánchez-Páramo, and Renos Vakis. Luis Miguel Chiriboga provided important inputs by discovering and interviewing users of the maps.

the challenges posed by the creation of a panel of poverty maps; these challenges arise from both a methodological and a process perspective; and (2) to examine how poverty maps may be used to inform policy decisions.

The main lessons learned from the Ecuadorian experience are the following:

- The sustainability of a poverty mapping process initiated by external actors and the usefulness of poverty maps in policy making within a country depend on the establishment of a working relationship with local counterparts and on strengthening local capacity.
- Training and the distribution of information about poverty maps should occur from the start of the preparation of the poverty maps, not after the maps have been completed.
- Poverty maps should be distributed through diverse media, including user-friendly compact discs, so that users may have access to the data and to geographic information system (GIS) applications and be able to display the data according to their needs.
- Poverty mapping should be complemented by research, in collaboration with local specialists, that documents differences between the various poverty maps available, the mapping methodologies used in the country, and the application of the maps in policy making.
- Capacity-building efforts should also target map users so as to illustrate other experiences and help users understand the application potential.

This chapter is organized as follows. The next section supplies background information on Ecuador, the availability of relevant poverty and household data, and the poverty mapping exercise. The subsequent section presents details on the methodologies involved in developing poverty maps, especially methodologies aimed at ensuring comparability among maps over time. The penultimate section describes the construction of poverty maps and the policy impact of the maps. The last section identifies the lessons learned through the experience in Ecuador.

Background

Ecuador produced four household surveys during the 1990s, the *Encuestas de condiciones de vida* (Living Standards Measurement Surveys, ECVs), which were carried out in 1994, 1995, 1998, and 1999. Ecuador also completed population censuses in 1990 and 2001. In this chapter, the first Ecuador poverty map (sometimes referred to as the 1990 poverty map) is the map that combines the 1994 ECV and the 1990 census. The second Ecuador poverty map (the 2001 poverty map) is the map that blends the 1999 ECV and the 2001 census.

The first Ecuador poverty map was developed when the government was considering the elimination of a subsidy on cooking gas and was seeking a tool for targeting compensatory transfers. A consultation with the World Bank on this issue coincided with the preparation by the Bank of a poverty assessment on Ecuador in the mid-1990s (see World

Bank 1996). The combination of these two goals became a pioneering research effort in poverty mapping. It evolved into a systematic initiative to develop small area estimation methodologies inside the World Bank and in collaboration with academics in Europe and the United States.

Because of the completion of the 2001 census and the availability of the 1999 household survey, there was a unique opportunity to undertake another poverty mapping effort. The second poverty map was thus initiated as a research exercise. During the process of the creation of the map, the exercise was integrated into the 2004 poverty assessment on Ecuador (see World Bank 2004). The construction of the 2001 poverty map was supervised by the same team of researchers that had worked on the 1990 map. Resources provided through a Norwegian trust fund and through the World Bank's poverty assessment in Ecuador supported the participation of a short-term consultant (an Ecuadorian national) who was responsible for the technical work.

The two poverty maps were constructed and funded by the World Bank, but there was little involvement of local counterparts during the process. Local capacity building was limited, and it occurred mostly at the distribution stage.

During both experiences, World Bank staff interacted with the directors of the *Instituto Nacional de Estadísticas y Censos* (National Institute of Statistics, INEC) and with local professionals in relevant areas of poverty analysis. INEC provided access to relevant data and support in all questions on the data, including the consistency checks on cartographic maps during the period between the two censuses.

Despite its technical support, INEC was not an active counterpart in the actual drafting process for the poverty maps. When consulted about the possibility of taking on a role in the creation of the second poverty map, INEC directors explained that the institution was not able to devote the staff time required for training and active involvement in the process. They indicated that the institution's mandate was to produce rather than use or analyze data. INEC publishes periodic reports containing descriptive summaries of INEC's main surveys, but it did not have staff specialized in data analysis or poverty. Nonetheless, INEC directors have often expressed their support for poverty mapping.

Another local entity that was involved in and consulted on technical issues during the preparation of the 2004 poverty assessment and the second Ecuador poverty map was the *Sistema Integrado de Indicadores Sociales del Ecuador* (Integrated System of Social Indicators of Ecuador, SIISE). SIISE is housed within the Ministry of Social Welfare. It is the technical agency that analyzes statistical data for the Ministries of Education, Health, Labor, and Social Welfare. During the drafting of the poverty assessment, SIISE staff were frequently consulted on technical issues related to the 1999 ECV, including design, documentation, and the calculation of variables. Indeed, a SIISE senior staff member was a coauthor of a chapter in the 2004 poverty assessment. However, SIISE did not participate directly in the preparation of either of the poverty maps.[1] In recent years, SIISE and its staff have expressed interest in building capacity in poverty mapping within their institution. However, no concrete training or capacity-building initiative has been established by SIISE and the World Bank on poverty mapping. One of the main limitations faced by SIISE is the size of the institution; it is fairly small, and this would make it difficult for SIISE to devote substantial staff time to poverty mapping.

Preparation of Poverty Maps: Technical Aspects

A central goal in constructing the 2001 poverty map was to make the map comparable to the 1990 map so as to enable users to track changes in small area estimates of poverty over the decade. Achieving comparability across the small area estimates of poverty presented methodological challenges. These included issues such as establishing comparability across the different consumption expenditure methodologies used in two surveys, establishing comparability across the different enumeration areas of the censuses and the surveys, and establishing comparability across surveys and censuses that had not been carried out on the same year.

One of the first problems was the fact that each of the ECVs produced during the 1990s had incorporated changes in the consumption modules in the survey questionnaires. For example, in the 1994 and 1999 questionnaires, important differences existed in the recall periods on some consumption goods, as well as in the level of aggregation of food items, durable goods, and consumption goods.

The 1999 ECV differed in three other aspects from previous surveys. First, due to costs, it excluded one of the three continental geographical regions of the country, the sparsely populated El Oriente Region (the East), which consists of six provinces (of the country's 22) and around 5 percent of the total population of Ecuador. Second, the 1999 survey was collected over a period of 11 months, while the previous surveys had been collected during a single annual quarter. Lastly, the survey was carried out during an unstable period of high inflation that preceded a major financial crisis.

For these reasons, considerable thought was given to using the 1998 ECV instead of the 1999 ECV in the construction of the second poverty map. Since not all the comparability problems would be resolved by using the 1998 survey, the choice was ultimately made to favor the proximity of the 1999 survey and the 2001 census in terms of chronology, and, so, the 1999 survey was selected.

The two poverty maps were constructed following the small area estimation methodology proposed by Elbers, Lanjouw, and Lanjouw (2003). Consumption models were estimated for each of the geographical divisions that the surveys had been designed to examine. The maps illustrated measures of poverty and inequality, including standard errors, for parishes, cantons, and provinces.[2] For four of the largest cities in the country, Cuenca, Guayaquil, Loja, and Quito, INEC was able to reconstruct information on neighborhoods from the census tract data. The 2001 map therefore included an additional layer of data and produced welfare estimates down to the neighborhood level in these cities.

These various issues are now discussed in detail. This section then concludes by presenting the main findings from the two poverty mapping exercises.[3]

Comparability in consumption expenditure methodologies

The use of poverty measures based on consumption aggregates that are not comparable may lead to erroneous inferences about changes in welfare over time. A considerable methodological literature documents this issue (see, for example, Deaton and Kozel 2005; Lanjouw and Lanjouw 1997, 2001). For this reason, assessments of changes in poverty that are based solely on the raw consumption aggregates from each of the four ECVs would be inaccurate. Thus, the first step in the analysis of the changes in poverty throughout the decade was to establish comparability between the 1994 and the 1999 consumption aggregates and poverty lines.

To establish comparability, we decomposed total expenditures (TE) in 1994 and 1999 into two subcomponents:

$$TE = CE + NCE \qquad (8.1)$$

Comparable expenditures (CE) was defined as the set of goods in the consumption aggregate that had been identified in exactly the same way in the 1994 and 1999 ECV questionnaires. Noncomparable expenditures (NCE) represented the difference between TE and CE. Lanjouw and Lanjouw (1997) have shown that the headcount ratio does not change as the definition of consumption changes from CE to TE when the following assumptions hold: (1) CE and NCE are increasing in TE and (2) the budget share of CE declines as TE increases. Analysis of data from the 1994 ECV and 1999 ECV has confirmed that expenditure patterns in both surveys are consistent with these two assumptions.

To construct comparable poverty lines for 1994 and 1999, the starting point was the poverty rate for 1994 reported by the World Bank (1996), a headcount ratio of 0.35. This headcount ratio was mapped to the distribution of CE_{94} to find the corresponding value of comparable expenditure. We called this value $Z_{CE, 94}$ (the CE poverty line). This value was then mapped to the distribution of total expenditure, and, by averaging the value of TE_{94} in the neighborhood containing the household where $CE_{94} = Z_{CE, 94}$, we found $Z_{TE, 94}$ (the 1994 TE poverty line). We used the consumer price index to deflate $Z_{CE, 94}$ to its value in 1999. We called this poverty line $Z_{CE, 99}$. Finally, by averaging the value of TE_{99} in the neighborhood containing the household where $CE_{99} = Z_{CE, 99}$, we derived $Z_{TE, 99}$ (the 1999 TE poverty line).

Table 8.1 presents the results of this exercise. The top panel of the table shows the figures constructed using the comparable consumption aggregate, CE, while the bottom panel uses the measure of total consumption, TE. Poverty estimates are not significantly different across the top and the bottom panels, which suggests that the properties of the distributions of CE and TE allow comparison.

In the collection of systematic rounds of household survey data, countries face a trade-off between the frequency with which they update their survey instruments and the comparability of the estimates they will be able to produce from the data. The lesson learned from the experience in Ecuador is that, while it is preferable to maintain

Table 8.1 Poverty Incidence, Ecuador

Continental region	1994		1999	
	Poverty	Standard error	Poverty	Standard error
Comparable consumption aggregate				
Nationwide without El Oriente	0.34	0.03	0.51	0.03
La Costa (the Coast)	0.32	0.03	0.48	0.03
La Sierra (the Highlands)	0.36	0.03	0.54	0.03
Total consumption aggregate				
Nationwide without El Oriente	0.36	0.04	0.52	0.03
La Costa	0.35	0.04	0.51	0.03
La Sierra	0.36	0.04	0.54	0.03

Source: Compiled by the author using data from 1994 ECV and 1999 ECV.

consistency in the survey instruments, it is also important to document all the changes and adjustments that are undertaken over time. Moreover, during the analysis stage, specific corrections, such as the one described here, are crucial in making sure that the survey data are actually comparable. While these steps may be time consuming, they should never be neglected.

Comparability in enumeration areas

Changes in the national map and establishing comparable enumeration areas

A major challenge in the construction of the second poverty map in Ecuador was the documentation of the changes in the country's cartographic map to ensure that the same census tracts were classified within the same geographical units over time. The task required several months of work and considerable support from INEC. The objective was to establish comparability across administrative units (census tracts, parishes, and cantons) in the two population censuses and surveys. The main problem was that, between 1990 and 2001, the cartography and administrative map of Ecuador had undergone important modifications. New provinces, parishes, and cantons had been created, and the borders of others had been redefined. Unfortunately, there was no systematic centralized record of these changes at INEC or elsewhere documenting the administrative unit to which each particular census tract had belonged when the various surveys and censuses had been carried out. It was therefore necessary to invest a considerable amount of time tracking down each of the changes on actual paper maps and documenting them. When the second poverty map was produced, comparable administrative maps had been reconstructed down to the level of the provinces and cantons, but not the parishes. Therefore, cantons were the lowest level of aggregation in the comparable 2001 poverty map.

The main lesson from this experience is the importance of maintaining a central database to document systematically all changes in the structure of census tracts or other administrative units and the dates when these changes occur. INEC is the natural entity that should be responsible for this task. One of the main challenges for INEC would be to establish a system of regular updates to the database so as to build up a computerized institutional record. This process should not be particularly costly given that INEC already periodically publishes lists of all the parishes, cantons, and provinces (known as the *division político-administrativa,* which is usually published annually). The documentation on changes in the structure of census tracts would simply be an additional level of refinement in this tool.

Urbanization

The poverty estimates shown in table 8.1 suggest that, at the national level, the incidence of poverty increased significantly between 1994 and 1999. The magnitude of this increase was similar across La Costa (the Coast Region) and La Sierra (the Highlands Region). However, when these data are disaggregated into urban and rural locations, the regional differences become more pronounced. Several factors underlie these differences. First, there have been changes in the distribution of poverty. Second, a process of urbanization has occurred, which means that there has been a redistribution in populations across territories. There have also been administrative changes in the national map.[4] Finally, problems have arisen because of the lack of consistency in the definitions of rural and urban locations used in the sampling frames.[5]

Imputing poverty figures for El Oriente

To save on costs, the household sample in the 1999 ECV did not include El Oriente. Although El Oriente is not densely populated and is small in relative terms (accounting for only about 4.4 percent of the national population, according to the 2001 census), it has unique economic, social, and institutional characteristics. Unfortunately, because of the lack of data, it was not possible to measure the special structural relationships between welfare and the characteristics of households in El Oriente for the 2001 poverty map.

Two options were explored to resolve this problem. The first was to apply one of the models estimated for the other survey units (for example, rural Costa or rural Sierra) to El Oriente census data to recover poverty figures. This option was validated using 1990 data, but the results were unsatisfactory. The ranking of the parishes in terms of poverty based on models for other geographical divisions differed significantly from the ranking based on the model estimated using data on El Oriente.

A second option was to estimate poverty based not on household attributes, but on parish attributes that could be constructed from the census. Using poverty estimates for parishes for which survey and census data existed, one might estimate the structural relationship between average parish per capita expenditures (and the headcount ratio) and parish variables. The exercise was performed and then validated using the 1990 poverty map. While the 1990 data showed that the correlation between the true rural headcount numbers and the predicted numbers in El Oriente was not low (0.77, while a rank correlation was 0.71), it was not possible to quantify the margin of error in the prediction.[6]

Given that neither of the two alternatives for producing poverty estimates for El Oriente was fully satisfactory, the region was not included in the final version of the 2001 poverty map that was distributed in the country. The main lesson learned from this experience is that, in poverty mapping, there is no adequate substitute for nationally representative survey data.

Comparability across surveys and censuses in different years

Although it was judged that the 1994 and 1999 ECVs contained the best data available for exploring the evolution of poverty and its correlates during the 1990s, the surveys were conducted, respectively, four years after and two years before the censuses used in producing the relevant poverty maps.

The poverty mapping methodology involves deriving structural relationships between household and neighborhood welfare and assets. Optimally, the household survey and population census used should correspond to the same time period or, if they refer to separate time periods, to time periods that vary little in terms of structural changes. Unfortunately, this is not the case in Ecuador.

The use of censuses and household surveys for different years in the construction of a poverty map entails an assumption that returns to assets have not altered appreciably during the interval between the two periods. Making such an assumption is always problematic in a country that has faced many shocks, as Ecuador did in the 1990s. Especially between the 1999 survey and the 2001 census, there were important changes in the Ecuadorian economy, including a major financial crisis and the adoption of the U.S. dollar as the nation's official currency.

Figure 8.1 depicts the evolution of real per capita gross domestic product in Ecuador over the decade. The large bubbles mark the periods when censuses or household surveys were conducted. While the change in per capita gross domestic product is larger between 1990 and 1994 than between 1999 and 2001 (that is, 6.6 percent versus 3.5 percent), 1999 was a peculiar period. That year, the financial crisis was at its worst and the economy took a plunge.

Until recently, the 1999 ECV was the latest household survey carried out by the government.[7] When the 2001 poverty map was being constructed, the 1999 ECV was considered the best source of relevant data. Even if the crisis had

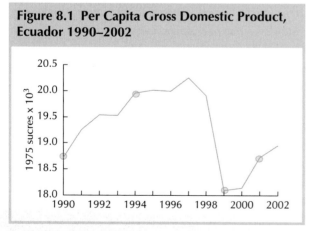

Figure 8.1 Per Capita Gross Domestic Product, Ecuador 1990–2002

Source: Compiled by the author.

altered the returns to household assets significantly, there was no other instrument on hand for attempting to assess the magnitude of the change. Moreover, because most of the variation in the development of poverty estimates arises from census variables, the expectation was that the poverty estimates based on the 1999 ECV and the 2001 census would be closer, in terms of accuracy, to the actual poverty situation during 2001 (the year of the census) than to the situation during 1999 (the year of the household survey). Since the next ECV was not expected to appear until late 2006 or thereafter, several years following the 2001 census, the best available option was to use the 1999 ECV for the 2001 poverty map.

Findings

This section briefly summarizes the main poverty estimates from the panel of poverty maps. Since it is unusual for comparable small area estimates of poverty to be available on a country, the purpose of presenting the results is to illustrate the type of information that may be produced by an exercise of this sort.

Table 8.2 summarizes the poverty estimates aggregated according to geographical survey units for the 1990 and 2001 poverty maps. For 2001, the table reports both the best possible estimates of poverty (based on total expenditures) and the estimates based on comparable expenditures that may be used to analyze poverty changes over the 10-year period. These estimates have been derived from consumption equations that have been solved using, as the dependent variable, the comparable expenditures (*CE*) according to geographical units. Since the explanatory variables in this model are the same as the ones in the model in which the dependent variable is total expenditures

Table 8.2 Headcount Ratio from Poverty Maps, Ecuador 1990 and 2001

Region or area	1990 TE		2001 CE		2001 TE	
	Estimate	Standard error	Estimate	Standard error	Estimate	Standard error
Nationwide	0.410	0.020	—	—	—	—
Without El Oriente	0.387	0.019	0.452	0.023	0.451	0.024
Quito	0.222	0.021	0.243	0.016	0.185	0.020
Guayaquil	0.382	0.018	0.386	0.028	0.337	0.027
Urban La Costa	0.258	0.015	0.464	0.013	0.464	0.021
Urban La Sierra	0.213	0.017	0.467	0.029	0.459	0.022
Rural La Costa	0.505	0.025	0.504	0.017	0.587	0.026
Rural La Sierra	0.528	0.019	0.617	0.034	0.663	0.028
Urban El Oriente	0.192	0.020	—	—	—	—
Rural El Oriente	0.598	0.026	—	—	—	—

Source: Compiled by the author from the 1990 and 2001 censuses and the 1994 and 1999 ECVs.
Note: La Región Insular (the region formed by the Galápagos Islands) and areas without fixed boundaries are included as part of rural La Costa.
— = no data are available.

(*TE*), it is not surprising that the estimates are close.[8] The shaded columns show the comparable poverty figures.[9]

Table 8.2 indicates significant increases in poverty in three areas: urban La Costa, urban La Sierra, and rural La Sierra. The increases are particularly dramatic in the first two areas, where the incidence of poverty doubled over the period. This is in clear contrast to what occurred in rural La Costa, Guayaquil, and Quito, where the incidence of poverty did not show significant changes over the decade. More highly disaggregated parish maps may be found in annex 8.1.

Distribution of Poverty Maps and the Policy Impact

Distribution

The 2004 poverty assessment (World Bank 2004) reports the results of the 1990 and 2001 poverty map exercises. The assessment provides a formal channel through which the information in the poverty maps may be communicated to the government. The maps, which have been geo-referenced, are displayed in the main report. In addition, data tables containing estimates for the cantons and provinces are included in annex. The report is available on the Web site of the World Bank.[10] However, no special compact disc with images or interactive poverty maps has been produced for distribution in Ecuador.

The publication of the poverty assessment was accompanied by numerous activities to disseminate the results. More specifically, the 2001 poverty map was presented during two workshops in Quito in October 2003. The first workshop was targeted at a large audience of potential users, including government workers, representatives of the nongovernmental sector and the donor community, and local government leaders. Around 130 individuals attended the workshop, where presenters explained the purpose of poverty maps and how they are constructed. A major focus of the workshop was discussions on how to interpret the maps and on potential uses and applications.

The second workshop was targeted at a smaller, more specialized audience of about 50 individuals. It centered on the technical aspects of the construction of the 2001 poverty map, especially the assumptions, methodology, and data involved. There were discussions on the trade-offs that one must make in building a panel of poverty maps, in particular those related to establishing comparability over time. Also examined were the reasons behind the differences among the poverty mapping methodologies developed by the World Bank and others based on unmet basic needs analysis or principal components analysis. Each of the steps in the poverty mapping methodology was explored in great detail.

The applications of poverty maps were illustrated during both workshops. One of the presentations concentrated on the agricultural productivity maps that were constructed for the poverty assessment and the process of overlaying these maps on poverty maps. Another presentation examined the geographical distribution of food poverty and malnutrition and discussed the preliminary results of a study conducted by a local researcher who had been developing malnutrition maps as part of a project for the Food and Agriculture Organization of the United Nations that was being carried out in collaboration with the World Bank poverty assessment team.

The format of the two workshops combined presentations and question-and-answer sessions. Each workshop lasted a half day. The workshops were organized prior to the publication of the poverty assessment report; so, other than the PowerPoint presentations, no additional poverty map materials were distributed at the workshops or later among the attendees.

Information on the 2001 poverty map was also disseminated through two additional channels. First, SIISE was provided with a complete set of the data. SIISE is the main government agency in charge of producing, compiling, and analyzing data on poverty in Ecuador. Every year, it produces a compact disc containing a wide range of socioeconomic indicators at various levels of disaggregation on the country. This is the most widely used source of disaggregated indicators produced in Ecuador. However, the World Bank poverty maps have never been included on a SIISE disc. Part of the reason is that the discs incorporate maps on unmet basic needs that have been developed and produced by SIISE (see elsewhere below), and there are discrepancies between the two map instruments in the assessment of levels of poverty and in the poverty rankings of parishes. Another reason is that SIISE staff considered the 2001 poverty map inadequate because it did not have reliable data on El Oriente. There has been no systematic effort by SIISE or the World Bank to follow up on this problem and document the discrepancies. The World Bank and SIISE maintain an active collaboration in other areas of policy analysis, especially issues related to the targeting, monitoring, and evaluation of social assistance programs. We believe that, as the data from the new round of the ECV (2005–06) are released, there will be increased demand by SIISE for World Bank technical assistance in poverty measurement, and this mapping issue will come again to the fore.

The second main additional channel for the dissemination of the 2001 poverty map is the Center for International Earth Science Information Network at Columbia University's Earth Institute. The center published the Ecuador poverty maps on its poverty mapping Web site.[11] The Web site presents a compilation of small area poverty data for a number of countries. Users have access to the data in Excel tables or in graphical representation through maps in Portable Document Format. The center is expected to make related GIS data available to users in the near future.

The discussion of the poverty maps in the 2004 poverty assessment (World Bank 2004) is presented mainly in sections on the evolution of poverty and the profile of the poor. However, the information gained through the poverty maps is also used in other sections of the report, for example, in the chapters on rural productivity and on targeting in social assistance programs. Specifically, the assessment finds as follows:

- The poverty maps are used to explore baseline correlates of changes in poverty in cantons during the decade. The findings suggest that poverty increased the most in areas that had better endowments and in which the incidence of poverty was initially lower. This is consistent with the urban focus of the 1999 financial crisis.

■ The poverty maps are laid over agricultural productivity maps, and the analysis indicates that cantons exhibiting higher productivity show lower poverty, especially in rural areas and among households relying on the agricultural sector for livelihoods.

■ The poverty maps are also laid over regional data maps on the coverage of health and education services and social assistance to highlight the benefit incidence and targeting of expenditures in these sectors.

In addition, the data and the experience gained through the Ecuador exercise have been used in numerous research and academic publications on poverty mapping methodologies, the properties of poverty maps, and welfare-related analyses (see, for instance, Araujo et al. 2005; Elbers et al. 2004, 2007; Elbers, Lanjouw, and Lanjouw 2004).

The poverty assessment and documents relating to the dissemination effort are available on the World Bank Web site (see endnote 10).

Alternative poverty maps produced in Ecuador

In addition to the 1990 and 2001 poverty maps created by the World Bank in Ecuador, there have been local efforts to produce disaggregated indicators of welfare. These initiatives have employed methodologies different from the ones developed by the World Bank, and the maps have been drafted locally. The distribution of the related data has been extensive, and many users have access to the data in various formats. This is particularly true of the maps on unmet basic needs that are part of the SIISE compact disc, the principal and most popular source for socioeconomic data in the country. For these reasons, these maps (and not the ones produced by the World Bank) are commonly used for socioeconomic analysis and policy making in Ecuador. The discussion at the end of this section suggests specific actions that may help position the World Bank poverty maps as complements (or even alternatives) to these other tools.

The maps on unmet basics needs

Along with the 1990 and the 2001 censuses, Ecuador produced two poverty maps based on an index of unmet basic needs. The index is a weighted average of five household-level variables: (1) characteristics of the dwelling, (2) access to basic services, (3) the dependency ratio, (4) the presence of school-age children who are not attending school, and (5) crowdedness, which is measured by the number of persons per room.

The index exhibits limitations in methodology and in the variables used to construct it. As a result, its correlation with consumption poverty is only partial (see figure 8.2). Some of these limitations are as follows:

■ The index variables tend to be of a structural nature, while consumption poverty is likely be cyclical.

■ The index measures the poverty of households based on one or more unmet needs, though the impact of the lack of satisfaction of different needs on welfare is not necessarily identical.

- While the index allows the ranking of localities according to their unmet basic needs, it does not produce a measure of the precision of this estimator.
- The maps on unmet basic needs share comparability problems with the cartographic maps of Ecuador. They are therefore not comparable with each other in a strict sense.
- Unmet basic needs and consumption poverty describe different aspects of poverty. These are reflected in the distinct evolution of these two variables over time. Specifically, while consumption poverty has been found to have increased during the 1990s, structural poverty decreased as measured by the index of unmet basic needs.

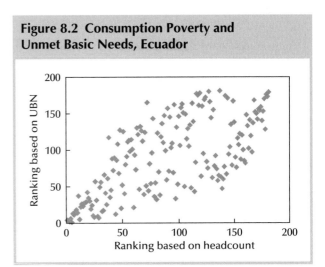

Figure 8.2 Consumption Poverty and Unmet Basic Needs, Ecuador

Sources: Compiled by the author. Data on unmet basic needs are from SIISE 2003.

The Infoplan project and map

The Infoplan planning information system project was initiated by the government within the President's Office of Developmental Planning to house geographically disaggregated socioeconomic data on poverty, health, education, employment, and the environment. The original project within the President's Office of Developmental Planning was supported through the World Bank's Modernization and State Technical Assistance Program and by other donors. The institutional support has not been steady, however. Infoplan is currently housed under the National Planning and Development Secretariat and is supported by the national association of municipalities and by the United Nations Population Fund. It is worth noting that, despite the institutional and political changes, the team that originally developed Infoplan established partnerships with local governments, nongovernmental organizations, and other researchers to sustain the project and produce the compact discs and update the databases.

The poverty map produced through Infoplan relies on principal components analysis. It combines the 1995 ECV and the 1990 census. Infoplan data are disseminated on compact discs and through various publications. The compact discs include GIS software that allows users to combine and map data. Users may select from a large list of indicators and display them one at a time in tables at different levels of geographical disaggregation. Users are also able to access the data online. The Web application permits users to construct maps by overlaying the poverty maps and visualizing other socioeconomic and environmental indicators. However, there is no application on the Web site that allows users to download the maps or the data directly into other programs such as Excel or GIS applications.

SelBen

SelBen is the largest national database on the beneficiaries of social assistance programs. Though not a poverty map, it is briefly discussed in this section because some have argued that the availability of SelBen may be one reason the number of policy applications for poverty maps is small in Ecuador.

The motive for the construction of the first poverty map in Ecuador in the mid-1990s was the government's need for a tool for geographical targeting in the allocation of compensatory transfers. In the late 1990s, an attempt to eliminate the compensatory transfers failed. As part of this process, a program of targeted cash transfers was created, the *bono solidario* (support benefit), which, in 2003, was retargeted and reformed into a conditional cash-transfer program, the *bono de desarrollo humano* (human development benefit).

To determine eligibility for the *bono de desarrollo humano,* a large investment was made to create a beneficiary selection system, SelBen. The main component of the system is a comprehensive database on households. The system is used to collect detailed information on household assets, carry out a proxy-means test, and compute scores through principal components analysis to determine eligibility for government programs. It now constitutes the most important tool for the targeting of social benefits on individuals.

SelBen covers over two-fifths of the households in the country. All rural parishes have participated in the SelBen census. In urban areas, on the other hand, a geographical targeting exercise was performed to select the census tracts where SelBen data would be collected. Targeting in urban areas is based on two instruments: first, the map on unmet basic needs derived using the 1990 census and, second, additional census variables measuring household access to public utilities such as running water and sewerage. The rankings among geographical units that have been produced according to census data are verified and validated by local authorities, who have a say in the choice of areas to be included or not included. Infoplan and World Bank poverty maps are not used for geographical targeting in SelBen, not even as a cross-check.

SelBen has been designed for individual household targeting, but it is not a substitute for poverty maps. Indeed, policy practitioners and others who use poverty data and who have been interviewed for this report acknowledge this. Specifically, they recognize that "SelBen risks becoming politicized and clientelistic, which is a risk that poverty maps do not have"; "poverty maps are helpful in geographical targeting, while SelBen is helpful in second-stage individual targeting"; "SelBen is very expensive to update; it includes the entire population of the country"; "SelBen is not a poverty map; it is an instrument that serves a different purpose."

One of the main goals of poverty mapping when it was first conceived and developed in Ecuador was to produce tools for targeting subsidies and social benefits. The decision to use SelBen and the maps on unmet basic needs as the main targeting tools and policy instruments in the social sectors has had implications for the large-scale policy applications of alternative targeting tools, such as the poverty maps created with the small area estimation methodology.

Policy informed by poverty maps

Given that the 2001 poverty map was disseminated through workshops, we decided to track down and interview individuals who had attended the two October 2003 workshops to discover whether and how they use poverty maps in their work. The goal of the interviews was also to learn how poverty maps and the dissemination of poverty maps might be improved to serve the needs of policy practitioners and the local development community. Two interview formats were designed for attendees at the two workshops: one focused on policy and applications, the other focused on a technical audience.[12] This section summarizes the main findings. While the initial interview formats were designed to distinguish between the poverty maps developed using the World Bank methodology and the other poverty maps available on Ecuador, it was established in practice that users tended to confuse the source of the poverty maps they had used. For this reason, unless otherwise specified, the results presented here refer to all poverty maps that are available; no attempt has been made to differentiate based on the source of the maps.

Poverty map users: policy and other applications

Of the 129 workshop attendees on the original list, it was possible to interview only 69 (53 percent). There was one main reason for this outcome: many people were no longer working in the organizations that had participated in the workshops in 2003, and it was not possible to locate them. In fact, of the 69 people who were interviewed, only 47 were still at the same organizations (36 percent of the 129 workshop attendees).[13] Clearly, a large majority of professionals active in policy, project management, and development in Ecuador do not hold permanent appointments, but work on short-term contracts with governmental and nongovernmental institutions. The steady rotation of technical staff needs to be taken into consideration by the World Bank in the distribution of publications targeted at this audience and in any capacity-building exercise. This finding supports the need to concentrate on building institutional capacity, as well as individual capacity.

It is worthwhile highlighting another factor, too: the overall profile of the people who attended the workshop. Most of these individuals were middle-aged professionals in institutions and sectors that might use poverty maps and other geo-referenced socioeconomic data. At an average age of 47, they had all completed tertiary education, and a considerable share reported that they had received some type of postgraduate degree. Of those interviewed, 38 percent were economists; 14 percent were health and education professionals; 10 percent were engineers; 10 percent were sociologists; and 6 percent were mathematicians. At the time of the interviews, 51 percent were government employees; 20 percent were with international organizations or donor agencies; 19 percent were academics; and 10 percent had jobs in nongovernmental organizations.

Given these professional backgrounds and affiliations, it is not surprising that 75 percent of the interviewees reported working with data frequently. When they were asked about the main source of the data they used, 39 identified SIISE, and 31 INEC. (More than one answer was possible.) Nine interviewees acknowledged using data produced by the World Bank. Other data sources included the central bank, ministries, and the interviewees' own organizations.

Among the interviewees, 94 percent possessed copies of the compact discs that are produced by SIISE and that contain socioeconomic data. This indicates that compact discs may be the most effective instrument for disseminating data in terms of exposure and coverage. It also highlights the great value of including World Bank poverty mapping data in the next version of the SIISE compact disc. A similar share of the interviewees recalled seeing a poverty map of Ecuador. Among these, 82 percent said they had used such a map at least once, but only 52 percent reported having access to digital versions. This shows that nearly half the interviewees were unaware that maps on unmet basic needs are included on the SIISE compact discs.

The survey found that 38 of the people who had used a poverty map had relied on the SIISE maps on unmet basic needs, while 9 had used the Infoplan map, 7 the ones produced by the World Bank, and 15 had used maps created by other entities.[14] (More than one response was possible per interviewee.) Those individuals who said they had never used poverty maps gave as the main reason their lack of access to the maps, their lack of understanding of the methodology behind the maps (and therefore skepticism about the value of the maps), or, for targeting purposes, their preference for the SelBen database.

All the interviewees were supportive of efforts to increase the distribution of poverty maps. By a large majority, they felt it would be most useful to make the maps available on compact discs. However, almost half the interviewees also insisted that it was important to complement the digital medium with hardcopy publications, given that access to computers is limited in Ecuador. One-third of the interviewees thought the data and map updates should be put on a Web site for ready access and download.

The interviewees also supplied suggestions on actual and potential applications for poverty maps in their work. These have been organized into three categories, which are summarized in box 8.1. Because of the design of the interviews, not much detailed information was collected on the specific applications. However, the box is interesting for the perspectives it provides on the broad range of uses for poverty maps.

The following is a more detailed description of actual poverty mapping applications revealed through an examination of the transcripts of the interviews:

1. *Project location:* A former staff member at the local office of the International Labour Organization had used the Infoplan poverty map in annual planning, especially

---

BOX 8.1   **Actual and Potential Poverty Map Uses: Policy and Applications Audience**

Development and policy work

- Targeting in governmental and nongovernmental projects
- Allocation of effort and resources, and allocations in projects and policy interventions
- Background information on regions and areas
- Determining differential tariffs on public utilities
- Program design and impact analysis
- Benefit incidence in public policy
- Local government applications
- Budget and investment allocations and approval processes
- In conjunction with other targeting tools such as SelBen
- Benchmarking and the establishment of baselines to assess changes in poverty
- The design of poverty reduction strategies
- Social policy design
- In conjunction with malnutrition and food security maps in estimating vulnerability and the costs of reducing incidence
- To foster transparency and government accountability
- Regional planning
- Identification of public investment priorities
- Sample stratification

Meeting institutional needs

- Verifying data provided by others
- Evaluation based on service coverage in areas where this is critical
- Planning future service coverage
- Cross-reference data for the media

Academic uses

- Research
- Identification of research topics and research areas for student theses
- As a teaching aid

---

in determining the location of projects in employment, microfinance, and small- and medium-enterprise development. Interestingly, the individual, who held a high-level position in planning at the Ministry of Labor at the time of the interview, acknowledged that he had not used poverty maps since leaving the International Labour Organization.

2. *Urban development:* The Centro de Investigaciones CIUDAD, a local nongovernmental organization involved in urban development, uses the Infoplan poverty map in planning urban reconstruction projects in historic neighborhoods, including assessing the socioeconomic impact of the projects.

3. *Food security maps:* A consultant with the World Food Programme used both the Infoplan poverty map and the maps on unmet basic needs to construct a map on food security and food vulnerability.

4. *Geographical targeting and donor projects:* The Italian Cooperation has used the maps on unmet basic needs to identify the 50 poorest parishes in the country. These parishes have been deemed eligible for development aid as part of a debt exchange program with the Italian government.

5. *Targeting the allocation of educational inputs:* The National System of Education Statistics within the Ministry of Education has used the maps on unmet basic needs in geographical targeting for the construction of new classrooms, school laboratories, and technical training equipment in schools in the poorest regions.

6. *Location of early childhood development interventions:* The *Organización de Rescate Infantil,* a national network of day-care centers, is one of the largest early childhood development programs in the Ministry of Social Welfare. It undertakes interventions in health care, nutrition, food programs, and early stimulation. The staff use the SelBen database to determine eligibility for the program and the maps on unmet basic needs to select new center locations.

7. *Internal planning at the Ministry of Social Welfare:* Various ministry programs and agencies have used the maps on unmet basic needs for internal planning in the distribution of their inventory of social assistance programs and services.

8. *Targeting investments at the Ministry of Health:* According to an interviewee who works at the government office responsible for the Millennium Development Goals, the Ministry of Health uses one of the poverty maps to identify the 200 poorest parishes for targeted investments to enhance the quality of health care services.

9. *Targeting at the Emergency Social Investment Fund:* The Emergency Social Investment Fund was created in March 1993. It finances small projects that are managed and implemented by local governments and local parish organizations. The fund targets project allocations using Infoplan data and the maps on unmet basic needs to identify parishes with higher poverty rates.

Poverty map users: technical aspects

The second set of interviews was carried out among a smaller group of persons. (Only seven interviews were completed.) The interviewees had participated in the poverty mapping workshop that emphasized methodological issues and were experts in poverty and inequality measurement. They had a thorough understanding of poverty data in the Ecuadorian context.

The focus of the interviews was to learn the views of these people on (1) the usefulness of World Bank involvement in poverty mapping given the other local efforts and methodologies and (2) activities that might render the World Bank contribution more relevant to local needs.

The main messages from these seven interviews may be summarized as follows:

- It is important to maintain World Bank involvement in poverty mapping. The quality of the Bank's methodologies relative to the maps developed locally is widely acknowledged.
- The interviewees agreed that it is crucial to institutionalize the poverty mapping exercise and to maintain updated maps as a complement to the investment in the SelBen database.
- The interviewees felt that the World Bank usually invests excessive resources in methodologies and product preparation, including in the case of the poverty maps, and not enough resources in product distribution.
- The interviewees were critical of the lack of a systematic effort to build local capacity in poverty mapping; they said this lack has translated into a lack of local ownership and continuity.

More specific information was gathered through the interviews to illustrate each of these issues. Regarding the first point, the interviewees emphasized that the quality of the World Bank poverty mapping methodology has been validated internationally. They noted, for example, that it is possible to quantify the precision of the Bank's estimates. The interviewees acknowledged that the software developed by the Bank has made poverty mapping less complicated to implement and more user friendly. They also liked the fact that structural relationships between welfare and the explanatory variables had been derived directly from the data.

However, the interviewees expressed some skepticism about the poverty maps developed by the Bank. Some preferred the maps on unmet basic needs, which are based on actual census averages and not on estimates. The interviewees pointed out that the 2001 World Bank poverty map did not include El Oriente. They considered this a major shortcoming for policy applications focusing on national issues. Several stressed that the Bank should support a technical assessment documenting the differences among the poverty maps on Ecuador, the results of related analyses, and the advantages and disadvantages of the various methodologies. Another suggestion was that all urban poverty maps should be disaggregated below the parish level. Urban parishes in most cities comprise tens of thousands of people, and policy makers require finer instruments in reaching decisions.

On the second point, the institutionalization of the poverty mapping exercise, the interviewees highlighted the benefits of the availability of an adequate tool for targeting geographical areas, which may sometimes be preferable to and politically more acceptable than targeting individuals. They also mentioned the advantages of the use of the two types of targeting jointly (for example, in two stages so as to combine geographical and individual targeting). The interviewees acknowledged that the value of poverty maps extends beyond targeting. For example, they stressed the importance of using poverty maps to validate SelBen data.

Regarding the third point, which concerns the distribution of World Bank products, particularly poverty maps, the interviewees expressed various perspectives. One criticized the Bank for producing "an academic environment around methodological aspects of the maps without opening up a space for discussion of the tools and their implications." Another interviewee highlighted the importance of investing in the distribution of poverty maps, saying that, "Only if more people know how the maps are constructed and how they may be applied in analysis will their use increase." The Bank should disseminate user-friendly techniques not only for the construction of such maps, but also for the use of the maps in generating graphic displays and overlays on socioeconomic indicators.

In relation to building local capacity, the interviewees argued that the World Bank should work on poverty mapping in close partnership with national public and private sector organizations so that local capacity is established and incentives are created for public and private organizations to compete in producing high-quality statistical data. More than one interviewee said that, although the World Bank has produced two poverty maps in Ecuador, there will be no local capacity to update these poverty maps when the data for the 2005–06 ECV become available "because the methodology is not easy, and the Bank has not worked in close partnership with local organizations on poverty mapping." On the positive side, the interviewees recognized that the new ECV represented an opportunity to establish fresh partnerships and collaboration between the World Bank and local institutions.

Lessons for the Future

The Ecuadorian experience in poverty mapping has provided many lessons on ways to strengthen the process of the creation and distribution of poverty maps so as to establish national ownership of the maps and enhance their use in policy decisions. The experience has also represented an opportunity for further collaborative work as the new household survey data become available. This survey is likely to create demand for a new, updated poverty map.

In anticipation of this process, a workshop on poverty measurement and the related methodologies was organized by a local private interdisciplinary research group in February 2005. Participants included governmental and nongovernmental organizations, development banks, and other external agencies. One of the most positive outcomes of this meeting was the endorsement by the attendees of a proposal issued to the government to create a technical group on poverty matters. The mandate of this group would be to (1) identify relevant methodological guidelines for poverty measurement, (2) produce official estimates on poverty and inequality for the country based on consumption expenditure data, and (3) ensure that there is continuity and consistency in data collection so that poverty might be monitored over time.

It is likely that Ecuador will engage in a new poverty mapping experience in the near future. The most important lessons that should be drawn from the analysis in this chapter and incorporated in such a future process are as follows:

1. *The importance of local capacity building:* In retrospect, it is clear that the World Bank poverty maps should have been created through a process that built local capacity. This is probably one of the main reasons for the lack of local ownership of the maps. It will be important to establish partnerships with local counterparts early on in the coming process. Agencies with different sets of skills and comparative advantages will be able to play strategic roles as counterparts at different stages. For example, given its technical capacity and experience, SIISE might become heavily involved in the development and distribution of the maps. In building local capacity, it will be crucial to transfer not only knowledge, but also the software, user manuals, and documentation that counterparts will need to produce poverty maps on their own.

2. *Dissemination activities:* Future dissemination activities should be carried out at several stages of the process. This will promote ownership among potential users of the maps early on. Moreover, user feedback and demands in terms of the presentation and dissemination of the data may be incorporated within the process in a timely fashion. It will also be important to organize workshops and other events for the distribution of the maps and other material on poverty mapping.

3. *Creation of a compact disc:* The dissemination of the poverty map should involve a serious investment in making the data accessible to users. A Web site and a compact disc that is widely distributed are likely to be the most effective means to reach users. Data should be accessible in tables that may be easily transferred onto spreadsheets or into a GIS. These digital media might even incorporate interactive GIS applications that allow users to produce their own maps and overlay socioeconomic variables at different levels of disaggregation. It is crucial that the material be user friendly, and users must be able to export the tables and maps onto other software platforms. The digital media should also include thorough documentation on the construction of the poverty maps, and this might also be distributed in a hardcopy version. It would be useful to incorporate some of these digital applications into the next version of the SIISE compact disc containing socioeconomic data that are already popular among the policy-making and academic community.

4. *Research that informs the local policy community:* Because several poverty maps already exist on Ecuador, there should be systematic collaboration between the World Bank and local researchers to document and inform the public on (1) the properties and the similarities and differences between the World Bank maps, the maps on unmet basic needs, and the Infoplan map, as well as their advantages and limitations in specific policy applications, and (2) the properties, advantages, and specific experiences with the use of various targeting instruments, including, specifically, geographical targeting and targeting on individual households.

5. *Policy uses of poverty maps:* The distribution activities might be supported through workshops designed to illustrate national and international applications of poverty maps in policy making. These workshops would also provide a good opportunity for the World Bank to benefit from feedback provided by poverty map users.

Annex 8.1 Ecuador Poverty Maps

Figure 8A.1 Incidence of Poverty by Parish, Ecuador 2001

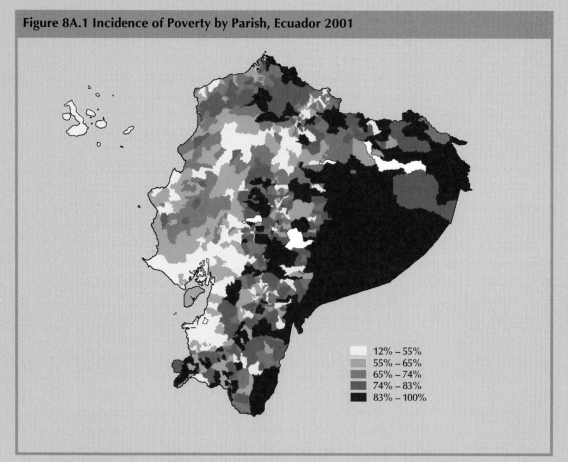

Source: Compiled by the author based on the 2001 total consumption poverty map.

Figure 8A.2 Incidence of Poverty by Canton, Ecuador 1990 and 2001

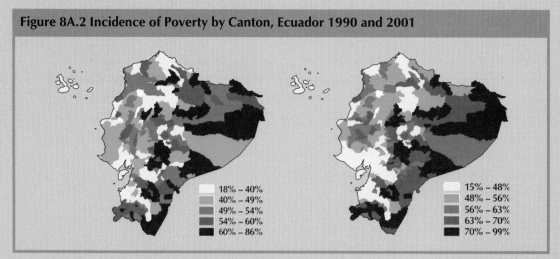

Source: Compiled by the author based on the comparable consumption poverty maps.

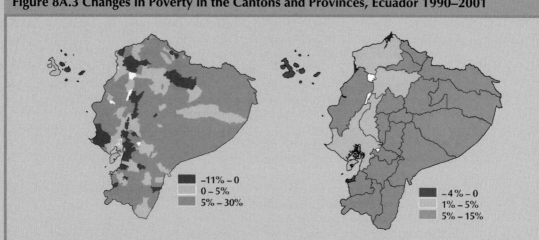

Figure 8A.3 Changes in Poverty in the Cantons and Provinces, Ecuador 1990–2001

-11% – 0
0 – 5%
5% – 30%

-4% – 0
1% – 5%
5% – 15%

Source: Compiled by the author based on the comparable consumption poverty maps.

Notes

1. In addition to its interaction with SIISE and INEC during the drafting of the maps, the World Bank was in frequent informal contact with Carlos Larrea, a local academic who has led valuable research on poverty measurement and the spatial distribution of welfare. His work on the Infoplan planning information system project is described elsewhere in this chapter. During the development of the 2001 poverty map, Larrea was preparing a malnutrition map for the Food and Agriculture Organization of the United Nations. The World Bank team shared with Larrea and his team relevant mapping data (with INEC authorization), methodological documents, and the poverty mapping software.
2. Ecuador is organized into 22 provinces, which are divided into 220 cantons and 995 parishes (*parroquias*). Throughout this chapter, the term "urban" encompasses parishes that are capitals of cantons (*cabecera cantonal*). Those parishes that are not capitals of cantons are classified as rural. In addition, for the purposes of the poverty maps, all census tracts in urban parishes, including urban peripheries (*zonas urbanas periféricas*), are classified as urban. This is the only difference between these urban-rural population figures and the ones produced by INEC.
3. A more detailed account of the methodology behind the panel exercise may be found in World Bank (2004).
4. According to data provided by INEC, 49 cantons were created between 1990 and 2001. (There was a total of 220 cantons in 2001.) The factors involved in the creation of new cantons are complex. While new cantons respond to population growth in rural parishes, which requires changes in local administrations, political issues are also involved since the creation of new cantons must be approved by Congress. Moreover, when a canton is created, a rural parish becomes a canton capital, and other, neighboring rural parishes in the same or other cantons are annexed to the new canton.
5. Specifically, the 1994 ECV included small rural towns, but no dispersed rural settlements. These were added to the sample starting in 1995. However, it is worth adding that, in favor of consistency, the sampling frames for all four surveys were based on the 1990 census.
6. The maps included in the annex use these estimates to illustrate the distribution of poverty in El Oriente.
7. The fieldwork for the most recent ECV commenced in November 2005, and data were to be collected for 12 months. The final sample is to be representative not only of all regions, but also of each of the 22 provinces, including urban and rural areas.

8. The figures in the 1990 poverty map revealed that the differences in the incidence of poverty in parishes derived from models using CE and TE were negligible. A comparison of the results of the two methodologies showed that the parish headcounts were less than two standard deviations apart. On the other hand, the 2001 exercise revealed that the headcount derived using TE as the dependent variable was systematically larger than the headcount derived using CE as the dependent variable.

9. Although, for parishes, differences between the 2001 poverty map derived using TE and the one derived using CE were statistically significant in a number of instances, it is worth noting that, in table 8.2, the geographical unit figures vary by less than two standard deviations.

10. http://wbln1018.worldbank.org/LAC/LAC.nsf/ECADocbyUnid/3DF59DABF75 E40E085256EA6006C59F6?Opendocument.

11. http://www.ciesin.columbia.edu/povmap/.

12. The interviews were carried out in November and December 2005 by Luis Miguel Chiriboga. The policy and application group was interviewed by phone, and the technical group, for which the lists of questions was much longer, was interviewed in person.

13. All the individuals in the technical group of interviewees that had attended the second workshop in 2003 had changed institutions.

14. To our knowledge, none of these other entities have ever produced poverty maps. So, these responses represent recall problems, or it may be that one or the other poverty map has also been issued through third parties.

References

Araujo, María Caridad, Francisco H. G. Ferreira, Peter F. Lanjouw, and Berk Özler. 2005. "Local Inequality and Project Choice in Ecuador's Social Investment Fund, 1993–97." Draft working paper, September, Development Economics Research Group, World Bank, Washington, DC.

Deaton, Angus, and Valerie Kozel. 2005. "Data and Dogma: The Great Indian Poverty Debate." *World Bank Research Observer* 20 (2): 177–99.

Elbers, Chris, Tomoki Fujii, Peter F. Lanjouw, Berk Özler, and Wesley Yin. 2007. "Poverty Alleviation through Geographic Targeting: How Much Does Disaggregation Help?" *Journal of Development Economics* 83 (1): 198–213.

Elbers, Chris, Jean O. Lanjouw, and Peter F. Lanjouw. 2003. "Micro-Level Estimation of Poverty and Inequality." *Econometrica* 71 (1): 355–64.

———. 2004. "Imputed Welfare Estimates in Regression Analysis." Policy Research Working Paper 3294, World Bank, Washington, DC.

Elbers, Chris, Peter F. Lanjouw, Johan A. Mistiaen, Berk Özler, and Ken Simler. 2004. "On the Unequal Inequality of Poor Communities." *World Bank Economic Review* 18 (3): 401–21.

Henninger, Norbert, and Mathilde Snel. 2002. *Where Are the Poor?: Experiences with the Development and Use of Poverty Maps.* Washington, DC: World Resources Institute; Arendal, Norway: United Nations Environment Programme–Global Resource Information Database.

Lanjouw, Jean O., and Peter F. Lanjouw. 1997. "Poverty Comparisons with Non-Compatible Data." Policy Research Working Paper 1709, World Bank, Washington, DC.

———. 2001. "How to Compare Apples and Oranges: Poverty Measurement Based on Different Definitions of Consumption." *Review of Income and Wealth* 47 (1): 25–42.

SIISE (Integrated System of Social Indicators of Ecuador). 2003. *Sistema Integrado de Indicadores Sociales del Ecuador.* CD-ROM, version 3.5. Quito: Information and Analysis Unit, Technical Secretariat, Ministry of Social Welfare.

World Bank. 1996. *Ecuador Poverty Report.* World Bank Country Studies Series. Washington, DC: World Bank.

———. 2004. *Ecuador Poverty Assessment.* Report 27061-EC, Poverty Reduction and Economic Management Sector Unit, Latin America and the Caribbean Region, World Bank, Washington, DC.

9

Indonesia's Poverty Maps
Impacts and Lessons

YUSUF AHMAD AND CHOR-CHING GOH

ABBREVIATION

BPS	*Badan Pusat Statistik* (the national statistical office)

Country Context

Indonesia is a large country of over 200 million people. While it was quite successful in reducing poverty between 1960 and 1990, some 37 million people were still living in abject poverty at the end of that period, surviving on less than a dollar a day in 1990.[1] In 1994, the government explicitly identified poverty reduction and elimination as a national objective for the first time, in the Sixth Five-Year Development Plan. Since then, there have been four major antipoverty programs.[2] However, the design and implementation of these programs have been hindered by the lack of poverty information at geographically disaggregated levels.

The authors would like to thank the following for taking time to provide helpful suggestions, insights, and feedback: Happy Dudy, Rusman Heriawan, Amir Kahar, Soedarty Surbakti, and Dedi Walujadi of Badan Pusat Statistik; Agus Chamdun and Herawati of the Ministry of Social Affairs; Sumedi A. Mulyo and Pungky Sumadi of Bappenas; Nafi and Widjanarko of the Ministry of Finance; Atmarita of the Ministry of Health; Bambang Irianto, Kasi, Lucy, Singgah Raharjo, and Betty Sinaga of the Ministry of Education; Sujana Royat and H. Tonno Supranotos of the Coordinating Ministry for People's Welfare; Sara Evaliyanti and Yenny Suryani of Catholic Relief Services; Noriko Toyoda of the United Nations Development Programme; Spriyadi of the United Nations Children's Fund; Yanti of Oxfam; Sonja of the Center for International Forest Research; Lisa Kulp of the Asian Development Bank; and Timothy H Brown, Tomoki Fujii, Emmet O'Malley, and Menno Pradhan of the World Bank.

As in other countries, poverty statistics based on surveys are only representative at the regional and urban or rural levels in Indonesia. There have been several attempts to produce poverty estimates for lower administrative units. For instance, the Presidential Instruction on Disadvantaged Villages Program of 1994–97 was the first major effort to produce small area poverty estimates nationally. The aim of the program was to classify all villages in Indonesia as either poor or nonpoor. Other attempts included a complete enumeration of all villages and village characteristics in the country (village potential statistics, or PODES; see elsewhere below) and the classification of all families in Indonesia into five welfare categories that was carried out by the Family Planning Coordination Board. However, these efforts were expensive, and some operations still suffered from undercoverage among villages and inconsistency in data gathering.

By early 2000, the government was expressing immense interest in the poverty mapping approach developed by a World Bank research team (Elbers, Lanjouw, and Lanjouw 2003). This approach combines information from a household survey and a population census to estimate the economic welfare of small areas. It does not involve much additional cost because the requisite data sources already exist, that is, household surveys, population censuses, and other, auxiliary databases. Furthermore, the small area estimates of welfare are accompanied by measures of precision (such as standard errors and confidence intervals). These estimates of welfare (for example, poverty and inequality) may be represented on high-resolution maps, which are therefore commonly called poverty maps. The disaggregated information on these maps is useful in identifying the share of the poor or the incidence of poverty, and this, in turn, may inform budget allocations and program design and targeting.

The Mapping Process

In the first phase of its assistance for poverty mapping in Indonesia during 2002–03, the World Bank hired a local entity, the independent SMERU Research Institute, through an Asia-Europe Meeting grant to help guide the staff at *Badan Pusat Statistik* (BPS), the national statistical office, in the production of poverty maps on three provinces: East Java, East Kalimantan, and Jakarta. The main objective of the pilot phase was to test the feasibility of applying the poverty mapping approach in Indonesia and provide step-by-step training to the BPS. At the time, the 2000 population census data were not yet available for the entire country. The results of the first phase are presented in Suryahadi et al. (2005). Then, in the second phase (2003–04), BPS staff produced poverty estimates disaggregated to the district (regency or city, *kabupaten* or *kota*), subdistrict (*kecamatan*), and village (*desa* or *kelurahan*) levels on the rest of the 27 provinces that were mapped. The World Bank continued to support the BPS through the Asia-Europe Meeting Trust Fund by providing expertise, hardware, and advice, as well as support in the dissemination of the poverty maps to local governments.

The mapping exercise relied on three sources of data, namely, the consumption and core modules of the 1999 household survey (the socioeconomic survey known as Susenas), the 2000 population census, and the 1999 village census (PODES).[3] All the data were collected by the BPS. The data on household consumption and household characteristics used in the mapping were obtained from Susenas, and additional information on villages was gleaned from PODES.

The exercise was the first occasion on which all these data sets were combined, and one major problem was discovered: the village codes are not identical in all three data sources. The BPS should possess a master list of all villages and keep track of changes in administrative divisions (such as the merging or the partitioning of villages), and, in theory, all the villages in Susenas and the population census should also exist in PODES. However, because of decentralization, the BPS has not kept up with the changes in these lowest administrative units, and a number of villages (as many as 10 percent of the villages in four provinces) do not match in the three data sources. To overcome this shortcoming, BPS staff imputed information on the missing villages using averages at the subdistrict level.

All the poverty estimates on provinces, districts, and subdistricts were within acceptable limits. However, the results at the village level need to be viewed with caution because the precision in poverty headcounts varies greatly across villages within individual provinces. Some village estimates suffer from high standard errors, and more village-level information will be required to improve the precision. Figures 9.1 and 9.2 present two examples of the poverty maps.

Many people have expressed the opinion that the maps are out of date because they are partly based on the population census, which only occurs once in a decade. However, this problem is being addressed by the World Bank research team given that a methodology to revise the maps between census years is being developed and tested in several countries in the region, including the Philippines and Thailand.

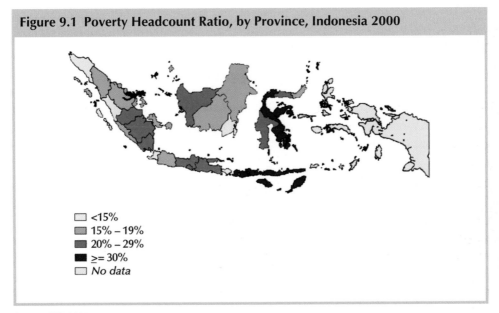

Figure 9.1 Poverty Headcount Ratio, by Province, Indonesia 2000

☐ <15%
■ 15% – 19%
■ 20% – 29%
■ >= 30%
☐ *No data*

Source: BPS 2004.

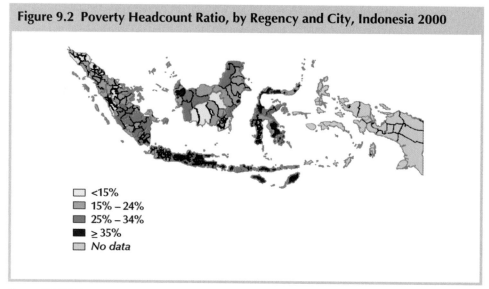

Figure 9.2 Poverty Headcount Ratio, by Regency and City, Indonesia 2000

Source: BPS 2004.

Another shortcoming noted by users is the fact that the maps only contain estimates of poverty and inequality, but do not contain information on other indicators of interest. However, this criticism misunderstands the poverty mapping approach. The methodology does not exclude the estimation and mapping of other indicators. Thus, for example, the World Food Programme and the BPS have created follow-up nutrition maps on the entire country. Other applications abound elsewhere, for instance, the health status maps on children in Cambodia, the caloric maps in Nepal, and the measurements of welfare among minority groups such as artisanal fishermen in Thailand and the disabled in Uganda.

Impacts: Actual Poverty Map Applications

Since their distribution in December 2004, the national poverty maps of the BPS have been used in various applications by government agencies, donors, and nongovernmental organizations (NGOs).

Ministry of Finance, budget estimates of unconditional cash transfers to the poor

In 2005, the government of Indonesia decided to cut fuel subsidies. The resulting increase in fuel prices would particularly affect the poor, and the government planned to cushion this negative shock by providing unconditional cash transfers to the poor. The Ministry of Finance used the poverty maps to estimate the budget for the cash transfers.

Ministry of Education, selection of beneficiary areas

The Ministry of Education has several programs targeted at helping vulnerable groups. The ministry has used the poverty maps to select beneficiary areas for these programs, which include the Skills-for-a-Living Program (*Kecakapan Hidup*), the Mainstream Gender in Education Program, and the Prevention of Women Trafficking Program. The Skills-for-a-Living Program, for example, has an annual budget of Rp 125,000,000 (approximately US$13,000) and seeks to help young unemployed Indonesians who are poor, out of school, and without marketable skills. The program provides these unemployed youth with training to acquire vocational and social skills so they may become self-sufficient and use the skills to find jobs. The participants are between 15 and 35 years old. Based on their positive experience with the ease of use of the maps, the Ministry of Education has recommended that other divisions also use the poverty maps for area targeting in their programs.

Ministry of Social Affairs and the United Nations Development Programme, cross checking and referencing

The Ministry of Social Affairs has a positive perception of the poverty maps and uses the small area poverty estimates to cross-check the information in its own database (for example, the nonmonetary dimensions of poverty). The ministry and the BPS have an ongoing collaboration whereby the BPS collects and updates information every year for the ministry's database. The United Nations Development Programme also uses the maps to cross-check its own information and other data it acquires from the Coordinating Ministry for People's Welfare and various line ministries for budget planning and targeting for its programs.

World Food Programme, production of follow-up nutrition maps

High-level staff at the World Food Programme have recognized that the poverty mapping experience has given the BPS the know-how and capacity to produce follow-up nutrition maps efficiently for its projects. The nutrition maps are used to select beneficiary areas.

Bina Desa

Bina Desa Secretariat (the Indonesian Secretariat for the Development of Human Resources in Rural Areas) is an NGO that operates in the field of empowerment and human resources in Indonesian villages. It has used the poverty maps of the BPS, but finds that the lack of other correlates such as population and locality variables on the maps is a limitation. More information, including a population profile, would be needed so that the maps may also be used for health insurance, scholarship initiatives, and other types of programs.

The local development planning board in Yogyakarta Province, identification of poor districts

The local development planning board in Yogyakarta Province has used the BPS poverty maps to identify poor districts (*kabupaten*) in the implementation of its Community Empowerment Program (*Pemberdayaan Masyarakat*).

The World Bank

Within the World Bank, the environment team is using the poverty maps to help guide their policy advice to the Indonesian government under the Forest Law Enforcement and Governance Initiative. In particular, the maps are providing information on poor people living in forested areas, poor people living within the State Forest Zone, and the relationship between forest coverage and poverty incidence.

The Bank's infrastructure team has used the poverty maps of East Java Province to prepare the East Java Strategic Infrastructure and Development Reform Program. The program provides loans and technical assistance to the provincial government through a combination of investments and supporting policy measures to attract investment and promote growth. The maps have been especially useful in identifying the poorest areas in East Java, notably, along the southern coast.

In addition to the various applications cited above, other impacts of the poverty maps include the increased awareness of the usefulness of poverty maps as a tool in geographical targeting. This awareness has generated a demand for updated and richer maps. The current poverty maps are limited to a few indicators (poverty and inequality). The government has realized that, to enhance the usefulness of the maps, complementary maps of other dimensions of poverty are needed. The Ministry for National Development Planning has been a leading advocate for creating a set of maps that encompass a range of core indicators. The ministry has begun discussions with other line ministries and donors about building a new set of maps under the Development of Data Systems and Analyses for Regional Planning Initiative.

Many officials have indicated that the poverty maps have highlighted the issue of poverty and energized the government to focus on poverty reduction. The poverty maps have also raised the profile of the BPS; it is increasingly being perceived as an institution committed to poverty reduction. Since the publication of the poverty maps, the BPS has been invited to participate in planning and strategy development at several ministries. For example, when the Ministry of Finance decided to implement the cash transfers program after terminating fuel subsidies, the BPS was one of the organizations consulted about the feasibility of the transfers at the subdistrict level.

Impacts: Potential Poverty Map Applications

During discussions with officials, we have also learned that small area estimates of poverty and inequality may be helpful in the following programs.

Kecamatan Development Program

The Kecamatan Development Program aims at reducing poverty in rural communities and improving local governance. The first phase of the program began in 1998 and ended in 2002. The second phase ran from 2002 to 2006. The program provides block grants of Rp 350 million to Rp 1 billion (US$40,000 to $114,000) directly to subdistricts and villages for small-scale infrastructure and social and economic activities. The current criteria for identifying poor districts are not very clear, and the poverty maps might be a helpful tool in identifying poor subdistricts in a consistent, systematic manner.

Unconditional and conditional cash transfers

Anticipating that the October 2005 removal of fuel subsidies and subsequent price increases would have a major impact on lower-income households, the government rapidly designed and implemented a short-term unconditional cash transfer program for 15.5 million poor and near-poor households. The transfers began on October 1, 2005, and ran for a period of three months. Initially, some officials suggested that the cash transfers might be given to village leaders for distribution based on the poverty maps. However, Indonesia's vice president decided that the cash transfers should be given to individual households directly.

The program is set to go forward again following evaluation. It has evolved into a conditional cash transfer system as part of a larger antipoverty agenda. Conditional cash transfers provide money to poor families contingent upon the fulfillment of certain criteria, such as investments in human capital (for example, as measured through school attendance or regular visits to health centers by children). Conditional cash transfer programs have two main objectives—immediate income support and the longer-term accumulation of human capital—and serve as a demand-side complement to the supply of health and education services. Currently, the program uses the poverty census to channel funds to the poor, but the leakage is substantial, and the poverty census is an expensive exercise. The poverty mapping methodology might help identify key correlates of poverty that would facilitate proxy-means testing, and it would be much cheaper than a poverty census.

Local governments and NGOs

Many of the representatives of government agencies who were interviewed had never heard of the poverty maps, but, when they were told of the maps, most acknowledged that such a tool would be useful in their programs. A primary potential user is local governments. A significant portion of the national budget is given to local governments for ultimate distribution. With proper training, local governments might make good use of the poverty maps for the allocation of resources among their administrative units.

Other potential users of the maps are the donor and NGO communities. These communities fund a wide range of poverty programs in the country. Oxfam International, for example, has many area-targeted projects in Indonesia and is well connected with local

NGOs. While Oxfam representatives had heard of the poverty maps, they had never received a copy of the report or seen the maps. Oxfam might use the maps for site selection and might also promote the use of the maps among their partnering NGOs. Similarly, most of the NGO representatives interviewed had never heard of the BPS poverty maps, but they believed the maps might become an important tool for targeting. In particular, most NGO projects are carried out at the district level, and a tool such as the poverty maps that facilitates selection among poor districts should be appealing.

Lessons

1. Consultation and effective dissemination are needed to dispel skepticism, foster dialogue, and encourage use.

In Jakarta on December 23, 2004, shortly after the poverty maps had been completed, the BPS held a seminar to disseminate the findings. Participants at the seminar included officials at ministries and other government agencies, local government officials, and representatives of donor organizations and NGOs. Some 1,000 hard copies of the poverty map reports were distributed. Subsequent to the seminar, dissemination was also carried out through eight provincial seminars funded by the local BPS offices in eight provinces: Bali, Bengkulu, East Java, East Kalimantan, North Sumatra, Semarang (Central Java), South Kalimantan, and South Sulawesi.

The demand for the information reflected in the maps appears to be high among lower administrative units. However, the BPS was constrained by funding limitations from distributing the maps more broadly to such units. A workshop to educate local BPS staff, as well as the staff of local development planning boards, on the methodology and on applications of poverty maps would have been immensely helpful. Without full understanding of the maps, local BPS staff must rely on the central BPS office to explain and promote use of the maps. Local development planning boards are the primary implementation agencies for a wide range of programs, and, thus, educating them about the maps might enhance the propoor impact of their projects and investments.

Many government agencies still harbor doubts about the mapping methodology and its reliability and robustness. One reason is that they feel that the process lacked inputs from end users during the early stages of development. Many said they were not given any opportunity to provide suggestions or feedback before the maps were completed. Thus, the participation of and consultation with stakeholders throughout the production of poverty maps are crucial not only to educate users and to raise awareness about the maps and the mapping methodology, but also to promote wider demand for the end product and institutionalize the mapping process.

The BPS is the producer of the maps, but the maps need a champion in a government agency that plans or implements the country's antipoverty programs. The Ministry for National Development Planning would be an ideal candidate. Sri Mulyani Indrawati, the minister of development planning in 2004 (and currently the minister of finance), was one of the few who understood the wide-ranging applications of poverty maps and urged government agencies to use them.

It appears that the potential applications of the poverty maps are not being conveyed effectively. For instance, somewhat ironically, the poverty maps produced by SMERU Research Institute and relying on the identical methodology have been more favorably received and accepted (see below). Many representatives of NGOs and donors said they knew about the SMERU poverty maps, but not those of the BPS. One main reason is that SMERU has been effective at dissemination. Maps produced by SMERU have been available on the Web, as well as on interactive compact discs, and SMERU's data formats are user-friendly. On the other hand, the BPS maps are only available in those 1,000 hard copies distributed at the national seminar, and there is no information about the maps on the BPS Web site.

2. In fulfilling the goal of building local capacity, avoid the creation of parallel, potentially competing maps.

There are two sets of poverty maps on Indonesia, and they have relied on the same methodology. One has been prepared by SMERU Research Institute, and the other has been prepared by the BPS. During the pilot phase of the mapping exercise (2002–03), SMERU was hired by the World Bank and the BPS as a local consultant to produce maps for three provinces, while training BPS staff on the methodology. The understanding was that, during the second and final phase, SMERU would supervise the BPS as the latter completed maps on the rest of the country. However, subsequently, in 2005, SMERU, in collaboration with the Ford Foundation, completed maps on the rest of Indonesia, while the BPS, with World Bank technical assistance, was also producing maps for the rest of the country. It would have been helpful to hold discussions, share experiences, and compare results, but both the BPS and SMERU carried out their work on their own without much interaction. Moreover, the existence of the parallel sets of poverty maps published only months apart has created much confusion and undermined the BPS initiative. The experience in other countries suggests that reliance on international consultants avoids this potential conflict of interest between local consultants and the government. However, such a reliance may also hinder local capacity building. A more constructive approach might be to obtain prior agreements that the local consultants will partner and collaborate with the government and that the end product will be a joint effort.

3. Ensure the internal cohesion of the agency that produces the maps.

In Indonesia, as in many other countries, the poverty mapping exercise has involved the merging of several data sets for the first time. In other countries, merging different data sets is synonymous with asking different divisions of the national statistics office to work together to produce a single product. This may represent a challenge because the division of labor is not obvious. In Indonesia, however, the question became which division should produce the poverty maps, the Mapping Division or the Poverty Division. In the end, the project was assigned to the Mapping Division, which does not have the requisite skills in statistical analysis, the experience in policy advisory services, or familiarity with antipoverty programs. Meanwhile, the people in the Poverty Division with the appropriate expertise felt alienated. This limited the outreach and impact of the maps.

4. Make potential users aware of the wide-ranging applications of poverty maps and emphasize that poverty maps are complementary to (rather than a substitute for) other antipoverty information tools.

Partly because of the internal controversy within the BPS over the production and ownership of the poverty maps, when the vice presidential directive was issued to carry out a poverty census, many in the BPS embraced this endeavor with great enthusiasm and viewed the census as a substitute for the poverty maps. However, given the particular uses of poverty maps, the two tools should be considered complementary.

While the poverty maps facilitate geographical targeting over targeting on households or individuals, the mapping methodology is able to provide considerable information about correlates of poverty at the household or individual level. Thus, indirectly, poverty maps also contribute to understanding the proxy determinants of poverty that the poverty census seeks to obtain. In particular, the poverty mapping process illustrates a rich set of variables suitable for proxy-means testing.

Unlike the population census, the poverty census is not an enumeration of all households in Indonesia. The poverty census was completed in three months at a cost of US$40 million. Many users have expressed concern about the limitations and the quality of the poverty census. For example, the lists of poor households in villages were supplied by village leaders, and their perception may have been subjective and rather arbitrary. This is complicated by the fact that many households are near poor, and it is difficult for local leaders to identify the difference accurately.

Given that the poverty census data are now available, the BPS may consider undertaking an analysis to compare the data reflected in the poverty maps and the data collected through the poverty census. Despite some of the limitations in the poverty census, this exercise would yield a great deal of information and offer the opportunity to validate the findings shown in the poverty maps.

Conclusions

There is evidence that the poverty maps of Indonesia have been used by government agencies and the donor and NGO communities. The number and types of applications might have been greater if there had been more consultations at the beginning and more effective dissemination at the end. The lack of participation of potential users during the mapping process has created resistance to the maps and skepticism about their utility. The broad-ranging uses of the maps were not effectively conveyed to users, who were, in most cases, frustrated with the difficult formats of the maps and their unavailability on the Web or in electronic copies.

The poverty mapping exercise has been particularly successful in encouraging local capacity building. The World Bank transferred the know-how to a local research institution that, in turn, guided BPS staff step-by-step in the poverty mapping methodology during the pilot phase. Subsequently, BPS staff produced the maps for the other provinces in Indonesia on their own under the supervision of the World Bank team.

In addition to the concrete uses and applications of the poverty maps, the poverty mapping exercise and the dissemination of the maps have had other impacts. The government has renewed its focus on poverty issues, and the issue of identifying and locating the poor has been debated. A discussion of poverty monitoring has been reinvigorated. Government agencies have come together to discuss the need to undertake concerted efforts to compile more reliable and timely poverty information to support government policies. Spearheaded by the Ministry for National Development Planning, the government is taking steps to create a database encompassing the monetary and nonmonetary dimensions of poverty so as to help improve regional and local planning.

Notes

1. This is the US$1-a-day poverty line adjusted for purchasing power parity.
2. These programs are the Presidential Instruction on Disadvantaged Villages, which aimed at accelerating poverty reduction in less developed villages across Indonesia; the Family Welfare Development Programs, designed to intensify the poverty reduction effort; the Income-Generating Project for Marginal Farmers, which sought to increase the incomes of small farmers through self-help groups; and the Twin Urban and Rural Kecamatan Development Programs, which provided block grants to poor subdistricts to reduce rural and urban poverty.
3. For an explanation of the data sources for the mapping exercise, see Suryahadi and Sumarto (2003). PODES is a complete enumeration of all villages in the country that has been constructed by the BPS. This village census collects information mainly on the presence (or absence) of infrastructure and facilities such as roads, health facilities, schools, market facilities, water supplies, electricity, telephone links, public toilets, and so on.

References

BPS (Badan Pusat Statistik). 2004. *Peta penduduk miskin Indonesia, 2000* [Poverty map 2000]. Jakarta: Badan Pusat Statistik.

Elbers, Chris, Jean O. Lanjouw and Peter F. Lanjouw. 2003. "Micro-Level Estimation of Poverty and Inequality." *Econometrica* 71 (1): 355–64.

Suryahadi, Asep, and Sudarno Sumarto. 2003. "Poverty Mapping Effort in Indonesia." Paper presented at the Ad Hoc Expert Group Meeting, "Poverty Mapping and Monitoring Using Information Technology," United Nations Economic and Social Commission for Asia and the Pacific, Bangkok, August 18–20.

Suryahadi, Asep, Wenefrida Widyanti, Rima Prama Artha, Daniel Perwira, and Sudarno Sumarto. 2005. "Developing a Poverty Map for Indonesia: A Tool for Better Targeting in Poverty Reduction and Social Protection Programs." SMERU Research Report, February, SMERU Research Institute, Jakarta.

10

Poverty Maps and Public Policy in Mexico

LUIS F. LÓPEZ-CALVA, L. RODRÍGUEZ-CHAMUSSY, AND MIGUEL SZÉKELY

ACRONYMS AND ABBREVIATIONS

HDI	Human Development Index
INEGI	*Instituto Nacional de Estadística, Geografía, e Informática* (National Institute for Statistics, Geography, and Informatics)
UNDP	United Nations Development Programme

In Mexico, as in many other countries, there is a need for more accurate information for the design and evaluation of public policy. In the context of macroeconomic analysis, we may access data on income, interest rates, exchange rates, and so on, but, when we move to the realm of microeconomic policy, the lack of information becomes evident. In the case of social policy and poverty alleviation interventions, we usually have nationally representative surveys at specific levels of aggregation, such as rural versus urban population, or national poverty rates. If we wish to fine-tune policy regionally to deal with clusters of poverty or backward regions, the only available source of information is often the census, which, in the case of Mexico, has been shown generally to be imprecise in terms of household income and expenditure data.[1]

Through a joint effort by the *Secretaría de Desarrollo Social* (Ministry of Social Development), academics, and the office of the United Nations Development Programme (UNDP) in Mexico, poverty maps became available in 2005. Because of this and because

---

The authors would like to thank Hector Sandoval for his assistance in carrying out interviews with around 50 relevant actors on the use of poverty maps.

of the growing use of data on poverty and inequality, as well as human development indicators, awareness has increased on the need to sharpen policies for specific local interventions. A program in Mexico to target policies on the 50 municipalities with the lowest levels of human development and highest poverty rates has been a direct result of this awareness.

The traditional source of information for the measurement of poverty in Mexico has been the *Encuesta Nacional de Ingresos y Gastos de los Hogares* (National Household Income and Expenditure Survey). The survey was carried out in 1984, 1989, and 1992, and has been carried out every two years since then. The survey allows the estimation of poverty at the national level, as well as in rural and urban areas generally. As the disaggregation increases, the standard errors of the indicators begin to rise, such that estimates become unacceptably imprecise even for the states (Soloaga and Torres 2003). It has thus become apparent that more accurate estimates of poverty, inequality, income, and consumption at lower levels of disaggregation would be excellent tools for improving policy design.

When the decision was taken to pursue the poverty mapping project, several other events had already occurred favoring the attainment of this goal, though the process still faced hurdles. The first event was the arrival of a new staff member at the Office of the President of Mexico. Formerly with the Research Department at the Inter-American Development Bank, this individual, Miguel Székely, had been exploring poverty mapping for some time and wanted to establish a partnership with academics in Mexico who were also interested in the methodology. Through the Office of the President, a meeting was therefore organized involving the participation of selected researchers and an advisory group at the World Bank. The mapping methodology was reviewed. A workshop was held, and a Mexican team started looking into specific data requirements.

This team later moved to the Ministry of Social Development, where the direct relevance of the project to policy design was immediately appreciated. Especially because of the interest generated during the launch of the first *Human Development Report* on Mexico (UNDP 2002), the participation of UNDP Mexico attracted external institutional support and helped bring the project to completion.[2]

This chapter describes the process, obstacles, and outcomes of the poverty mapping project in Mexico. This is a story of innovation. The process involved the intervention of academics, the Ministry of Social Development, and an external agency, the UNDP. The strengths of each of the agents joined to bring the process to fruition. The description of poverty mapping in Mexico, the use of the mapping output in policy analysis and public advocacy, and the perceptions of academics, policy makers, and politicians in Mexico on the potential importance of this tool are the themes of the chapter.

The Evolution of Poverty and the Need for Disaggregation

The reduction in poverty in Mexico in recent years, a trend that started during 1996–98 after the peso crisis, has gained a great deal of attention in academic and public policy circles in Mexico and abroad. Several explanations have been hypothesized for the success in reducing poverty, among which the following are the most common:

- The importance of macroeconomic stability and changes in the relative prices for essential goods
- The recovery of sustained positive growth rates
- The consistency and expansion of well-targeted social expenditure policies, such as the Progresa-Oportunidades conditional cash transfer scheme
- The increase in remittances from migrant members to poor families

Recent trends in household poverty in Mexico are illustrated in tables 10.1 and 10.2.

Research has focused on analyzing the overall time trends, but only recently has there been an emphasis on the fact that the reduction in poverty is occurring mainly in the rural sector and that poverty in the urban sector has been persistent. Reductions in poverty rates in the rural sector have also been accompanied by a reduction in inequality.

In any case, the discussions about the design and implementation of specific social programs such as Progresa-Oportunidades made clear that it would be impossible to understand trends in poverty properly without the regional dimension. The need for disaggregated data was evident.

Disaggregated information was available in Mexico on social indicators, but not specifically on poverty. The three most important indicators that have been developed and used in Mexico in recent years are the marginality index (National Population Council), a so-called welfare index (*Instituto Nacional de Estadística, Geografía, e Informática* [National Institute for Statistics, Geography, and Informatics, INEGI]), and the deprivation index, which was used during the implementation of the budget reform of 1997.[3] These indexes are all based on census or population count information and are multidimensional. They differ in the dimensions included and the way they are aggregated. For example, the marginality index relies on factor analysis. All of them, however, use income information directly from the census, which makes them susceptible to the usual criticism, that is, that the census has not been designed as an instrument for the collection of data on income. Using it for this purpose results in an inaccurate account of the phenomenon, which becomes especially important when the policy objective is related to regional targeting. Combining census information and household survey data turns out to be an obvious option in this case.

At least two important institutional changes in the last decade have also prompted the need for better data at a low level of disaggregation. In the late 1990s, a path-breaking budget reform took place in Mexico that established a new mechanism to distribute a larger share of federal resources to states and municipalities based on specific socioeconomic and demographic criteria. Later, in 2003, the General Law on Social Development was passed in Congress. Among other steps, the law required data on poverty in municipalities to be made available at five-year intervals.

Table 10.1 Trends in Poverty Incidence among Households, Mexico 2000–02

Poverty	Headcount		Standard error		$P_{2002}-P_{2000}$				
	2000	2002	2000	2002	Incidence change	Difference in standard error	Z-statistic	Significance level	Significance
National									
PL1	18.6	15.8	0.7418	0.8605	−2.789	1.136	−2.455	0.0070	yes
PL2	25.3	21.8	0.8583	0.9687	−3.542	1.294	−2.736	0.0031	yes
PL3	45.9	43.0	1.0698	1.2061	−2.865	1.612	−1.777	0.0378	yes
Rural									
PL1	34.1	28.5	1.5681	2.1064	−5.564	2.626	−2.119	0.0171	yes
PL2	41.4	36.6	1.7174	2.3109	−4.780	2.879	−1.660	0.0484	yes
PL3	60.7	57.2	1.7358	2.8962	−3.573	3.377	−1.058	0.1450	no
Urban									
PL1	9.8	8.5	0.7334	0.5746	−1.251	0.932	−1.342	0.0898	no
PL2	16.2	13.3	0.9449	0.7276	−2.886	1.193	−2.420	0.0078	yes
PL3	37.4	34.9	1.3562	1.0189	−2.510	1.696	−1.480	0.0695	no

Source: López-Calva et al. 2005.
Note: PL1 corresponds to what is officially called food poverty, PL2 to capabilities poverty, and PL3 to asset poverty.

Table 10.2 Trends in Poverty Incidence among Households, Mexico 2002–04

| Poverty | Headcount | | Standard error | | P_{2004}–P_{2002} | | | | |
	2002	2004	2002	2004	Incidence change	Difference in standard error	Z-statistic	Significance level	Significance
National									
PL1	15.8	13.7	0.8605	0.5269	−2.145	1.009	−2.126	0.0167	yes
PL2	21.8	19.8	0.9687	0.6475	−1.993	1.165	−1.710	0.0436	yes
PL3	43.0	39.6	1.2061	0.8541	−3.423	1.478	−2.316	0.0103	yes
Rural									
PL1	28.5	22.3	2.1064	1.4853	−6.196	2.577	−2.404	0.0081	yes
PL2	36.6	29.4	2.3109	1.8751	−7.155	2.976	−2.404	0.0081	yes
PL3	57.2	48.8	2.8962	2.3141	−8.340	3.707	−2.250	0.0122	yes
Urban									
PL1	8.5	8.7	0.5746	0.3781	0.116	0.688	0.168	0.5668	no
PL2	13.3	14.2	0.7276	0.4183	0.899	0.839	1.071	0.8579	no
PL3	34.9	34.2	1.0189	0.5593	−0.670	1.162	−0.576	0.2822	no

Source: López-Calva et al. 2005.
Note: PL1 corresponds to what is officially called food poverty, PL2 to capabilities poverty, and PL3 to asset poverty.

Institutional Changes That Have Reinforced the Need for Data

Two institutional perspectives that require more finely disaggregated data on poverty have recently become significant within a legal context in Mexico: first, the federalist perspective and, second, the growing awareness of the need to maintain continuity in social policy and in policy evaluation across political cycles.

Decentralization

Mexico has recently experimented with two major reforms aimed at strengthening a decentralized approach to development. The first reform, passed by Congress in 1983, sought to enhance the policy-making authority of local governments. In 1997, after a long process of negotiation between the federal government, state governments, and coalitions of local governments, a second major push toward a more decentralized system was undertaken in the country. This second reform was the result of a decisive effort by the federal government to transfer funds to local governments for specific development initiatives such as infrastructure development. The resources going directly to local governments have increased substantially since then (see figure 10.1). Persistent questions that have been raised during this process are: How are funds to be allocated across states and municipalities? How is this to be done objectively so that the political slant is eliminated as much as possible? There was a clear need for accurate poverty data at the local level.

The decision was therefore taken to use the deprivation index (see above), despite the drawbacks in the quality of the data on incomes and the greater weight assigned to population segments and marginality, rather than poverty itself.

The public discussion has since focused on ways to improve the procedures for the allocation of funds. According to a recurring argument, accurate information on poverty at the local level is needed for the establishment of an allocation system that is more progressive.

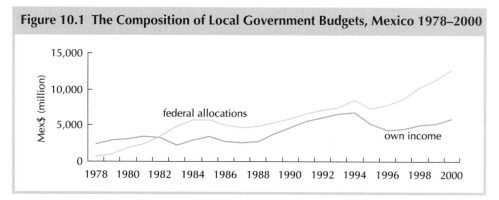

Figure 10.1 The Composition of Local Government Budgets, Mexico 1978–2000

Source: Cabrero 2003.

The search for continuity in policy and policy evaluation

In 2003, Congress passed the General Law on Social Development, which is aimed at providing institutional stability for social policy and establishing rules for social policy evaluation. The law covers social rights, the development of budgets for social initiatives, the evaluation of specific policies, and the measurement of poverty and deprivation. The law requires information to be collected on poverty at the state level. It also requires information on poverty in municipalities to be published at least every five years. Because the National Household Income and Expenditure Survey does not supply information disaggregated at the municipal level that is statistically accurate, INEGI was faced with the obvious problem of complying with the law and gathering poverty data down to the municipal level in a cost-effective way. Poverty mapping methodologies seemed an option.

The Mapping Process and Its Diverse Dimensions

In 2001, government officials asked academics and the World Bank to join in launching a poverty mapping project in Mexico. The initial project was undertaken by the Office of the President and El Colegio de México. Eventually, after key actors moved to the Ministry of Social Development and academics were invited to take the lead in drafting the first *Human Development Report* on Mexico (UNDP 2002), the project moved as well to the Ministry of Social Development and UNDP Mexico. This partnership was cemented through a formal agreement between the two organizations, in collaboration with INEGI. The involvement of UNDP Mexico in support of the internal agreements within the public administration fostered a politically neutral approach within the project. The project aimed at producing poverty measures, indicators of inequality, and human development indexes (HDIs).

A serious obstacle remained, however. The methodology required that the mapping team have full access to the census. INEGI usually makes census information available solely in the form of cross-tabulations and aggregated data. Information at the level of households is never made public, mainly because of confidentiality and privacy laws. The Ministry of Social Development and INEGI negotiated for almost 18 months to determine procedures so that the team would be able to exploit the census. According to the agreement that was finally reached, the database would be made available to the Ministry of Social Development only for the purpose of composing the maps. Codes would be attached to households so as to protect personal identities, while permitting all relevant data to be manipulated. The United Nations system in Mexico also reached a general collaboration agreement with INEGI that may be invoked to update the poverty maps when the need arises.

First: applying the technique

The technique used in Mexico has followed Elbers, Lanjouw, and Lanjouw (2002). The stages are described below.

Zero stage: the selection of variables

In Mexico, both a census and a household survey are available for the same year (2000). Standard tests have been required to ensure that these sources are comparable (see annex 10.1).

Stage one

The first-stage estimation involves modeling household per capita income at the most disaggregated geographical level for which the household survey is representative. In the case of the National Household Income and Expenditure Survey, this is the national level, broken down into rural and urban sectors.

So as not to force the parameters into a single nationwide model, the country was divided into five groups of states to produce a stratification according to the levels of marginality rather than any criterion of geographical proximity. Statistical tests showed that it was possible to divide the 32 federative entities into five groups. The fact that these groups were selected according to indexes of marginality rather than according to geographical proximity created some resistance from public officials. How might one justify the inclusion of Mexico City and Nuevo León in a single "region" even though they are far apart in geographical terms? The justification was purely methodological: to minimize heterogeneity. It was more important to create statistical groupings rather than geographical groupings. The results would then have higher precision, but the regions could not be used in these groupings for any sort of geographical purpose. The approach was accepted, with the caveat that the five combinations should not be called regions, but statistical groupings. The exercise was therefore carried out with the help of INEGI, and states were clustered together according to marginality indexes, proceeding from high to low index scores.

For each geographical region and area (rural and urban), the first-stage estimation produced an association model of household per capita income for a household in the location, where the explanatory variables were a set of observable characteristics, as laid out in the model. Ten variants of the model were estimated.

Stage two

In this stage, the first-stage parameters that had been estimated were combined with the observable characteristics of each household in the census to generate incomes and simulated disturbances (see López-Calva et al. 2005). For each simulation, a set of first-stage parameters was used. In this way, a set of coefficients was obtained. Finally, the poverty maps were developed illustrating the relevant indicators, including incidence of poverty, poverty gaps, severity of poverty, inequality, and HDIs. Figure 10.2 is a map showing poverty incidence by state. The consistency with other indicators was also analyzed (see figure 10.3).

Second: filling technical and institutional requirements

At least five ingredients were critical in guaranteeing that the project to construct poverty maps on Mexico was feasible.

Figure 10.2 Poverty Headcount Ratio by State in Mexico

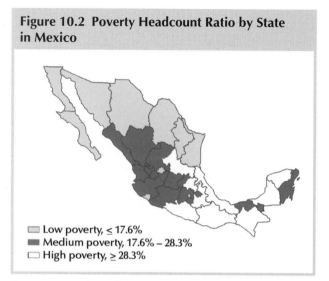

Low poverty, ≤ 17.6%
Medium poverty, 17.6% – 28.3%
High poverty, ≥ 28.3%

Source: López-Calva et al. 2005.

Data and methodological requirements

The first precondition in seeking to establish the feasibility of the project to construct poverty maps was the existence of good, reliable census and household survey data. Fortunately, INEGI is a well-regarded institution that has been producing statistical data for decades, and the two basic inputs for the construction of the poverty maps—the census and the household survey—were among the most respected products of the institution.

The second precondition was the existence of a well-accepted methodology for estimating poverty. During 2002–03, the Mexican government adopted a methodology that had been proposed by an independent committee of seven renowned academics; thus, when the time came to define poverty lines for the poverty map, the relevant procedures had already been tested and integrated with sufficient success to avoid rehashing a debate on the definition of poverty. Moreover, the work of the independent committee on poverty measurement and the publication of the official methodology contributed to a boost in the demand for accurate poverty data on states and municipalities.

Technical capacity

The three technological requirements for the construction of the poverty maps were (1) the existence of skilled human capital able to engage in the technical process of deriving income and consumption data using small area estimation methodologies, (2) the existence of an appropriate technical appreciation of the importance of the new instrument, and (3) the availability of adequate computer equipment, software, and data processing time.

In Mexico, meeting these preconditions was guaranteed partly because the original initiative had been undertaken by a qualified team that was supported by academics. The team followed no particular training routine. The principal researcher and two research assistants studied the technical needs and methodological requirements. The World Bank team provided key input during a workshop held to clarify details of the technique and to share the poverty mapping software. Likewise, INEGI and the Ministry of Social Development supplied essential technical assistance, including all the software required to manage the large database.

Administrative capacity

It was also necessary to guarantee the availability of adequate administrative capacity. The UNDP was key in maintaining this capacity throughout the three-year life of the project. Likewise, there had to be enough personnel involved on a steady basis so as to

Figure 10.3 Consistency with Other Indicators, Mexico 2000

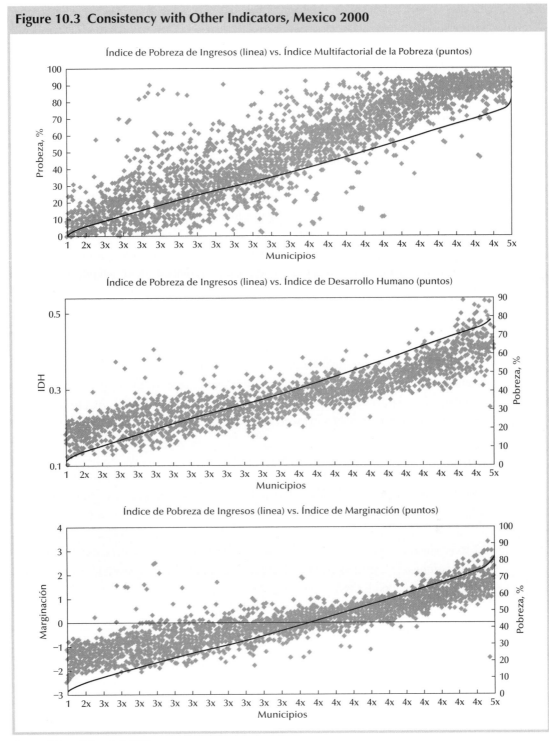

Source: López-Calva et al. 2005.

be able to carry out the substantial amount of data processing. Specific staff were assigned to the poverty mapping exercise. Junior staff (research assistants) from the *Human Development Report* team at UNDP Mexico and staff at the Ministry of Social Development devoted part of their time to this endeavor. Thus, the cost of the project was shared by the UNDP and the ministry.

Institutional arrangements

It was critical for the Ministry of Social Development and UNDP Mexico, which took the lead in the poverty mapping effort in Mexico, to establish an agreement with INEGI to gain access to the relevant data and the processing capacity. Similarly, for technical support, it was vital to guarantee World Bank assistance throughout the process and to elevate poverty mapping to a mainstream project within the Ministry of Social Development. Because the decision was made to take advantage of geographic information system techniques and use geo-referenced data in targeting social programs and responding to natural disasters, maps were developed for other purposes as the mapping process became more refined. These various tools allowed decision makers to rely on more detailed information in fine-tuning policy.

Budget

Of course, the project would not have been successful or even possible without adequate financial resources. Specific budget allocations were made for the projects, both in the Ministry of Social Development and the UNDP. UNDP Mexico played a major role by securing a permanent budget and meeting any shortfalls in the government contributions.

Data publication

The data produced through the project were used widely within the Ministry of Social Development and at the UNDP, but public access was delayed for several reasons. When the UNDP published HDIs on municipalities, the decision was made not to include detailed data on poverty so as not to interfere in the cooperative interaction between the ministry and local government institutions, mainly with regard to the allocation of funds. Eventually, in 2005, data on poverty at the local level in 2000 were posted on the ministry's Web site.

Third: political economy considerations

The identification of key partners and of individuals and institutions that might have an interest in a project or might oppose or resist it helps one to understand the potential benefits and drawbacks of a project and facilitates the establishment of conditions favoring a successful outcome. The data produced through a project of this sort are instruments of power in certain areas of public action. Therefore, it is important not to impose a new methodology, but to create a fresh, open pathway in the design of public policy and in public advocacy. Concretely, the following issues should be addressed:

- *The power of information:* Information is a means to power. It is possible that the construction of the poverty map would increase substantially the power of the groups and individuals involved in the mapping process and in distributing the related data. It is therefore critical to engage individuals and groups in the process that are at ease with sharing data rather than monopolizing data so as to increase their power. Thus far, the approach in Mexico has been successful in that the mapping data are shared widely within the Ministry of Social Development, though the maps are not well known and are rarely used in other government offices or in public forums. Greater emphasis should now be placed on disseminating the information more widely and spreading awareness about the related techniques in such a way that they may be understood by nonexperts.

- *Poverty mapping as an additional tool:* Alternative methods for creating tools similar to poverty maps were already available in Mexico when the poverty maps were being developed, for instance, marginality indexes and principal components analysis. Researchers who have developed applications based on these other tools have sometimes tended to view the new project as threatening. It is therefore important to emphasize that poverty maps are an additional tool rather than necessarily a better tool. This approach has helped attract others to cooperate in the endeavor and use the mapping data. For example, designers of other indexes, such as the marginality index, joined the mapping team and came to appreciate the complementarity of the indicators. Likewise, INEGI is now one of the main supporters of the use of poverty maps.

- *Create demand:* Creating demand for the final product during the early stages of the project in Mexico proved to be important along the way. Without the support of potential users, it would have become difficult to find resources for a project that initially seemed excessively expensive and time intensive to some of the relevant actors. Even today, though other groups in the Ministry of Social Development have become acquainted with the usefulness of the mapping information and are more willing and able to use it, the data and methodology are still not widely disseminated among government, academia, or the public.

- *Incentives for producers:* The production of poverty maps is a time-intensive activity. It is therefore worthwhile to create incentives for the team working on the project. For example, the possibility of writing up an innovative project in an academic publication or specialist journal played an important role in Mexico by stimulating the young professionals and academic researchers involved. Among public officials, the potential for the creation of additional tools for policy making represented an incentive.

The participation of INEGI, the UNDP, and the *Human Development Report* team was also an incentive in that it enhanced the visibility of the project. It was clear that a specific product would be developed and that the timeline would be respected. The loss in credibility caused by a failure to abide by the agreements with these partners would have been too great.

The Use of Poverty Maps

Poverty maps have definitely improved the way in which social policies are planned and implemented in Mexico. We present concrete examples in this section. The examples highlight the use of poverty maps in policy design and implementation and in public advocacy on specific policies.

The application in policy design and implementation

The first example relates to budget allocations. In Mexico, as in many other developing countries, a portion of the central government budget is transferred to state and municipal governments for decentralized allocations. This has especially been the case since the reform of the late 1990s discussed elsewhere above. The financing has been distributed to each entity according to criteria that are typically proxies for poverty indicators, since local poverty estimates hare not normally been sufficiently accurate.

The information made available through the poverty maps represents a general quality improvement. The data are technically more sound than the criteria that have been used for decades. The appearance of the maps therefore rekindled a debate on whether the method for distributing the budget should be modified. This debate was already ongoing because the urgent need for improvement had been obvious, but now that the new data are available, it has also become obvious that changing the allocations to local governments might lead to a touchy political problem. Since the size of the overall budget would remain the same, any reallocation would produce winners and losers. The probable losers would naturally oppose any modification in the status quo. Nonetheless, the poverty map has successfully placed the issue to the forefront, and Congress will likely take it up at some point. The key discussion may revolve around whether the current allocation system is progressive and the extent to which the maps may help lessen any regressivity.

The second example relates to targeting in welfare programs. For several years, the Ministry of Social Development lacked a specific program aimed at reducing poverty in urban areas through the provision of infrastructure in part because the technology for targeting such an intervention was inadequate. In densely populated areas such as cities, poverty maps may supply detailed information on poverty within communities and even neighborhoods, making refined targeting possible. Relying on indicators of the concentration of poverty among neighborhoods in the main cities of the country, the Habitat Program has thus now been launched in Mexico. The program identifies city areas with the highest concentration of poor people and directs a series of integrated actions at these areas to improve standards of living among the inhabitants of slums and the neediest neighborhoods.

Likewise, used in conjunction with geographic information systems, detailed poverty maps are now being applied widely in social development programs, including those that tend to favor alternative techniques, to help identify the geographical areas in which particular policy interventions may have their greatest impact. A good illustration is Liconsa, a milk subsidy program that has been running for more than 50 years and that, guided by poverty maps, is now able to pinpoint priority areas for intervention in a transparent way for the first time.

Using mapping outputs for public impact

The municipality is the appropriate geographical unit for the analysis of local development. HDIs have been calculated for municipalities in Mexico based on census and household survey data for 2000. The indexes were published in 2004. This was the first time that HDIs were made available at the municipal level in a format that might be used by the general public.

The examination of human development at the municipal level revealed great inequalities. Thus, if municipalities were to be classified as countries in the world ranking according to the international HDI, Benito Juárez, one of the boroughs of Mexico City, would have an HDI similar to that of Italy, whereas Metlatonoc, a municipality in the state of Guerrero, would have an HDI similar to that of Malawi.

Some of the information that emerged from the publication of the HDIs had an important public impact. For example, 11.3 percent of the inequality in human development in municipalities across the nation is accounted for by the health component of the index, 31.2 percent by the education component, and 52.1 percent by the income component. On the other hand, most of the inequality in human development may be attributed to differences in development within federal states (64.1 percent); the inequality across states is not as significant (35.8 percent). Inequality in human development at the national level may be explained mainly by the low HDIs in the states of Veracruz (8.9 percent), Oaxaca (7.1 percent), Chiapas (6.9 percent), Puebla (6.3 percent), and Guerrero (6.1 percent), and in the State of México (not to be confused with the capital of the country or the surrounding territory, 5.0 percent).

For the first time, discussions about poverty and inequality in specific states in Mexico became possible based on income data, as well as nonincome indicators in terms of their consistency with income data (see figure 10.3). The publication of the municipal HDIs and a compact disc containing the poverty data fostered public awareness about the importance of regional inequalities and the need for more disaggregated analysis. As a result of the mapping, discussions on marginality, access to services, and other indicators have been enriched. In particular, because of the importance of the income component in the HDI, it became evident that the economic determinants of development and income inequality among municipalities and regions and the way these determinants have evolved over time should be reviewed in light of the new data. During the first year, there were more than 1,900 downloads from the Web page where the information had been posted. Multilateral organizations, public officials, and academics requested the income and poverty estimates, as well the HDIs.

Fresh analyses have been generated. National labor market studies have found new details confirming that labor markets in the various regions of the country have distinctive features (Hernández Laos 2005). The labor markets of Mexico City and the large northern regions are relatively more well integrated, and they are relatively more competitive than those of the center and south or southeast regions. Geographical mobility within the country and abroad is more feasible for individuals with higher educational attainment. Labor mobility eases the demographic pressure on local labor markets, but also clearly reflects the lack of local labor demand. Other studies have found that the concentration of economic activities among municipalities declined between 1989 and 2000, even while inequality persisted among states. The increased concentration of fixed capital investment in certain municipalities has played a key role in maintaining inequalities.

Public policy responses have also been prompted. One immediate use of the poverty maps was the estimation and publication of HDIs by the UNDP. HDIs had previously been calculated on the basis of census data on incomes, but, because the census was not considered adequate on incomes, the HDIs were not regarded as a reliable tool for policy making. However, shortly after the publication of the HDIs based on data from the poverty maps, the president of Mexico announced a special plan to reduce poverty and promote human development by concentrating government efforts on the 50 municipalities that presented the highest poverty rates and the lowest HDIs according to this newly published information. Seven ministries operating 12 different, but related programs are now focusing efforts on the poor in these 50 municipal areas. The high visibility of the new HDIs was certainly a factor in this outcome. One of the candidates for president had started his campaign in 2005 precisely in the municipality that exhibited the lowest level of development in the country according to the poverty mapping exercise.

The federal plan of action against poverty required coordination among actors in a way that had not been observed in Mexico for many years. The priorities, objectives, and criteria for selecting geographical areas for targeting had typically been unique to each ministry and program. The establishment of common criteria now had two important positive outcomes. The first was that the budget allocations flowing to the 50 municipalities were increased substantially. Many of the municipalities experienced budget inflows that were unprecedented for a single year. The second outcome was the benefit of greater coordination. When each government agency has different objectives and criteria, programs are isolated one from the other, and, although they might generate a positive impact each on their own, their impact is generally less than if they had been combined with other programs to trigger multiplier effects. The accuracy of the poverty mapping played no small part in the more positive result.

The application of poverty maps

Novelty often generates skepticism among key actors. This resistance must be addressed to guarantee the use of a new tool in improving day-to-day processes such as planning and policy implementation. The use of poverty mapping in policy making has highlighted several interesting phenomena relating to political economy, as follows:

- *Ideological resistance:* The creation of poverty maps relies on data processing and econometric estimation techniques that sometimes appear obscure to people who are involved in local planning processes in which beneficiary communities and households participate in decision making. Indeed, in our case, doubts were frequently raised about the effectiveness of a tool developed by bureaucrats in Mexico City to reduce poverty, which they hardly knew or understood. To face this challenge, it was important to emphasize that poverty maps are one of many possible tools for policy making and that, rather than replacing other tools, such as local planning through community participation, they enrich these other processes. People working in private interdisciplinary research groups and nongovernmental organizations have been exposed at workshops to this principle of the complementarity of the maps and other quantitative and qualitative tools, but an aggressive strategy is still needed in this respect.

■ *Acceptance of results:* When used in distributing budget allocations, poverty maps inevitably generate winners and losers, and it is common for the losers to try to discredit the new technology simply because its application might imply fewer resources for them in the future. For example, in Mexico, a new policy initiative undertaken by the president shifted the target of welfare programs toward the 50 poorest municipalities identified through the use of the poverty maps. This shift generated opposition. Without the endorsement of the World Bank, the UNDP, and academics, it might have been difficult to defend poverty mapping as a valuable tool for improving policy making.

■ *The effective life of poverty maps:* Once a poverty map has been estimated, its effective life span depends on the gap between the latest household survey and the next census. Data eventually become outdated, and using outdated data may lead to errors in policy decisions. It is important to remember that poverty maps are imperfect tools; like other statistical techniques, they will only be as good as the data underlying them.

Are Poverty Maps Perceived as Useful? Are They Being Used by Other Agents?

We developed a questionnaire and carried out in-depth interviews with relevant actors in various realms to examine how poverty maps are perceived in Mexico. For the interviews, we approached staff at the Ministry of Social Development, the Ministry of the Economy, the Ministry of Finance and Public Credit, and the Ministry of Labor, people involved in the Progresa-Oportunidades program, distinguished academics, and members of Congress.

Actors involved in social policy

The interviewees involved in social policy making were all aware of the poverty maps and the impact of small area estimation methodologies in the design of public policy. Indeed, they told us that the mapping data help in analyzing whether social expenditure reaches the poor and in evaluating the effectiveness of the targeting of programs, especially at the municipal level. However, we learned that these people do not use poverty maps at all in carrying out their own routine activities. Only a few of the interviewees had actually used them and then merely to obtain a snapshot of the poor in Mexico. The main reason they do not use the maps is their lack of experience with the methodology. They are more familiar with, for example, the marginality index published by the National Population Council. In the case of Progresa-Oportunidades, the program staff use the information generated through that program.

Other government actors

Few people in the ministries of finance and public credit, labor, and the economy knew about the poverty maps. None of them had used the maps. Other government actors who were familiar with the poverty maps agreed that the maps are definitely helpful in the design of public policy and in targeting social expenditure. They also said that the poverty maps may be used to determine whether subsidies or investments for infrastructure should benefit one region or another. The members of Congress whom we approached all felt that this sort of information may be extremely important in the design and analysis of public policies, especially income redistribution policies and policies aimed at raising household incomes. However, none of the members of Congress had ever had occasion to use the maps, and none of them were aware that this kind of mapping information is available for Mexico. They did express interest in learning more about the methodologies behind the maps and the characteristics of the maps.

Academics

Mapping methodologies are not well known among academics. Only half of the academics who were interviewed said they were aware of the existence of poverty maps. They all agreed, however, that this disaggregated information is unquestionably useful in the design of public policy and, in particular, in the targeting of poverty reduction policies. They said a seminar should be organized locally to demonstrate the methodologies, compare poverty mapping with other options, and make the maps available for more analysis.

Updating Poverty Maps: Selected Issues

The success of the poverty maps and their widening application will inevitably raise new questions and lead to the identification of other uses.

If poverty maps are seriously applied to enhance the effectiveness of welfare policy and the targeting of government action toward the poorest households and most impoverished areas of a country, we would expect poverty to be reduced precisely among these households and in these geographic spaces. In fact, to be able to evaluate whether a poverty map has actually exercised a positive impact on poverty reduction, it would be necessary to remap poverty in states and municipalities periodically. This is, in our opinion, the natural next step in the evolution of poverty maps.

This is an important challenge, since, strictly speaking, updating a poverty map requires access to a population census and a household survey for the same (or a proximate) year. Because population censuses are commonly carried out about every 10 years, there is a usually a significant lag between censuses and household surveys.

One alternative is the use of older censuses and newer household surveys to update existing maps. Although this approach might generate useful information, it also introduces additional errors in poverty estimates, and the errors grow as the time lag becomes greater. It is an imperfect method.

In Mexico, however, supplementary population counts are conducted between censuses, which means that there is a new census for 2005, though it has produced less information than the regular full-scale censuses. An ongoing project has been examining the possibility of updating the poverty maps based on data from 2000 using the narrower information made available through the population count of 2005. This might permit the creation of a new, though less detailed set of maps that would be helpful in analyzing the dynamics of poverty and inequality at the local level. Thus far, the results have been promising.

Lessons Learned

Poverty mapping methodologies have been applied successfully in Mexico. They have become an important tool especially because of the needs and requirements created by recent institutional changes, such as the decentralized budget reform and the General Law on Social Development. Undoubtedly, they will be used in analyzing the dynamics of local development, especially once the maps have been updated and the analysis has been able to focus on trends in poverty at the state and municipal levels.

Nonetheless, even in this context in Mexico, poverty maps have not been accepted as a substitute for welfare and deprivation indicators in local resource allocations. They are being used for policy design at the federal level, and the methodology has been applied to estimate local HDIs. The information has been made public by academics and government officials. Partly as a result of the greater awareness, specific policy responses have been prompted, such as the program to assist the 50 municipalities with the lowest HDIs in the country.

We have presented information on the various ways in which poverty maps have been used to inform policy dialogue and interventions. We have also analyzed the views of various actors who have had contact with the poverty maps or who are likely to have the opportunity to use the poverty maps because of their professional activities. The main findings from our personal in-depth interviews are as follows:

- Although not all the interviewees knew about the new methodology, they all agreed that poverty maps contain valuable information that should be taken into account in the identification, design, and evaluation of public policy.
- The maps are not seen as a substitute, but as a complement for other tools of analysis and policy design.

Poverty maps have been used in welfare policy design and to build public awareness on poverty in Mexico. Our questionnaires and surveys have shown, however, that the maps and the related methodologies need to become more well known within the federal government and academia, and, especially, among local governments.

Annex 10.1 The Process for the Selection of Variables

The following illustrates the process undertaken in the selection of information from the 2000 census and the 2000 household survey on variables for inclusion in the poverty maps on Mexico (see López-Calva et al. 2005):

- The census questionnaire and the survey questionnaire were compared to identify those questions that were identical or similar conceptually. Whether the questions were directed at the same population groups was considered. For instance, if questions sought to provide information on household literacy, the responses were considered only if they applied to the same age groups in both questionnaires.
- The distributions of the variables identified and selected through the above method were statistically compared. The comparison of the sample means against the population means for the selected quantitative variables was based on tests of statistical significance. Variables that were not rejected were considered for the modeling. Qualitative variables were selected if the mean value of the census variable was within the confidence interval of the corresponding survey variable. The statistics from the national household survey were recalculated for each of the newly defined statistical regions and according to rural and urban areas.[4]

The variables that turned out to be both conceptually and statistically comparable in the National Household Income and Expenditure Survey in 2000 and the 2000 census were the following:

- *Housing characteristics:* water access, electricity access, fuel for cooking, construction materials used in floors, construction materials used in walls, construction materials used in ceilings, room used for cooking, connection to a sewage system
- *Household appliances and other equipment:* telephone, radio, television, videocassette machine, blender, refrigerator, washing machine, water heater, automobile or van, computer
- *Sociodemographic characteristics:* sex, age, marital status, kinship, school attendance, literacy, education
- *Labor characteristics:* labor force participation, employment, hours worked, position

Notes

1. The census in Mexico has questions on income, though income tends to be misreported because the census instrument is not designed appropriately to capture it.
2. Since 2001, when the idea of the map was first being explored, the support of Peter Lanjouw and the World Bank team has been crucial.
3. The deprivation index is known in Spanish as the *índice de masas carenciales*. Hernández and Székely (2005) provide a detailed description of the three indexes.
4. The division by statistical region is discussed in the subsection on the first-stage estimation (Stage one).

References

Cabrero, Enrique. 2003. "Los cambios en la agenda de políticas públicas en el ámbito municipal: Una visión introductoria." Working Paper, DTAP 129, Centro de Investigación y Docencia Económicas, Mexico City.

Cortés, F. 2005a. "La pobreza en el periodo 2000–2004." Unpublished working paper, Centro de Estudios Sociológicos, El Colegio de México, Mexico City.

———. 2005b. "Identificación de los mecanismos de aversión de la pobreza en el agro, 1992–2002." Unpublished working paper, Centro de Estudios Sociológicos, El Colegio de México, Mexico City.

De Janvry, Alain, and Elisabeth Sadoulet. 2001. "Income Strategies among Rural Households in Mexico: The Role of Off-Farm Activities." *World Development* 29 (3): 467–80.

Elbers, Chris, Tomoki Fujii, Peter F. Lanjouw, Berk Özler, and Wesley Yin. 2004. "Poverty Alleviation through Geographic Targeting: How Much Does Disaggregation Help?" Policy Research Working Paper 3419, World Bank, Washington, DC.

Elbers, Chris, Jean O. Lanjouw, and Peter F. Lanjouw. 2002. "Micro-Level Estimation of Welfare." Policy Research Working Paper 2911, World Bank, Washington, DC.

Hernández, Daniel, and Miguel Székely. 2005. "Medición del bienestar en México en los inicios del siglo XXI." In *Números que mueven al mundo: la medición de la pobreza en México*, ed. Miguel Székely, 85–103. Mexico City: Editorial Porrúa.

Hernández Laos, Enrique. 2005. "Mercados regionales de trabajo en México: estructura y funcionamiento." *Denarius* 1: 35–124.

López-Calva, Luis F., Alvaro Meléndez, Ericka G. Rascón, Lourdes Rodríguez-Chamussy, and Miguel Székely. 2005. "Poniendo al ingreso de los hogares en el mapa de México." Ministry of Social Development, Mexico City.

López-Calva, Luis F., and Lourdes Rodríguez-Chamussy. 2004. "The Evolution of Poverty and Inequality in Mexico 1992–2002." Unpublished working paper, World Bank, Mexico City.

Soloaga, Isidro, and Mario Torres. 2003. "Agricultural Growth and Poverty Reduction." Conference working paper, Food and Agriculture Organization of the United Nations, Rome.

Székely, Miguel, and Ericka G. Rascón. 2005. "México 2000–2002: Reducción de la Pobreza con Estabilidad y Expansión de Programas Sociales." In *Números que mueven al mundo: la medición de la pobreza en México*, ed. M. Székely, 309–58. Mexico City: Editorial Porrúa.

UNDP (United Nations Development Programme). 2002. *Informe sobre desarrollo humano, México 2002*. Mexico City: United Nations Development Programme and Mundi-Prensa México.

11

The Poverty Mapping Application in Morocco

JENNIE LITVACK

ACRONYMS AND ABBREVIATIONS

BAJ	*Barnamaj al Aoulaouiyat al Ijtimaiya* (Social Priorities Program)
DEC	Development Economics Vice Presidency (World Bank)
DH	dirham, the Moroccan currency
INDH	National Initiative for Human Development

Overview

Since 2002, the World Bank has been providing technical assistance to Morocco in the production and analysis of poverty maps. The work is considered highly successful. It has been successful because of the high degree of interest of the Moroccan authorities, the high-quality technical support provided by the Bank, and the policy dialogue that has accompanied the technical exercise from the early days.

The Moroccan government requested the technical support of the World Bank in 2002 to learn how to use poverty mapping techniques and produce a detailed, disaggregated map of poverty throughout the country. The request came from a small technical unit, the Observatory of Living Conditions, lodged within the Statistics Directorate at the Planning Commission. The Bank had helped establish this unit under a poor-area project—*Barnamaj al Aoulaouiyat al Ijtimaiya* (Social Priorities Program) or simply the BAJ—and had provided technical assistance to staff in poverty measurement. The contact person at the commission had read the Bank literature on poverty maps and initiated the new request.

At the time, the Bank was scheduled to undertake a poverty report that would be due the following fiscal year. This would provide the Bank with a period of about 18 months to complete the work, a much longer period than is usual for producing poverty reports.

This turned out to be important in our efforts to improve the impact of our work because it enabled the emergence of an active dialogue on poverty targeting—that is, how to improve targeting in social spending—to accompany the preparation of the poverty map and the poverty report. Thus, when the map and the report were completed, there was already substantial interest in these issues.

The traditional method of disseminating Bank analytical work focuses on the distribution and discussion of a report, whereas our process allowed us to focus on the issues, stimulate internal debate, and, eventually, produce a report that might be used concretely by decision makers to advance antipoverty policy. A few subjects were chosen for deeper enquiry; they all related to understanding the spatial aspects of poverty and growth and ultimately led to the publication of the Bank's poverty report on Morocco, "Strengthening Policy by Identifying the Geographic Dimension of Poverty" (World Bank 2004). So, the task budget was used not only to support research and the publication of a World Bank report, but also to support technical assistance and the production of Morocco's first detailed poverty map.

The task team leader and the outreach specialist (both based at the field office in Morocco), in addition to working closely with our technical counterparts at the Observatory of Living Conditions, made a significant effort to define and situate the report with the appropriate counterparts such that, when the poverty map and other analyses were ready, it might have a substantial policy impact, rather than remain a study on the shelf, as some have characterized previous reports.

We identified a principal counterpart for the report at the Ministry of Finance who was well respected throughout the government, civil society, and the palace (where important decisions are often taken). Locating a primary counterpart at the Ministry of Finance may seem questionable for poverty work, but, in fact, the ministry was a key supporter of the poverty mapping process because of its interest in improving the efficiency of social expenditures through better targeting. This counterpart had been following the progress of other reform agendas and the preparation of a multiyear report focused on Morocco's development over the past 50 years (see Kingdom of Morocco 2006). He was able continually to inject ideas about poverty targeting, including the spatial element of targeting in both rural and urban areas, into these processes so that the poverty map and poverty targeting were already being considered within the government and at the palace.

In addition, we visited and maintained contact with key individuals in several ministries who would benefit from the poverty map, such as the ministries of social development, family, and solidarity; health; education; agriculture, rural development, and fisheries; and interior. We tried to formulate a steering committee comprised of these individuals, but it was difficult to maintain interest and promote discussions on the topic until the poverty map had actually been produced. Nonetheless, the individual meetings that we had with each potential member of this steering group, the one-on-one conversations our principal counterpart had with key people in the government and at the palace, and the multiministerial technical seminar we conducted on poverty mapping and map applications helped sensitize people to the value of the upcoming poverty map. By the time the first poverty map was published, key policy makers had been sensitized to the significance of poverty maps. This may have helped highlight the importance of poverty maps to the ultimate decision maker in Morocco, King Mohammed VI.

Household survey data had previously permitted poverty to be disaggregated only into the general categories of rural or urban areas, and it was already clear that poverty was concentrated in rural areas. Yet, pockets of poverty obviously existed within urban areas, and many rural areas were prospering. To design effective government policies to address poverty, a much finer understanding of the geographical distribution of poverty was necessary.

The perceived need for finer geographical targeting of the poor was intensified because of two factors: one related to national security issues and the other to economic management. First, a series of suicide bombings in Morocco in May 2003 shocked people. The terrorists were home grown and came from urban slum neighborhoods. Renewed attention was focused on the vulnerability of the urban poor and the phenomenon of rural-urban migration. More information was needed on pockets of poverty and vulnerability in Morocco. Second, because of a growing budget deficit, there was strong pressure to make public expenditures more effective. Program impact evaluation had generally been inadequate, but now the desire to minimize benefit leakage to the nonpoor had become strong.

The poverty mapping program proceeded for almost a year on two levels: technical and policy. Both these levels were vital. The technical focus would permit a full transfer of the capacity to construct poverty maps to Moroccan experts, and the policy focus would stimulate interest in the potential utility of the poverty maps for policy purposes.

The Bank's expert from the Development Economics Vice Presidency (DEC) worked closely with the small technical unit charged with preparing the poverty map. The first expert mission focused on explaining the poverty mapping methodology and beginning the process of checking the available household survey and census data to identify matching variables. During this mission, the Bank arranged with the Ministry of Finance to host a seminar among relevant officials in various ministries to examine the international experience in poverty mapping, as well as issues in poverty targeting. At the seminar, the Bank provided an overview of poverty mapping techniques and how these have been applied within countries. The presentations set the stage for a dynamic discussion among actors in Morocco who otherwise might not have had such an opportunity for mutual reflection. Overall, this had been the strategy all along for reaching out to stakeholders involved in poverty and social sector analysis, stimulating discussions within a country on targeting, sensitizing actors to the spatial aspects of poverty, and creating a commonly perceived need for transparency and objectivity.

Subsequent technical missions focused on the steps necessary to produce poverty estimates at the commune level. Since capacity building and technology transfer were key objectives at this stage, the Bank's DEC expert worked for a full week with technical counterparts in the Statistics Directorate during one mission. He explained many details and walked the counterparts through each phase of the preparations for the poverty mapping. At the end of each mission, the expert left a point-by-point report on all that had been accomplished. Toward the end of the poverty mapping preparation process, the United Nations Development Programme funded a three-week trip to Washington by a Moroccan expert to work closely with DEC.

Throughout the process of capacity building and the technical preparation of the map, the task team leader stayed in close contact with the principal counterparts in the government who understood the big picture importance of the poverty maps. She kept them informed on the progress and shared early findings that would be interesting from a policy perspective, for example, that some urban communes did show significant poverty and that poverty rates varied greatly among neighboring rural communes. Rather than retreating from the potential political sensitivities involved in exposing such findings, the task team leader and the principal counterparts searched out these useful bits of information. Without high-level political involvement, it is difficult to advance technical agendas; if the maps were to have an impact on policy, they had to appeal to important decision makers who would be able to use them to realize the country's policy goals.

One major question throughout the process was whether or not the government, particularly the Planning Commission, which was responsible for producing the poverty maps, would make the data publicly available. Given its long history of extreme caution in releasing data, the government was skeptical about the idea of publishing the maps. Indeed, the provision of objective, transparent information on poverty in communes might (and eventually did) lead local leaders to question how the central government had determined the targets of poverty programs and public expenditures more generally. In any country, the release of this sort of disaggregated data would be a sensitive issue, but, in a country such as Morocco that had always been especially hesitant about releasing data on internal problems, there was an added incentive toward secrecy: the incentive of tradition.

The Bank encouraged the Planning Commission to publish the data by agreeing to pay the publication costs and by giving the commission due credit for the technical work. When the poverty estimates were ready, the Bank and the government interviewed potential publishers and agreed on a company, and then the Bank engaged directly with this company to publish the maps. The map publication was entirely a government product.

Each map report, which includes colored, glossy map inserts, has been distributed along with an interactive compact disc containing an attractive presentation of the maps (accompanied by classical music) and a user-friendly interface. On the compact disc is a map of the country divided into regions, each of which opens to reveal provincial maps and then commune maps. A user simply clicks on the region or province to see the next geographical level. Clicking on the commune maps causes a host of poverty statistics to pop up. The detailed maps have been published by the government (as well as in the World Bank poverty report).

There was full country ownership of the maps and the related poverty estimates. The Bank's technical support was gratefully acknowledged in the mapping report, but credit was given largely to the Planning Commission for the work. This helped buttress the technical standing of the commission and elevated the reputation of the local technicians who were working with poverty data. The Bank encouraged this outcome by suggesting, whenever approached, that the media should pose their questions to the relevant people at the commission rather than the Bank. The Bank made this conscious effort to play down its role so as to enhance the country ownership of the mapping products and, hopefully, foster greater policy integration. The Bank also organized a major launching event for the poverty maps at which the planning commissioner and the Bank's Morocco country director gave opening speeches. At the event, Bank experts and Moroccan counterparts at the Statistics Directorate provided technical presentations on the mapping work.

The World Bank poverty report was published two months after the government's poverty map report (see World Bank 2004; Planning Commission 2004). Both publications provided analysis of other issues besides the spatial aspects of poverty and inequality, such as the impact of agricultural reform and the progress achieved in girls' education. The Bank's poverty report did not reproduce the specific commune poverty estimates, but, rather, cross-referenced the government publication. It explained the poverty mapping methodology and provided examples for the provinces.

The Moroccan government decided to construct a second, updated poverty map. This time, it had the technical knowledge to take the lead in preparing the map, and the Bank provided the team with ongoing technical assistance by e-mail. The second, updated poverty map was completed in September 2005, about 18 months after the first had been finished. It was based on the 2000–01 National Household Consumption Survey and the 2004 census. While the objective of the first poverty map had been to obtain a detailed idea of the spatial distribution of poverty and test the local capacity to generate small area estimates, the objective of the second map was more ambitious: to update the estimates and related data and to create a tool for targeting. The second poverty map became publicly available in March 2006 after several months of delay.

Access to the data continues to be an issue in Morocco. While the Bank gained access to the detailed data from the second poverty map in March 2007, the data are not yet available to others in government or to the scientific community in Morocco.

Technical Aspects of the Poverty Mapping Exercise

Like the construction of poverty maps elsewhere, the poverty map methodology applied in Morocco involved three stages. During the first stage, the household living standards survey and the population census were subjected to close scrutiny with an eye toward identifying a set of common socioeconomic variables such as educational attainment, housing characteristics, and access to basic services. In the second stage, the household survey was used to develop a series of statistical models of per capita consumption and the common variables identified in the preceding stage. Different models were estimated in the household survey data set for each region or groupings of regions and separately for rural and urban areas. In the final stage, the parameter estimates from the previous stage were applied to the population census and used to predict consumption for each household in the census. Once such a predicted consumption measure was available for each household in the census, summary measures of poverty, inequality, and vulnerability (that is, poverty according to a higher poverty line) were estimated for a set of households in the census. Statistical tests were performed to assess the reliability of the poverty estimates that had been produced.

When the poverty map exercise had been completed for all regions or groups of regions, the resulting estimates of poverty and inequality and the related standard errors at a variety of levels of geographical disaggregation were projected onto geographical maps using geographic information system mapping techniques.

Certain aspects of the survey and census required special consideration and called for additional techniques. These and other points are now examined. (For more details on the topics in this section, see World Bank 2004.)

Data sources

The first poverty map on Morocco was developed on the basis of the 1994 population census and the 1998–99 household survey. Given that these two data sources did not refer to the same time period, the interpretation of the mapping results is somewhat problematic: did the poverty map produced on the basis of these two data sets refer to 1994 or to 1998? Certainly, poverty rates may have changed in numerous localities throughout the country during this four-year period. On the one hand, there had been relatively slow growth since 1994, which implied that changes had been few; on the other hand, rural-urban migration may have occurred, and poverty rates may thus have risen in urban areas and perhaps shifted within rural areas, too. So, it was difficult to say that the estimates reflected one year or the other. The poverty map might instead be interpreted as providing a snapshot of the geographical distribution of poverty for the period of the mid- to late 1990s. Likewise, the second poverty map, completed in September 2005, relied on the 2001 household consumption survey and the 2004 population census and therefore reflected the poverty situation in the early 2000s. (For the sake of clarity, most of the technical comments below refer to the first poverty map. It may be assumed that similar comments are generally applicable also to the second map.)

Morocco is organized into 16 regions, 61 prefectures and provinces, and 1,497 communes. Urban communes are further subdivided into districts and subdistricts. Whereas previous national poverty assessments were able to measure poverty fairly accurately only down to the level of the province, the first poverty map covered the communes. Subsequent analysis has indicated that this may be appropriate for geographical targeting in rural areas, but urban areas may require a lower level of disaggregation. Thus, the second poverty mapping exercise drew on the census to generate urban poverty estimates at the subdistrict level. Additional analysis to decompose inequality is still necessary to determine if this is now an appropriate level for targeting.

Poverty lines

The mapping exercise relied on different poverty lines (urban and rural) to measure poverty and vulnerability. The poverty line for rural areas was set at DH 3,037 per person per year, while that for urban areas corresponded to DH 3,922 (at 1998 prices). Note that, even at this considerably higher poverty line for urban areas, poverty rates are generally much greater in rural areas than in urban areas. In any case, these two poverty lines are best viewed as conservative. They are associated with a national poverty headcount rate of around 17 percent. Since many households may not fall under the poverty line, but may lie slightly above it and thus be more vulnerable to shocks than the rest of the population, a second set of lines was used to gauge this sort of vulnerability. There is a body of literature exploring definitions of vulnerability. In the case here, as in the World Bank poverty update on Morocco (World Bank 2001), vulnerability reflects the percentage of the population falling under a level of consumption that is 50 percent higher than the level at the poverty line.

Dropping all households without residence

A decision was taken to drop from the census data set all households that were not living in a fixed residence (the *sans abri* or homeless). This decision was taken because the household survey did not include such households, and the models estimated in the household survey were therefore not likely to apply readily to these households. Moreover, a number of the explanatory variables in the survey models were linked to household characteristics (access to water and so on), and these were missing among the homeless. Note that this segment of the population is not terribly large as a rule, but, in the very south of the country (in both urban and rural areas), it is somewhat more important quantitatively, presumably because of the existence of a nomadic population in the south. The population for which the poverty map estimates are believed to hold thus refers to a (large) subset of the overall population of Morocco.

Sampling structure of the census

One of the features of the 1994 census data is that only 25 percent of the responses to the questionnaires were computerized. This 25 percent sample was not selected on a purely random basis. Rather, provinces with small populations were entered completely; in medium-size provinces, one in two questionnaires were entered; in larger provinces, one in four questionnaires were entered; and, in the largest provinces, only one in ten questionnaires was computerized. The implication of this feature of the census data is that the poverty map estimates are likely to be slightly less precise than would have otherwise been the case. However, because the population-related structure underpinning the census sample ensures that the smallest provinces are well represented in the data, the overall impact of this issue on poverty mapping was considered rather modest.

Estimating poverty in regions not covered by the household survey

The household survey sample was stratified down to the regional level, and a distinction was made as well between urban and rural areas within each region. There are 16 regions in Morocco, and, given the limited sample size of the household survey (about 5,000 households), this implies that there are some regions in which few households were sampled (less than 100). Consumption models were thus estimated on nine geographical domains that were built on the basis of three to five geographically contiguous regions each and that included separate domains for rural and urban areas. The southernmost domain comprised the regions of Oued Ed-Dahab-Lagouira, Layoune-Boujdour-Sakia El Hamra, Guelmin-Es-Semara, Souss-Massa-Draaa, and Marrakech-Tensift-Al-Haouz. Oued Ed-Dahab-Lagouira and Layoune-Boujdour-Sakia El Hamra are in large desert areas with fairly sparse populations; in any case, the 1998 household survey did not sample Oued Ed-Dahab-Lagouira and Layoune-Boujdour-Sakia El Hamra, and even Guelmin-Es-Semara comprised a sample of fewer than 100 households. Consumption models for this geographical grouping were therefore based only on Guelmin-Es-Semara, Souss-Massa-Draaa, and Marrakech-Tensift-Al-Haouz, and the model parameters were assumed to apply to Oued Ed-Dahab-Lagouira and Layoune-Boujdour-Sakia El Hamra as well. This is not an assumption we were able to validate independently, and, as a result, estimates on these regions should be viewed as more tentative than those produced on other regions.

Accuracy of the poverty estimates

In addition to producing estimates of poverty and vulnerability (headcount, poverty gap, and squared poverty gap), the poverty mapping project also estimated two additional measures that are relevant to the analysis of welfare: average per capita consumption and per capita consumption inequality. The inequality measure that was used for this purpose is the general entropy–class inequality measure with a parameter value of 0.5. This inequality measure is less computationally intensive than the more commonly used Gini coefficient, but has been found to be quite satisfactory for purposes of summarizing inequality.

How accurate are the poverty estimates? We have addressed this question by comparing the poverty estimates produced through this method and regional data from the household survey. We have concluded that, on the whole, poverty has been sufficiently precisely estimated to permit meaningful comparisons down to the commune level.

Results, Analysis, and Implications for Policy Use

The poverty map estimates pointed to a marked heterogeneity of poverty across communes. Some communes have high concentrations of poverty; some have none. This finding itself was interesting because prior research on the household survey data had permitted only a regional analysis. Other studies had examined poverty at the provincial level, albeit never in a nationally consistent way, and poor-area development programs had already been designed at the provincial level. That poverty varied greatly not only among provinces, but also within provinces was an eye opener for policy makers and led to a reappraisal of targeting strategies. Whereas the major poor-area development project, the BAJ, had relied on province-level targeting, the new information on poor communes provided the government with fresh insights into the possible design of a more finely targeted program, the National Initiative for Human Development (INDH).

In itself, these estimates of local poverty are interesting, but not useful for policy purposes. Further analysis is necessary to understand the true potential for geographical targeting. Specifically, is geographical targeting appropriate, and, if so, what government programs should be targeted to which localities? The Bank pursued these questions through analysis first, through dialogue second, and, now, through the development of a sectorwide approach.

The poverty mapping techniques produced estimates of poverty and inequality in provinces and communes. Subsequent analysis has drawn on both estimate levels.

Analysis of inequality

The poverty map revealed heterogeneity in household consumption across communes, but it might also be used to examine inequality within communes. To what extent is overall inequality in Morocco attributable to the fact that communes differ from one another in average per capita expenditures? Does inequality *within* communes account for an important share of the overall inequality?

These questions may be readily investigated on the basis of a decomposition of inequality into a between-commune component and a within-commune component. The former asks how much overall inequality would remain if it were assumed that, within communes, all individuals had the same consumption level (equal to the average per capita consumption level of the commune), and, hence, the only variation in consumption that one might observe would be attributable to differences in average consumption levels between communes. The latter component asks the analogous question about how much overall inequality would remain if differences between communes in average per capita consumption were assumed away.

The decomposition exercise in Morocco revealed a remarkably high degree of inequality. This is attributable to differences between administrative units such as communes and districts, particularly in rural areas. This is probably caused, at least in part, by the tremendous variation in terrain and geographical characteristics that is typical of

Morocco. The findings may be contrasted with those observed in other countries in which similar exercises have been carried out. It is clear that Morocco stands out as something of an outlier in that geographical differences across localities, especially in rural areas, play a particularly important role in understanding consumption inequality.

Unlike in rural areas, there is a great deal more heterogeneity in living standards within urban communes. A decomposition analysis of the main cities shows that not much inequality may be explained by differences between urban communes. Generally, this is not surprising because the communes are much larger in urban areas. The signs of inequality in cities are likely to appear among much smaller units such as neighborhoods or even at the household level. The major exception is the city of Fez. There, we see enormous disparities between communes, especially between those in the *medina* (the walled old city) and those in the new city. Indeed, almost 40 percent of the inequality measured in Fez may be attributed to differences between communes. The corresponding figures are 19 percent for Rabat-Salé, 14 percent for Agadir, 13 percent for Casablanca, 12 percent for Meknès, 5 percent for Tangier, and 4 percent for Marrakech.

Additional examination of commune poverty reveals that, although much inequality may be attributed to differences across communes, there is also inequality within communes. Moreover, the inequality tends to be higher within poorer communes than within the less poor communes. There should be no presumption that poorer communes are somehow more homogeneous than communes with higher per capita consumption levels.

This analysis of inequality led us to believe that geographical targeting at the commune level may, indeed, represent a good way of reaching concentrations among the poor in rural areas, while lowering leakage to the nonpoor. This would not be the case in urban areas, where communes are too heterogeneous to use geographical targeting unless this might be done at a much smaller level or in combination with other targeting mechanisms.

Analysis of local conditions and government programs

The poverty map was telling us where the pockets of poverty were located, and the inequality analysis was telling us that commune-level targeting in rural areas may make sense. Yet, we still needed to understand what interventions were required in which localities and how we might deliver them. More insights into local conditions were necessary, as well as a deeper vision into the effectiveness of existing government programs. It was decided that more analysis of the correlation between poverty and other small area data, including public expenditures, might help the line ministries assess their sectoral targeting strategies. (For more details, see World Bank 2004.)

The poverty maps were useful for this analysis as well. Indeed, poverty map estimates are most useful when they are combined with other detailed small area data, such as information on education (schools, enrollment rates, the availability of school meal programs or school cafeterias, literacy rates), health (the distribution of health centers, access, doctors or nurses per capita, nutrition levels, infant mortality rates), infrastructure (roads, electricity grids, potable water, irrigation systems), safety net programs (*Promotion Nationale,* a public works program aimed at increasing employment and building small-scale infrastructure; *Entraide Nationale,* a governmental organization that serves as administrative headquarters for welfare agencies), and development programs (the BAJ, the Social Development Agency, nongovernmental development organizations, and so on), as well as natural conditions that may affect welfare (rainfall, topography, desertification).

We combined the disaggregated measurements produced through the poverty mapping exercise with other data to obtain a deeper understanding of localities, the changes in social conditions, the reasons conditions have changed, and the effectiveness of government programs in reaching the poor. Such a local database should be maintained and updated periodically given that the combination of poverty estimates and information on the other characteristics of localities is most helpful in designing government projects and programs. (After completing this exercise, we decided to add a final chapter to the mapping report that focused specifically on problems in data collection, consistency, and coordination.)

With much effort, we developed a database of provincial poverty estimates, as well as other province-level data such as human development indicators, infrastructure, geographical conditions, and public expenditures. Basically, we sought to include all variables that might help explain why some areas were poor. We examined simple correlations between provincial poverty rates and social indicators, as well as the degree to which social outcomes, inputs, and other indicators are correlated across provinces. Maps of the spatial distribution of these variables helped to indicate particularly lagging regions where attention was urgently needed and to elucidate issues regarding the geographical distribution of past spending.

We used statistical decomposition analysis to examine in more detail the extent to which changes since 1994 have benefited the poor, the nonpoor, and girls, in particular, and why school enrollment rates have improved in some areas more than in others. We complemented this analysis of school enrollment among girls through a qualitative study examining cultural and institutional issues that may not be picked up in quantitative analysis. This led to a descriptive picture of the distribution across provinces of spending on various antipoverty programs and other programs.

Once again, we then carried out a statistical decomposition analysis exploring the distribution of spending across poor and nonpoor groups in rural and urban areas and the province-level characteristics that influence such allocations.

Finally, we summarized the key findings and suggested ways of continuing and improving this type of analysis so important for results-based government. More details on the analysis and results are provided below.

First, we asked if public expenditures for poverty reduction programs and development programs were being targeted at poorer provinces. The answer was almost always no: the distribution of expenditures per capita across provinces did not seem to reflect the levels of provincial poverty or other measures of nonincome poverty.

Despite a lack of targeting on the provinces, it is still possible that, within provinces, funds were reaching poor households (which exist in all provinces regardless of the provincial poverty ranking). Unfortunately, we were unable to examine this issue because survey information on household program participation was unavailable. This should be an important area of focus for improvement in future household surveys to assess targeting performance.

In the absence of such household information, statistical techniques have been developed to infer how well public program expenditures are targeted at poor households (see Ravallion 2000). In essence, the distribution of public expenditures to provinces (ranked by their poverty level as determined through the poverty mapping exercise) permits one to make inferences about the underlying differences in the average per capita amounts going to the poor and nonpoor. Such differences are referred to as the targeting differential. Targeting performance is measured by exploiting the spatial variance in both spending and poverty incidence across provinces. The targeting differential is estimated by regressing a specific program's per capita allocations across provinces on the province-level poverty measures. This gives a measure of how well program allocations match the provincial poverty map. Our results are based on allocations across provinces and the extent of propoor geographical targeting at the provincial level only. We are unable to identify province-specific differences in targeting performance (which would require spending and poverty data at the subprovincial level such as by commune). Nonetheless, given the data currently available, this methodology permits an assessment of targeting performance relative to the poor.

For our analysis, the targeting differential methodology was extended so that it might be applied separately to rural and urban areas of Morocco. It was used to assess how well expenditures on poverty and development programs are targeted at poor zones in each of those sectors. Provincial per capita spending allocations were regressed on the provincial rural and urban headcount indicators.

The most striking finding of this analysis was that many government social development programs have been successful at reaching poor rural areas. Perhaps most encouragingly, the gains in school enrollments (across primary and secondary schools) have been strongest among the rural poor and among girls. The BAJ program and school meal programs have helped create the proper conditions for attracting poor children to attend school. The significance of the school meal programs is confirmed by the qualitative study. This suggests that the programs should be expanded.

While improvements have been evident among the poor in rural areas, they have not been so evident among the poor in urban areas. For urban areas, we noted a strong bias in most government programs toward the nonpoor. This leakage may be caused by the strong political influence of the urban nonpoor (who may generally not be so wealthy). It may also be caused by the fact that urban areas are much more heterogeneous than rural areas. Poor and nonpoor live more closely together in urban areas, such that geographical targeting will be less effective there than in the more homogeneous rural areas. It is therefore possible that the poor living in urban areas have been classified as nonpoor and are actually benefiting from these programs. It is also possible that the rich benefit from programs located in poor rural areas. But, again, the data necessary to examine this issue of mistargeting do not exist.

Many of Morocco's poverty programs currently rely on geographical targeting. Successfully targeting the poor, particularly in urban areas, may require much better local data on the characteristics of poor households, as well as the development of targeting indicators other than location. At any rate, the results of this empirical analysis are certainly worth noting. They highlight that the urban poor may be falling between the cracks and receiving a disproportionately low share of the allocations linked to government poverty reduction efforts. (This database is available from our team members at DEC. It contains two time periods for data pertaining to school enrollments among girls.)

The Implications for Targeting Strategies

The results of the analysis of inequality have important implications for targeting strategies in rural and urban areas. In trying to achieve cost-effective targeting, policy makers worry about two kinds of targeting errors: type 1 errors refer to cases in which intended beneficiaries such as the poor are missed; type 2 errors refer to cases in which benefits leak to unintended households or persons such as the nonpoor. Narrowly targeted programs run mainly the risk of the former type of error. An example in Morocco is the RAMED (*Régime d'aide médicale aux personnes économiquement faibles*) health care insurance scheme for poor households. Broadly targeted programs run the risk of the latter type of errors. An example is represented by bread subsidies in Morocco.

For technical and political economy reasons, it is extremely difficult to identify individual poor households. However, in most countries, using geographical areas as proxies for household poverty would lead to large type 1 and type 2 errors because of the heterogeneity within localities. In Morocco, this would be less of a problem because, as the results here suggest, the differences in poverty outcomes across rural areas are large. The findings here therefore indicate that geographical targeting might be a reasonable approach for reaching the poor in rural Morocco and limiting type 2 errors (leakage to the nonpoor).

Leakage will inevitably be substantial if targeting is done at the provincial level in rural areas (for example, in programs such as the BAJ). Nonetheless, given the differences in poverty between provinces in the same regions, this may still be an appropriate targeting strategy in some cases. However, the findings suggest that geographical targeting at the commune level is likely to represent an improvement on targeting at the provincial level. Since inequality still exists within poor communes, the geographical targeting is often best complemented by other forms of household targeting, including, for instance, self-selection based on benefits that would be appealing only to the poor, within-area means testing, and related demographic characteristics. Alternatively, the provision of commune-level public goods rather than household transfer benefits might be an option.

Given that the costs of targeting may rise dramatically with disaggregation and given the difficulty of administering targeted programs down to the commune level, a two- or three-stage targeting strategy may make the most sense. This might involve the allocation of central funds to poor provinces, which would then be responsible for administering the targeting of these programs to poor communes. A third stage might involve provinces and communes distributing a portion of the funds through some form of household targeting.

Generally, a requirement that provincial allocations of central funds to communes be based on objective, transparent, and comparable data across communes, including poverty map estimates, may help enhance the targeting of poor communes. This is so partly because it may reduce a couple of problems common in many countries, that is, capture by local provincial elites or the allocation of public funds to communes based on subjective criteria that do not properly cover the poorest communes.

At any rate, the poverty map exercise provides estimates not only of poverty, but of inequality, and these estimates may be used to inform targeting strategies, too. There are costs involved with all methods of targeting, and this issue must be examined carefully for each program.

In Morocco, urban areas represent a special case. The analysis indicates that urban communes show a much higher level of heterogeneity than do rural areas. Using solely the commune as a proxy for poverty in urban areas will lead to high levels of leakage to the nonpoor. Much more detailed knowledge of the characteristics of poor households is therefore necessary in urban areas. Alternatively, programs need to be designed to enable self-selection. Geographical targeting may still be appropriate, but it is more likely to be at the level of individual neighborhoods or even blocks within neighborhoods. Identifying micropockets of poverty or nongeographical characteristics of urban poverty may be accomplished through citywide household surveys. This will be particularly important in the larger cities, each of which has been aggregated into one unified municipal structure since September 2003. Because poverty may be concentrated in various pockets throughout a city, in different arrondissements, for instance, a further disaggregation of household welfare and of access to services within the arrondissement is warranted. This will be important in limiting the risk of type 1 errors (mistargeting by overlooking some pockets of poverty) and type 2 errors (benefit leakage to wealthier urban areas where the benefit is least needed). The exception is the city of Fez, where the differences among communes are enormous, and geographical targeting on poor communes is a useful and practical first step for reaching all poor households.

The Impact of the Poverty Map on Policy

The impact of the poverty maps on Moroccan social policy has been strong and direct. Indeed, Morocco is a case where the analytical work involved in constructing the poverty maps has led to a major government social initiative. The poverty maps were released in June 2004. This was followed by the publication of the World Bank poverty report in the fall (see World Bank 2004). The Bank report presented analyses of poverty, inequality, and targeting at the local level. In May 2005, King Mohammed VI launched the INDH, which he referred to as "the program of my reign." The government announced that US$1 billion would be allocated to the program, half of which would go to efforts to target extra resources to the poorest 360 rural communes and poorest 250 urban neighborhoods. The king had made numerous speeches about his desire to improve social conditions by encouraging policies that are more responsive to local needs (*une politique de proximité*), but, apparently, the poverty maps provided him with the objective information needed to launch a specific effort. (While the king never directly mentioned the poverty maps, the policy initiative he proposed was based on commune-level targeting, which is only possible through the new information provided by the maps.)

In addition to using the poverty maps for targeting purposes, they were also beginning to play an interesting role in promoting local governance. Indeed, even the first poverty map supplied citizens and local government officials with transparent, objective information on the relative poverty ranking of the areas in which they lived. This empowered citizens to question the government allocations to their communes and hold government officials accountable for any lack of equitable treatment in the geographical distribution of government programs.

We learned about this outcome from counterparts. These people reported that several governors who had been surprised by some of the poverty map data had undertaken site visits and had confirmed the data. Our counterparts were delighted to learn that the poverty maps might thus contribute to a much broader agenda of transparency and good governance. While this had not been the primary objective of the poverty mapping exercise, it is an important objective as the kingdom moves forward on a path to greater democracy.

These benefits of poverty maps—transparency and objectivity—are also constraints on local politicians and other officials who find it useful to have discretion over the allocation of public funds. Some of this discretionary flexibility may be good, however. The implementation of the INDH will therefore be based on the poverty map data, but will allow a little room for flexibility so that provincial governors may allocate resources in the way they believe makes the most sense. Instead of simply taking the poorest 360 rural communes, all rural communes with poverty rates above the national average (about 550 communes) are eligible for INDH targeting. The governors may select communes from within that group. This seems to be a political compromise whereby poor communes will certainly be selected; however, they may not be all the very poorest. This decision was reached by the INDH national steering committee and was presented to the Bank as irreversible. The Bank's view was that the decision was acceptable from a targeting perspective, but that it was unsatisfactory from the perspective of good governance because it weakened the transparency and objectivity of the INDH.

The poverty maps will also be used for planning in various sectors. For example, a reform of water tariffs is being considered in Morocco to encourage greater efficiency, conservation, and equity. A Bank poverty and social impact analysis will draw on household data to gauge the effect of the proposed tariffs on households, but targeting at the commune level is a much more realistic strategy in rural water supply, particularly in Morocco, where poverty in rural communes is significantly more homogenous than in other countries. Finally, the World Bank is now working on a second generation of studies that will analyze the use of poverty maps in assessing the dynamics and determinants of local poverty.

The Sustainability of the Poverty Map

Morocco and the Bank have much about which to be proud. The Bank provided top-quality technical assistance, and the Moroccans acquired a sophisticated antipoverty technique and formed and developed a unit that will be able to complete future poverty maps with little outside help. Indeed, while the Bank constructed much of the first poverty map as it explained each step to the counterparts, the second map was completed entirely within the government, and the Bank served only a long-distance advisory role by responding to e-mail queries. The Bank was also used by the planning commissioner to perform quality control over the work of his staff. The poverty map has become a high priority for the government. The funding for the first map was supplied largely by the government, though the Bank provided the technical assistance and paid the cost of publishing the report. The preparation and publication of the second map were financed entirely by the government.

Technically and financially, the mapping techniques appear sustainable. However, additional work will be necessary to disseminate the methodology and explain it so as to ensure that there is adequate public understanding and the estimates remain credible.

The Bank assisted the government in launching the first poverty map, and the methodology was explained in the press. The estimates were generally accepted as credible at that time. Nonetheless, officials in various ministries still question how the poverty map may be drawn from the census if the census contains no information to measure consumption or poverty. Or, they question the accuracy of estimates that combine census and household survey data that are different in nature. Clearly, public awareness must be renewed regularly.

Lessons Learned

Lessons learned from the Morocco case include the following:

1. It is necessary to have a strong government commitment to the poverty maps if they are to be accepted and used to influence policy in the country.
2. It is important to secure multiyear financing to ensure the preparation of the poverty map, as well as the accompanying dialogue—in this case, individual discussions with many different actors, seminars, policy relevant analysis of poverty map results, and so on—so that the poverty maps may be understood by reformers and used to advance social policy and programs. In Morocco, a two-year funded poverty report

was accompanied and followed up by programmatic economic and sector work that enabled capacity building and a sustained dialogue on poverty with the government, the palace, and civil society.

3. A strong relationship and trust between technicians and their ministry or other organization and the Bank are important in ensuring the quality of the poverty maps and the proper use of the results in analysis.

4. Work should be conducted with local counterparts as closely as possible in the preparation of the poverty maps. These counterparts should be given as much credit as possible so that there will be local ownership of the results.

5. The intimate involvement of the task team leader and the DEC expert enabled technical and policy channels to be pursued effectively. The task team leader was based in Morocco and worked with the Bank's outreach expert to enable close cooperation with clients so as to ensure the relevance of the analysis to the issues. The sustained commitment of the DEC poverty map expert ensured that the lengthy technical assistance process was consistent and coherent.

6. Poverty maps are political documents because they remove some of the discretion that policy makers may feel they require; they increase transparency; and they may impact the allocation of public expenditures. This means that some people will gain and some people will lose power and resources. Rather than shying away from the political nature of poverty maps, teams should embrace this political aspect and try to identify key reformers and other actors who may use the maps to affect changes for the benefit of the poor.

7. If the technical work on poverty maps evolves within a particular project, it is important to possess the ability to form multisectoral teams to pursue operational details. It is important not to allow the dialogue on targeting to become locked into a particular project since many issues may not be addressed through a single project.

8. It is important to work at a technical level and at a policy level during the poverty mapping exercise. Both levels are likely to influence the usefulness and the impact of the maps.

References

Kingdom of Morocco. 2006. *50 ans de développement humain et perspectives 2025* (*50 Years of Human Development and Prospects to 2025*). http://www.rdh50.ma/fr/index.asp.

Planning Commission. 2004. "Carte de la pauvreté communale." Report, Planning Commission, Rabat.

Ravallion, Martin. 2000. "Monitoring Targeting Performance When Decentralized Allocations to the Poor are Unobserved." *World Bank Economic Review* 14 (2): 331–45.

World Bank. 2001. "Main Report." Vol. 1 of "Kingdom of Morocco: Poverty Update." Report 21506-MOR, Human Development Sector, Middle East and North Africa Region, World Bank, Washington, DC.

———. 2004. "Kingdom of Morocco Poverty Report: Strengthening Policy by Identifying the Geographic Dimension of Poverty." Report 28223-MOR, Social and Economic Development Group, Middle East and North Africa Region, World Bank, Washington, DC.

12

Poverty Maps in Sri Lanka
Policy Impacts and Lessons

TARA VISHWANATH AND NOBUO YOSHIDA

ACRONYMS AND ABBREVIATIONS

DCS	Department of Census and Statistics
DS	Divisional Secretariat
HIES	Household Income and Expenditure Survey

Poverty in Sri Lanka is marked by spatial heterogeneity. The poverty headcount ratio in Colombo District in 2002 (6 percent) was less than a sixth of the ratios in Badulla and Monaragala Districts (37 percent). The regional disparities in the pace of poverty reduction is even more striking. The poverty headcount ratio in Colombo District *declined* by 10 percentage points between 1990–91 and 2002, while the ratio in Puttalam District *rose* by almost 10 percentage points during the same period. Further disaggregation would be needed to uncover fully the spatial heterogeneity of poverty in Sri Lanka; there is a widespread perception that many pockets of severe poverty remain or are emerging even in Colombo District.

The growing regional inequality and slow poverty reduction are not the results of inaction by the government of Sri Lanka. Indeed, the government has a long history of social welfare programs. The most significant one now is the *Samurdhi* (prosperity) transfer program. In 2005, the expenditures of the Ministry of Samurdhi amounted to 0.6 percent of the country's gross domestic product; about 90 percent of this was spent on the transfer program. The issue is therefore not inaction, but rather the identification of ways to improve the targeting of social welfare programs through the development of an accurate, objective database to locate the poor and measure the extent of deprivation.

In May 2003, the World Bank proposed a poverty mapping exercise to the Department of Census and Statistics (DCS), which agreed to undertake the exercise in close collaboration with the Bank.[1]

The poverty maps of Sri Lanka have had a wide impact. Maybe one of the most important impacts was the use of the maps by the Ministry of Samurdhi to select 113 of the poorest Divisional Secretariats (DSs) when the ministry initiated the reform of the Samurdhi transfer program for the poor. This did not happen in isolation; it was an outcome of the tireless efforts of the DCS to disseminate the results of the poverty mapping exercise to the public and, especially, government officials. Now, many officials are aware of poverty maps as important monitoring instruments. The Sri Lanka poverty maps are accepted widely because the DCS has taken this lead in dissemination. DCS staff are able to explain the technical aspects of poverty maps and deal with the political sensitivity of the maps. The World Bank's long-term commitment to capacity building within the DCS, which began well before the poverty mapping exercise, and the World Bank's supportive role in dissemination have also contributed to this success.

The objective of this chapter is to share some of the experiences involved in the poverty mapping exercise in Sri Lanka with potential future practitioners so as to facilitate their work and enhance the policy impact of poverty maps. The chapter is organized as follows. The next section portrays major technical issues faced during the mapping exercise. The subsequent section illustrates the main findings of the exercise. The section thereafter supplies information on other applications of the poverty maps. The ensuing section outlines the process of the mapping exercise in detail. The penultimate section describes important policy impacts. The final section concludes.

Building a Poverty Map, Technical Considerations

The DCS agreed to use a standard poverty mapping methodology, the small area estimation method developed by Elbers, Lanjouw, and Lanjouw (2003). The Census of Population and Housing conducted in 2001 and the Household Income and Expenditure Survey (HIES) conducted in 2002 were chosen for the analysis. The poverty mapping exercise followed a standard procedure depicted in the World Bank guidelines. The following issues turned out to be a major challenge in Sri Lanka.

First, there are some mismatches in the location codes used in the 2001 census and the 2002 HIES. The location codes were changed in the 2001 census, and the HIES 2002 was supposed to implement the same codes. However, the team found codes at the DS unit level and many at the Grama Niladhari level in HIES 2002 that are different from the codes in the 2001 census. For the small area estimation method, such mismatches are critical and need to be resolved before initiating the analysis. To solve this problem, census and HIES sampling frame specialists were called in and asked to match the location codes manually. After this time-consuming matching work had been completed, it was possible to use the same location codes with the HIES and census data.

Second, the HIES 2002 focuses on consumption and income among households, but does not include much information on education, health, or housing conditions. Since the 2001 census contains detailed information on housing conditions, if the HIES 2002 had covered housing conditions more thoroughly, the predictive power of the consumption models used for the poverty mapping exercise would have improved substantially. On the other hand, the HIES has a large sample size relative to the population of Sri Lanka: the HIES sample was 20,100 households, while Sri Lanka's population in the 17 districts where the HIES was fielded has been estimated at around 18 million people. The large sample size allows consumption models to follow consumption patterns more closely.

Third, the data entry process was slow. When the work was initiated in September 2003, the full sample of the 2001 census was not yet available; instead, only 5 percent of the sample was available for the analysis. The team needed to use the 5 percent sample to develop programs and train the DCS staff. When the full sample data finally became available in April 2005, DCS staff were able to estimate poverty headcount ratios at the DS level.

Results of the Poverty Mapping Exercise

Before we present the results of the poverty mapping exercise in Sri Lanka, it is worth noting certain limitations on the use of the maps. Poverty mapping is a powerful statistical tool for identifying pockets of poverty that may not be observable through aggregated or national poverty statistics. The results may be used to improve targeting in poverty reduction programs and help identify the causes of severe deprivation. However, we must be careful in using the results, particularly in the actual design of poverty programs. In many cases, poverty maps are only indicative of problems. To discern clear policy implications, additional well-designed surveys or analyses are often needed.

Figure 12.1, a map of poverty headcount ratios at the DS level, illustrates some interesting geographical characteristics of poverty incidence. First, as expected, poverty headcount ratios are substantially lower in Colombo District and neighboring areas. Second, high rates of poverty are much more common in areas in the deep south (Sabaragamuwa, Southern, and Uva Provinces) than in areas more to the center and north of the country (North Central and North Western Provinces). (Note that the darkest areas of the map denote projected poverty headcount rates of 36 percent and above, compared to the country's average of 22 percent.) Third, the map highlights the pockets of extreme poverty in almost all parts of Sri Lanka, including districts with low aggregate poverty rates. For example, some DSs in the southern part of Western Province (Kalutara District) suffer from severe deprivation, and similar pockets of extreme poverty exist in North Central and North Western Provinces (for example, in parts of Anuradhapura, Kurunegala, and

Figure 12.1 Poverty Headcount Ratio at the DS Level, Sri Lanka

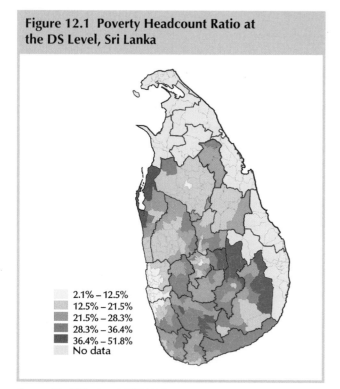

2.1% – 12.5%
12.5% – 21.5%
21.5% – 28.3%
28.3% – 36.4%
36.4% – 51.8%
No data

Source: World Bank and DCS 2005.

Figure 12.2 Estimated Distribution of the Poor, Sri Lanka

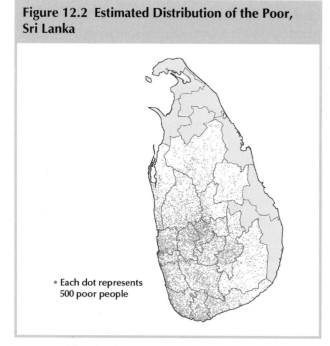

• Each dot represents 500 poor people

Source: World Bank and DCS 2005.

Puttalam Districts). Fourth, extreme poverty seems to be concentrated in Sabaragamuwa Province and, especially, Uva Province.

However, high headcount ratios do not always indicate that there is a large *population of poor people* in a DS since the poverty headcount ratio in an area depends on the area's total population, as well as the number of poor people. Figure 12.2 illustrates this clearly. Thus, for example, even though the headcount ratio in Colombo District is only 6 percent, the population of poor people in the district is high, especially in Colombo city areas, because of the large population. Furthermore, the coastal areas from southern Gampaha District to the western part of Hambantota District record high numbers of poor people despite the relatively low headcount ratios. On the other hand, many of the DSs in Monaragala District record the highest headcount ratios in the nation, but there are lower numbers of poor people because of the low population density. This illustrates the danger of relying *only* on poverty headcount ratios in designing poverty reduction programs. In Sri Lanka's case, targeting all antipoverty programs on poor districts in the deep south, for instance, would run the risk of missing large numbers of the poor in districts that are more well off on average, including the capital city of Colombo.

Colombo District witnessed a significant reduction in poverty incidence between 1990 and 2002, as table 12.1 shows. But figure 12.3 suggests that, even in Colombo District, there are

Table 12.1 Estimates of Poverty Headcount Ratio by District, Sri Lanka

Province	District	1990–91 (%)	1995–96 (%)	2002 (%)
Western	Colombo	16	12	6
	Gampaha	15	14	11
	Kalutara	32	29	20
Central	Kandy	36	37	25
	Matale	29	42	30
	Nuwara Eliya	20	32	23
Southern	Galle	30	32	26
	Matara	29	35	27
	Hambantota	32	31	32
North Western	Kurunegala	27	26	25
	Puttalam	22	31	31
North Central	Anuradhapura	24	27	20
	Polonnaruwa	24	20	24
Uva	Badulla	31	41	37
	Monaragala	34	56	37
Sabaragamuwa	Ratnapura	31	46	34
	Kegalle	31	36	32

Source: Data from the HIES 1990–91, 1995–96, and 2002 (DCS).

Figure 12.3 Poverty Headcount Ratio at the Grama Niladhari Level in Colombo District, Sri Lanka

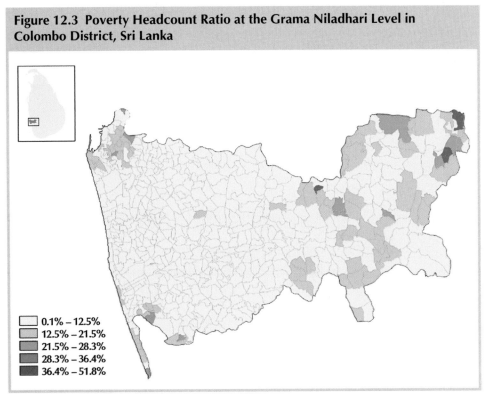

0.1% – 12.5%
12.5% – 21.5%
21.5% – 28.3%
28.3% – 36.4%
36.4% – 51.8%

Source: World Bank and DCS 2005.

some pockets of poverty that are concentrated in the eastern part of the district and Colombo city (the northwest of the district). Figure 12.4 shows that there is a concentration of poor people in the population in Colombo city, while the poor population is more sparse in the eastern part of Colombo District.

Further Analysis Using the Poverty Maps

Accessibility and poverty

Geographical isolation as measured by the distance to the nearest market or city seems to be highly correlated with poverty incidence. To illustrate this relationship in detail, figure 12.5 shows an accessibility index for each DS. The accessibility index is calculated for every point as the sum of the population of surrounding cities and towns, inversely weighted by the travel time on the road network to each town. It requires data on the populations of major cities and towns and a detailed road map, which are both available from a recent assessment of the investment climate in Sri Lanka (World Bank and ADB 2005).

Figure 12.5 shows that the areas surrounding Colombo District in Western Province (the blue areas on the lower left side of the map) are well connected to cities and markets,

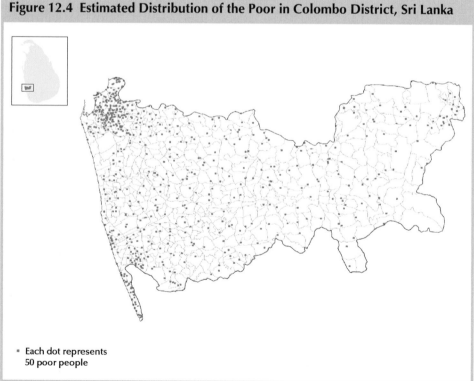

Figure 12.4 Estimated Distribution of the Poor in Colombo District, Sri Lanka

▪ Each dot represents
50 poor people

Source: World Bank and DCS 2005.

while, for example, most of Uva Province (the yellow and light green area near the lower right corner of the map) is geographically isolated. Apparently, as one travels away from the area surrounding Colombo, the accessibility index becomes lower.

A comparison of figures 12.1 and 12.5 clearly indicates a negative correlation between the poverty headcount ratio and the accessibility index. For example, the coastal areas surrounding Colombo District record a high accessibility index and a low poverty headcount ratio, while many DSs in Monaragala District (in Uva Province) are poor and geographically isolated. A simple regression verifies the observation that there is a significant negative correlation between the two indexes.[2] More research will be needed to identify the extent to which lack of accessibility explains poverty incidence in remote areas.

Drought and poverty incidence

It is well known that the agricultural sector remains one of the major sources of livelihoods in all provinces except Western Province and that agricultural wage employees are vulnerable. Thus, a natural disaster such as flooding or drought may have serious consequences on livelihoods and result in sharp rises in poverty incidence.

Figure 12.6 shows rainfall anomalies in 2001. These are defined as the percentage deviation of rainfall in 2001 from the average annual rainfall over the previous 30 years. The figure shows that some areas were severely

Figure 12.5 Accessibility Index, Sri Lanka

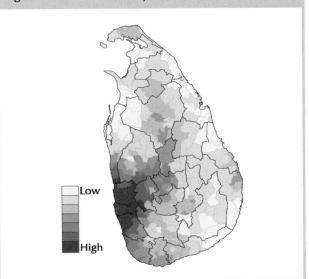

Source: World Bank and DCS 2005.
Note: The map shows the mean of the access values for all points that fall into a given DS unit. (See the text for more details.) This accessibility index is a measure of potential market integration. It reflects the quality and density of local transportation infrastructure. Included in the analysis are 185 cities and towns.

Figure 12.6 Rainfall Anomalies, Sri Lanka 2001

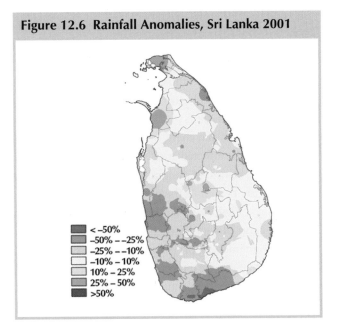

Source: World Bank and DCS 2005.
Note: The figure shows the rainfall in 2001, less the average rainfall over the previous 30 years. The red areas were drier in 2001. The blue areas were wetter in 2001. The figure has been computed using only stations for which there are data for the 30-year period and for 2001.

affected by drought in 2001, especially most of Hambantota District and the southern part of Matara District (both in Southern Province; the areas in question are shown in bright red in the figure). Drought does not necessarily raise poverty incidence; the impact also depends on other factors—such as the availability of good irrigation systems, the crops cultivated, and the diversity or the lack of diversity in occupations—that affect the vulnerability of the people to rainfall anomalies. For this reason, it is difficult to hypothesize about the links between rainfall anomalies and poverty incidence, especially in the absence of information about the other factors and panel data allowing the measurement of the impact of drought.[3]

Nonetheless, we may find a rough correlation between poverty incidence and drought-affected areas if we compare the poverty map (figure 12.1) and the drought map (figure 12.6). For example, Hambantota District (Southern Province; red and orange areas at the bottom in figure 12.6) and the southern parts of Kalutara District (Western Province; orange and yellow areas at the lower left in figure 12.6) were affected by severe drought and recorded high poverty incidence according to poverty headcount ratios. Although these visual links suggest that specific areas of the country are likely to be vulnerable to such events, more careful analysis needs to be performed to measure the impact of this vulnerability on poverty.[4]

Assessing the impact of the tsunami on poverty

Poor people are more vulnerable to natural disasters. They are less capable of coping with such disasters and also of recovering from them. There is a real concern that the tsunami catastrophe that struck the Indian Ocean in late December 2004 may irreparably worsen the situation of the poor and generate higher poverty rates in Sri Lanka. Special care thus needs to be taken to ensure a smooth recovery process among the poorest and most vulnerable people.

It has been widely presumed that the killer waves struck some of the poorest areas of the nation, but there is no clear information linking poverty and tsunami damage specific to the affected areas. Detailed poverty profiles and information on disaster damage will be critical in designing and targeting medium- and long-term reconstruction efforts for the benefit of the poor in these areas.

Figure 12.7 illustrates poverty headcount ratios for affected areas in Galle, Hambantota, and Matara Districts (Southern Province). The related data have been produced through an ongoing project involving the DCS through which an extensive geo-referenced database on the effects of the tsunami disaster will be constructed. Note that the figure shows poverty headcount ratios only for DSs that *include tsunami-affected Grama Niladhari divisions.* Data on poverty incidence in entire DSs would be misleading since most areas in the DSs were not affected by the tsunami; on the other hand, most of the Grama Niladhari divisions have populations that are too small to yield statistically reliable estimates. Grouping several Grama Niladhari divisions within each DS therefore enables the estimation of poverty headcount ratios with a reasonable amount of precision.

It is possible to see from the figure that, before the tsunami struck Sri Lanka, most of the affected areas in Hambantota were poor, and some of those in Galle were also poor. However, most of the affected areas in Matara were not particularly poor relative to average national and district poverty headcount ratios. These results suggest that there is substantial variation in poverty incidence among affected areas in Southern Province, which should be taken into account in designing or prioritizing long-term tsunami reconstruction projects.

Building Capacity to Sustain the Poverty Mapping Exercise

One of the most important objectives of the mapping exercise has been to incorporate poverty mapping into the regular poverty monitoring framework of the DCS. Our goal is to help ensure that the DCS not only produces poverty maps, but is also able to repeat the exercise in the next round of the census.

However, it is not easy to ensure the sustainability of the poverty mapping exercise. For example, if technical assistance is not provided to the DCS, poverty mapping might easily become a one-time effort by outsiders because the data and technical requirements are substantial. Moreover, without large-scale dissemination of the results, it will be difficult to gain political support to sustain the effort over decades and foster the expansion of a community of poverty map users and stakeholders.

Figure 12.7 Poverty Headcount Ratios in Parts of Southern Province, Sri Lanka

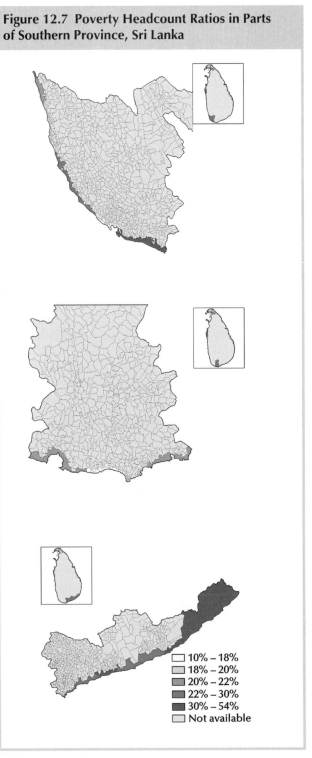

10% – 18%
18% – 20%
20% – 22%
22% – 30%
30% – 54%
Not available

Source: World Bank and DCS 2005.

Capacity building within the poverty mapping exercise in Sri Lanka has been comprehensive. The capacity-building process supported by the World Bank has covered a wide range of activities, including improving data entry facilities, establishing a geographic information system (GIS) laboratory, providing training on a range of estimation and simulation methods and mapping techniques, selecting affordable, but effective software, and creating user-friendly methods to apply the software to the task. A series of dissemination workshops has also been planned in Colombo and other districts.

The poverty mapping exercise has been the outcome of an ongoing technical assistance program on poverty monitoring with the DCS. The program has also included assistance in reaching a consensus on an official poverty line for Sri Lanka, the organization of workshops to disseminate the poverty line and the poverty maps, and support for a potential expansion of the HIES to cover other indicators for monitoring social sector outcomes. In July 2005, the DCS and the World Bank held a workshop in Colombo to present the official poverty line and the results of the poverty mapping exercise. The Bank will continue to support the DCS in the broad dissemination of the poverty maps.

Needs assessment for poverty mapping in Sri Lanka

At the start of this project, we conducted a thorough needs assessment. We identified the following areas for an intensive effort at capacity building and technical assistance:

■ Updating the data entry facilities for the 2001 population census was necessary. The population census is one of the most important components of the poverty mapping exercise, but the entry and processing of population data were slow because of the limited space and facilities at the DCS. Without significant upgrades in the DCS facilities, the poverty maps would have had to be based only on the 5 percent census sample that was available at the time.

■ A well-organized GIS was not ready. The existence of such a GIS would not only help maximize the range of applications for the poverty maps, but also improve the accuracy of the maps. However, in Sri Lanka, geographical information was spread out across various government agencies and research organizations. This made the timely preparation of geographical information for the poverty mapping exercise and for the dissemination of the results difficult.

■ No official poverty line had been generally accepted in Sri Lanka. At the time the poverty mapping exercise was initiated, several poverty lines had been created by various institutions, but there was no consensus on trends in poverty and the geographical profile of poverty. Without a single, widely accepted, and official poverty line, the uses for the poverty maps might be limited.

■ DCS staff had not been exposed to relevant issues and techniques in econometrics or to the general-purpose statistical software (such as SAS or Stata) that the small area estimation method calls for. This meant that the latest statistical software packages had to be purchased, and the staff had to undergo substantial training in econometrics and statistical software application.

How these issues have been addressed

Updating the data entry facilities and creating the GIS laboratory

The DCS and the World Bank team prepared two proposals for an economic reform technical assistance project: one to upgrade the data entry facilities at the DCS (submitted in October 2003) and another to set up a GIS laboratory (submitted in April 2004). The submission of the second proposal was delayed in part because we were waiting for the needs assessment by our GIS expert in December 2003. All the equipment for the data entry and data processing upgrades was provided in November 2004, and all the equipment for the GIS laboratory was provided only in May 2005. The delays were understandable given the interruptions caused by the general election in April 2004 and the tsunami in December 2004, but there were misunderstandings involved in the delays as well.[5]

At the new facilities, the entry and cleaning of the 2001 census data were completed in March 2005. This was sooner than expected given the nearly six-month delay in the work on the facilities.

Establishing an official poverty line

In May 2004, work on a new poverty line was finalized through a collaborative effort of DCS staff and the World Bank team. Previously, many poverty lines had been used in studies conducted by various organizations. To resolve all the issues in determining the official poverty line for Sri Lanka, a consultative approach was adopted to engage stakeholders in the country and in the donor community, including Central Bank staff, university professors, and international poverty specialists at the World Bank.

A workshop was convened in March 2004 to examine relevant poverty estimation methodologies and to discuss issues with an expert on international best practice. Based on recommendations emerging from the workshop, a detailed analysis was undertaken by a poverty study group at the DCS in which two international consultants supported by the World Bank team participated. The group explored the HIES data collected in 1990–91, 1995–96, and 2002 and identified an appropriate methodology for consistent measurement of poverty trends across time and space.

The new official poverty line has helped resolve some of the confusion in poverty profiles and trends, and it has enhanced the usefulness of the poverty maps. Another notable outcome of the process is the ready ability of DCS staff to update the official poverty line, which has motivated them to take up the far more difficult analytical tasks required by the poverty mapping exercise. The results, along with detailed explanations, are available on the DCS external Web site (http://www.statistics.gov.lk/). The fact that, in their analyses, academic researchers, government departments, and the Central

Bank use the official poverty line and the poverty estimates produced by the DCS is proof these have been widely accepted.

Training

Intensive training on the small area estimation methodology was provided by experts in poverty mapping. Poverty mapping requires careful work in creating common and cluster-specific variables; selecting optimal models of household consumption and the distributions of cluster- and household-specific errors; and mapping poverty and other geographically referenced information. Training needs to cover all these areas.

The DCS chose a group of statisticians to take part in the training. The World Bank team provided three separate two-week periods of training to the group between 2003 and 2005. For the rather lengthy data analyses, the World Bank team developed a set of Stata programs to automate many of the steps involved in the small area estimation method. These programs eased the training significantly because the number of adjustments in the data by the DCS statisticians was dramatically reduced. The DCS staff succeeded in producing poverty estimates for DSs using the 5 percent sample of 2001 census data in December 2004 and the full sample of census data in 2005.

However, only a few staff members actually acquired a strong command of the programs. It would be worthwhile to introduce the DCS staff to the World Bank's new poverty mapping software, PovMap, which would reduce the length of the process dramatically. Because most of the staff understand the concepts behind the small area estimation methodology, it should be easy for them to implement the analysis using the new software. The new software would be especially helpful now that the DCS has expanded the HIES questionnaire, given that this expansion might prevent DCS staff from simply and incorrectly applying the existing programs to update the poverty maps during the next round of the census.

GIS software is essential for overlaying poverty statistics on DS or Grama Niladhari boundary maps. The software may be used to conduct simulations to estimate average distances and times to reach main roads (see elsewhere above). Basic training in GIS software was provided by the vendor. Around 20 staff members attended the course. Currently, the DCS is actively producing GIS databases, as well as various kinds of maps, such as food vulnerability maps, poverty maps, accessibility maps, and drought maps.

Dissemination of poverty maps and other results

A dissemination workshop was held in Colombo in July 2005 shortly after the completion of the poverty mapping exercise. The workshop was organized jointly by the DCS and the World Bank to display the detailed maps and illustrate the proper application of the maps in planning and policy making. The audience consisted of staff from the Central Bank and various nongovernmental organizations, as well as local researchers. The experts of the DCS and the World Bank discussed the context, the technical issues, and the uses and limitations of poverty maps. The response was positive and improved the visibility of and trust in the work of the DCS.

The DCS took the lead in the dissemination process. For example, the director of the DCS presented the poverty maps to many government officials. He also presented the poverty maps at a conference organized by a research institute at which many people from nongovernmental organizations and the local academic community participated.

A series of dissemination workshops in other districts are being planned to present the poverty maps and promote the creation of a network of long-term users. Because of their visual and intuitive appeal, poverty maps may be easily misapplied. Stressing the limitations of poverty maps is therefore important. Poverty maps should be used only as an indicative first step in planning poverty programs. They are not substitutes for actual targeting mechanisms, particularly at the household level.

Besides the workshops, the DCS has prepared a user-friendly Web site containing poverty maps and a brief description of the methodology. The DCS and the World Bank have also drafted a policy note on the technical aspects of the exercise, the interpretation of the results, and the limitations of the maps and distribute the note at conferences.

The Impact of the Poverty Maps on Policy

The poverty maps have not only enhanced public awareness of the significant regional inequalities in Sri Lanka, but also encouraged policy makers to take appropriate steps to address the severe deprivation that still prevails in rural and remote areas. The poverty maps are now widely accepted within government, nongovernmental organizations, and the local academic community and among donors in Sri Lanka. The maps are having an effect on policies, lending strategies, and research. In particular, the poverty maps and the map illustrating the accessibility index (see figure 12.5) are influencing World Bank projects, such as road projects. The poverty maps have also helped revive the government's initiative to improve targeting in the Samurdhi transfer program and have been used to identify the poorest 113 DSs so that the government might raise benefits there. This has been a result of the careful dissemination of poverty maps by the DCS, with World Bank support, and the World Bank's long-term technical assistance for Samurdhi reform.

The Samurdhi welfare program and reform process

Social welfare programs have a long tradition in Sri Lanka. Among the current programs, the Samurdhi transfer program has the highest budget share in welfare spending among poor families. However, a number of studies point to large-scale mistargeting and the exclusion of poor households in the Samurdhi program.[6] The program apparently misses more than 35 percent of the households in the poorest 20 percent of the population, while reaching 12 percent of the richest 20 percent of the population. Given that Sri Lanka's poverty headcount ratio is around 23 percent, this indicates that the program suffers from substantial undercoverage of the poor, as well as large leakage to the rich. Such large errors in targeting dilute the positive impact of the program on the poor and are evidence of serious distortions in the welfare budget.

In response to a request by the government, the World Bank has been providing nonlending technical assistance for Samurdhi welfare reform since 2003. This World Bank technical assistance has consisted of two major components: (1) a reorientation in the selection of program beneficiaries from subjective eligibility criteria to a formula-based system that allows for greater objectivity and (2) the creation of the institutional capacity to support the changes in the selection process.

A change in government in March 2004 altered the pace and sequence of the steps in implementation. Since December 2004, the revamped targeting system is being implemented in northern, conflict-affected areas where the Samurdhi program had not previously been active.

Samurdhi reform in the south

The reform in the south was stalled until recently because it involves the transformation of an existing system. The poverty maps contributed to reviving this implementation process. The director general of the DCS presented to government officials a comparison between the poverty maps and an allocation map for Samurdhi transfers. This clearly illustrated the large-scale mistargeting in the south. The government announced the Samurdhi reform in the south in early 2006.

In late 2005, the minister of Samurdhi had taken the important step of publicly acknowledging the need to target the Samurdhi program only on the poor. Steps were initiated to encourage nonpoor beneficiaries to give up their beneficiary status voluntarily. In early 2006, the government announced a considerable increase in the allocations for Samurdhi transfers. The increase in payments amounted to 50 percent (beginning in January 2006) for all current beneficiaries in the 113 DSs selected according to the information in the poverty maps; moreover, 100 DSs were to be added soon. The increase in the transfers was sensible, given the widely held view that the transfers had been too small to improve living conditions adequately among poor households. The higher payments made improvements in the targeting in the program all the more important. Reform efforts continue to improve the coverage of the poor by the Samurdhi transfer program.

Concluding Remarks

This chapter helps clarify the extent of regional disparity in poverty incidence in Sri Lanka, particularly by locating pockets of deprivation, even in districts that are better off on average. The analysis in the chapter provides a nuanced interpretation of headcount ratios in urban and rural areas showing that urban areas may have significant populations of poor people, but relatively low headcount ratios, while remote rural areas may have high headcount ratios that do not necessarily translate into high numbers of poor people.

Although these results should be useful for designing poverty reduction programs, it is equally important to stress the limitations. First, poverty headcounts are derived from simulations, and these are associated with imputation errors. While the method is useful for broad ranking across geographical areas and communities, it is not a good substitute for other methods to identify poor households for more precise benefit targeting. Second, poverty headcounts are typically based only on data on household consumption, and these do not adequately capture other attributes of poverty. Third, poverty headcount estimates do not explain the causes of poverty. Well-designed surveys and careful analyses are needed to obtain proper diagnoses of the attributes and causes of poverty; such information is essential in designing appropriate interventions.

The poverty mapping exercise in Sri Lanka offers lessons for other countries in the region on the technical feasibility and the potential uses of poverty maps. Perhaps the most important lesson from the experience in Sri Lanka is that the process matters. Given the relevant technical resources available through the World Bank, the production of a poverty map is not difficult or time consuming. However, it is still difficult to ensure the wide acceptance of poverty maps among governments, the private sector, and donors.

In Sri Lanka, poverty maps are increasingly being recognized by policy makers and government officials as useful tools for poverty measurement. This is largely the result of the initiative of the DCS in spreading awareness and convincing potential users. Poverty maps are often politically sensitive because they may alter and otherwise affect design and targeting in ongoing social welfare programs. Since DCS staff are alert to the technical and political issues, the leadership of the DCS at the dissemination stage has been effective in avoiding unnecessary debates and any political backlash.

To continue this process, additional capacity building at the DCS is essential. The comprehensive assistance of the World Bank in supplying software, hardware, and hands-on training has successfully fostered this capacity-building process. In Sri Lanka, the partnership between the World Bank and the DCS has clearly been fundamental to the successes of the poverty mapping exercise so far.

Notes

1. Sri Lanka has 17 districts on which poverty estimates are already available through the Household Income and Expenditure Survey (HIES). Each district covers a relatively large area, which implies that poverty estimates at a lower level—such as the Divisional Secretariats (DSs) or below—will be necessary to capture fully the extent of heterogeneity. But there is a practical problem in achieving this: neither the HIES nor the Census of Population and Housing is appropriate for producing statistically reliable poverty estimates for geographical areas smaller than districts. For example, the 2002 HIES covered a sample of 20,100 households, a number that was designed to be representative at the district level. However, the number is not sufficient to produce reliable poverty estimates at lower levels. In contrast, the census of 2001 may be disaggregated to a lower level, but it does not include information on household consumption and income.
2. The R^2 for a regression of the poverty rate of DSs on the accessibility index is 0.21, which is high considering that this regression with a *single* variable is being used to explain variations in poverty rates at the DS level.
3. Rainfall is generally concentrated in southeastern Sri Lanka. High mountains cover the south-central part of the country. Note that there does not seem to be an obvious association between poverty incidence, land elevation, and typical rainfall.
4. To clarify the direction of causality in the case of rainfall, for example, it would be useful to compare poverty maps with rainfall anomalies in other years.

5. We submitted two proposals: one to upgrade the data entry facilities and the other to set up a GIS laboratory at the DCS. Officials with the economic reform technical assistance project thought the two were a single proposal and neglected to process the latter proposal, which delayed the launch of the laboratory. After inquiries from the DCS and the World Bank, the officials understood what had happened and started processing the proposal for the laboratory.

6. See Glinskaya (2000) and Narayan, Vishwanath, and Yoshida (2006) for more analysis.

References

BBS (Bangladesh Bureau of Statistics) and WFP (United Nations World Food Programme). 2004. "Local Estimation of Poverty and Malnutrition in Bangladesh." Report, Bangladesh Bureau of Statistics and United Nations World Food Programme, Dhaka, Bangladesh.

Bigman, David, and P. V. Srinivasan. 2002. "Geographical Targeting of Poverty Alleviation Programs: Methodology and Applications in Rural India." *Journal of Policy Modeling* 24 (3): 237–55.

DCS (Sri Lanka, Department of Census and Statistics). 2003. "The Department of Census and Statistics Announces the Official Poverty Line for Sri Lanka." Department of Census and Statistics. http://www.statistics.gov.lk/poverty/OfficialPovertyLineBuletin.pdf.

Elbers, Chris, Jean O. Lanjouw, and Peter F. Lanjouw. 2003. "Micro-Level Estimation of Poverty and Inequality." *Econometrica* 71 (1):355–64.

Fujii, Tomoki. 2003. "Commune-Level Estimation of Poverty Measures and Its Application in Cambodia." Draft research paper, United Nations University–World Institute for Development Economics Research, Helsinki.

Gibson, John, Gaurav Datt, Bryant J. Allen, Vicky Hwang, R. Michael Bourke, and Dilip Parajuli. 2005. "Mapping Poverty in Rural Papua New Guinea." *Pacific Economic Bulletin* 20 (1): 27–43.

Glinskaya, Elena. 2000. "An Empirical Evaluation of the Samurdhi Program." Background paper for *Sri Lanka: Poverty Assessment,* Report 22535-CE (2002), Washington, DC, World Bank.

Henninger, Norbert, and Mathilde Snel. 2002. *Where Are the Poor?: Experiences with the Development and Use of Poverty Maps.* Washington, DC: World Resources Institute; Arendal, Norway: United Nations Environment Programme–Global Resource Information Database.

Hentschel, Jesko, Jean O. Lanjouw, Peter F. Lanjouw, and Javier Poggi. 2000. "Combining Census and Survey Data to Trace the Spatial Dimensions of Poverty: A Case Study of Ecuador." *World Bank Economic Review* 14 (1): 147–65.

Mistiaen, Johan A., Berk Özler, Tiaray Razafimanantena, and Jean Razafindravonoma. 2002. "Putting Welfare on the Map in Madagascar." African Region Working Paper Series 34, World Bank, Washington, DC.

Narayan, Ambar, Tara Vishwanath, and Nobuo Yoshida. 2006. "Sri Lanka: Welfare Reform." In *Poverty and Social Impact Analysis of Reforms: Lessons and Examples from Implementation,* ed. Aline Coudouel, Anis A. Dani, and Stefano Paternostro, 149–212. Washington, DC: World Bank.

Narayan, Ambar, and Nobuo Yoshida. 2004. "Poverty in Sri Lanka: The Impact of Growth with Rising Inequality." PREM Working Paper Series SASPR-8, Poverty Reduction and Economic Management Sector Unit, South Asia Region, World Bank, Washington, DC.

World Bank. 2002. *Sri Lanka: Poverty Assessment.* Report 22535-CE. Washington, DC: Poverty Reduction and Economic Management Sector Unit, South Asia Region, World Bank.

———. 2004. *Sri Lanka: Development Policy Review.* Report 29396-LK. Washington, DC: World Bank.

World Bank and ADB (Asian Development Bank). 2005. *Sri Lanka: Improving the Rural and Urban Investment Climate.* Colombo, Sri Lanka: World Bank; Manila: Asian Development Bank.

World Bank and DCS (Department of Census and Statistics). 2005. "A Poverty Map for Sri Lanka: Lessons and Findings." Policy Note 35605, Poverty Reduction and Economic Management, South Asia Region, World Bank, Washington, DC.

13

Thailand's Poverty Maps
From Construction to Application

SOMCHAI JITSUCHON AND KASPAR RICHTER

ACRONYMS AND ABBREVIATIONS

B	baht, the Thai currency
BMN	basic minimum need (a data set)
NESDB	National Economic and Social Development Board
NRD2C	National Rural Development Committee Survey (a data set)
NSO	National Statistical Office
POREP	Poverty and Social Registration Program

Poverty reduction is about improving the well-being of disadvantaged families, sharing the benefits of growth across communities in villages and cities, and connecting remote regions within the country and with the rest of the world. This agenda has played a central role in Thailand's development model. There is little doubt that commitment to poverty reduction by policy makers, businesses, and civil society has contributed to a remarkable record of poverty reduction over recent decades. Yet, questions and concerns have been raised about the effectiveness of economic policies in supporting growth in household income and providing communities with access to basic services. While poverty reduction policies may be a force for good, they also have to be implemented properly.

The motivation for the case study in this chapter is to look at one aspect of these issues: how small area estimation poverty maps might become an essential tool for poverty eradication in Thailand. The chapter is organized around four topics: Thailand's impressive

The authors gratefully acknowledge the excellent research assistance of Wanchat Suwankitti.

record in poverty reduction over the last 15 years, the need for poverty maps to direct public interventions to eradicate poverty during the second half of this decade, the constraints on the policy applications of poverty maps, and steps for promoting the use of poverty maps in policy making in the future.

Rapid Poverty Reduction

Strong national record

Thailand's economic record is impressive by any standards. The economy expanded from US$56 billion in 1987 to over US$140 billion in 2004 (in constant 2000 prices). Gross national income per capita rose by over 125 percent over the same period, increasing from US$1,060 to US$2,400. Worldwide experience shows that the most powerful force for the reduction of income poverty is broadbased economic growth. Using the series of nationwide cross-sectional Thailand Household Socio-Economic Surveys, we have been able to trace poverty from 1988 to 2002 at the provincial, regional, and national levels. In spite of the Asian crisis and population growth, the national poverty headcount, defined as the share of people living in households with income below the poverty line, fell from 32.6 percent in 1988 to 11.4 percent in 1996, while the number of the poor dropped from 17.7 million to 6.8 million over the same period. In the aftermath of the Asian crisis, the poverty rate rose to 14.2 percent up to 2000, when 8.8 million people were poor, before it declined with the economic recovery and dropped for the first time below 10 percent, representing 6.2 million people, in 2002.[1] Thailand has already reached its Millennium Development Goal poverty target of halving the poverty headcount between 1990 and 2015 (NESDB 2004). In addition, the target of the government's Ninth National Economic and Social Development Plan (2002–06) of reducing poverty incidence to under 12 percent was also met ahead of time.

Increasing regional poverty concentration

Thailand's poverty has stark regional features: poverty is highest in outlying regions and lowest in Bangkok and surrounding areas. Yet, poverty reduction has extended all across the country. Relative to the levels in 1988, the proportional reduction in poverty has been largest in Bangkok, followed by the Central, South, and North regions; the reduction was slowest in the Northeast. Because poverty is falling more rapidly in other regions, it has become more concentrated in the Northeast. One in two persons who were poor were living in the Northeast in 1988; the share of the poor in the total population was one in three at that time. The Northeast accounted for roughly one-third of the total population in 2002, but its share of the poor had increased to three in five. This translates into 3.8 million people living in the Northeast who are poor, compared to only 2.3 million in the rest of the country.

The provincial variations in living standards are even starker than the regional differences. Provinces (*changwat*) with low poverty rates exist alongside provinces with high poverty rates. While the Northeast and the South include the very poorest provinces, these regions also contain wealthy provinces where poverty incidence is less than 7.5 percent (see figure 13.1). Provinces with high poverty headcounts also tend to have large populations and, hence, a large number of poor people. While the Northeast includes provinces with little poverty, such as Chaiyaphum, Nong Khai, and Ubon Ratchathani, it also has the poorest provinces with the largest number of poor people, such as Buriram, Sisaket, and Surin. This is an important difference with the North, the second poorest region in Thailand. In the North, the provinces with the highest poverty incidence, such as Mae Hong Son, Tak, and Uthai Thani, tend to be remote and sparsely populated. Hence, they contribute only moderately to the national poverty rate because of low population density.

Unpacking Spatial Poverty

The small area estimation poverty map

The government is aspiring to eradicate poverty nationwide. As part of its ambitious Millennium Development Goal–Plus agenda, it is aiming at reducing the poverty headcount to below 4 percent by 2009 (NESDB 2004). Meeting this goal will be a significant challenge because maintaining progress is a different task from launching progress. The easy gains are being exploited, but improvement is becoming more difficult to achieve. As Thailand's provincial, regional, and national poverty rates have fallen, the focus has shifted to the remaining pockets of poverty. Poverty maps are therefore an aid in reaching the poverty reduction objective. They help to make visible those poor who are otherwise hidden behind the averages of large regional aggregations. There are huge differences in the abilities of families to cover basic needs not merely across regions, say, the Northeast relative to the Center, and provinces, such as Mae Hong Son relative to Chonburi, but also within provinces and within districts (*amphoe*).

Small area estimation techniques allow the construction of poverty measures at the district and village levels that are comparable to the poverty measures at the provincial, regional, and national levels. The main motivation behind the use of such methods is to combine the advantages of population censuses (extensive coverage of the population) with the advantages of household surveys (reliable expenditure and income data).[2] In response to a 2002 request by the National Economic and Social Development Board (Thailand's national planning agency, the NESDB) and the National Statistical Office (NSO), the Thailand Development Research Institute drew on technical expertise from the World Bank to derive Thailand's first small area poverty map, which was based on the 2000 population and housing census and the 2000 household socioeconomic survey. Since then, the institute and the NSO have completed the 2002 small area poverty map and have launched the 2004 map.

Figure 13.1 Poverty Headcount Ratio and Distribution by Province, Thailand 1988, 1994, and 2002

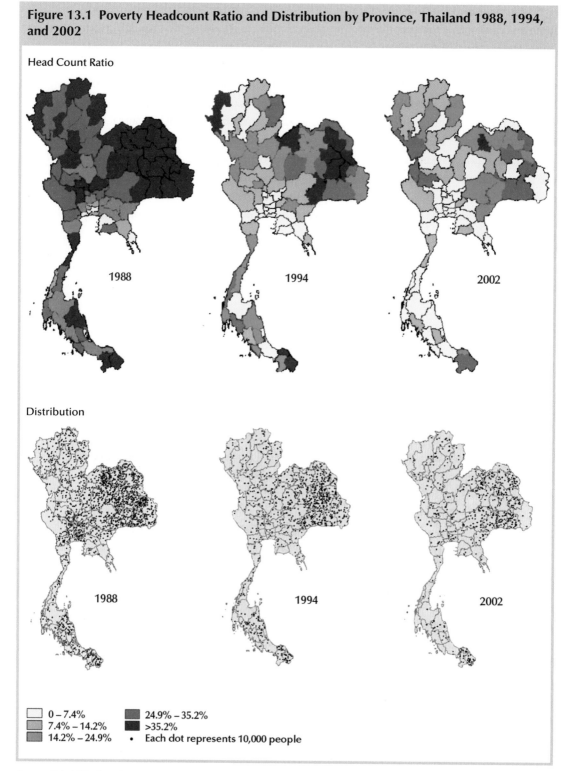

Source: World Bank and NESDB 2005.

Versions of the 2000 and 2002 maps were constructed separately for income and consumption. To reflect geographical differences in the determinants of poverty, separate models were estimated for each province, including a division by rural and urban areas. In addition, Bangkok was divided into four areas. There were thus 154 model estimations (75 provinces, each divided into urban and rural areas, plus the four Bangkok areas), replicating the number of strata in the household socioeconomic survey. Judging from standard goodness of fit measures such as the adjusted R^2, the models performed well.

The following paragraphs briefly discuss three challenges encountered in the creation of the small area poverty maps in Thailand.

Software

A basic requirement for estimating small area poverty maps is access to appropriate software. Thailand's 2000 population census collected information on each of the country's 62 million inhabitants. Until now, SAS software was the first choice for constructing small area poverty maps because of its ability to handle large data sets and sophisticated file management tasks. However, the standard leasing arrangements for SAS software impose a high financial burden on government agencies. For example, the NSO had to delay the preparation of the 2004 poverty map because of a lack of funds. SAS representatives finally granted the NSO a substantial discount on the license fee for one year, but this arrangement may not always be renewed in coming years.

In addition to the expensive license fee, SAS poses another issue. While the software is superior in data handling, it is not well suited for computationally intense tasks. For example, for the 2000 poverty map, SAS required more than three hours to complete the Bangkok model and almost two full days to estimate all 154 models. Given the estimation of separate poverty maps for both consumption and income and the choice of up to five different distribution forms for the error terms, as well as possible mistakes in data preparation, these calculations quickly became a heavy burden on the agency in charge of maintaining and updating the poverty maps.

Fortunately, a team at the Development Research Group of the World Bank has created a feasible alternative to SAS. The Windows-based PovMap software calculates poverty and other welfare measures much more quickly than does the SAS software. However, the PovMap interface for data preparation tasks such as merging files and transforming variables is cumbersome. These initial tasks may be accomplished using SAS or more affordable software such as Stata or SPSS.

Locality matching

Another challenge is the work involved in matching the area identification codes in the data sources used in the construction of small area poverty maps. Clearly, the localities in one data set have to be matched to the identical locality in another data set. As the NSO is the producer of both the population census and the household socioeconomic survey, it uses the same location identifier for both data sets. Nonetheless, three difficulties remain. First, merging variables from other data sets into the exercise, such as the Ministry of

Interior village surveys, requires a lengthy and ultimately imperfect matching process based on, for example, village and district names. Second, the number of localities, especially of small units such as villages and subdistricts (*tambons*), tends to change frequently over time as administrative units are partitioned or combined. For example, the numbers of villages and subdistricts in the 2002 and 2004 socioeconomic surveys increased relative to the 2000 population census because communities were split into separate villages. The rise in the number brought about changes in the coding. Furthermore, numerous rural communities were upgraded to municipality status between 2000 and 2004. Because of such changes, it took more than two months to match accurately the rural and urban communities cited in 2000 and the new rural and urban communities cited in 2004. Third, geographical locations have not been systematically coded according to a standard geographic information system, which limits one's ability to combine poverty measures and other data. For instance, of the 16,000 target villages identified by the NESDB and the Ministry of Interior, it was possible to match only 14,218 villages on the 2000 small area poverty map.

Capacity building

One objective of the Thailand poverty mapping initiative has been to foster institutional development and capacity building in counterpart agencies so as to establish greater ownership and sustainability in the results. Emphasis has therefore been placed on process as a key input for impact, while balancing this objective with the need to deliver timely analytical work of high quality. The focus on capacity building has thus shifted in line with the progress on the project and the lessons from earlier phases in the training. The training initiatives selected for staff at the NESDB and the NSO during the pilot stage of the development of the poverty map of 2000 were replaced by systematic formal training over a three-month period for the poverty map in 2002. At the end of this training program, each trainee was able to operate the SAS-based programs to build the poverty map, but the capacity building remained limited in key regards. In particular, some participants lacked the basic statistical and software knowledge to understand key steps in the development of poverty maps, modify the programming codes with confidence, or ensure adequate matching of areas across data sets. Furthermore, the NSO and the NESDB did not have sufficient institutional capacity to train new staff when there was attrition among the poverty mapping experts. Based on these lessons, the ongoing training program for the poverty map in 2004 was substantially revised in four aspects: the training period was extended to five months; the number of trainees was increased from six to ten; the trainees formed three three-member teams, each with an adequate skill mix in terms of statistical and software knowledge; and the three teams were given assignments after each training session. These adjustments increased the satisfaction in the training program for both the instructor and the trainees.

Dissemination

The small area poverty maps have been distributed through two channels: at the national level and among the provinces. The NESDB and the NSO, which are the agencies with core responsibility for policy planning and policy evaluation, have introduced line ministries to the poverty maps as an additional tool for poverty policy evaluation. Meanwhile, the NSO has established guidelines for provincial statistical offices so as to promote the use of the poverty maps in the context of local poverty reduction efforts, and it has placed background material on the maps on its Web site in Thai.

Findings

The small area poverty map of 2000 confirmed that there are large differences between poor and nonpoor communities within provinces. A relatively small number of subdistricts account for a large share of all the poor people. For example, the poorest third (34 percent) of all subdistricts and the poorest sixth (16 percent) of all villages and urban blocks accounted for more than two-thirds (70 percent) of all the consumption poor in Thailand (see figure 13.2). Over two-thirds (71 percent) of the subdistricts and over half of all villages and urban blocks (53 percent) in the Northeast showed a poverty incidence that was at least 50 percent in excess of the national average.

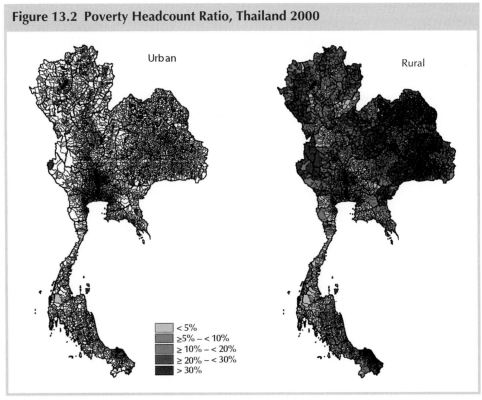

Figure 13.2 Poverty Headcount Ratio, Thailand 2000

Urban

Rural

< 5%
≥5% – < 10%
≥ 10% – < 20%
≥ 20% – < 30%
> 30%

Source: Jitsuchon 2004.
Note: The maps reflect the consumption approach.

Roadblocks to Application

The case for small area poverty maps

The previous section discussed how household survey data may be combined with census data to derive poverty estimates at the district, subdistrict, and village levels across the whole of Thailand. While there are other data sources for regional information on living standards, the small area poverty map approach has one important advantage: it gives the same poverty measure for districts and subdistricts that is used at the provincial, regional, and national levels to monitor the progress in poverty reduction. This consistency should make this method appealing to policy makers. It provides confidence that one is talking about the same thing whether at the national level or the village level.

Three examples illustrate how a poverty map may contribute to reaching the goal of a country free of poverty. First, the knowledge of poverty incidence at a detailed spatial scale has the potential to enhance the geographical targeting of interventions to improve people's lives. The impressive record of poverty reduction in Thailand has heightened the need to target the remaining pockets of poverty in the country. In the past, policies with broad coverage in sectors or areas where most poor persons were known to reside were effective in reducing poverty. For instance, the wide urban-rural divide implied that policies aimed at raising agricultural productivity would generally be successful in lifting many poor people out of poverty. Today, with the share of poor people below 10 percent, some rural areas are fairly prosperous, and broad policies alone have become unsuitable for poverty reduction. Policy makers may thus draw on small area poverty maps in planning public investments in education, health, sanitation, water, transportation, and other sectors. Such information may also help promote the decentralization process in Thailand, which will lead to a shift in expenditure responsibilities from the central government to local governmental or nongovernmental agents. In addition, it may assist in the design of fiscal transfer schemes from richer to poorer areas.

Second, poverty maps may be combined with other available geographically disaggregated data—such as geographical databases of transport infrastructure, the location of public service centers, access patterns to input and output markets, and information on natural resource quality and natural disasters—to yield a rich array of information relevant for poverty analysis and policy making. These data may also be used to evaluate the impact of government projects. By combining a detailed poverty map with a project spending map, one may infer whether it is the poor or the nonpoor who will benefit the most.

Finally, a poverty map may assist communities in the development of local poverty reduction strategies. It provides local stakeholders with the facts that are required for local decision making and for negotiation with government agencies. Poverty maps thus become an important instrument for local empowerment.

Despite the large potential for application, small area poverty maps have made little progress in becoming standard tools among civil servants, planners, and politicians. The

NESDB and the NSO have used poverty maps as a tool for monitoring poverty at the national level, and the NSO has held several national seminars and workshops to introduce poverty maps to provincial statistical officers, as well as potential external users. While these efforts have increased the awareness about poverty maps in provinces, institutional and political impediments prevent a more widespread use.

The institutional roadblock

There is no unique definition of poverty and no perfect indicator to measure changes in poverty over time. Poverty is a state of deprivation involving many dimensions, from limited income to vulnerability in the face of shocks. Small area poverty maps are based on objective measures of household income and the consumption basket. The advantage of this approach is comparability across space and time. But the approach also has important weaknesses. Perhaps the most important criticism is that it is tied to a material concept of poverty. It does not incorporate directly other dimensions of well-being, such as empowerment and happiness. These latter notions of poverty were central, for example, in Thailand's Ninth National Economic and Social Development Plan, which embraced the principle of the sufficiency economy (see box 13.1). In addition, the approach pays no attention to the people's own perception of poverty. While statistics may tell us that economic growth has made the population more well off, the people may actually feel less well off due to the many changes that have accompanied economic development. Finally, the poverty maps are aggregated from household-level indicators and do not make any direct reference to community-level indicators, such as village infrastructure or crime rates.

BOX 1 3 . 1   The Sufficiency Economy

The philosophy of the sufficiency economy stresses the middle path as an overriding principle for appropriate conduct by the populace at all levels. This applies to the conduct of families and communities, as well as the nation in development and administration so as to modernize in line with the forces of globalization. Sufficiency means moderation, reasonableness, and the need for immunity through adequate protection from negative impacts arising from internal and external changes. To achieve this sort of sufficiency, an application of knowledge with due consideration and prudence is essential. In particular, great care is needed in the utilization of theories and methodologies in planning and implementation at every step. Meanwhile, sufficiency is also essential for strengthening the moral fiber of the nation so that everyone, particularly public officials, academics, and businesspeople at all levels, adheres first and foremost to the principle of honesty and integrity. In addition, a way of life based on patience, perseverance, diligence, wisdom, and prudence is indispensable in creating balance and developing the capacity to cope appropriately with critical challenges arising from extensive and rapid socioeconomic, environmental, and cultural changes in the world.[3]

Such views on poverty are reflected in two separate data sets. Since 1982, the Community Development Department of the Ministry of Interior has collected the basic minimum need (BMN) and the National Rural Development Committee Survey (NRD2C) data sets (see box 13.2). These two data sets form the foundation of the ministry's community information system at the village, subdistrict, district, and provincial levels. They have three advantages. First, they provide extensive information on a locality's demographic, physical, economic, and social conditions to local administrations for the design of programs and projects on housing, law and order, health, education, poverty, social protection, and culture. Second, the data are updated frequently: the BMN annually, and the NRD2C biannually. The indicators collected are adjusted every five years in line with the national development plans, thereby ensuring that the NESDB may draw on the BMN and the NRD2C as monitoring tools. For the Ninth National Economic and Social Development Plan, the NESDB and Community Development Department worked together to develop, in 2003, a list of poor target villages based on the NRD2C. These villages became the primary focus of poverty reduction efforts by the Ministry of Interior and the NESDB. Third, the data are collected through a bottom-up process involving local administrations from the village level up to the provincial level and covering every village in the country. This ensures the ownership of the information by local stakeholders.

The availability of alternative poverty measures begs the question: how do their rankings compare? Comparisons between the small area poverty maps and the BMN and NRD2C reveal stark differences in the levels and patterns of measured poverty. Figure 13.3 shows the classification of villages in rural areas according to the 2000

BOX 13.2   Data Collection for the BMN and NRD2C Data Sets

The BMN collects household information on life quality to assess the level of happiness in society. A village committee supervises the data collection through village volunteers who conduct household interviews using a structured questionnaire. The data are first processed by the local offices at the subdistrict, district, and provincial levels, then aggregated by the board of the Community Development Department at the national level, and finally approved by the Ministry of Interior's Life Quality Development Facilitation Board. During the Ninth National Economic and Social Development Plan period, the BMN consisted of 37 indicators covering health, housing, education, the economy, ways of life, and participation.

The NRD2C measures the living conditions of people in rural areas. A village-level data collection working group, consisting of the members of the village committee, the village head, and local government officials, fills out the relevant questionnaire by relying on up to 10 key informants. As in the BMN, the data are then sequentially aggregated and cross-checked at the various administrative levels. The latest NRD2C comprises 30 indicators covering infrastructure, employment, health, knowledge and education, community strength, and natural resources and the environment. Along each dimension, villages are classified into three groups (least developed, somewhat developed, and most developed). Villages identified as least developed in more than 10 dimensions are included in a list of poor villages.

poverty map on household income and the 1999 NRD2C list of target villages. If one restricts attention to villages identified in both the NRD2C and the poverty map, one counts 14,218 NRD2C target villages, equal to over one-fifth of all rural villages. To replicate the share of poor villages in the small area poverty map, we impose a cut-off in the poverty headcount of 30 percent so as to group villages into the poor and non-poor categories. Among the NRD2C target villages, no more than one-third are also classified as poor according to the poverty map. Among the NRD2C nontarget villages, almost one-quarter are labeled poor in the poverty map. Put differently, assuming that the classification of the small area poverty map reflects the true situation in Thailand, the NRD2C targeting exhibits a type 1 error (labeling a poor village as nonpoor) of 66 percent and a type 2 error (labeling a nonpoor village as poor) of 24 percent.

The sharp differences in village poverty assessments in the NRD2C and the small area poverty map naturally raise the issue: which of the two data sets is likely to be more accurate? One approach to investigating this issue is field validation. As part of the poverty mapping project, the Thailand Development Research Institute conducted two visits to selected villages on which the NRD2C and the small area poverty map evaluations diverged. Information was collected through interviews with local officials, entrepreneurs, and residents; observations on economic conditions, including in housing, commercial activity, geographical characteristics, and water; and reference to official documents such as tax records. The findings suggest that the poverty maps are more accurate than the NRD2C.

Two main factors have distorted the NRD2C classifications. First, the NRD2C ranking is affected by criteria not directly related to the economic well-being of a village. For example, one village was put on the NRD2C target list because of its weak agricultural endowments, but the village did not depend on agriculture for its well-being, and most villagers commuted to nearby urban communities for work. Second, some village committees appeared intentionally to underreport economic conditions

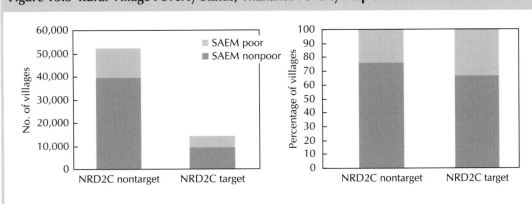

Figure 13.3 Rural Village Poverty Status, Thailand: Poverty Map of 2000 and NRD2C of 1999

Source: Jitsuchon 2004.

Figure 13.4 Comparison of Subdistrict Poverty Status in Thailand: 2002 BMN and 2002 Poverty Map

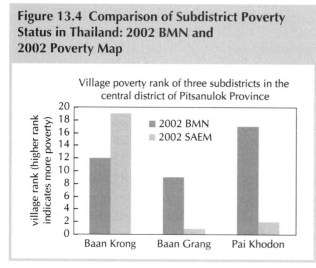

Village poverty rank of three subdistricts in the central district of Pitsanulok Province

■ 2002 BMN
■ 2002 SAEM

village rank (higher rank indicates more poverty)

Baan Krong   Baan Grang   Pai Khodon

Source: Jitsuchon 2004.

in their villages to qualify as target villages. These included villages with vast agricultural lands of good quality, abundant water supplies, and adequate housing conditions. They were typically situated closer to district centers and were more well represented in subdistrict councils.

Field validations of the BMN data set arrived at similar conclusions. Figure 13.4 compares the 2002 poverty rankings of three subdistricts relative to other subdistricts in the Central District of Pitsanulok Province. The BMN suggests that Baan Grang and Pai Khodon are relatively poor subdistricts, similar to Baan Krong, while the small area poverty map indicates that the first two are relatively well off and much less poor than Baan Krong. The field validation supported the poverty map ranking. Interviews with villagers and key informants and observations of village infrastructure and economic activity established that Baan Grang and Pai Khodon were clearly more prosperous than their neighboring subdistricts, including Baan Krong. The land of Baan Grang and Pai Khodon is more suitable for rice growing; land plots are larger; and water is more abundant. Farmers grow rice almost year round. The major economic problem was the shortage of farm workers. By contrast, Baan Krong was less well off because rice growing was possible at most only twice a year in some selected areas, and farming was less mechanized.

While the field trips confirmed that small area poverty maps are likely to be more accurate than the BMN and the NRD2C, the maps are equally prone to errors whenever core determinants of a village's livelihood are not captured in the model. For example, rubber tree growing has become an important source of income for villages in the South over the last decade because of a vast expansion in rubber tree plantations and the sharp rise in rubber prices on the world market. Yet, the 2000 poverty map was unable to incorporate information on rubber tree growing because this information was missing in the underlying data sets. Similarly, in some areas of the Northeast, older family members receive substantial remittances from younger family members who have migrated for work to Bangkok and other urban centers, but the poverty map did not reflect this income source adequately. The information on remittance income in the socioeconomic survey is inaccurate, and the asset variables included in the model failed to capture the wealth of these households sufficiently. This resulted in an overestimation of the poverty in such localities.[4]

The BMN and the NRD2C are clearly valuable tools for local policy making. At the same time, they have major shortcomings. First, the traditional focus of the BMN and the NRD2C is rural areas, although the BMN has also been covering urban areas since 2006. While poverty was, indeed, an almost exclusively rural phenomenon in the past, large-scale rural-to-urban migration, especially in and around Bangkok, has made urban poverty an important concern in today's Thailand. Second, an inconsistency is introduced if one monitors poverty at the national level through income or consumption measures relative to a monetary poverty line, while monitoring it at the local level through the BMN and NRD2C indicators. Third, there are concerns about the accuracy of the information in the BMN and the NRD2C because of uneven interpretations in the questionnaires. For example, household income is evaluated in a single question, and questions on ways of living involve subjective assessments. Furthermore, village committees have an incentive to underreport living standards to qualify for public funds. Field verifications have generally confirmed that the small area poverty map rankings are more reliable, although missing information on local economic activity also poses a problem in those rankings.

The political roadblock

The government has embraced the objective of eradicating mass poverty by the end of this decade. To reach this goal, the government adopted a number of grassroots policies in 2001, including the Village Fund, the People's Bank, asset capitalization, and the B 30 health care scheme. The extent of the government's poverty effort may be gauged by the volume of resources spent on all antipoverty programs. Total expenditure on all antipoverty programs was approximately B 35 billion in fiscal year 1998/99, which constituted 4.2 percent of total public expenditure and 0.74 percent of gross domestic product. It increased substantially, to 10.4 percent of public expenditure and 2.3 percent of gross domestic product, in fiscal year 2001/02. However, many of the programs have limited coverage or significant benefit leakage to the nonpoor because they cover large populations. Improved targeting through better criteria for the allocation of resources is essential if the number of the poor is to be reduced. For example, the Village Fund was launched in 2001 as a revolving fund of B 1 million (about US$23,000) that was to be distributed to about 70,000 villages nationwide over a three-year period. A key characteristic of the program is that it covers every single village in the country, regardless of whether the village is poor or nonpoor. In fact, the bulk of the beneficiaries of the program are nonpoor households. The poverty impact of the Village Fund would be increased if the same resources were allocated in a more targeted fashion toward poor villages or if loans were provided at more favorable terms to low-income households.

One way to illustrate the implications of the lack of targeting is to investigate the reduction in the poverty gap under an assumption of perfect targeting.[5] The poverty gap is the average shortfall in the consumption of the poor relative to the poverty line, multiplied by the poverty headcount ratio. Considering the rural population only, this gap equaled 3.1 percent in 2002. Assuming that the transfer is both perfectly targeted and fully consumed, the sum of all poverty gaps across rural individuals is the minimum amount of the income transfers needed to bring all the rural poor up to the poverty line. Under this scenario, an income transfer of B 25.2 (or B 0.031, times the rural poverty line of B 813) per person per month would be required to eliminate poverty. The total annual volume of income transfers for rural poverty eradication would then be B 13.1 billion (or B 25.2, times 12 months, times 43,300,000 persons). This is equivalent to no more than 1.3 percent of central government spending in fiscal year 2001/02, or just one-sixth of the estimated budget spent on the Village Fund. By contrast, maintaining perfect targeting within regions, but assuming that the transfer amount is allocated according to current public expenditure patterns, the Northeast would receive only 30 percent rather than over 60 percent (its share in national rural poverty), and poverty in the Northeast would fall by only half. If the sum were evenly spread across the rural population (as in the Village Fund), the Northeast would obtain 40 percent, and poverty in the Northeast, rather than being eliminated, would fall by less than two-thirds.

In addition to the Village Fund and other grassroots policies, another recent government poverty reduction initiative is the Poverty and Social Registration Program (POREP), which was launched and run nationwide in 2004 (see box 13.3). Through the program, all poor persons were invited to register at their district branch of the Ministry of Interior and fill out a form stating the major reasons for their poverty. After verification of the information provided, local governments were supposed to design tailored assistance for each registered person. A number of problems hampered this initiative, including the initiative's links to Thailand's established social welfare system, the time lag between registration and reduction measures, and the shortcomings in the implementation of the assistance programs. In addition, there were issues in terms of the initiative's reliability as a poverty database. An immediate concern is that such a program may involve substantial leakage to the nonpoor because of the overreporting of poverty problems. At the end of the registration period, about eight million persons had registered, which was about the same as the number of poor people living below the revised national poverty line in 2004. However, the POREP database refers to *individuals* rather

---

BOX 13.3   **The POREP Initiative**

The government launched POREP, a nationwide poverty registration program that lasted from January 5 to March 31, 2004. Under the scheme, more than eight million people throughout the country registered as poor persons at district branch offices of the Ministry of Interior and reported on their economic and social problems. The registration distinguished seven categories among the poor: landless people, the homeless, workers in illegal occupations, destitute schoolchildren, victims of fraud or other deception, indebted persons, and persons with housing problems. The district offices passed the roster of the poor on to the village committees for assessments of their validity. The assessments were conducted publicly and case by case in each community.

than *households*. Curiously, there are no statistics available on the number of households with members who are on POREP lists. Given that the average household size in Thailand is about five members, it is evident that the group of households with members who are registered as poor is much larger than the number of households considered as poor according to the household socioeconomic survey since individuals are counted in one, and households in the other. The 2004 household socioeconomic survey found

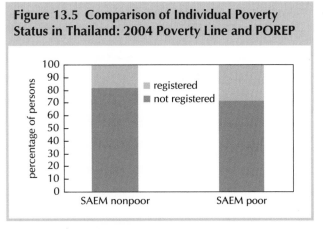

Figure 13.5 Comparison of Individual Poverty Status in Thailand: 2004 Poverty Line and POREP

Source: Jitsuchon 2004.

that only one in ten persons on POREP lists is poor according to the poverty line criteria (see figure 13.5). In addition to the leakage to nonpoor households, POREP also failed to cover most poor households. Almost three out of four people among the poor had not registered.

The inconsistency in the number of the POREP-registered poor and the number of the income-poor according to the national poverty line is also evident in comparisons across provinces. Figure 13.6 shows the provincial estimates of the poverty headcount ratio in the Northeast region, based on POREP registrations and the 2002 household socioeconomic survey. These two measures differ greatly at the provincial level. In particular, the POREP estimates tend to be too high in provinces with low poverty headcounts, such as Ubon Ratchathani. In general, the POREP estimates vary from one province to another much less than the survey data: the respective standard deviations are 3.3 and 11.2.

Beyond the problems of the inclusion of nonpoor persons and the exclusion of poor persons, it is too early to tell whether POREP has been successful in improving the living standards of those people whom the program has assisted. The government is still in the process of providing help to the registered poor. Most importantly, it is not known whether the families that have been supported have escaped poverty at least in the short term if not the long term. While direct and practical assistance is clearly useful, families are often poor because of a multitude of related factors. In many cases, there is no silver bullet for solving poverty, and one-off assistance will not lift households permanently out of poverty. This suggests that incorporating geographical targeting into the design of a range of antipoverty programs might greatly aid program effectiveness.

The Way Forward

The government has embraced the objective of eradicating mass poverty by the end of this decade. Geographical targeting may become a powerful tool in reaching this goal.

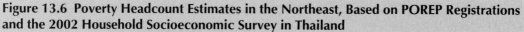

Figure 13.6 Poverty Headcount Estimates in the Northeast, Based on POREP Registrations and the 2002 Household Socioeconomic Survey in Thailand

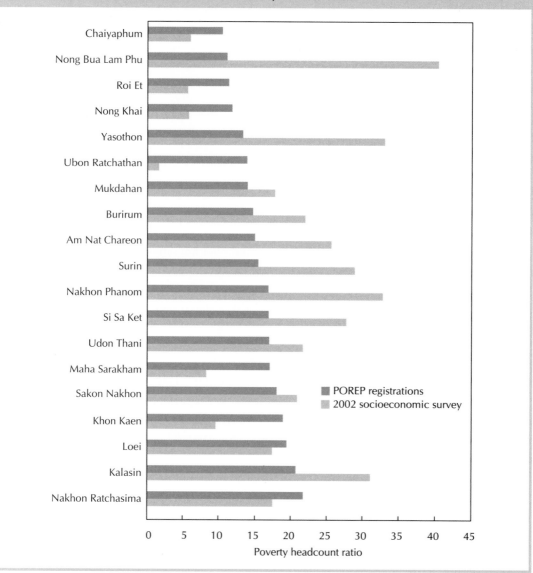

Source: World Bank and NESDB 2005.

The close overlap between poor areas and areas with large populations is an exceptional feature of poverty in Thailand and contrasts with the more common pattern in other countries where high poverty occurs in sparsely populated areas. The targeting of public resources on a small number of provinces, subdistricts, and villages would allow Thailand to achieve significant progress in meeting the goal of eradicating poverty. By adopting such a targeted approach, the government would be able to use its limited resources to help the neediest people. The design of efficient programs that are tailored to

Thailand's specific conditions presents a challenge that government agencies must confront. In too many projects and programs, the careful design of the general project structure and a meticulous evaluation of total costs and benefits are still followed by much less scrupulous attention to decisions about where—in which specific province, district, or village—to implement the project.

Political economy considerations influence the design, implementation, and outcome of social programs. Although the need for targeting on poor villages and poor households is clear enough, it also entails an important difficulty. By reducing the number of recipients, such targeting reduces the political support for using taxes to fund redistribution. Instead, the government's grassroots initiatives support rural areas, but they do not differentiate between poor and nonpoor villages. While this makes these programs politically more sustainable, it dilutes the effect on poverty.

Another roadblock to the application of targeting is linked to the prominent role of the Ministry of Interior in the government's poverty eradication programs. To implement these policies, the Ministry of Interior relies crucially on its own data collections, the BMN and the NRD2C. These data sets have important advantages: they have a track record of more than two decades, are well understood by civil servants around the country, rely on complete coverage instead of sampling techniques, are collected every two years, and integrate a broad range of economic, social, and cultural information at the household and community levels. However, the data are difficult to access, are considered unreliable because of inaccurate reporting by respondents, are a curious hybrid of objective and subjective indicators, and draw summary assessments based on arbitrary simple averaging across the underlying indicators.

Given these shortcomings, it is important to reconcile the evidence offered in poverty maps with the findings in the BMN and the NRD2C. The ambitious approach would be a statistical reconciliation of these data sources so as to derive a single poverty map. The less ambitious approach would be to use the poverty maps as a verification tool for the BMN and the NRD2C. For example, areas identified as nonpoor in the BMN and the NRD2C, but as poor in the poverty maps might also qualify for government assistance.

Such reconciliation will be possible only when poverty maps have become a recognized alternative to the BMN and the NRD2C. This will require a number of technical and institutional advances: (1) a routine procedure must be agreed upon to update poverty maps at least biannually; (2) the technology for updating poverty maps must become financially affordable; (3) the government agency charged with updating and distributing the poverty map must acquire the expertise to do so; (4) there must be full cooperation among producers of all alternative poverty maps and databases and among current and potential users; and (5) the accuracy of the poverty maps must be enhanced through steady improvements in estimation by the producers and through regular feedback from users.

To fulfill these requirements, the followings steps would need to be taken. First, the NSO executive board should endorse the routine updating of small area poverty maps as new household socioeconomic survey data become available. Such a commitment will require assurances about the financial sustainability of the poverty mapping project, which will entail finding cost-effective alternatives to the SAS software and a wider acceptance of poverty maps among potential users. It will also require advances in the methodology because updating small area maps on the basis of an old census and a new survey is still in the experimental stage. (Much of the initial work on this extension to the methodology has been done in Thailand.)

Second, while the NSO staff has made great strides in building its capacity to generate poverty maps, the NSO has not systematically developed the area identifications that allow easy merging across data sets and time periods. Third, government agencies should collaborate in the application of poverty maps. This would involve greater cooperation between the NSO (the main producer of data and the generator of the poverty maps), the NESDB (the government's planning agency, which has an important role in formulating and evaluating poverty reduction policies), the Ministry of Interior (the producer of the BMN and NRD2C data sets and the main employer of the relevant local administrative staff), and line ministries such as the Ministry of Health, the Ministry of Labor, the Ministry of Education, and the Ministry of Social Development and Human Security.

Three and a half years of experience with small area poverty maps in Thailand suggest the following process lessons:

- Creating ownership goes hand in hand with capacity building. Creating ownership enhances the likelihood that small area poverty maps will be put to use in policy contexts. Yet, ownership hinges on making sure that institutional learning occurs. This requires building up sufficient statistical, technical, human, and financial capacity within local institutions to generate the maps. While this approach increases the transaction costs and prolongs the process, it ultimately pays off in terms of mutual learning and policy impact.
- Developing a common understanding among government partners on objectives and a common framework right from the outset is essential in maintaining focus and having an impact in the longer run. Ultimately, the policy impact of better monitoring and evaluation through small area poverty maps depends on the commitment of policy makers to the poverty reduction agenda.

Notes

1. Reductions in poverty continued up to 2004, but a change in the definition of the poverty line has rendered the new 2004 numbers incompatible with the previous numbers. Based on the new poverty line, the poverty headcount fell from 21 percent in 2000 to 11 percent in 2004, and the number of the poor declined from 9.5 million to 7.1 million over the same period (World Bank 2005).
2. The provincial poverty maps shown in figure 13.1 draw exclusively on the household socioeconomic survey, without any reference to population census data. This approach is justified because the socioeconomic survey is representative at the provincial level. However, even at the provincial level, the small area estimation methodology leads to greater precision in the poverty estimates.

3. This is an unofficial translation of a working definition of sufficiency compiled from remarks made on various occasions by King Bhumibol Adulyadej, approved by him and transmitted through his principal private secretary to the NESDB on November 29, 1999. See NESDB (2004).

4. Because of a recent revision in the household socioeconomic survey questionnaire (Jitsuchon, Chandoevwit, and Kakwani 2006), future surveys will provide more details on remittance income and wealth, such as the value of houses, land, and financial assets. It is also important to remember that the econometric approach of the small area poverty maps in deriving poverty estimates provides some protection against omitted variable bias to the extent that the other explanatory variables capture the impact of the missing indicator.

5. Perfect targeting implies that all individuals living below the poverty line and only such individuals will receive transfers equal to the shortfall of the consumption of these individuals below the poverty line. If one assumes that these income transfers are entirely consumed in all cases, then one may conclude that, after the transfers, all previously poor individuals will have a consumption level equal to the poverty line and that no individual who had been living above the poverty line would have received any transfer. The numbers that follow in the text are hypothetical; few developing countries would choose to continue making income transfers to the poor in perpetuity. Perfect targeting is impossible in practice: besides the lack of complete information that would be needed to implement perfect targeting, not all transfer income is consumed, and transfers to the poor based on a shortfall in consumption (or income) relative to a poverty line have significant disincentive effects.

References

Alderman, Harold, Miriam Babita, Gabriel M. Demombynes, Nthabiseng Makhatha, and Berk Özler. 2001. "How Low Can You Go?: Combining Census and Survey Data for Mapping Poverty in South Africa." *Journal of African Economies* 11 (2): 169–200.

CDD (Community Development Department). 2003. "Guidelines for Using Community Information Systems." Report, Community Development Department, Ministry of Interior, Bangkok.

———. 2005. "Thai Rural Villages from 2005 NRD2C Data." Report, Community Development Department, Ministry of Interior, Bangkok.

———. 2006. "Community Information Systems Guidelines." Report, Community Development Department, Ministry of Interior, Bangkok.

CDD (Community Development Department) and NESDB (National Economic and Social Development Board). 2003. *Targeting Poverty in Villages during the Ninth Plan (2002–2006)*. Bangkok: Community Development Department, Ministry of Interior, and Office of the National Economic and Social Development Board.

Demombynes, Gabriel M., and Berk Özler. 2002. "Crime and Local Inequality in South Africa." Policy Research Working Paper 2925, World Bank, Washington, DC.

Demombynes, Gabriel M., Chris Elbers, Jean O. Lanjouw, Peter F. Lanjouw, Johan A. Mistiaen, and Berk Özler. 2002. "Producing a Better Geographic Profile of Poverty: Methodology and Evidence from Three Developing Countries." WIDER Discussion Paper 2002–39, United Nations University–World Institute for Development Economics Research, Helsinki.

Elbers, Chris, Jean O. Lanjouw, and Peter F. Lanjouw. 2000. "Welfare in Villages and Towns." Tinbergen Institute Discussion Paper TI2000-029/2, Tinbergen Institute, Amsterdam.

———. 2003. "Micro-Level Estimation of Poverty and Inequality." *Econometrica* 71 (1): 355–64.

Ferriera, Francisco H. G., Peter F. Lanjouw, and Marcelo Neri. 2000. "A New Poverty Profile for Brazil Using PPV, PNAD, and Census Data." Textos para Discussão 418, Department of Economics, Pontifícia Universidade Católica, Rio de Janeiro.

Hentschel, Jesko, Jean O. Lanjow, Peter F. Lanjouw, and Javier Poggi. 1998. "Combining Census and Survey Data to Study Spatial Dimensions of Poverty." Policy Research Working Paper 1928, World Bank, Washington, DC.

Jitsuchon, Somchai. 2004. "Small Area Estimation Poverty Map for Thailand." Paper presented at the SMERU Research Institute and Ford Foundation International Seminar, "Mapping Poverty in Southeast Asia," Jakarta, December 1–2.

Jitsuchon, Somchai, Worawan Chandoevwit, and Nanak Kakwani. 2006. "A Redesign of Thailand's Household Survey." Unpublished research paper, March, United Nations Development Programme, New York, and World Bank Institute, Washington, DC.

NESDB (National Economic and Social Development Board). 1992. *Information System for Rural Development in Thailand.* 2nd ed. Bangkok: Office of the National Economic and Social Development Board.

———. 2004. *Thailand Millennium Development Goals Report 2004.* Bangkok: Office of the National Economic and Social Development Board and United Nations Country Team in Thailand.

Supachalasai, Supat. 2001. "Constructing a Targeting Map for Budget Allocation and Evaluation in Thailand." Research paper, Office of the National Economic and Social Development Board, Bangkok.

World Bank. 2005. "Thailand Economic Monitor." Report, November, World Bank Thailand Office, Bangkok.

World Bank and NESDB (National Economic and Social Development Board). 2005. *Thailand Northeast Economic Development Report.* Bangkok: World Bank Thailand Office and Office of the National Economic and Social Development Board.

14

Poverty Mapping in Vietnam

ROB SWINKELS AND CARRIE TURK

ACRONYMS AND ABBREVIATIONS

CEM	Committee for Ethnic Minorities
D	Dong, the Vietnamese currency
GSO	General Statistics Office
ICARD	Information Center for Agricultural and Rural Development
ILSSA	Institute of Labor Science and Social Affairs
Molisa	Ministry of Labor, War Invalids, and Social Affairs
NEU	National Economics University
VHLSS	Vietnam Household Living Standards Survey
VLSS	Vietnam Living Standards Survey

Background

Over the past decade, Vietnam has witnessed a rapid reduction in poverty. Data from the Vietnam Living Standards Survey (VLSS) and the Vietnam Household Living Standards Survey (VHLSS), conducted by the General Statistics Office (GSO) in 1993, 1998, 2002, and 2004, show that the poverty rate fell by almost two-thirds, from 58 percent in 1993 to 20 percent in 2004. This was largely due to the sound propoor policies adopted by the government. But these successes have been achieved without a mechanism for targeting assistance to the poor that would meet international standards.

Tara Bedi, Aline Coudouel, Peter Lanjouw, and Roy van der Weide have supplied substantial and helpful comments on this chapter.

A continuation of such rapid poverty reduction is likely to require better targeting of transfers to poor areas and poor people. While a number of targeted programs are in place, there is increased recognition in Vietnam that the targeting procedures used in these programs need to be strengthened. Weak targeting mechanisms mattered less in the past, when poverty levels were high and even flawed targeting processes were likely to capture large numbers of poor people. As poverty rates decline, however, targeting becomes more challenging. The government is therefore enthusiastic about exploring more sophisticated techniques to improve the impact of targeted expenditures. In recent years, efforts have been undertaken to test one such promising tool: the small area estimation methodology and the production of highly disaggregated poverty maps. This chapter aims to document the experiences in Vietnam with poverty mapping based on this methodology and assess the impact of the resulting poverty maps on policy making and targeting.

Various government agencies and other stakeholder agencies have shown interest in poverty mapping using the small area estimation methodology. This is so for two broad reasons. First, they have desired to see whether local poverty estimates produced by the Ministry of Labor, War Invalids, and Social Affairs (Molisa) might be verified through alternative and, possibly, more reliable methods. Second, they have wished to determine whether such local poverty estimates might then be used to improve targeting.

The VLSS and VHLSS have enabled reliable estimates of trends in poverty at the national and regional levels, as well as trends in social outcomes among various groups in society. Still, the size of the samples in the 1993 and 1998 VLSS were insufficient to generate poverty estimates for each of Vietnam's 64 provinces. This changed when the number of enumeration areas and the sample size were expanded for the 2002 and 2004 surveys, making it possible to estimate poverty rates in the provinces, albeit with large standard errors ranging from 1.5 percent to 5.5 percent. However, no mechanism existed for producing reliable and comparable poverty estimates for each of the 625 or so districts and each of the 10,000 or so rural communes and urban wards.

While VHLSS data have played an important role by serving as a source of information in the poverty policy debate, official government poverty estimates have not (until very recently) been based on the VHLSS. Instead, poverty estimates were based on nation-wide annual counting exercises, whereby the number of poor people was counted by Molisa officials in each commune and ward across the country, and lists with the names of the poor were drawn up. A household was declared poor if its income was less than a low rice-based poverty line, and incomes were supposed to be measured using a detailed household questionnaire.

In reality, however, the number of people who were declared poor depended signif-icantly on the poverty reduction targets for that particular year. These targets were set in advance for each administrative unit (usually a standard 2 percent reduction per year). The number of poor people actually listed also depended on the resources that were available for assisting the poor under national targeted programs. The official poverty line that was applied tended to differ across provinces because the provinces were given the freedom to set higher poverty lines if they had the resources available to address poverty among larger numbers of people.

Lists were updated annually, and local community meetings were frequently held to decide who would be declared poor and who had moved out of poverty. These meetings often made household income measurements unnecessary. The commune and ward poverty rates that emerged from this exercise were aggregated at the district level, then at the provincial level, and, finally, at the national level.

Because these poverty counts were not based on one standard methodology applied throughout the country using an independent measurement tool, such as the VHLSS, but were subjectively defined through a political process driven by targets set by higher authorities, the poverty rates were not comparable across administrative units. As a consequence, the data on local and national poverty rates used in official government reports were not reliable, a finding which has been confirmed by recent research (see Nguyen and Rama 2006).

Not only did the local poverty rates distort intercommune differences, but they were also generally too low. The poverty line that was applied reflected only the minimum amount of rice necessary for survival. It did not reflect other food and nonfood consumption needs. In 2002, the value of the official poverty line used in the Molisa methodology was roughly D 90,000 per person per day, which is US$0.19, or US$0.92 valued at a purchasing power parity of 4.9. This is insufficient to meet minimum basic needs in Vietnam. The VHLSS 2002 used a poverty line of D 159,788, which is approximately 1.8 times higher.

The difference in official and VHLSS-based poverty rates may be easily demonstrated by provincial poverty maps derived according to the Molisa or the GSO methodology. Figure 14.1 illustrates how the Molisa data result in lower levels of poverty and a more compressed range of poverty rates across the country.

The lack of reliable poverty rates at the provincial and subprovincial levels that are compatible with the VHLSS estimates stimulated an interest in alternative approaches for estimating poverty rates at these levels.

During the 1990s, the government was placing greater emphasis on two national targeted antipoverty programs through which it was channeling increasing resources. These were the Hunger Eradication and Poverty Reduction Program and a program targeting poor communes that has come to be known as Program 135 after the number of the decision that established it. The former, coordinated by Molisa, was designed to deliver benefits such as subsidized credit, school fee exemptions, and free health care to individuals who live in households defined as poor through the Molisa-led process described above. Program 135 is coordinated by the Committee for Ethnic Minorities (CEM) and makes grants to communes in exceptionally difficult circumstances. The grants are provided mainly for investment in small-scale infrastructure. Communes are identified using a number of criteria, including local geography, the concentration of poor households, the presence of ethnic minorities, and deficiencies in infrastructure.

Figure 14.1 Provincial Poverty Incidence by Molisa and the GSO, Vietnam 2002 and 2003

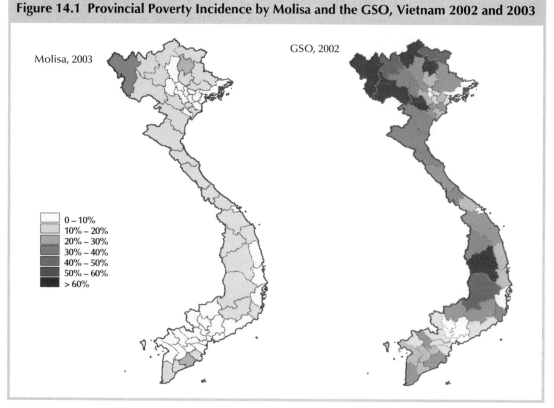

Sources: Administrative data from Molisa; GSO estimates.
Note: The GSO estimates rely on the VHLSS; the GSO data (right) have standard errors ranging between 1.5 and 5.5 percent.

This chapter will next discuss the preparations and the process for the production of small area estimation poverty maps. Thereafter, it offers an overview of the main technical aspects, the key findings, the impact of the maps, missed opportunities, and the sustainability of the process. The chapter concludes with a summary of the lessons learned.

Arrangements and Process

During 1997, the International Food Policy Research Institute developed a poverty map of rural districts in Vietnam using techniques related to the small area estimation methodology. This map relied on the 1993 VLSS to estimate the likelihood of poverty among rural households as a function of a series of household and farm characteristics and then calculated district averages for these characteristics from the 1994 agricultural census to predict district poverty rates (see Minot 2000). In 1999, a census was completed by the GSO. The World Bank and the International Food Policy Research Institute made use of a 3 percent sample from this census, together with the 1998 VLSS, to develop a provincial poverty map using the small area estimation methodology (see Minot and

Baulch 2002, 2004). This generated the first reliable set of provincial poverty estimates for Vietnam and demonstrated that the small area estimation methodology might be made to work using the available data sets and that the generation of more disaggregated poverty estimates and maps was possible if a larger portion of the census became accessible.

Institutional arrangements

In 2002, the International Food Policy Research Institute and the Institute of Development Studies, in partnership with the Information Center for Agricultural and Rural Development (ICARD), submitted a proposal to the World Bank on a collaborative effort to generate disaggregated poverty estimates. This would include district and, possibly, commune poverty estimates and district poverty gap and inequality estimates and maps. The proposal would require a 33 percent sample of the 1999 census. Eventually, funding was arranged through the New Zealand Agency for International Development. At the suggestion of ICARD, the proposal included a large capacity-building component for Vietnamese researchers and government officials. It required that the participating international researchers, instead of doing most of the work themselves, as they had done during the earlier provincial mapping exercise, would take a step back this time and play the role of mentor.

A poverty mapping steering committee was established, led by the director of ICARD. The committee included representatives from the key agencies that are involved in anti-poverty programs, such as Molisa, the Ministry of Finance, and the Ministry of Planning and Investment, in addition to the GSO. Each agency was asked to send three English-speaking representatives to form the 12-member Interministerial Poverty Mapping Task Force. The members were to be trained in poverty mapping techniques. The GSO was asked to send one local staff member experienced in quantitative analysis to act as a cotrainer during some of the training sessions, together with two local economists: one from the National Economics University (NEU) and one from the Institute of Economics. One local geographic information systems specialist from Hanoi Agricultural University was also recruited for the training program.

Training and capacity building

Over the first six months of the project, three one-week training sessions were organized by ICARD and the international experts: one on statistical analysis using the Stata software package, one on geographic information systems using ArcView, and one on poverty mapping. Between these training sessions, subgroups of participants were given assignments to practice what they had learned. Supervision over these assignments was provided by the international experts over the Internet and by the World Bank in Hanoi. Following the final training session, a somewhat smaller group was formed consisting of the analysts who had performed well during the final training. This smaller group worked together to generate the remaining detailed estimates and to produce the maps and a report. The result of this capacity-building approach was a capable local expert on the small area estimation methodology and a wider group of people who understood and, with some help, would be able to produce poverty maps.

Attempts to update the original analysis

In the course of 2003, data from a new household living standards survey, the 2002 VHLSS, became available. This made it possible to reestimate the coefficients representing the relationship between household characteristics and consumption expenditure. These coefficients might then be used to revise the household expenditures estimated on the basis of the household characteristics covered in the 1999 census. The Institute of Labor Science and Social Affairs (ILSSA), which is affiliated with Molisa, submitted a proposal to the World Bank to investigate the possibility of updating the maps using reestimated coefficients. The World Bank provided support, mainly through a local poverty mapping specialist from the NEU who guided the ILSSA team through the various analytical steps (see Nguyen et al. 2004a).

Later in 2004, the ILSSA requested help from the World Bank in a renewed effort to test a method for updating the poverty map. This was to be done by using a minicensus in pilot communes to update the household characteristics covered in the 1999 census and on which the poverty mapping estimates were based. This involved testing a bottom-up approach, whereby data would be collected on household characteristics locally to update poverty rates using poverty mapping techniques. The ILSSA also proposed exploring whether the census variables might be applied as proxy indicators to identify poor households. If the test proved successful, then the cumbersome and unreliable Molisa poor household income census would be replaced by a much simpler minicensus to collect data on only 10–15 household characteristics.

In the field, a simple questionnaire on asset ownership was used to identify all rich and all very poor households. These two extreme sorts of households were eliminated from the sample. The remaining households were subjected to a more detailed questionnaire covering household characteristics that was used to estimate household expenditures. To verify these estimates, data were also collected on household expenditures and incomes using simplified versions of the VHLSS questionnaire. Nine communes were included in the field test. Separate tests were run using the 2004 VHLSS to estimate regional and provincial poverty rates directly through expenditures and through estimated expenditures using household characteristics. The results of this work were presented at a World Bank conference in Cambodia on the uses and impact of poverty maps in February 2006 (see Nguyen et al. 2006).

Overlaying the poverty map with other information

The team that originally produced the national poverty map also produced various overlays for this map, including information on market access. Subsequently, the ILSSA team and the NEU economist overlaid the poverty map with information on the 2,500 or so communes where Program 135 funds had been distributed. The results of this exercise were presented to Program 135 officials (at CEM) by the local research team during a workshop. The CEM officials subsequently requested training in poverty mapping techniques for 10 CEM staff. A three-week training session was provided by the local poverty mapping specialist from the NEU and was completed in the summer of 2004.

Producing an updated provincial map

When the provincial authorities of Ho Chi Minh City decided to conduct a midterm population census in 2004, the provincial statistics office approached the World Bank for help with data tabulations and analysis. The idea of using this census, in combination with the 2002 VHLSS, to develop a provincial poverty map quickly emerged. The relevant information for poverty mapping was collected for 10 percent of the sample. It was hoped that the map would be completed in time to feed into the next Ho Chi Minh City five-year plan (2006–10). A collaborative effort was undertaken that included the Institute of Economic Research of Ho Chi Minh City and the provincial statistics office, with technical leadership and training provided by the poverty mapping specialist from the NEU.

Technical Aspects

Accounting for regional differences

Seventeen household characteristics that appear in both the 1998 VLSS and the 1999 census were adopted for use in the poverty mapping analysis. Separate regression models were estimated for urban and rural Vietnam. Earlier attempts to derive separate estimates for seven rural strata and two urban strata had produced unconvincing results, and this approach was dropped. The team considered that this use of only two consumption models, one rural and one urban, for the whole country was somewhat unsatisfactory; it seems unlikely that returns to each of the rural (or urban) household characteristics would be the same across the entire country. As an alternative, the regression models included dummy variables for each of the regions to account for regional differences. As a result, the estimated poverty rates for neighboring districts or communes with similar characteristics, but on opposing sides of a regional boundary, sometimes showed unrealistically large differences. This is especially so on the border between the poor Central Highlands and the rich Southeast.

Large confidence intervals for small communes

The national poverty estimates derived through the poverty mapping exercise using a 33 percent sample of the census were very close to those using a 3 percent sample of the census, as well as to those estimates derived directly from the 1998 VLSS. The 95 percent confidence intervals of the provincial poverty estimates using 33 percent of the sample averaged ±5.2 percent. This figure was only slightly higher for the district estimates, at ±5.8 percent, but significantly higher for the commune estimates, at ±8.1 percent. Half the commune estimates showed a confidence interval between ±6.6 percent and ±10 percent. One-quarter of the communes (mostly the smaller ones) showed confidence intervals greater than ±10 percent. Clearly, the commune estimates should be treated with caution and should not be used as the sole criterion in targeting resources.

Intracluster correlation

One of the weaknesses of the poverty mapping methodology applied in Vietnam is the failure to account for the possibility of intracluster correlation in the disturbance terms from the first-stage regression model estimated using the VLSS data. Failure to accommodate for this possibility may mean that standard errors are underestimated. Elbers, Lanjouw, and Lanjouw (2003) recommend that specific steps be taken to minimize the influence of location effects by incorporating into the underlying consumption model variables that are explicitly intended to control for such effects. For example, they recommend that a set of means calculated on the basis of the unit record census data at the level of the primary sampling unit be inserted into the estimation model. The international experts who led the Vietnam poverty mapping exercise adopted this method at a later stage and found that it did not have an important impact on the estimates.

Access to census data

Raw data from the 1999 Population and Housing Census are not available to the public. However, samples of the data may be purchased from the GSO following submission and acceptance of a formal request spelling out in detail the variables needed and the purpose for which the data will be used. To keep costs down at first, only a 3 percent systematic sample was bought from the GSO, which was deemed sufficient for generating estimates at the provincial level. When the data appeared suitable for the application of the small area estimation methodology, the interest in producing more disaggregated poverty maps grew. This meant a much larger sample of the census data was needed. The poverty mapping proposal submitted to the World Bank by the International Food Policy Research Institute, the Institute of Development Studies, and ICARD to produce higher-resolution poverty maps therefore included a budget item for purchasing a 33 percent systematic sample from the GSO. This was the largest proportion of the population census the GSO was willing to make available. This is unlikely to change in the near future.

Outdated census data

An important weakness of the national high-resolution poverty maps relates to the fact that the census and survey data on which they have been based were collected in 1999 and were thus four years old at the time the mapping results were made available and distributed in 2003. In a country where poverty has been declining at an average of 3.5 percentage points per year, such poverty data may no longer be regarded as relevant (see below). In addition, because Vietnam is witnessing rapid migration, in particular from rural to urban areas, population data from the census are also likely to become out of date quickly. The 2004 midterm population census in Ho Chi Minh City showed that immigration there had been much more significant than originally thought and that administrative records on this phenomenon were incomplete.

Incomplete survey coverage of mobile urban population groups

The poverty maps estimated for Ho Chi Minh City in 2005 were based on the 2004 provincial census and the 2002 VHLSS. The estimation models were based on the 2002 VHLSS data from the urban sample in the Southeast (the region in which Ho Chi Minh City is located). Given the uniqueness of Ho Chi Minh City, it would have been better to use only the data from urban Ho Chi Minh City, rather than data from the whole region, to estimate the regression coefficients. But the urban data provided unsatisfactory results. One of the key problems is the failure of the VHLSS survey to capture urban poverty sufficiently accurately. Although the survey sample is based on household lists from the census and is, in principle, updated using local administrative records, this approach might be problematic in reality given that these records are incomplete and seem to miss large parts of population groups that are more mobile. This is corroborated by the 2004 Ho Chi Minh City population census. Given that these mobile groups are likely to constitute a large fraction of the urban poor, omitting them from the living standards survey sample would have led to biased estimates of the regression coefficients and thus, ultimately, of the small area poverty estimates on this city. Unless the VHLSS is able to cover urban poverty adequately, producing reliable poverty maps for urban areas will be difficult.

Conflicting methods for measuring poverty

Official poverty rates in Vietnam are not based on the VHLSS, which is used, in combination with the population census, to produce the poverty maps (see elsewhere above). Given the unofficial nature of the VHLSS poverty estimates, the poverty maps have suffered from a similar unofficial status. However, Molisa has come under increasing criticism from various parts of the government for its approach to poverty measurement, and the VHLSS approach is finding gradual acceptance as a more reliable method among planners and policy makers at the national level. This represents an opportunity to seek more official recognition for subnational small area poverty estimates and maps.

Explaining the methods to nonspecialists

Lastly, the poverty mapping techniques follow rather complex procedures that are difficult to explain to policy makers. The estimation techniques tend to be regarded as a black box, and this has led to doubts about the validity of the estimates.

The Findings of the Poverty Mapping Exercise

Dissemination

The small area poverty estimates on districts and communes using the 33 percent sample of the 1999 Population and Housing Census and the 1998 VLSS became available in mid-2003. They were presented to the poverty mapping steering committee by members of the Interministerial Poverty Mapping Task Force at a workshop held at the Ministry of Agriculture and Rural Development. Later that year, the results were presented at a larger forum to which all members of the Poverty Task Force were invited. At that time, the Poverty Task Force constituted the main mechanism for interaction among the government, donors, and nongovernmental organizations on poverty policy work.

Reports in Vietnamese and English that described the methodology and the main findings were distributed at these events (see Minot, Baulch, and Epprecht 2003). Various large, colorful, poster-sized poverty maps were also distributed. Compact discs were produced that included all the poverty, poverty gap, and inequality estimates and other data on communes, districts, and provinces. The discs allowed users to make their own maps for areas of the country that were of particular interest to them.

Since the workshop, the maps, reports, and compact discs have been reissued many times and circulated widely. Several of the maps have been reproduced in other documents, including publications of the World Bank, other donors, and NGOs. They have also been reproduced in a national newspaper and shown on television. The maps were presented to a large number of researchers and officials in various places throughout the country as part of an exercise to disseminate the 2003 World Bank poverty assessment. Currently, the maps are available on the Web site of the Institute of Policy and Strategy for Agriculture and Rural Development as part of an online socioeconomic atlas of Vietnam (see http://agro.gov.vn/news/default.asp).

Key findings

The poverty maps provide estimates of poverty headcounts for provinces, districts, and communes. Large color maps have been reproduced using these estimates. The maps provide a striking visual account of the depth of poverty in the mountains to the north, the upland areas along the coast, and the Central Highlands. They show much lower levels of poverty in the Southeast (where Ho Chi Minh City is located), other lowland areas, the Mekong River Delta, and the Red River Delta. These findings may not be surprising to those already familiar with the VHLSS data. Nonetheless, there appears to be a strong correlation between poverty and geography rather than between poverty and administrative boundaries, a link that is not evident from a list of provincial poverty headcounts. The maps also provided a visual account of inequality in Vietnam for the first time, a topic of much concern to policy makers. The maps showed differences in poverty levels that were much starker than the differences indicated by the data that had been circulated previously. The district and commune poverty maps strongly support the argument that assistance should be targeted on less densely populated, largely forested, ethnic minority areas (for example, see figure 14.2). The poverty team at the World Bank routinely uses these maps, alongside a map of ethnicity from the population census, to show the correlation between ethnicity and poverty.

A second map was produced showing the density of poverty in Vietnam (see figure 14.3). This map indicates that the density of poverty is highest where the population density is highest, that is, in the two delta areas of Vietnam and along the coastal lowland areas. This map is almost an inverse of the map showing the incidence of poverty in that the poverty headcounts are highest in more sparsely populated areas. Some actors consulted as part of this review of the impact of poverty maps recalled the map on poverty density more clearly than the map on poverty incidence. When used on its own, this map supports an entirely different argument for resource allocation. When an objective is set to reach the maximum number of people living under the poverty line, the density map used alone suggests a pattern of resource allocation that would be targeted at the more accessible and more rapidly growing parts of the country. A third map, depicting the poverty gap across Vietnam, demonstrates that

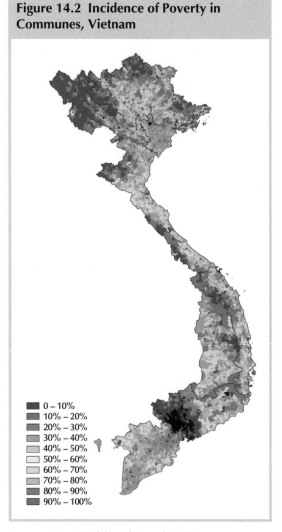

Figure 14.2 Incidence of Poverty in Communes, Vietnam

Legend:
- 0 – 10%
- 10% – 20%
- 20% – 30%
- 30% – 40%
- 40% – 50%
- 50% – 60%
- 60% – 70%
- 70% – 80%
- 80% – 90%
- 90% – 100%

Sources: Minot, Baulch, and Epprecht 2003.

poverty is not deep in the areas of greatest poverty density (see figure 14.3).

The poverty team in the World Bank uses these three maps together to demonstrate the message that, though large numbers of poor people reside in the deltas, their poverty is not extreme and is likely to be substantially reduced through continued rapid economic growth. By contrast, the areas with high poverty headcounts are experiencing much deeper poverty that is unlikely to be addressed in the medium term by continued growth alone. This message is reinforced by a map developed by World Bank staff in Vietnam from the same data set that shows the cumulative poverty gap, which multiplies the number of poor people in a district by the average poverty gap of that district (see figure 14.4). The poverty density maps are in the public domain and may be (and are) used individually to support alternative arguments for targeting.

Figure 14.3 Density of Poverty and Poverty Gap by District, Vietnam

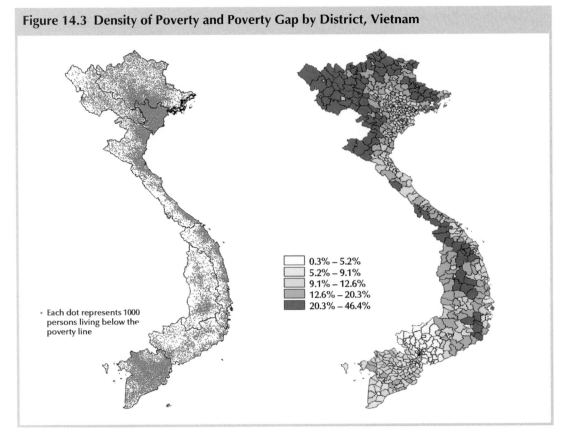

Sources: Minot, Baulch, and Epprecht 2003.

A further finding arises from the comparison of maps depicting the poverty headcounts in the provinces, districts, and communes (see figure 14.5). This shows the considerable heterogeneity within provinces in many parts of the country. Many rich provinces have several poor districts, while the reverse is true for several poor provinces. By extension, many richer districts include a large number of poor communes. A significant share of the budget is allocated by provincial governments, often using little more than population figures as a basis for determining the distribution across districts. We use these maps to show that more sophisticated criteria might be appropriate as a basis for allocating resources designed to tackle poverty.

Reactions to the initial findings

Reactions to the poverty maps were mixed across government authorities. Many researchers and officials found it helpful to have a visual account of inequality, an issue of great concern to the central government. Because the levels of poverty illustrated by the poverty

Figure 14.4 Cumulative Distance below the Poverty Line by Province and District, Vietnam

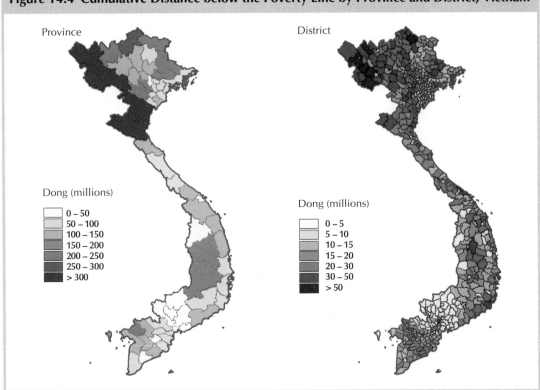

Province

District

Dong (millions)

	0 – 50
	50 – 100
	100 – 150
	150 – 200
	200 – 250
	250 – 300
	> 300

Dong (millions)

	0 – 5
	5 – 10
	10 – 15
	15 – 20
	20 – 30
	30 – 50
	> 50

Sources: World Bank estimates.

maps closely agreed with the fieldwork of researchers, many agencies found the maps quite credible and convincing. The least positive feedback came from Molisa, where misgivings about the maps arose from the following factors. First, the data used for the poverty maps came from sources that were different from the official poverty data. The official data were not, at that time, derived from the VHLSS, but through an entirely different process involving local counts of poor people (see elsewhere above). Despite misgivings about this traditional poverty measurement method in some parts of the government, most officials were reluctant to accept any method that deviated radically from official measures. The rather technical nature of the small area calculations also did not help win over the acceptance of government officials.

The two maps in figure 14.6 show the extent of the differences between the official poverty rates and the rates based on the small area estimation methodology. Both maps show estimates of poverty for 1999. The first picture comes from official Molisa sources. The second shows the poverty mapping estimates using the 1999 census and the 1998 VLSS. The levels of poverty indicated through the mapping exercise are much higher

Figure 14.5 Poverty Incidence by Province, District, and Commune, Vietnam

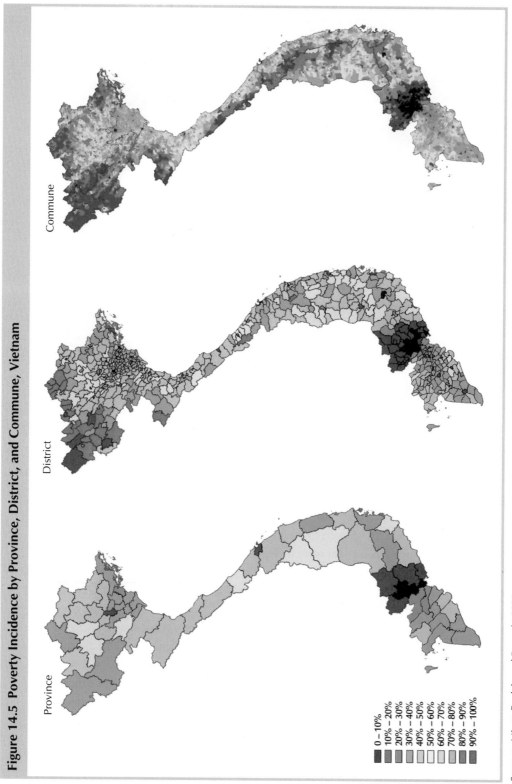

Province

District

Commune

0 – 10%
10% – 20%
20% – 30%
30% – 40%
40% – 50%
50% – 60%
60% – 70%
70% – 80%
80% – 90%
90% – 100%

Sources: Minot, Baulch, and Epprecht 2003.

Figure 14.6 Poverty by Province, as Estimated by Molisa and GSO, Vietnam 1999

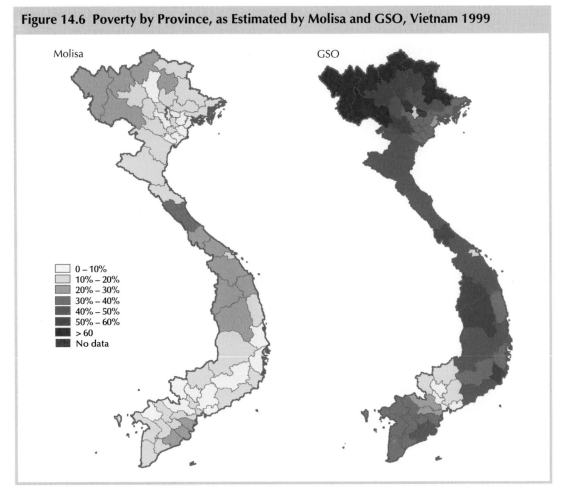

Molisa

GSO

0 – 10%
10% – 20%
20% – 30%
30% – 40%
40% – 50%
50% – 60%
> 60
No data

Sources: Molisa 2000; Minot, Baulch, and Epprecht 2003.

than the poverty found in the official data. The maps also show much higher levels of absolute inequality. This is perhaps the single strongest message that many people took away from the maps, probably because it matched their intuition and experience.

The differences in the sources for these poverty data are compounded by a second factor: timing. Because the official data are updated annually, Molisa already had 2002 estimates available as a basis for comparison with the 1999 poverty maps when the maps were released. Given the variations in data sources and timing, Molisa and a large part of the government were disinclined to adopt the messages emerging from the small area estimation poverty maps and rarely used the maps to guide their targeting decisions. Many government officials, however, found the findings interesting and wanted to know more.

One such agency is CEM, which requested training in poverty mapping techniques. It is now expressing interest in using any updates of the poverty maps as aids in targeting resources under its support efforts for poor communities. The GSO has included in the next agricultural census the variables used for the poverty mapping so that updates of the poverty maps may be produced ahead of the next full census.

Updating the poverty maps

The high level of interest of planners and policy makers in the poverty mapping methodology, especially if this methodology may lead to updated estimates, prompted the World Bank to support two attempts to update the poverty maps (see the section on Technical Aspects for a detailed description of the process). One attempt consisted of updating the maps using a new household survey that had become available. The second attempt tried to arrive at new poverty estimates by updating the census variables through fieldwork.

The team involved in the first attempt combined the 1999 census with the 2002 VHLSS. They found this approach unproductive. The estimated poverty rates were approximately the same as those based on the combination of the census and the 1998 VLSS. Given that, according to the direct measurements of consumption expenditure in the 2002 VHLSS, poverty had declined by 8.5 percentage points since 1998, the finding that poverty had remained constant was not credible. Although the relationship between expenditure and many of the household characteristics had changed, this had not led to a change in the estimated poverty rates. Clearly, lower levels of poverty had become manifest in changes in household characteristics. Without updates on the household characteristics, the new estimates would lead to the same poverty rates because the new estimates continued to rely on the same 1999 census data. However, the regression estimates showed that, between 1998 and 2002, rural poverty had become more strongly associated with a number of household characteristics. These included status as part of an ethnic minority and low educational attainment of the spouse. Also, for both rural and urban areas, some of the regional dummies became less strongly associated with higher household expenditures. Factors that are less region specific had obviously become more important in explaining poverty (see Nguyen et al. 2004a).

The effort to update the poverty maps through local data collection was conducted in nine communes. In all communes, the poverty rates estimated on the basis of expenditure measures gauged through household characteristics were much lower than the poverty rates estimated on the basis of the collected expenditure data. One reason for this appeared to be that the collected expenditure data were lower than the actual expenditures since the data were collected using simplified questionnaires (see Nguyen et al. 2006). This is likely to have led to an overestimation of poverty, making a comparison with the poverty mapping method impossible.

Looking forward, efforts to update the maps regularly will focus on ways to update the data on household characteristics (the census variables) because new surveys and updated estimates of coefficients seem to have little impact on the poverty estimates. Efforts to test methods to update the data on household characteristics so as to calculate new commune or district poverty rates should include more rigorous verification of the test results. This should include (1) direct poverty estimates calculated from reliable expenditure or income data on a large number of households in the area and (2) discussion with key local informants on the relative ranking of communes or districts by poverty level. Use might also be made of data from the 2006 agricultural census.

Using poverty mapping to identify proxy indicators

The use of household characteristics from the census as proxy indicators for poverty caught the imagination of staff at the ILSSA and Molisa. The targeted programs managed by Molisa are aimed at households or individuals, rather than small areas. The staff there wanted to test whether these household characteristics might be used to predict whether a household is poor or not. This test was conducted using data from the 2004 VHLSS. The results showed that the coverage rate of this method is only 57 percent, excluding 43 percent of poor households. The leakage rate is lower, suggesting that about one-quarter of the households are miscategorized as poor (see Nguyen et al. 2006). In short, this analysis showed that selecting poor households through poverty indicators might not be as straightforward as was thought.

Overlaying the poverty maps with information on program coverage

The overlay of the poor communes selected by the government for special assistance under Program 135 showed that nearly all selected communes were in poor areas and that nearly all poor areas were included, but that some gaps existed, particularly in the Northwest (see figure 14.7). The good coverage is partly caused by the fact that Program 135 focuses on remote communes, most of which are poor. In addition to remoteness from infrastructure and services, the selection criteria also include the proportion of ethnic minorities in the communes, which is also strongly associated with poverty. The gaps exist especially in areas that are to be flooded once a new hydropower dam is completed nearby. However, CEM was somewhat disturbed by the exposure of these gaps and wanted to study them more before commenting.

Producing an urban poverty map

The research team that produced the poverty mapping estimates for Ho Chi Minh City using the city's 2004 midterm provincial census found that there are very few people in the city who are living below the national poverty line. The use of a poverty line established by the Ho Chi Minh City authorities that is about two times higher than the national poverty line resulted in higher levels of poverty (2.6 percent, on average). The highest poverty rates were found in the outlying rural areas of Ho Chi Minh City. Differences in poverty among city districts were low and insignificant (Institute of Economic Research 2005). This is not in line with observations and other data that show that pockets of poverty exist in some urban wards of the city, especially in areas with large numbers of migrants. This finding is probably related to the difficulty in estimating an

Figure 14.7 Poverty Incidence in Communes with and without Program 135, Vietnam

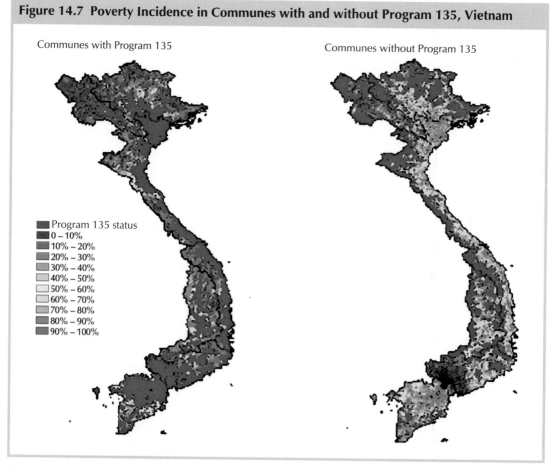

Communes with Program 135   Communes without Program 135

Program 135 status
- 0 – 10%
- 10% – 20%
- 20% – 30%
- 30% – 40%
- 40% – 50%
- 50% – 60%
- 60% – 70%
- 70% – 80%
- 80% – 90%
- 90% – 100%

Sources: Nguyen et al. 2004b.
Note: On left map, communes without Program 135 are shown in blue. On right map, communes with Program 135 are in blue.

expenditure equation for urban Ho Chi Minh City from the VHLSS, which, in turn, is likely to be caused by insufficient VHLSS coverage of urban migrants. In fact, the midterm census for Ho Chi Minh City indicated that the proportion of people with temporary registration status is 30 percent, whereas only 10 percent of urban residents in the urban southeast sample of the VHLSS (which is heavily dominated by Ho Chi Minh City) have temporary registration status, providing more evidence that the VHLSS leaves out greater proportions of more mobile population groups. This issue is now receiving the attention of the GSO.

Impact

Impact of the national poverty maps

The poverty maps were introduced primarily to promote well-informed debate on poverty and inequality by producing poverty estimates disaggregated at the subprovincial level.

The results showed that it was possible to use high-quality survey and census data to generate poverty estimates for provinces, districts, and communes and that the methodology might be used to aid in decisions about targeting. This demonstrated that there was potential to replace the cumbersome and unreliable annual income surveys and the counts of poor people conducted across the country by Molisa. There was no explicit objective to use the poverty maps to encourage revisions to any specific government policies.

As a preliminary step to drafting this chapter, the World Bank conducted a number of interviews and sent a brief questionnaire to people who had seen the poverty maps. The questions covered the exposure of these people to and use of the maps and their recall on the main messages of the maps. The questionnaire was sent to 17 donors, 12 journalists, 9 researchers, 5 NGO representatives, 3 independent development professionals, and 9 officials in Ho Chi Minh City. There were 46 respondents, who answered that they had used the poverty maps in the following ways:

■ *Improving their understanding of poverty.* Most respondents stated that they had used the main messages of the poverty maps in explaining poverty to their own organizations, in their dialogue with the government, and (particularly the NGOs) in their discussions with development professionals seeking to learn more about poverty in Vietnam. The journalists said they had used the maps as background for articles, sometimes reproducing the maps. Several researchers had used the maps in lectures or in publications. The maps were used as an aid in discussions in a number of organized forums, including the Poverty Task Force and the Partnership to Assist the Poorest Communes.

■ *Targeting resources.* A number of respondents at donor organizations and NGOs said they had used the poverty maps in allocating resources. This involved setting priorities for new programs, adjusting the allocation of resources in ongoing programs, and arguing for more propoor public expenditures within sectors where these organizations are active. One donor used the poverty map overlay of the communes selected for Program 135, which are actually the poorest communes and include nearly all poor communes in Vietnam, as a basis for providing budget support for one of the government programs that channels additional resources to poor communes. NGOs, in particular, used the maps as an advocacy tool to influence others to allocate resources in a more propoor manner. The Office of the National Assembly reported that it, too, had used the poverty maps to argue for more resources for poorer areas. Some respondents had used the maps to argue for the targeting of areas of dense poverty, rather than deep poverty.

■ *Rethinking poverty measurement techniques.* As a powerful instrument for generating debate about the different results from the use of different poverty data, the poverty maps have encouraged recognition that the official poverty measurement and targeting techniques relying on Molisa data are flawed. This was confirmed by subsequent research (see Nguyen and Rama 2004). The debate has led to the definition of a new poverty line that brings official poverty estimates much closer to the estimates derived from the household surveys. The debate has also prompted a series of investigations into new targeting techniques and demonstrated the need for more independent data sources, a need that had not been previously recognized.

Discussions with government agencies about the value of the poverty map exercise suggest that there have been a number of benefits arising from the process of preparing the maps. The institute leading the research argues that the approach to the work—the establishment of a multistakeholder task force—set a precedent for cross-agency collaboration that has since become normal in government operations. There had previously been little collaboration across government agencies in the production of analytical work, particularly in poverty analysis. Poverty analysis had previously been associated with the targeted Hunger Eradication and Poverty Reduction Program coordinated by Molisa, rather than with policy development across a range of sectors.

In addition, government agencies noted the capacity that the poverty mapping exercise had built. There are now a number of Vietnamese experts able to construct poverty maps with minimal outside support, indicating a sustainable improvement in the capacity to use poverty data to influence debate (see below on Sustainability). One government agency also argued that the poverty mapping exercise had changed the government's approach to presenting data more generally. The poverty maps were an inspiration for a whole range of other mapping exercises, which vividly illustrate a number of social trends and other trends. For example, following the success of the poverty maps, ICARD and the GSO collaborated to produce a socioeconomic atlas of Vietnam using the 1999 data. This atlas, which includes the poverty maps, allows easy, visual cross-referencing between the poverty headcount and other indicators, such as the presence of forest cover. Helvetas, the Swiss Association for International Cooperation, is now using mapping techniques in Vietnam to motivate discussion at a subnational level in support of a provincial planning process to develop a more sound evidence base and to become more propoor by mapping a range of administrative and other data.

Impact of the Ho Chi Minh City poverty maps

The results of the Ho Chi Minh City mapping exercise were made available at a dissemination workshop hosted by the Institute of Economic Research in December 2005. Representatives from the People's Council and from city departments, district officials, and researchers attended. Feedback from the attendees suggests that they found the poverty maps either "very useful" or "quite useful." Those most interested in using the maps as an instrument for policy design or resource allocation voiced concerns about the errors resulting from the absence of nonpermanent migrants from the Ho Chi Minh City sample of the VHLSS. They were interested in encouraging follow-up work that would reduce the likelihood of errors and that would investigate links between poverty and other indicators, such as access to basic services. Several officials mentioned that they had used the maps in internal reports, district plans, and research.

Missed Opportunities for Influence

A number of factors constrain the level of influence that the poverty maps have had in policy- and decision-making processes. The two most significant limitations relate to the timeliness of the maps and their relationship to official poverty data. The focus of the dialogue at the national level rather than locally and, perhaps, the failure to engage with certain organizations as early and as energetically as might have been desirable have also been important.

The timeliness of the maps and the conflict with official data

The poverty maps became available in 2003, around the time that the 2002 VHLSS data also became available. The 2002 VHLSS data showed clearly that rapid poverty reduction had continued and emphasized that the levels of poverty (though not the overall patterns of distribution) illustrated in the 1999 poverty maps were no longer accurate. While appreciating the higher levels of disaggregation available in the poverty maps, planners and policy makers within government were frustrated by the prospect of using old data as a basis for planning. Moreover, the fact that the poverty maps used nonofficial poverty data was an additional reason for reluctance to use the poverty maps formally in decision making or in government documents. These factors did not mean that the poverty maps were not used informally (even within the government) in framing debate and in identifying issues to be tackled. But they certainly inhibited the degree to which the maps were used formally, a problem that was recognized at the outset of the exercise. Even with hindsight, it is not clear what more might have been done. Arguably, the maps might have been produced more quickly had the balance of the work taken place outside the country, with less iteration and interaction with local officials. But this would have required trade-offs in capacity building and local ownership.

The maps are now well out of date and are used less frequently in presentations and publications. There is an urgent need to update them. The poverty team in the World Bank office in Vietnam is supporting a number of activities to produce updated maps. Official data at the national level might now be more closely aligned to the VHLSS, suggesting that the problems caused by the difference between the stories of poverty described in the VHLSS and the official data are less likely to arise in the future. Furthermore, the greater familiarity that now exists with poverty mapping techniques and the higher levels of enthusiasm for representing poverty data graphically suggest that updated maps would be well received.

Engagement at subnational levels

Though one of the most significant potential uses of the poverty mapping methodology lies in the ability to provide decentralized, subnational government agencies with reliable poverty estimates, little effort has gone into validating and promoting the poverty maps in the provinces. Large poverty maps may be found in central government and civil society offices in Hanoi, but they are very much less visible in offices in the provinces. Discussions on the poverty maps have generally taken place in Hanoi and are very frequently related to how the disaggregated picture of poverty should influence national decision making: for example, how the targeting of lagging regions by national agencies might be refined; how resource allocation criteria in the Ministry of Finance might be amended; and how inequality might be tackled more effectively.

The poverty maps were discussed at regional workshops as part of efforts to disseminate the poverty assessment produced in 2003. But the audience at these workshops consisted primarily of local researchers based at regional universities. A systematic attempt to disseminate the findings of the poverty maps to 64 provinces in a meaningful way would require considerable resources.

There might also have been a process to work with provinces to tackle the disparity between the districts and to reflect on improved resource allocation at the subprovincial level. This was not actively pursued, partly because the problems arising from the conflict between official poverty data and the VHLSS poverty data are compounded in the provinces because provincial officials have generally had less exposure to the VHLSS data. The Molisa estimates on poverty in the provinces and districts are available to provincial officials, but these officials are less likely to recognize an estimate derived from the VHLSS or the poverty maps. When discussions have taken place with local officials about the poverty maps, the officials have been disinclined to base their work on poverty data that they have not been authorized to use. Had some kind of validation exercise taken place in collaboration with local officials, the understanding of and commitment to the maps might have been more substantial.

The work carried out in 2005 in Ho Chi Minh City to combine the 2004 midterm Ho Chi Minh City census data and the 2004 VHLSS data has nonetheless generated considerable enthusiasm. This exercise produced poverty maps based on both the GSO poverty line and the higher, city-defined poverty line, and officials were able to compare the different views on poverty that resulted from the use of the different lines.

Engagement with key national agencies

One important national process that the poverty mapping exercise might have influenced was the targeting work that has directed the flow of resources for Program 135. CEM is responsible for identifying poor communes to be included in the program. It therefore has an institutional interest in assessing commune poverty levels. CEM did not participate in the poverty mapping exercise. The value of engaging with CEM and the potential for assisting CEM in developing more robust means of targeting poor communes were recognized about 18 months after the poverty maps had been released. By that time, the data on which the maps are based was five years old. CEM is now engaged in some of the follow-up work.

Though the Ministry of Finance was part of the multiagency task force that was established as a governance structure for the poverty mapping exercise, there was little effort put into following up on the main messages of the poverty maps with the ministry. The poverty focus of public expenditure has improved quite remarkably over recent years, whether or not poverty maps have played a role. In any case, the ministry remains receptive to new ideas and suggestions on the allocation of resources across provinces in ways that promote social equity.

Lastly, although GSO staff members have been trained as trainers in poverty mapping techniques and contributed to many of the subsequent training sessions for other agencies, the GSO has never been central to the actual production of the poverty maps. A more central role for the GSO might have facilitated access to census and other data. But the decision to move the production of poverty mapping estimates closer to the users, that is, the sector ministries, was deliberate. It aimed at making sure the efforts would more easily feed into decision making.

Sustainability

The 12 analysts of the Interministerial Poverty Mapping Task Force were closely involved in all the analytical work leading up to the preparation of the district and commune maps. As a consequence, they were able to explain the poverty mapping methodology to their colleagues and superiors in the respective ministries. However, only one of them, the NEU researcher, was able to conduct poverty mapping calculations without support from international experts. After the district and commune poverty mapping work was completed, the task force was no longer active. However, a series of follow-up activities have taken place since then. The original lead agency, ICARD, continued to produce maps of socioeconomic information from the census. But it was ILSSA that requested further training in poverty mapping techniques and in testing methods for updating the maps. Over the past two years, the NEU researcher has worked with a team of ILSSA researchers on a number of research topics. Foreign expertise was hired on only one occasion for this. The poverty work in Ho Chi Minh City was conducted entirely by Vietnamese experts.

In Vietnam, there is now a strong demand for poverty maps that may be updated regularly and that reflect local realities. Molisa wants to improve its targeting methods to address the weaknesses that have been exposed. It is interested in a method that enables the poverty maps to be updated from the bottom up through local data collection on household characteristics. Such a method might replace the ineffective income surveys and the reliance of Molisa on poverty reporting by local officials that is easily manipulated. CEM has communicated that it needs an updated map to conduct a midterm evaluation of its program to assist the poorest communes. This may perhaps be accomplished using the 2006 agricultural census. Little foreign expertise will be needed to meet these demands. However, support from international experts might still be required to test new approaches such as exploiting the panel component of expenditure surveys to update maps, using administrative data on population movements to take account of migration trends in new poverty maps, and verifying the methods for bottom-up poverty mapping techniques. External help might also be required to apply the small area estimation methodology to map other indicators such as vulnerability or nutrition.

The Lessons Learned

Together with other poverty analyses, the poverty maps have undoubtedly stimulated debates on trends in poverty, on the methodology underpinning poverty measurement, on the geographical dimensions of poverty and inequality, and on national resource allocation across provinces. The maps have led to increased demand for more independent data on poverty especially at the local level. The poverty team at the World Bank will continue to support efforts that provide reliable poverty data, disaggregated to the level where decisions are made. Future work in this area will respond to the lessons of the past 10 years of experience with poverty mapping. These lessons cover the following issues.

Keeping up with changes and developing second-generation poverty maps

Vietnam is a rapidly changing country. Poverty has fallen by more than 3.5 percent per year over the last 10 years. The population is becoming increasingly mobile. In this context, techniques that depend on census data that become available only every 10 years are not going to provide a dependable flow of updated information for policy makers. Though past attempts to update the poverty maps have not been successful, ongoing work that is focused on updating the data on household characteristics and correcting for past technical errors will likely deliver interesting results.

Improving outreach and use at subnational levels

The last few years have seen a growing focus on public expenditures to influence poverty. In particular, the Ministry of Finance has made efforts to revise the criteria and coefficients it uses in determining allocations across provinces. Remote and upland areas are increasingly favored in the allocation of the recurrent budget. However, little progress has been made below the provincial level. Population figures still seem to dominate in the calculations that determine how provinces allocate funds across districts and how districts allocate funds across communes. At these levels of decision making, access to reliable poverty data that local officials feel permitted to use and that they feel they may trust might make a difference in the way resources flow to poor areas.

Strengthening the validation process

Future activities in producing second-generation poverty maps will include a process that may generate more effective technical and political validation of the small area estimates, as well as a better local understanding and ownership of the numbers behind the maps. It is a significant challenge to reach out to 64 provinces in a meaningful manner using this kind of analysis. Nonetheless, the research with the ILSSA that sought to test the updating of poverty maps by collecting new data on household characteristics might have included an exercise to verify the results informally with key local informants. This would have been better than trying to compare the results with poverty estimates calculated from detailed income and expenditure data that appeared unreliable.

Improving the coverage of urban migrants in household surveys

The poverty mapping work in Ho Chi Minh City demonstrated how the incomplete capture of nonpermanent migrants in the VHLSS might influence poverty mapping estimates. There is a need to examine how the sample for the VHLSS may be made more inclusive of mobile populations. The extension of the work to ward-level differences has been important in improving the understanding of urban poverty. This work has also taught us that there might be a useful collaboration between statistics offices and research institutes outside Hanoi.

Maintaining the emphasis on capacity building

There has been a significant emphasis on capacity building throughout the poverty mapping work and among the team. This has paid off in the development of a small pool of Vietnamese experts who are confident in their ability to use poverty mapping techniques and a larger pool of Vietnamese experts who understand enough about the techniques to feel at ease with the products. Though working with local experts has meant that the maps have perhaps taken longer to produce than might have been the case had they been produced by a team of international experts, this approach has had benefits. It has meant that there is a team of experts available to explain the techniques in Vietnamese to more skeptical audiences. It means that dissemination and outreach may be carried out in Vietnamese and that requests for technical information may be satisfied quickly. If the people's committee of a province contacts the World Bank asking for a training course so as to understand and use the poverty maps, the existence of skilled local researchers means that it is possible to respond quickly and appropriately. Future work will continue to emphasize the need to build the skills of local researchers in these techniques.

Strengthening engagement with national agencies where it has been deficient

Future activities will engage more directly with CEM, an agency that has a functional role in identifying poor communes. CEM staff are currently defining a revised list of poor communes, but they are hopeful they will be able to use any updated poverty maps that become available as they review this list in 2008.

Continue responding to the demand for credible local poverty measurements

Replacing the currently flawed official poverty measurement approach with the poverty mapping methodology has never been a realistic objective. But the methodology has helped crystallize the debate at the local level and even at the level of national poverty measurement. The poverty mapping exercise has led to a search for reliable alternatives for the measurement of poverty to replace the current approach. The Ministry of Finance has expressed an interest in making subnational poverty rates part of its criteria for budget allocations. But it will do this only after a robust, reliable method has been identified that is accepted by subnational governments.

References

Elbers, Chris, Jean O. Lanjouw, and Peter F. Lanjouw. 2003. "Micro-Level Estimation of Poverty and Inequality." *Econometrica* 71 (1): 355–64.

Institute of Economic Research. 2005. "Report on Poverty Mapping for Ho Chi Minh City." Report, Institute of Economic Research, Ho Chi Minh City and World Bank, Hanoi.

Minot, Nicholas W. 2000. "Generating Disaggregated Poverty Maps: An Application to Vietnam." *World Development* 28 (2): 319–31.

Minot, Nicholas W., and Bob Baulch. 2002. "The Spatial Distribution of Poverty in Vietnam and the Potential for Targeting." Policy Research Working Paper 2829, World Bank, Washington, DC.

———. 2004. "The Spatial Distribution of Poverty in Vietnam and the Potential for Targeting." In *Economic Growth, Poverty, and Household Welfare in Vietnam,* ed. Paul Glewwe, Nisha Agrawal, and David Dollar, 229–72. World Bank Regional and Sectoral Studies. Washington, DC: World Bank.

Minot, Nicholas W., Bob Baulch, and Michael Epprecht. 2003. *Poverty and Inequality in Vietnam: Spatial Patterns and Geographic Determinants.* In collaboration with the Interministerial Poverty Mapping Task Force. Washington, DC: International Food Policy Research Institute; Brighton, United Kingdom: Institute of Development Studies.

Nguyen Nguyet Nga and Martin Rama. 2006. "Combining Quantitative and Qualitative Information to Assess Poverty Targeting Methods in Vietnam." Unpublished monograph, World Bank, Hanoi.

Nguyen Viet Cuong, Do Anh Kiem, Pham Minh Thu, Nguyen Bao Cuong, and Nguyen Thi Lan. 2004a. "Estimating Poverty Rates Using the 1999 Census and the 2002 VHLSS." Unpublished working paper, Institute of Labor Science and Social Affairs, General Statistics Office, and National Economics University, Hanoi.

———. 2004b. "Statistics Analysis and Mapping of the Relationship between Poverty Indicators and Communes Selected for Assistance under Program 135." Unpublished working paper, Institute of Labor Science and Social Affairs, General Statistics Office, and National Economics University, Hanoi.

Nguyen Viet Cuong, Nguyen Lan Huong, Lo Thi Duc, and Institute of Labor Science and Social Affairs. 2006. "Using Poverty-Proxy-Indicator Surveys to Update Poverty Maps and Identify the Poor: Evidence from Household Surveys in Vietnam." Paper presented at the Conference "Poverty Mapping: Impacts and Uses," Siem Reap, Cambodia, February 8–9.